Western Civilization

Mainstream Readings & Radical Critiques

VOLUME TWO

FROM THE FRENCH REVOLUTION TO THE PRESENT

JEFFRY KAPLOW

ALFRED A. KNOPF   NEW YORK

THIS IS A BORZOI BOOK
PUBLISHED BY ALFRED A. KNOPF, INC.

First Edition
987654321
Copyright © 1973 by Alfred A. Knopf, Inc.

Library of Congress Cataloging in Publication Data

Kaplow, Jeffry, comp.
    Western civilization.
    CONTENTS: v. 1. From the Greeks to the
enlightenment.—v. 2. From the French Revolution
to the present.
    1. Civilization, Occidental.   I. Title.
CB245.K32   1973   901.9   72-10009
ISBN 0-394-31688-6   (v. 2)

Manufactured in the United States of America. Composed by
Cherry Hill Composition, Pennsauken, N.J. Printed and bound by
The Kingsport Press, Kingsport, Tenn.

Cover design by Bob Silverman

ACKNOWLEDGMENTS

PAUL BARAN AND E. J. HOBSBAWM, "The Stages of Economic Growth" from *Kyklos* 14 (1961). Reprinted by permission of the publisher.

K. D. BRACHER, from *The German Dictatorship*. Copyright © 1970 by Praeger Publishers, Inc. Reprinted by permission of the publisher.

LOUIS CHEVALIER, "Violence and the Working Class in Paris, 1815–1848" from *Classes laborieuses et classes dangereuses à Paris pendant la première moitié du XIXe siècle*. By permission of Librairie Plon, and of Howard Fertig, Inc., whose own edition appears under the title *Laboring Classes and Dangerous Classes* (1973). The Fertig translation was not available at press time; the translation used here is by the editor.

ISAAC DEUTSCHER, from *The Unfinished Revolution: Russia, 1917–1967*. Copyright © 1967 by Isaac Deutscher. Reprinted by permission of Oxford University Press, Inc.

D. K. FIELDHOUSE, "Imperialism: An Historiographical Revision" from *Economic History Review* New Series XIV (1961). Reprinted by permission of the publisher.

ANTONIO GRAMSCI, from *Il Risorgimento*. Reprinted by permission of Giulio Einaudi, Turin; Lawrence and Wishart, London; and International Publishers Co., Inc.

E. J. HOBSBAWM AND R. M. HARTWELL, "The Standard of Living during the Industrial Revolution: A Discussion" from *Economic History Review* New Series XVI (1963). Reprinted by permission of the authors and the publisher.

DAVID HOROWITZ, "World War and Cold War" from *Empire and Revolution: A Radical Interpretation of Contemporary History*. Copyright © 1969 by David Horowitz. Reprinted by permission of Random House, Inc., and Deborah Rogers Ltd., London.

JEFFRY KAPLOW, "The Culture of Poverty in Paris on the Eve of the Revolution" from *International Review of Social History* XII (1967). Reprinted by permission of the publisher.

v

GEORGE F. KENNAN, "The Breakdown of the Tsarist Autocracy" from *Revolutionary Russia*, edited by Richard Pipes. Copyright © 1968 by Richard Pipes. Reprinted by permission of Harvard University Press.

GABRIEL KOLKO, from *The Politics of War: The World and United States Foreign Policy, 1943–1945*. Copyright © 1968 by Gabriel Kolko. Reprinted by permission of Random House, Inc.

HENRI LEFEBVRE, "The Commune and the Nature of Revolution" from *La Proclamation de la Commune*. Copyright © 1965 by Editions Gallimard. Reprinted by permission of the publisher.

KARL MARX, "The Civil War in France" from *Selected Works*. Foreign Languages Publishing House, Moscow.

————, from "The Eighteenth Brumaire of Louis Napoleon" from *Selected Works*. Foreign Languages Publishing House, Moscow.

FRANZ NEUMANN, from *Behemoth: The Structure and Practice of National Socialism, 1933–1944*. Copyright © 1942, 1944 by Oxford University Press. Published in 1963 by Octagon Books. Reprinted by permission of Farrar, Straus & Giroux, Inc.

NICOS POULANTZAS, "Fascism and Social Class" from *Fascisme et Dictature*. Copyright © 1970 by Librairie Francois Maspero, Paris. Reprinted by permission of Monthly Review Press and New Left Books, Ltd.

ROSARIO ROMEO, "The Risorgimento" from *Risorgimento e capitalismo*. Reprinted by permission of Gius. Laterza & Figli, Bari. Translated for this volume by Jill Carlton Manacorda.

W. W. ROSTOW, from *The Five Stages of Growth* (2nd ed.). Copyright © 1971 by W. W. Rostow. Reprinted by permission of Cambridge University Press.

ALBERT SOBOUL, "The Popular Movement and Bourgeois Revolution" from *The Parisian Sans-Culottes and the French Revolution, 1793–4*. Reprinted by permission of The Clarendon Press.

ERIC STOKES, "Late Nineteenth-Century Colonial Expansion and the Attack on the Theory of Economic Imperialism: A Case of Mistaken Identity" from *Historical Journal* Summer, 1969. Reprinted by permission of Cambridge University Press.

GEORGE V. TAYLOR, "Noncapitalist Wealth and the Origins of the French Revolution" from *American Historical Review* LXXII (January 1967). Reprinted by permission of the author and the publisher.

EDWARD THOMPSON, from *The Making of the English Working Class*. Copyright © 1963 by Edward Thompson. First published by Victor Gollancz, Ltd., London. Reprinted by permission of Pantheon Books, A Division of Random House, Inc.

LEON TROTSKY, from *The History of the Russian Revolution*. Published by Estaven Volkov.

CONTENTS

THE MEANING OF RADICAL HISTORY

To be radical is to take things at the root. Now, for man, the root is man himself.

> —MARX, *Contribution to the Critique of Hegel's Philosophy of Law*

It is easy to slide from "let us not oversimplify" into a theoretical justification, or a tacit assumption, of history as just one damn thing after another—a historical nihilism which is becoming fashionable today, for obvious sociological reasons. . . . I am impenitent in my conviction that it is right to try to see society as a whole, and wrong to consider men's work and thought as though they existed in separate self-contained compartments.

> —CHRISTOPHER HILL, in *Past and Present*, No. 29 (1964), 96–97

Learning without living doth but breed traitors as common experience too well showeth.

> —ELLESMERE, Lord Chancellor of England, early seventeenth century

The purpose of this book is indicated by its title, a confrontation between mainstream interpretations and dissentient radical views of the principal issues of European history. Although my sympathies are clearly with the radical side, there has been no attempt to set up straw men, nor has it been my intent to show the development of historical thought across time. Most of the material reprinted here is of very recent vintage, some 80 percent of it having been published since World War II. I have therefore not included selections from historians who, however great their contributions, have now been left behind because of the discovery of new evidence or because their conceptual schemes no longer attract approval or allegiance. I have focused rather on illustrating the many different ways of approaching the historical past. To do so, it is not always necessary to have opponents engage in direct debate about the significance of this or that trend or event. The confrontation is located at another level, a higher and more abstract one. The crucial question is this: What is important in history—which is to say, in society? What are the agents that, through human actions and their limitations, determine what happens in history? If we all agree, more or less, that causality is the proper concern of the historian, how are we to determine causes—and to establish a hierarchy among them?

The most important development in the historiography of the last fifty years has been historians' gradual assimilation, to a greater or lesser extent, of Marxist thought. At the very least, this has meant a renewed emphasis on what are known as social and economic "factors" in shaping human destiny. But there is a difference between allowing oneself to be influenced by Marx in this way (after all, he was not alone in preaching the lesson) and accepting Marxism as a system of thought. To follow the latter option is not, however, to accept as absolute truth everything that Marx said, much less the obiter dicta of what the Polish philosopher Leszek Kolakowski has called the Office, that is, the ideologists of the Soviet Union. The acceptance of Marxism as a system is the adoption of the method of historical materialism and, more specifically, of class analysis as a means for understanding what has happened in history. The first task men face is to create the conditions of their own survival, that is, the taming of nature and the making of a living, which are inseparable from one another. This is what Marxists call the process of producing and reproducing real life: the carving out of an environment, the perpetuation of the species, and the production of goods. In the course of this activity, men enter into relationships with one another that we call social relations of production, and those social relations most characteristic of a given time and place are said to constitute the dominant mode of production. All areas of human activity are construed to be part of, and dependent upon, these modes. History is thus the study of the totality of human activity, of men in society, of whole men taken at the root. In this light, the traditional distinctions between political, economic, social, and intellectual history, which presuppose the compartmentalization of human life, melt away.

One does not have to be a Marxist to accept the definition of history as the study of man in his total dimension. Marc Bloch, the great French medievalist whose theoretical work was an attempt to come to terms with Marxism while rejecting its basic assumptions, shared this point of view, as do his present-day disciples in the VIe Section of the Ecole Pratique des Hautes Etudes and on the review *Annales: Economies, Sociétés, Civilisations*. It is, however, incorrect to tax Marxism with being an economic determinism. The charge is the result of a basic misunderstanding, which is sometimes knowingly perpetuated. Marxism has nothing to do with economic determinism. It is, indeed, a determinism in the sense that it shows (1) that men are not totally free to do as they wish and (2) that consciousness is neither prior to, nor independent of, real life—that is, the social relations of production. In a narrow sense, one may be justified in speaking of a social determinism, but even then man remains the doer and the measure of all things. Economics and technology remain subordinate to the desires and perceptions of flesh-and-blood human beings who are, in turn, the products of a dialectical interaction between biology and society. For example: It may be said that in the nature of capitalism lies a tendency to expansion and to the maximization of profit. We do not, or should not, say that these tendencies work themselves out automatically. It is capitalists and bureaucrats who actually perform the task. And we cannot maintain that each one of them is motivated in a crude way by rapacity. The archetypal capitalist does not exist; he is always a particular person possessed of an ideology and world view peculiar to his time and place, motivated in complex ways. In short, he is a member of a class, even if he does not recapitulate in himself all of its characteristics.

But then what is a class? The proposed answers are so numerous as to make impossible even an attempt to catalogue them within the framework of this essay. I will content myself with citing what I consider to be the best contemporary definition. It is the work of the historian of the English working class Edward Thompson:

By class I understand an historical phenomenon, unifying a number of disparate and seemingly unconnected events, both in the raw material of experience and in consciousness. I emphasize that it is an *historical* phenomenon. I do not see class as a "structure," nor even as a "category," but as something which in fact happens (and can be shown to have happened) in human relationships.

More than this, the notion of class entails the notion of historical relationship. Like any other relationship, it is a fluency which evades analysis if we attempt to stop it at any given moment and anatomise its structure. The finest-meshed sociological net cannot give us a pure specimen of class, any more than it can give us one of deference or love. The relationship must always be embodied in real people and in a real context. Moreover, we cannot have two distinct classes, each with an independent being, and then bring them *into* relationship with each other. We cannot have love without lovers, nor deference without squires and laborers. And class happens when some men, as a result of common experiences (inherited and shared) feel and articulate the identity of their interests as between themselves, and as against other men whose interests are different from (and usually opposed to) theirs.

The class experience is largely determined by the productive relations into which men are born or enter involuntarily. Class-consciousness is the way in which these experiences are handled in cultural terms: embodied in traditions, value-systems, ideas, and institutional forms. If the experience appears as determined, class-consciousness does not. We can see a *logic* in the responses of similar occupational groups undergoing similar experiences, but we cannot predicate any *law*. Consciousness of class arises in the same way in different times and places, but never in *just* the same way.

We have here in outline the basic tools of Marxist historical interpretation. They ought to be handled with care, bearing in mind, as the historian of Southern slavery Eugene Genovese has said, that class analysis can "only serve as the basis for a much more complex analysis." Marxism is a method of perceiving social reality. Because this is so, there is a priori no single Marxist truth. The results arrived at by the application of Marxist techniques of analysis are liable to the normal rules of evidence and scientific critique. They are never acquired once and for all, but are constantly subject to revision.

The radical historian believes that history should be studied as the sum total of man's activity at a given time and place, and that a liaison must be established between the study of the past and our present concerns. He is a "why" rather than a "how" historian, systematically posing the "big" question about historical change: Why did it happen this way and not that? He challenges accepted ideas when he finds them inadequate and especially when they neglect the dimension of popular movements and class struggle. But the radical historian does not waste his time crying over the victims of past events, no matter how much sympathy he may feel for them. He is not iconoclastic and merely skeptical, nor does he engage in art for art's sake— activities readily tolerated by ruling classes and easily turned by them to their own advantage. The village atheist never did anyone any harm.

History is more than a simple intellectual exercise, a pack of tricks played upon the dead. It is a social science, and therefore the proper field, perhaps even the laboratory, in which to develop the analyses and ideas that form the very stuff of social change. As a social science, it does not pretend to "transcend time and place" in order to permit analogy, generalization, or prediction; only by having one's historical feet planted firmly in a specific context can one learn anything at all. We want not lessons from the past, but learning with which to change the world. Marx, who spoke of philosophers as having done nothing more than study the world, was only expressing in a different way what Ellesmere had said in the early seventeenth century and what today is called the necessity of integrating theory and practice into a revolutionary praxis.

The notion is a very simple one. It means activity aimed at shaping the future in liaison with a theoretical understanding of the basis of change. The man who practices without theory is doomed to failure, for he will be taking pot shots in the dark at an unknown target. The man who theorizes without practice is equally so, for lack of contact with the real world will render him sterile. It is not sufficient to look out on what is going on from the window of an ivory tower. But the conclusion is not that there can be no division of labor in this life, or that the historian is expected to lead the revolution. Even less has it anything to do with sopping up wisdom from the masses. The historian who abandons the study of history to enter the factory is as likely to hinder progress as to advance it.

There are those who argue that to speak of radical history is a contradiction in terms. Truth is one, they say, and our task as historians is to seek it out. For David Landes of Harvard and Charles Tilly of the University of Michigan, editors of the recent *History As Social Science,* ours is an age "that is beginning to fear and mistrust science and technology, that wants to substitute heart for mind, warmth for coolness, passion for reason." Radicals, they argue, wish to subordinate the dispassionate search for truth to political tasks, an attitude which is not only arrogant, but leads them into the dangerous byways of judging the credentials of the historian rather than the results of his inquiry.

To make the search for truth dispassionate is to take the guts out of what a historian does. Truth is a passion, and the fact that the converse is not true has nothing to do with the case. Only the jesting Pilates of this world, for whom truth is of no importance, can adopt an agnostic position. Recent events, of which the war in Indochina has been the most significant and catalytic, have created a new generation of activists who seek explanations of present horrors in historical study. They are no longer satisfied with traditional university fare and demand more meat on the bones of scholarship, by which they mean increased "relevance" to contemporary concerns. Relevance is a tricky and easily abused concept. When it is meant to discredit any scholarly endeavor not directly related to the cure of what ails us, it can be very ugly indeed. Moreover, to use it as a cudgel is in direct contradiction to conscious radical goals. In a "good" society—that is, one free from the imperatives of capital and class—it would presumably be both possible and desirable to allocate resources in such a way as to permit investigations of the most highly abstract and nonrelevant nature; and one cannot prepare the way for that society by suppressing such of its aspects as may already exist. But it is sometimes difficult to separate the error of mindless rhetoric from its context. As Bertolt Brecht once wrote in a poem addressed to future generations:

> Even the hatred of squalor
> Makes the brow grow stern.
> Even anger against injustice
> Makes the voice grow harsh.[1]

The important thing, it seems to me, is to refuse to countenance these errors, but at the same time not to fall into the trap of divorcing oneself from the young people whose responsibility they are. Their protest against the failures of the university, the historical discipline, and the role they are too often made to play in contemporary society is fundamentally healthy. There is a proper and an improper way of attacking the failings of traditional or mainstream history. If relevance is too often senseless and abusive, it nevertheless expresses a real concern and is a direct challenge to the idea of a value-free social science.

For the radical scholar qua scholar, this is the most basic issue. He argues that value-free social science cannot exist in a class society, where all knowledge is to some extent ideological. Although science may under certain conditions attain a measure of autonomy, like everything else it is socially conditioned. In this sense, one can speak of bourgeois science. It is not *bad* science (although one may disagree with it), but science of its time and place. By its very nature, it is a carrier of values. This is what the radical scholar asks be recognized. He demands both lucidity and mastery, the combination of which will allow us continually to deepen our understanding of the past.

Radicalism is not relativism. It does not maintain that one truth (interpretation) is as good as another, in the manner of the American historians Charles Beard (1874–1948), who was led by his view that objectivity was a "noble dream" to maintain that the past was ultimately unknowable, or Carl Becker (1873–1945), who made of Everyman his own historian and insisted on a skeptical distrust of them all. The radical historian refuses to make the question one of individual bias versus objectivity, so the argument that "bias can be overcome" has no significance. The point hinges rather on the question of ideology. Marxists and other sorts of radicals share a conviction that it is possible to analyze the past scientifically according to a set of theoretical principles and that their theory is more consonant with reality than any other. They operate under no illusions about their own objectivity. They recognize themselves as ideologists, and ideology, by definition, as a deformation of objective truth (assumed to exist, even though presently unattainable). But the quality of an ideology is measured by its capacity to furnish a coherent explanation of society and of nature— or in history, of events observed to have taken place in the past.

---

[1] From "To Posterity" in *Selected Poems* by Bertolt Brecht (New York: Harcourt Brace Jovanovich, 1959).

Social science is, then, thoroughly imbued with values, even when its practitioners cry most loudly that their aim is only to be detached and objective. The call for ivory-tower scholarship is itself expressive of a value set, and it is difficult to imagine that the kind of isolation from the outside world it implies will be without effect on the studies so undertaken. The radical maintains that there is something wrong with a system of values that incites professors to publish while others perish. Let me be clear: It is not what you study, but how you study it. No one should want to force a scholar of, say, ancient Greek philology to try to relate his work to the current political situation in Greece. What a radical is against is scholarship that castrates itself by willfully cutting itself off from areas of contemporary concern to which it has a legitimate relation. More generally, radicals oppose scholars who, as a matter of principle, make of their university or discipline a haven from the melee of the problems of this world.

There is also the matter of the perversion of science. Isolation from the real world finds its complement at the other end of the scale among scholars who use their knowledge for dubious ends. I refer, of course, to the kinds of labors that currently go under the name of defense research, in which, for example, the latest techniques of "objective" social science are used to develop counterinsurgency plans for keeping the natives quiet. This kind of thing has been going on ever since Woodrow Wilson, then president of Princeton University, announced the desirability of fostering liaisons between the universities and the state ("Princeton in the Nation's service"—1896). It, too, is a form of commitment, and I would be the last to gainsay it on that basis; I have no desire to consign the university and the state to their separate spheres. But I hold that commitment must not be blind, that the scholar is indeed responsible not only for the quality and accuracy of his work, but for the uses to which it is put. When those uses turn out to be the physical uprooting and even extermination of whole groups of people or the destruction of the physical environment, the refusal to be an accomplice becomes mandatory. To hide behind the skirts of science in order to legitimize—or even refuse to condemn—criminal acts is an act unworthy of a scholar.

The radical scholar is on the defensive these days. He wants the university to be kept safe from manipulation by the state, but he also wants to encourage his fellows to take positions on the major issues of the day not just as citizens, but also as scholars. In other words, he refuses to establish a dichotomy between the two functions of a single individual. In fact, he sees the union between them as the necessary condition of success in either. It is becoming more and more difficult to live as a whole man these days, for the pressures on the members of the university community to conform to the status quo are increasingly great. The price of freedom of thought seems to be the abandonment of freedom of action. But the one cannot survive without the other.

It is at this point that radical activism and radical scholarship meet in a shared concern for revolutionary change. There are many ways to promote that change. In this regard, the historian practices a privileged discipline, for it is one of those most directly related to the building of a new and better world. Without history, there can be no theory, and without theory, there can be no change. The praxis of the revolutionary intellectual takes place most of the time, but not exclusively, in his library and at his writing table. One kind of action is not better than another; although there may be moments when one is more needed than another, each is part of a whole. Everything depends on the attitude of the historian toward his work. If he is radical in his concerns and methods as we have defined them, he is likely to make a significant contribution to the common task. The truth, or what we can know of it, historical as well as actual, is always revolutionary.

This said, there is not necessarily a direct connection between a radical historiography and a commitment to a political movement, however much they might enrich one another. I have little or no idea of the political positions of the authors represented in this collection. It is as yet impossible to present a collection of essays by committed radical scholars that would attempt to offer a coherent overview of European history animated by a common political viewpoint and using the latest techniques; it is a weakness within whose bounds we have to operate. So it is only right to say that what we have here is more a set of challenges and suggestions than a single interpretive system.

I/THE FRENCH REVOLUTION

EVERY nation has its historical cliché. In France, the most popular one has to do with choosing sides in regard to the Revolution of 1789; the position taken is supposed to be indicative of a whole range of political options from that day to this. A cliché is not necessarily untrue, and this one would seem to have some very profound and still lively roots.

The French Revolution of 1789 overthrew the absolutist state, deprived the nobility of its dominant class role, abolished feudal social relations of production, and thus cleared the way for the development of modern capitalism and bourgeois society in France. It established the republican tradition, equality before the law, and the principle of careers open to talent. It replaced consumption and status by accumulation and dynamism as the ultimate social values. And it marked the entrance of the masses onto the stage of history.

There's the rub. Besides being the single most important series of events in the development of the class power of the bourgeoisie, the Revolution was also the moment when the peasantry and the urban working classes were able to put forth their claim to a voice in public affairs. For that reason, in the second half of the nineteenth century and well into the twentieth, the Revolution was the bogey of all right-thinking people, even of those whose class interests had been promoted by it. Earlier, many bourgeois and their historians had been willing to recognize the benefits of the Revolution, even to see it as the culmination of an ages-long struggle between the nobility and the third estate against despotism and for freedom. Counterrevolution was left to the survivors of the old regime who cultivated nostalgia even while integrating themselves, to a greater or lesser extent, into the ranks of the dynamic and conquering bourgeoisie. It was only when the fear of despotism began to be replaced after the Paris Commune by an even greater fear of anarchy (that is, proletarian power) that all the forces of conservation, whatever their origins, joined in a common attack on the heritage of 1789. No longer was it merely the Terror that had to be condemned as an excess or abuse of power, but the entire revolutionary experience which, in this version, was ultimately responsible for all contemporary miseries.

Not all the French intellectual elite accepted this simplistic game of cops and robbers; a large number (the republicans grouped around the Radical-Socialist party and others further to the left) did substantial battle to defend the Revolution, which they regarded as the "Mother of us all." In the course of the twentieth century, Mother has been the subject of increasing controversy among her children, all of whom are concerned to establish their legitimacy. But Mother, as befits a woman of her years, isn't talking. We are therefore obliged to believe what we will—or, rather, to interpret the events of the French Revolution in the light not only of the available sources, but of our philosophies of history and our current preoccupations. A subject like the French Revolution is not likely to be politically neutral until its successor revolution has been made.

The current argument is really twofold. First, there is the question of the character of the Revolution— was it bourgeois or not? Marxist and neo-Marxist historians (and others as well) have long considered "bourgeois" an appropriate word to use in this context. But did they mean that a group of bourgeois, defined as industrial capitalists on the model of the nineteenth century, were actually responsible for the revolutionary upheaval, or did they wish to indicate the meaning of the Revolution in a larger historical scheme of their own making, independent of personnel? The latter is a perfectly legitimate procedure and, for a Marxist, the only defensible one. But confusion of Marxists on this point has led to demands for clarification and critical analyses such as the one presented here by George V. Taylor of the University of North Carolina, whose researches on the economic history of eighteenth-century France have made important contributions to our knowledge.

The questions raised by Professor Taylor have ultimately to do with our understanding of capitalism as a mode of production and its place in a given social formation. Unless agreement on a working definition can be secured, we will continue to engage in fruitless argument. Since it is evident that the bourgeoisie in the old regime played a role different from their postrevolutionary successors, we have got to be careful to differentiate between the two classes. Furthermore, it would be foolish to seek to establish chronological concordance between the development of productive forces, the formation of a class, the creation of class-consciousness, and the outbreak of revolution. Not just vain, but mechanical and therefore incapable of accounting for historical reality. And last but not least, revolutions of both the bourgeois and the socialist varieties do not break out once and for all, to remain ever the same. They grow, and their leadership may pass from hand to hand even as their content changes. In that sense, they are permanent.

The last point ought really to be addressed to other contemporary critics of the Revolution and revolutionary historiography. The French historians François Furet and Denis Richet have recently argued that the leftward movement blew the Revolution off course. They accuse a "whole tradition of left-wing opinion" of falsifying history by describing "the very period when the bourgeoisie was unable to fulfill its ambitions as the 'ascendant phase of the bourgeois revolution.' " Their point has to be understood in the context of contemporary French politics, as they themselves have gone on to demonstrate in recent articles. In their view, French Marxists, and particularly those close to the French Communist party, in their eagerness to establish their own political legitimacy, have been misled into overestimating the value (and importance) of the Jacobin phase of the Revolution, that is, the year II, 1793–1794, when Robespierre and the Committee of Public Safety were in power, and the sans-culottes artisans and shopkeepers were exerting pressure on them to take ever more radical steps along the road to social revolution. The thesis is most specifically associated with the name of Albert Soboul, professor of the history of the French Revolution at the University of Paris. In the article reprinted here, he argues that, although not a class, the activity of the sans-culottes was essential to the preservation of the victories of the bourgeois revolution. The contradictions within their own ranks, which were the result of conditions as yet unripe for the triumph of popular revolutionism, led to their ultimate defeat, but only after the great threat of counterrevolution had been met and destroyed by the nation in arms.

It is, of course, possible to dispute the validity of this idea, as Furet and Richet do. It is another matter, however, to maintain that the writers under attack have, willfully or otherwise, falsified the history of the Revolution, a politically motivated and unverifiable accusation. More important, what the critics seem either to ignore or reject (and it is not clear which) is the Marxist theory of the hegemony of the masses in bourgeois revolutionary movements. From this point of view, it is not a contradiction to describe an advanced stage of a bourgeois revolution, when nonbourgeois personnel were particularly active and nonbourgeois measures were being enacted, as its ascendant phase. It is much less a question of personnel and conscious programs than it is of the relationships between the classes and fractions of classes contending for power. And by "ascendant phase" the Marxist necessarily refers to that moment when the bourgeois revolution most nearly surpasses itself. As to the "blowing off course," such a phrase indicates a penchant for determinism that makes Marxism seem absolutely voluntaristic by comparison, since it assumes a course prescribed by circumstance, history or some other force to which the popular movement did not adhere.

My own article is a first attempt to understand the background of revolutionary political response among the laboring poor.

George V. Taylor

1

Noncapitalist Wealth and the Origins of the French Revolution

To call the French Revolution of 1789 a "bourgeois revolution" invokes ideas which, by common consent, are inseparable from that phrase. It implies, for example, a social class created and nurtured by capitalism, with its wealth preponderantly capitalist in form and function and its values largely derived from capitalism. It implies that the relation of this class to the processes of production differed substantially from that of other classes and that, allowing for a reasonable number of eccentricities, the bourgeoisie showed an over-all unity of goals and outlook, related significantly to capitalism, that made its political action meaningful, powerful, and revolutionary. Stripped of these associations, the phrase "bourgeois revolution" (or "revolutionary bourgeoisie") loses most of its interpretive value, including particularly its involvement with a concept of economic change and class struggle ranging from the Middle Ages to the cold war and beyond.

The ideas that comprise this interpretation have now come under criticism, chiefly from Alfred Cobban. In his London inaugural lecture of 1954, in an article of 1957 on "The Vocabulary of Social History," and in his *Social Interpretation of the French Revolution,* Cobban argues that the concepts embodied in the words "bourgeois revolution" disagree with what research has brought to light. He believes that the phrase incorporates a self-confirming system of deception. Taken in its ordinary sense, it acts as a standard for selecting, interpreting, and arranging evidence, and because of this the research usually ends by confirming assumptions that creep in with the terminology. In the writings of Albert Soboul and the late Georges Lefebvre, Cobban finds assertions and data that can be turned against their conclusions, and

---

Editor's note: Citations to supporting evidence have been deleted and can be found in the original place of publication, *The American Historical Review.*

he attributes these discrepancies to unperceived conflicts between their premises and their evidence. As a corrective, he calls for a reform of the vocabulary, challenging, among other things, the equivalence of "bourgeois" to "capitalist," and of "noble" to "feudal," and there are others who share his dissatisfaction. I have myself found that there were under the old regime not one kind of capitalism but three, that in comparison with nineteenth-century capitalism they were relatively primitive, and that nobles held a heavy stake in two of them. It also seems clear that the speculation and stockjobbing of the 1780's at Paris, so conspicuously capitalist in appearance, was built not on the modernization of industry and trade but on the financial needs and policies of the monarchy. It was heavily penetrated by the nobles, and its center of gravity included the royal court as well as the Bourse. Herbert Lüthy complains that a "quasi-Marxist" preoccupation with capitalism as peculiarly bourgeois has obscured the capitalism of the court and the great nobles and diverted research from the study of the fortunes of the "grandees." Finally, in a recent article, Elizabeth Eisenstein shows that Lefebvre, in his *Coming of the French Revolution,* attributed the initial stimulus of the "bourgeois revolution" to a group of nobles, the Committee of Thirty, apparently without noticing the contradiction between their status and the class character of the revolution they were supposed to have set afoot.

All this suggests that what has long seemed a settled explanation of the French Revolution has become the source of growing dissatisfaction and is up for a reappraisal like that which J. H. Hexter has applied to the concepts of the gentry and the middle class in Tudor England. This reappraisal is far from complete. The range of topics involved in a full examination of the bourgeois revolution model is very broad; the issues are economic, social, political, and even intellectual. The problem can be taken up at several points. Cobban, in his *Social Interpretation,* reopens the question of how the bourgeois revolution was related (if at all) to that of the peasants, whether the Revolution strengthened capitalism or weakened it, and whether the real winners of the Revolution were not the landowners rather than the commercial-industrial entrepreneurs. Another issue is posed by recent studies of social structure that show wide ranges of property and income within each of certain vocational groups of the upper Third Estate and suggest that the members of each vocational category may have been distributed among two or more degrees of status. But the fundamental question is certainly whether the bourgeoisie of 1789, however defined, had any economic consistency that opposed it to other classes grounded in different forms of wealth. This paper has to do with distinctions between capitalist and noncapitalist wealth and what these imply about the revolution of the upper Third Estate, the movement that began with the demand for doubling the representation of the Third Estate and voting by head rather than by order. It also offers a way of explaining that revolution without having recourse to the present terminology.

There was in the economy of the old regime a distinct configuration of wealth, noncapitalist in function, that may be called "proprietary." It embodied investments in land, urban property, venal office, and annuities. The returns it yielded were modest, ranging between 1 and 5 per cent, but they were fairly constant and varied little from year to year. They were realized not by entrepreneurial effort, which was degrading, but by mere ownership and the passage of calendar intervals. Risk was negligible. Although bad harvests lowered rents in kind, they never destroyed capital, and the rents in money, like annuities and salaries of venal office, were payable regardless of natural hazards. In the proprietary sector investments were almost fully secure.

Historically and functionally, proprietary wealth was aristocratic. Under the old regime, gentility required a stable fortune that left one free to live with ease and dignity on his revenues. In the fortunes of the Toulouse nobles studied by Forster and of the magistrates of the Paris Parlement studied by Bluche it was precisely land, urban property, venal office, and annuities that furnished the income on which these families maintained their way of life. Two considerations discouraged nobles from investing in commerce. First, the social values of aristocracy included a notorious aversion to business as practiced by merchants, merchant manufacturers, and bankers. To invest in "trade" was to risk losing status. The only industries that nobles felt entirely free to develop were those rooted in the land and its resources and growing out of certain exploitations of the medieval fief—mines, metallurgy, paper, glass, and canals—and in developing these they adopted practices and forms of organization substantially different from those employed by the merchants. Second, the risks inherent in business endangered the solidity and continuity considered essential to wealth meant to support a family for several generations. Fundamentally, the fortune that best served the interests of an aristocratic family was an endowment. Like an endowment, it was carefully managed, and risk was kept to a minimum. The preference for this kind of wealth, based on ingrained social attitudes that have powerfully retarded French economic growth, survived the Revolution. When the Napoleonic aristocracy was established, a landed endowment or *majorat* was required of anyone raised to the peerage, and he and his heirs were forbidden to alienate it except in exchanges of land. Both before and after the Revolution, the social values of the old elite dominated the status-conscious men and women of the wealthy Third Estate. Avid for standing, they had little choice but to pursue it as the aristocracy defined it, and the result was a massive prejudice that diverted *roturier* [commoner] as well as noble wealth into comparatively sterile proprietary investments.

In describing this system of wealth, the word "proprietary" does better than "feudal." Cobban has pointed out that, in terms of property, "feudalism" could refer only to the seigneury. The seigneury, consisting of dues, monopolies, and rights surviving from the fief, was an order of property superimposed on property in fee simple, and it could be and was acquired by nonnobles. But seigneurial rights figured marginally in a larger preference for all long-term assets yielding secure revenues and standing, a taste for "property" in every form, not only seigneuries but domains, farms, *métairies* [farms leased on a sharecropping basis], meadows, fields, stands of timber, forges and mills that could be rented out, houses, buildings, venal offices, and loans of indefinite duration producing annuities called *rentes perpétuelles*. Such properties were enduring. Combined into endowments yielding assured revenues, carefully managed, they could be made to support a family indefinitely in a genteel style of living. They guaranteed a status, by no means exclusively noble, that Professor Palmer has called aristocratic. The term "proprietary" describes these fortunes not only because it is derived from "property" but also because it echoes the old regime term *propriétaire,* a prestige counter claimed by those who owned land, even in trifling amounts.

The fondness for land penetrated all levels of French society. Profoundly rural, most eighteenth-century Frenchmen had an atavistic attachment to the soil, and "living nobly" was habitually identified with at least seasonal residence in the country. The aristocracy by tradition and the wealthy urban groups by emulation showed an incurable esteem for rural property. The novelist Stendhal, raised in the 1780's at Grenoble, recalled his father, an *avocat au parlement* [a lawyer allowed to plead before the sovereign courts known as *parlements*], as a man constantly preoccupied with acquiring rural land and expanding his holdings. His father's wigmaker (*perruquier*), on missing an appointment with a client, would explain that he had been visiting his "domain," and his excuses were well received. People bought land yielding 1 or 2 per cent with funds that could have been deposited with merchants at 5, and borrowed at 5 to buy land that yielded 1 or 2. This passion for land was by no means limited to Grenoble. Nobles, *avocats, procureurs* [legal officers], financiers, officials, and merchants in all parts of France bought and held urban and rural properties that qualified them for local acceptance, advancement, and privileges. There were shopkeepers, artisans, and even peasants who invested in land and *rentes* that gave them small incomes for old age. In every town those without a business or profession who lived on such investments were taxed on a separate roll, that of the bourgeois,

and in 1789 in most towns they voted as a separate electoral group of
the Third Estate. A study by Vovelle and Roche shows that the qualification bourgeois disappeared during the Revolution from official acts,
and that persons listed under the old regime as bourgeois reappeared
in documents of the Directory and the Consulate as *rentiers* and
propriétaires, demonstrating as well as anything can that before the
Revolution the fiscal group called bourgeois was noncapitalist.

Nearly all wealthy landowners exploited their land indirectly,
through tenants. They saw their properties not as profit-making enterprises but as sources of rental income. Rent, in fact, was at the center
of all calculations. It was what determined the value of a property: as
rent increased, the value grew proportionately, so that, curiously
enough, the rate of return on capital remained about the same. Generally speaking, rental income seems to have ranged between 2 and 4
per cent of capital value, and Necker wrote in 1784 that the net revenue
from land was 2½ per cent, which is to say that, as an investment, land
provided the low but assured return typical of proprietary wealth.
When an eighteenth-century proprietor set out to increase the revenue
of his properties he thought not in terms of increasing the productivity
of the soil but of raising the rent, and in the late eighteenth century a
significant rise of the peasant population made this easy to do. As land
hunger grew and candidates for leases multiplied, rents rose hand-
somely. Labrousse has found that, from the base period 1726–1741 to
the "intercyclic" period 1785–1789, rural money rents advanced by
98 per cent, and in a paper on the royal domains submitted to the
Assembly of Notables in 1787 mention was made of "the Revolution
which, in twenty years, has nearly doubled the revenues of all land."
Where the rent was paid in kind, as in *métayage* [the practice of share-
cropping], the rise in rents is difficult to measure, but there is no doubt
that it took place. Forster has written that in the Toulouse region the
old phrase "half-fruits" that signified the owner's share was a euphe-
mism; at the end of the century the owners took as much as three-
fourths. It is perhaps possible to say that the French landowner of the
old regime was an exploiter of persons rather than of the soil. The
circumstances of the prerevolutionary period did nothing to change his
traditional attitudes. Indeed, by enabling him to raise his income
without raising production. they reinforced them.

If in the eighteenth century France had had an agricultural revolution comparable to that in England, it would be possible to speak of
agricultural capitalism and to discover an entrepreneurial mentality
that saw income as profit and was prepared to increase profits by investing in productivity. Unfortunately for the old regime, no such thing
took place. There was, of course, much interest among certain upper-
class intellectuals in British agricultural innovations, and, beginning

in 1750, there began to appear a large body of publications on the subject. Agricultural societies were formed, and experiments were undertaken. Nevertheless, the results were meager. The peasants distrusted innovations and sabotaged experiments, and proprietors who wished to install improvements failed because, in order to succeed, they would have had to learn to work and think like peasants, which was exactly what their values prevented them from doing. But it was not only the disinterest of landowners or their unfitness to provide leadership that aborted the French agricultural revolution. There were many other obstacles which, taken together, would have defeated the boldest plans of agricultural reform: the fragmentation of domains into small, dispersed parcels of property; the stubbornness with which country people defended common rights and broke down enclosures; the burden of the taille, which penalized initiative; the hostility of peasants to new crops, crop courses, and methods of cultivation; the tyranny of the leases, which fixed the crop courses in the old patterns; and finally the shortage of livestock, which assured a shortage of manure, which assured a shortage of improved meadows, which in turn assured a shortage of livestock. Given all these barriers to improvement, the proprietary mentality, with its noncapitalist orientation, was not terribly unrealistic. In 1788 the scientist-financier Lavoisier, a careful student of agriculture, told the provincial assembly of the Orléanais that the productivity of British agriculture was about 2.7 times that of French agriculture and that the capital invested per unit of land was two or three times greater in Britain than in France. He owned an experimental farm. In four years he had invested 120,000 livres in it. In his judgment, which would seem well established, the improvements needed to raise productivity in the Orléanais would require much more of an outlay than the proprietors could or would invest. All these deterrents—legal, psychic, and social—checked economic growth and increased the danger of breakdowns like that of 1788–1790, which in its origins was largely, though not wholly, agrarian and unleashed the rural and urban disorders of the common people, disorders without which the Revolution of 1789 could not have succeeded.

In the proprietary scale of preference, the passion for property in office was nearly as strong as that for property in land. A venal office was a long-term investment. Usually it brought a low but stable return, and, as long as the owner regularly paid the *droit annuel* [annual fee] (in earlier times the *paulette*), he could, under restrictions applicable to each office, sell it to a buyer, bequeath it to an heir, or even rent it out to someone, such as a judge, who, though admitted to practice, was unable to buy the required *charge* [public office]. The number and variety of venal offices that existed at the end of the old regime is incredible. An investigation that Necker launched in 1778 disclosed no less than 51,000 venal offices in the law courts, the municipalities, and the financial system, and their capital value, as revealed by voluntary declarations made under an edict of 1771, totaled 600,000,000 livres, although this should be increased by as much as 50 per cent because the declarations, taxable at 1 per cent per annum, were notoriously undervalued. These offices included those held by the personnel of the parlements and their chancelleries, the judges of the other royal courts, and the multitude of clerks, beadles, sergeants, surveyors, assessors, and concessionaires that surrounded these courts. They also included the offices held by the notaries and *procureurs,* who could practice their professions only by acquiring the appropriate *charges.* They did not, however, include the offices of the royal household, venal military appointments, or places in the financial companies and the higher financial concessions like those of the *receveurs généraux des finances* [chief tax collectors], and for these we should probably add another 200,000,000 or 300,000,000 livres to the total indicated above. Also excluded from these figures were the offices held by guild officials, inspectors, and masters, and particularly by the wigmakers. Given the present state of research we have no precise idea of how many adult males owned offices, but it would not be surprising to find that they came to 2 or 3 per cent of the total.

Ordinarily, the declared value of an office was only part of the cost of buying and exercising it. Nearly always, it was sold for a price higher than that recorded in the declarations and contracts, and the investment was increased by heavy taxes, fees for registration and reception, and the honoraria, gratuities, and *pourboires* [tips] that a candidate had to distribute to officials, clerks, beadles, and even doormen in obtaining his nomination. Philip Dawson has brought to light the case of a young *avocat* who in 1781 purchased a magistracy in the *sénéchaussée* [administrative district] of La Rochelle. In the contract of sale, filed with a notary, the price was put at 10,167 livres. But the buyer's notes show that he really paid 14,000 livres, plus another 4,150 in taxes, dues, fees, and gratuities, all of which means that the total investment exceeded the stated value of the office by 78 per cent. When an office gave admission to a profession, the disproportion between its acknowledged value and the full investment was apt to be still greater. In March 1787 the future revolutionary Danton bought the office of *avocat au Conseil du Roi* for 10,000 livres; at the same time, however, he paid the seller 68,000 livres for his practice, including the clientele and the accounts receivable. In short, the additional costs and professional outlays that accompanied investments in venal office raised the total French private funds committed to this purpose far above the more than 600,000,000 livres with which the Revolution compensated those whose offices it abolished.

Few venal offices were genuinely lucrative. On the 51,000 judicial, municipal, and financial offices covered by the 1778 investigation, the salaries, after deducting for the *droits annuels, vingtièmes* [royal tax on wealth], and transfer taxes (*droits de mutation*), averaged only 1 per cent of the values declared in 1771, although in most cases there were fees, perquisites, and gratuities that made up the interest on the declared capital. Whatever economic value they had depended on how the owners used the opportunities that accompanied them. For a notary or *procureur,* the income from a practice could constitute a very decent return on the total outlay. But for the magistrates it was likely to be a different story. Although it was taken for granted that a Parisian *conseiller au parlement* cleared 5 per cent per annum on his investment, the *présidents à mortier*[1] made only 2 per cent, and the First President, burdened with costs of maintaining the dignity of his position, probably spent more than he received. Generally speaking, an investment in office was an investment in standing. What made it desirable was the status, the respectability that it conferred. For a solid gain in prestige, the holders of *charges* would usually settle for a low return and even a loss of capital. In 1790, for example, the National Assembly was told that the magistrates of some parlements, by excluding *roturiers* from admission, had so narrowed the market for their offices as to reduce the purchase price from more than 50,000 livres to as little as 15,000. In effect, they sacrificed capital for status, which was not unnatural in a society afflicted with a mania for prestige. Apparently, it meant a great deal to be a *lieutenant-civil,* a *lieutenant-criminel,* a *procureur du roi,* a *grand-maître des eaux et forêts,* or even a *conseiller au grenier à sel.* To the *roturiers* it meant still more to acquire an office that gave noble rank. According to Necker, there were more than four thousand of these, although perhaps half of them, like the magistracies of the parlements, were inaccessible to commoners. For example, a *secrétaire du roi* was ennobled by his office and, if he held it twenty years or died possessed of it, acquired *noblesse transmissible* [nobility that can be passed on to one's heirs] for his heirs and descendants. A *trésorier de France* enjoyed *noblesse personnelle* [nobility for the possessor alone]; although his family did not share this, there was nothing to prevent him from bequeathing his office to his eldest son, and it appears that some of these offices gave *noblesse transmissible.* According to Necker, there were 900 *secrétaires du roi* attached to the chancelleries of the parlements and 740 places that one takes to be those of the *trésoriers de France* in the financial apparatus.

---

[1] The *conseiller au parlement* and the *président à mortier* were judges in the Parlement, the latter having a superior grade in the hierarchy.—*Ed.*

Nothing indicates that the propensity of these offices for creating new nobles had been cut off at the end of the old regime.

In addition to land, urban properties, and office, proprietary wealth was invested in *rentes*. In the broadest sense, a *rente* was an annual revenue that one received for having transferred something of value to someone else. A *rente foncière* was rent for land. A *rente hypothécaire* was an annuity the payment of which was secured by property. A *rente perpétuelle* was an annuity of indefinite duration, terminated only when the debtor chose, on his own initiative, to refund the principal and thereby free himself from paying the *rente*. A *rente viagère* was a life annuity: the principal was entrusted to someone who paid the annuity until the person or persons named in the contract died; at that point the principal became finally and irrevocably his. Because the *rente viagère* was essentially a speculation that destroyed all or part of the capital accumulated for a family endowment, most of those living on proprietary wealth believed it reckless and immoral, and a man who converted his fortune into life annuities was considered to have defrauded his heirs.

To an American student, the rationale of this vocabulary is elusive. Everything is clarified, however, by the fact that the vocabulary took shape during the late Middle Ages, when those who wished to borrow, and those who wished to lend, had to find ways of disguising loans at interest so as to circumvent the laws against usury. The terminology of the *rente* made this possible, at least during the sixteenth and seventeenth centuries. One spoke, for example, of purchasing a *rente:* this modulated the smell of avarice and exploitation by making it seem that the lender, who bought the *rente,* had solicited it from the borrower, who sold it, and obtained it on the borrower's terms. The vocabulary also improved appearances by assimilating all these transactions to land rents, which were undoubtedly on the right side of the law. Schnapper has shown that the *rente perpétuelle* began as an annual rent paid to a seller of land by a buyer who could not furnish the full price and, in effect, paid rent on that part of the property he did not own. In the sixteenth century, however, the *rente perpétuelle* acquired an existence apart from real-estate transactions. It then became a perpetual annuity paid for a grant of capital that an investor (the lender) "abandoned," and this was its legal character through the end of the old regime. In the contract, whatever the parties may have agreed verbally or in separate instruments, to stipulate a time of repayment was forbidden, and no such stipulation could be enforced in the courts, for the Church insisted upon a permanent alienation of the capital. Only the borrower, the "seller" of the *rente,* could decide whether the capital would be restored, and, if so, when. No doubt, if he failed to pay the *rente* he could be forced into ceding property that might equal or even exceed the original capital, and perhaps there were other pressures that creditors could employ. Whatever the truth may have been, it seems probable that in the eighteenth century many borrowers gave assurances that the capital would be repaid at a stipulated time. Those who lived up to these assurances probably did so in large part so as to protect their credit and reputations.

The indefinite duration of the *rente perpétuelle* ruined it for commerce, industry, banking, and the short-term credits that the financiers furnished the royal treasury. In these sectors, advances at interest were indispensable, and, although they were nominally illegal, the parties were shielded from prosecution by a national conspiracy, abetted by the administration, to keep the usury laws from being invoked. Merchants gave and took interest on the balances of their accounts with one another and paid interest on time deposits put up by investors. Bankers took interest for many kinds of accommodations. The King, himself, violated the usury laws, and there was even a royal rate of interest which, since the time of Louis XIV, was fixed at 5 per cent. Under these circumstances it is difficult to see why the archaic *rente perpétuelle* survived. It survived, of course, because it met most of the demands for long-term credit operations in the traditional or proprietary sector, where there were few pressures for collection and payment and where people took satisfaction in avoiding the questionable practices of *traitants* and *commerçants* [businessmen]. Its proper domain was that of accommodations within and between families and investments in annuities sold by municipalities, provincial estates, and the royal treasury. Although economically obsolete, it not only survived, but left a mark on the management of royal and private wealth. Among other things, it engendered that characteristic insouciance toward debt for which the old regime was famous and induced a dangerous negligence in royal finance. "The abundance of claims and credits of indefinite duration," writes Schnapper, "is a characteristic trait of old economies. The creditor prefers a fixed revenue to a capital for which he cannot easily find use. The debtor, himself, never repays because he does not have sufficient monetary means." It is impossible to read this without thinking of the old French royal debt and the bankruptcy in which it finished. On January 1, 1789, the registers of the Paris Hôtel de Ville showed 52,119,537 livres in *rentes perpétuelles* to be paid out during the year, of this more than 44 per cent represented annuities on funds borrowed before 1721. In large part, the chronic and ultimately fatal disinclination to amortize the long-term debt is attributable to the fact that the capital of a *rente perpétuelle* did not have to be repaid. Neither, of course, did that of a *rente viagère*. It was therefore easy to drift into bankruptcy. Only when

service on the long-term debt was so large as to make deficits inescapable would a controller general have to consider refunding principal, but then, of course, he would find it impossible to pay. That
was precisely the quandary of the controllers general of finance after
the American war.

It should now be clear that there was a fairly consistent pattern of noncapitalist wealth, that it was traditionally aristocratic, and that "feudalism" is a bad name for it. It was governed by institutional survivals
and social values that opposed the progressive and expansive tendencies of capitalism, preferring rent to profit, security to risk, tradition
to innovation, and, in terms of personal goals, gentility to entrepreneurial. skill and renown. It displayed nearly all the traits of what
Rostow has called a traditional society, one dominated by landowners
and their values and governed, as far as production was concerned, by
pre-Newtonian modes of thought. All these institutions, values, and
fixations promoted, as Rostow has suggested, a "long-run fatalism"
and a "ceiling on the level of obtainable output per head." In England, no doubt, such deterrents to growth existed, but in ways that are
not yet clearly explained they were being outflanked or overcome. In
France, however, they flourished. The question of why there should
have been such a disparity deserves much more study than it has
received.

Compared with proprietary wealth, eighteenth-century commercial
capitalism seems a vastly different thing. In commerce, banking, and
domestic industry fixed assets were negligible, and investments were
put into circulating wealth. Goubert has written of the Motte family
of Beauvais:

One is tempted to write that what was always important to those mer-
chants-born [marchands-nés] was wealth in motion, the rather intoxi-
cating impression that must have come to them from the merchandise,
credits, and cash that moved, circulated, fluctuated, and constantly transformed themselves: a kind of ballet of linens, paper, and money.

This engaging description of commercial wealth is justified by entrepreneurial records in many archives. At Lyons merchants rented the
houses and warehouses in which they did business. With the armateurs
[ship owners] of Bordeaux and Marseilles, ships were short-term assets;
bought by a syndicate organized to finance the voyage, the ship was sold
at the end of the venture, sometimes at auction, sometimes simply to
the syndicate the armateur had formed for the next voyage. Industrial
machinery was simple and made mostly of wood. In textiles, which
accounted for about two-thirds of industrial production by value, it

was owned chiefly by the artisans to whom the work was distributed, and when merchants loaned it to them it was not serious enough to warrant carrying in the accounts. All this explains why the ledgers of the old regime carry no accounts for depreciation costs. The day of heavy fixed commercial and industrial investment was yet to come.

Risk, nearly unknown in the proprietary sector, was a central fact of business life. The merchant speculated in commodities, paper, and credit, and, no matter how prudent he was, his fate depended largely on events he could not control. Shipwrecks, acts of war, sudden changes in style, unforeseeable bankruptcies, or unfavorable shifts in exchange rates could wipe him out, and if it was bad luck that broke him it was largely good luck that made him rich. Established merchants, known for caution and probity, went under, while new men, starting with borrowed money and the savings of a clerk's salary, became well to do. Commerce, therefore, was a zone of fortune building and social mobility. But because it lacked the stability of the proprietary sector, it was dangerous for established wealth. "All that I have seen," wrote the Comte de Villèle, ". . . leaves me with the opinion that every man with an acquired fortune who desires only to keep it, must keep at a distance from people, of whatever class or profession they be, who strive to make a fortune; . . . he must avoid all business, all relations with them, because they will not fail to make him their dupe. Furthermore, to each man his *métier,* as the proverb says: look at the proprietor trying to speculate, and at the merchant trying to enter agriculture. . . . Never have I participated in the least speculation."

Finally, in contrast to proprietary wealth, business capital gave low dividends in prestige. The public image of the merchant that Molière exploited rather brutally in *Le bourgeois gentilhomme* was profoundly ignoble, and it afflicted the merchants themselves with feelings of inferiority that probably troubled them more than the contempt they actually encountered. To some extent their unhappiness was self-induced. In 1700–1701 merchant deputies to the Council of Trade complained that merchants were held in low esteem, that the public ignored the superior status of a wholesale merchant or banker, and that because of this their sons avoided business and their daughters preferred nonmerchants as husbands. "Our young people," wrote one of them, "concentrate on the social graces rather than on the really substantial things in life, [and] our children are ever fearful lest it become known that their fathers were once merchants." About thirty years before the Revolution the Abbé Coyer wrote: "Only the Merchant perceives no luster in his career, & if he wants to succeed in what is called in France *being something,* he has to give it up. This misunderstood expression does a lot of damage. In order to be *something,* a large part of the Nobility remains nothing." The merchants felt that the intense practical training of business, the constant supervision and attention it required, and its remoteness from the leisure and finesse of the proprietary round of life kept them from cultivating the social and intellectual qualities that brought respect. Savary, whose *Le parfait négociant* remained throughout the eighteenth century a desktop oracle of business practice and morality, warned merchants not to educate their sons in the liberal arts and not to let them mingle with young nobles and men of the robe in the *collèges,* because the self-esteem they would acquire in those milieux would ruin them for trade. Because these attitudes existed, anyone who remained in business, no matter how creditably he lived, suffered some discount in prestige. Even in the values of the Third Estate, diverse as they may have been, esteem was associated with proprietary wealth. Capitalism, which offered neither the assurance nor the standing that went with land and office, was simply a way, direct and dangerous, of getting rich.

The merchants, although they complained of the prejudices against trade, had to accept them as part of the status system and ground rules in the competition for standing. That is why they so often diverted profits into the purchase of country properties and offices, and why so many of them, once enriched, converted their commercial fortunes entirely into proprietary possessions. At an appropriate stage, the richest and most ambitious bought offices that conferred nobility. The members of the Danse family, linen merchants of Beauvais, constantly put business profits into country properties, acquired nobility, and, in 1757, liquidated their last partnership. During the Revolution, like other nobles and wealthy commoners, they lost their seigneurial dues, but purchased *biens nationaux* [lands confiscated from the Church and the emigré nobility] and remained until the Second Empire a family of provincial gentlemen. But this is only a sample of what was going on. The conversion of commercial capital into proprietary wealth was a regular feature of French history, from the sixteenth century to the eighteenth and even beyond. Apparently, the purpose of succeeding in business was to get the means of becoming a proprietor and a gentleman, and both Colbert and Necker, a century apart from one another, complained that this tendency drained off commercial and industrial capital and undermined economic growth. In order to counteract this, the government frequently authorized nobles to enter maritime and wholesale commerce and banking, thereby permitting ennobled merchants to continue in trade without losing status. This remedy, however, was only partly effective. It protected the juridical status of an ennobled merchant, but, since it had little impact on social values and attitudes, his sons were likely to drift into the administration, the armed forces, the judiciary, or country life, where sooner or later their ignoble origins would be forgotten.

There is no conclusive way of comparing the mass value of proprietary and business wealth in prerevolutionary France. Beginning with
what passed in those days for statistics, supplementing them with estimates made by well-informed men who say little about their derivation, making inferences on assumptions which, though reasonable, can
be endlessly debated, one concludes that the traditional modes of
property—land, buildings, office, and *rentes*—accounted for more than
80 per cent of French private wealth. This indicates a substantial preponderance for the proprietary sector. It is in no way astonishing. The
day of heavy fixed industrial investment in factories and railroads,
which would have altered the balance, lay far ahead. Meanwhile, most
Frenchmen lived on the land, which yielded most of the taxable
income and the gross national product. That is why the *économistes*
not unreasonably attacked agricultural problems first, often to the
neglect of the others.

For our purposes it is desirable to know the relative weight of the
two kinds of capital not only for the society as a whole but in the upper
Third Estate. Unfortunately, studies of the notarial records are not
sufficiently advanced to show this. For the moment, all one can do is
count persons, and from this it appears that even in the most heavily
commercialized cities the proprietors and professional men in the
Third Estate outnumbered the merchants. At Bordeaux, the second
most active port, there were 1,100 officials, professionals, *rentiers*, and
property owners against only 700 merchants, brokers, and sugar
refiners. At Rouen, a prime center of industry, banking, and maritime
and wholesale trade, the administrative and judicial officers, professionals, and proprietors-*rentiers* outnumbered the merchants and
brokers by more than three to one. At Toulouse, an agricultural, legal,
and ecclesiastical capital, the ratio was about eleven to four, but the
four included merchants who for the most part traded on small capital
and in little volume and did much retail business, so that one hesitates
to call them capitalists. There is, however, a further consideration.
Because the merchants and industrialists owned, along with their
commercial capital, considerable proprietary wealth, we could, with
better data, divide them fractionally between the two sectors, and, by
such a procedure, the share of commercial and industrial capital in
the upper Third Estate would seem much lower than the impression
we get by counting heads.

Soundings like these are merely straws in the wind, but they drift
always in one direction. They confirm what seems to have been implicit
in the consciousness of eighteenth-century France—that even in the
well-to-do Third Estate proprietary wealth substantially outweighed
commercial and industrial capital. This would not have surprised a
Frenchman of the old regime and should not surprise us. The reason

for stressing it here is to lay the ground for an assertion that is fundamental in analyzing the causes of the Revolution: there was, between
most of the nobility and the proprietary sector of the middle classes,
a continuity of investment forms and socio-economic values that made
them, economically, a single group. In the relations of production
they played a common role. The differentiation between them was not
in any sense economic; it was juridical. This situation, in the historiography of the Revolution, has received practically no serious attention
and remains, in Orwellian language, an "unfact." The reason for this
is that it contributes nothing to what Cobban rightly calls "the established theory of the French Revolution," the theory that the Revolution was the triumph of capitalism over feudalism. In that context the
configuration of proprietary wealth that pervaded both the second
and Third Estates has no place and remains unwanted, unused, and
therefore, in effect, unknown.

It deserves, however, to be recognized, and its claims are strengthened by bringing forward a second unfact: that a substantial number
of nobles participated as entrepreneurs in commerce, industry, and
finance. There was indeed, before the Revolution, a *noblesse commer-
çante,* though not, perhaps, the one that the Abbé Coyer called for in
1756. Provincial, military, and court nobles, peers, and members of
the royal family invested in the General Farm, speculated on the
Bourse, and developed and exploited mines, canals, and metallurgical
establishments, including the great foundry of Le Creusot. On the
other hand, there was, to reverse the phrase, a *commerce anobli,* a
sizable group of merchants ennobled through the municipal offices of
certain cities and the two thousand or more venal offices that conferred
nobility on the buyers. For the most part, these ennobled merchant
families were in a transitional stage. As enterprises were liquidated, or
generations arose that were no longer trained for business, they
dropped out of trade to live, as other nobles did, on their revenues.
All the same, merchants or not, they were nobles and sat in the noble
assemblies of 1789. To sum up, there were nobles who were capitalists.
There were merchants who were nobles. As the proprietary wealth
traditionally identified with aristocracy extended far down into the
Third Estate, so the capitalism traditionally identified with the
wealthy Third Estate penetrated into the second, and into its highest
ranks.

This means that the old diagram by which we envision prerevolutionary society must be changed. There was a clear juridical boundary
that separated nobles from commoners, and a commoner crossed it by
registering a legal document, his letters of nobility. On the other hand,
the frontier between capitalist and proprietary wealth ran vertically
through both orders. The horizontal line marked a legal dichotomy,

the vertical line, an economic one. To think of them as coinciding, even roughly, is to misunderstand the situation completely. The concept of two classes, at once economically and juridically disjunct, can be sustained only by ignoring the weight of proprietary wealth in the Third Estate and that of capitalism in the second, or, in other words, by continuing to ostracize them as unfacts.

From this follow two important conclusions. The first is that when the word bourgeois is used to indicate a nonnoble group playing a capitalist role in the relations of production it includes less than half the well-to-do Third Estate and excludes the proprietary groups that furnished 87 per cent of the Third Estate deputation to the Estates-General. In other words, it embraces only a minority of the upper middle classes and explains almost nothing about the origins of the revolutionary leadership. In this sense it should be discarded as inadequate and misleading. But there are other senses, loaded with eighteenth-century implications, in which the word will continue to be employed because it alone translates what the documents have to say. One may, for example, speak of bourgeois who lived nobly on their revenues and comprised a fiscal category; these constituted a small portion of the Third Estate and counted entirely in the proprietary group. One may also speak of bourgeois as persons who, being inscribed in the registers of the bourgeoisie of a town, enjoyed what Anglo-Saxons call "the rights of the city," including political advantages and fiscal exemptions worth having, but in this sense the bourgeoisie included nobles and noncapitalist commoners and was not entirely of the Third Estate. Finally, one may adopt a peasant usage, applying the word bourgeois to townsmen who collected rents in and near the village and were felt to be an alien and adverse interest. All three meanings convey realities of the old regime and are useful on condition that one makes clear which of them he has in mind.

The second conclusion is that we have no economic explanation for the so-called "bourgeois revolution," the assault of the upper Third Estate on absolutism and aristocracy. No one denies that such an assault took place or that it left a powerful imprint upon French society. The struggle for the doubling of the Third Estate and the vote by head, the demand for a constitution and an elected legislature, the intimation of political equality in the Declaration of the Rights of Man, the liquidation of intendancies, provinces, parlements, fiscal inequalities, forms of nobility—all these, put in series with the emigration, the expropriation of Church and *émigré* wealth, and the Terror, have to be made credible on some basis. By one of the unexamined postulates of current historiography we expect them to be explained by a conflict of social classes and the contradictions between a "rising" economic order and the order that it challenges. The position taken here is that we have now learned enough to see that this cannot be done, that to divide the wealthy elements of prerevolutionary society into a feudal aristocracy and a capitalist bourgeoisie forces the concealment of too much evidence, and that the whole classic concept of a bourgeois revolution has become impossible to sustain.

This leaves in our interpretation of the Revolution a somewhat painful void. Our instinct is to fill it with a new class struggle interpretation like Cobban's "revolution of the propertied classes," which explains some results of the Revolution but not, apparently, its origins. There may, however, be more plausibility in a political approach than in a reorganization of social categories. The gist of such an approach can be set down in two propositions that probably amount to the same thing. First, the struggle against absolutism and aristocracy was the product of a financial and political crisis that it did not create. Second, it was essentially a political revolution with social consequences and not a social revolution with political consequences. Because these assumptions suggest a backward step in historiography, it will take a few paragraphs to make them respectable.

The Revolution resulted from a bankruptcy that left the monarchy discredited and helpless. The disclosures of the first Assembly of Notables shocked everyone capable of reacting to public affairs, set off an expanding discussion of reforms, and raised hopes for a national regeneration. The government's reform program, which threatened privileges and seemed tainted with the supposed negligence and dishonesty of the Controller General Calonne, was rejected by the Notables. For more than a year the parlements and other constituted bodies opposed it. This resistance, the so-called *révolte nobiliaire,* taught the upper Third Estate the language, tactics, and gallantry of opposition. It made the convocation of the Estates-General inevitable. When in August 1788 this convocation was announced (along with a partial suspension of payments), there was thrust upon the nation a new political issue: whether royal power would pass to the privileged orders or would be shared with those who, until then, had been disfranchised. By inviting his subjects to advise him on how to organize the Estates-General, the King precipitated a landslide of publications that touched off a growing outcry for the doubling of the Third and the vote by head. This generated a political struggle between democracy, as Palmer has defined it, and aristocracy, substantially as he has taught us to understand it. The stakes were very high. They included the question of at whose expense the financial problem would be solved, and whether careers in the military, the clergy, and the judiciary, and, above all, in politics would be opened to commoners, rich and poor, whose main resources were talents, education, and ambition.

In explaining the democratic assault on despotism and aristocracy it is unnecessary to conjure up a social struggle rooted in economic change. The paralysis of the monarchy, the apprehensions of the taxable groups and creditors of the state, and the hopes and ambitions of the professional classes, combined with the slogans, myths, and images generated by the struggle, seem quite enough. The revolutionary mentality was created by the crisis. It was, in fact, the writing of the *cahiers* that forced a crystallization of issues and their formulation in ideological terms. For the mass of the upper Third Estate, the schools of revolution were the electoral assemblies of 1789, not the salons and *sociétés de pensée* [intellectual societies] of the old regime.

What this interpretation restores is the sense of an unplanned, unpremeditated revolution that in many ways exceeded the aims expressed in the *cahiers de doléances* [list of grievances] of March and April 1789. Take, for example, the abolition of nobility, which may be understood here as aristocracy constituted juridically as an order. If in the spring of 1789 the upper Third Estate had seen nobility as an intolerable institution it would certainly have called for its destruction. But this was never attempted until the revolutionary leadership had concluded, from more than a year of political experience, that the nobility was an incorrigible enemy of the new regime. Certainly there was friction in the quarrel of 1788 over how the new provincial estates would be constituted and whether nobles and commoners would deliberate there together. It was intensified by the dispute over how the Estates-General should be organized. But in the spring of 1789 middle-class feelings toward nobility were still benign. Far from wanting to abolish nobility, the Third Estate wished to rehabilitate it. One reads in the Third Estate *cahiers* of the major towns and cities that nobility was to be reformed, that nobles should be given opportunities to replenish their fortunes, and, still more remarkable, that nobility must be saved from adulteration by abolishing the venal offices and making ennoblement depend not on money but on service to the nation. Then came the quarrels and confrontations of 1789, the destruction of the constituted bodies, and the reform of the army and the Church, which was dispossessed to protect the creditors of the state. These events made the opposition to the Revolution, inside and outside the National Assembly, formidable. In all three orders it developed considerable strength. On June 19, 1790, after a year of struggle, nobility, as such, was abolished in order to disarm and probably to punish the most conspicuous element of the opposition. Nothing in the *cahiers* forecasts such a decree. The intention to smash the legal basis of nobility and, along with it, the whole system of language, symbols, images, and formalities that reinforced the subservience of the lower groups, was a product of the revolutionary crisis, not a cause. To argue that it came about through long years of economic change, class formation, and the gradual growth of class consciousness in a bourgeoisie that played a capitalist role in the relations of production is not only out of keeping with the evidence, but superfluous.

The present crisis in the interpretation of the French Revolution results from the maturing of social history as a discipline. This specialty, in its present form, was virtually created in France. Its methods are as distinctive as the sources it employs, and its findings are most convincing when expressed in quantitative form. Applied to the history of the Revolution, it has yielded a mass of data on economic interests and conditions, standards of living, population change, corporate structures, social values, and the complex mentalities found at various levels of society. Much of this material disagrees with the vocabulary in use when the effort began. But the vocabulary is still in force. The problem is how to rescue the data from a language that misrepresents it and imprisons it in categories that can no longer be justified.

Although interest in the social history of the Revolution is very old, its progress as a specialty began during 1901–1904, when Jaurès published the first four volumes of the *Histoire socialiste* and procured the establishment of the Commission of the Economic History of the Revolution. "It was Jaurès," Lefebvre once wrote, "who habituated historians to see [in the Revolution] a fact [that is] social and, consequently, of economic origin." Jaurès had no doubt that the Revolution was the political triumph of a bourgeoisie matured by the growth of capitalism, and, with an erudition that is astonishing, given the literature available to him, he rewrote the history of the Revolution on this theme. Lefebvre, who avowed a deep indebtedness to Jaurès, never renounced this view. In the first two paragraphs of *Quatre-vingt-neuf*, paragraphs that dominate the reading of the whole book, he identified the "primary cause" of the Revolution as a conflict between an aristocratic society, grounded historically in the ascendancy of landowners, and a new class, the bourgeoisie, enriched on liquid forms of wealth. In this passage Lefebvre left no doubt that capitalism was the economic basis of the bourgeoisie and the source of its growing power. Out of this socio-economic configuration had come, he said, the ideology of the philosophes and the *économistes,* expressing the values and aspirations of a revolutionary class. These developments were fundamental. The royal bankruptcy and the aristocratic resistance that forced the King to convoke the Estates-General were treated as an "immediate cause" which explained many of the characteristics of the Revolution and why it began when it did.

Lefebvre's work, however, led him to modify considerably the original overview of Jaurès. Writing in 1932, he found that overview already too simple. As an explanation, he observed, it was credible only when supplemented with the financial crisis, the *révolte nobiliaire,* and the economic distress that produced the popular disturbances without which the Revolution could not have succeeded. In *Quatre-vingt-neuf,* passing well beyond the thesis announced in the preface, he described four revolutions: aristocratic, bourgeois, popular, and peasant. In *La Révolution française,* the synthesis that he contributed in 1951 to the series "Peuples et civilisations," he described an aristocratic revolution, a bourgeois revolution, and a popular revolution, the last being composed of a Parisian revolution, a municipal revolution, and a peasant revolution; all these were treated under the heading "L'avènement de la bourgeoisie en France" [the coming of age of the bourgeoisie in France]. He was also troubled, far more than less perceptive historians, by the problem of relating the bourgeoisie, with all its diversity, to the derivation assigned it in Jaurès' writings and his own preface to *Quatre-vingt-neuf.* Twice he wrote that it was not "homogeneous." In *La Révolution française* he saw it as composed of bourgeois living on investments in land and, to some extent, liquid capital; holders of venal offices; financiers, maritime merchants, and manufacturers; a "middle class" or *petite bourgeoisie* of tradesmen and petty officials; and a bourgeoisie of intellectual capacities ranging from savants and artists to law clerks and office employees. The determinants of status, he believed, included birth, corps, vocation, and, occasionally, talent. In his last study, an analysis of the urban society of Orléans, he laid out social categories in terms of order, vocation, and wealth or income, but Soboul tells us that he was not satisfied with either the method or the results. It is not difficult to see why. Classification by wealth conflicted with classification by role, and both conflicted with classification by order. Nearly a fifth of the nobles who enjoyed revenues of more than five hundred livres per year, for example, were merchants and sugar refiners; "bourgeois" by vocation, they shared the privileges of the second estate. To put the matter another way, half the refiners and a third of the merchants named in the tax rolls of 1791 were nobles; giving priority to the system of orders, Lefebvre classified them with the nobility. The Third Estate he divided into a *haute bourgeoisie* and a large category called *moyenne et petite bourgeoisies,* but for lack of tax rolls did this entirely on the basis of vocations and corporate groupings. All non-nobel merchants, refiners, brokers, officials, and manufacturers were assigned to the *haute bourgeoisie,* although Lefebvre observed that, if the tax rolls had survived, some of them would have had to be demoted. On that principle, of course, the same documents would have elevated many professional men from the lower group to the higher. Finally, one reads that the *cahier* of the Third Estate of the *bailliage* [administrative district] was drawn up by the elite of the bourgeoisie, but that elite, a political entity, remains unreconciled with the socioeconomic groupings.

Apparently, what the emerging data have made impossible is to equate the identifiable leadership of the upper Third Estate—the "revolutionary bourgeoisie"—with a social class that played a common role in the relations of production, or, more precisely, owned the instruments of production in an emergent capitalist economy. Soboul, in his masterful study of the sans-culottes, faced a comparable situation. He found the sans-culottes a political bloc composed of diverse economic elements; he therefore pronounced them not a social class. The same step may now be taken with regard to the "revolutionary bourgeoisie." Jeffry Kaplow has, in fact, moved toward this solution by defining the bourgeois on juridical and political lines. They were, he says, well-to-do people excluded from the privileges of the nobles and from powerful positions in the state, the army, the Church, and the parlements. Yet they had access, not enjoyed by the common people, to local political office. "They were beginning to become conscious of themselves as a class," he observes, "and shared a definite set of values." That is certainly true. Yet, if this is a social class, it is not one in the sense recognized by the last two generations of social scientists in this country. Nor is it the bourgeoisie as we commonly think of it.

Hexter has recently pointed out that one of the peculiarities of historical rhetoric is the use of words that he calls "evocative" because they signal the historian to summon up whole categories and sequences of associations with which professional thought identifies them. Terms like "aristocracy," "bourgeoisie," "feudalism," "capitalism," and "social class" have this quality. It is what gives them interpretive value. Each is freighted with implications that make it operative in the machinery of the bourgeois revolution model, so that, as Cobban points out, to accept the language is to accept the theory. In ordinary usage, whoever says "class" is heard to say "productive role," and whoever says "bourgeois" is heard to say "capitalist." Unless he adds an emphatic disclaimer, he should expect to be understood in this sense. But even emphatic disclaimers can be ineffectual if, as in the case of "class" and "bourgeois," special meanings have been welded on by more than thirty years of writing, teaching, and discussion. Under those circumstances, there is little prospect of revising professional usage. That is particularly true of a vocabulary which, among many millions of the world's people, has a content that is ideologically obligatory and is thereby frozen into alliance with an obsolete interpretation. Obviously, the project of solving this problem by giving new meanings to old words is more or less utopian. The phrases "bourgeois revolution" and "revolutionary bourgeoisie," with their inherent deceptions, will have to go, and others must be found that convey with precision and veracity the realities of social history.

Albert Soboul

2

The Popular Movement
and Bourgeois Revolution

In the final analysis, the 9 Thermidor constitutes a tragic episode in the conflict of classes within the former Third Estate. But, to place it in the right perspective, we need to remember that the Revolution was fundamentally a struggle between the European aristocracy and the Third Estate as a whole. In this struggle, it is hardly surprising that the French bourgeoisie should have played the leading role. The Revolutionary Government, founded upon an alliance between the montagnard bourgeoisie and the Parisian sans-culotterie, had been given the task of defending the Revolution against the aristocracy both within France and beyond her frontiers. As far as the Montagnards were concerned, it was perfectly natural that the Revolution should have placed the bourgeoisie in control of the nation's destiny; but, in any case, this was not the immediate problem. Solely concerned with victory, the Montagnards—particularly the Robespierrists—realized that the Third Estate would have to remain united as it had been in 1789. This explains the alliance with the sans-culotterie which made possible the installation of the Revolutionary Government during the summer of 1793. It also explains why this government—at least until the spring of 1794—should have been so anxious to arbitrate between the interests of the bourgeoisie and the popular movement; to share the necessary sacrifices between them; and to intervene immediately either of them threatened to undermine the policy of national defence. It was a question of directing the entire resources of the nation for war.

On the basic issues—hatred of the aristocracy and the will for victory—the Parisian sans-culottes wholeheartedly supported the Revolutionary Government: the measure of this support can be judged from the fact that on 13 Vendémiaire and 18 Fructidor, setting aside their own legitimate grievances, many of them assisted the Thermidorean bourgeoisie to crush the counter-revolution. But differences of opinion on other vital issues rapidly alienated the sympathy of the

Parisian sans-culotterie; and although these differences can be traced to the consequences of the war, they nevertheless reveal, quite clearly, the incompatible interests of two distinct social categories.

On the political level, the war created the need for an authoritarian régime. The sans-culottes showed that they were fully conscious of this by playing an important part in the creation of such a government. But it soon became apparent that the democratic ideas favoured by the Montagnards and the sans-culotterie were not designed to meet the particular problems which arose: this was especially true of the kind of democracy practised by the sans-culotterie which, moving spontaneously towards the exercise of direct government, was incompatible with the conduct of a war. The sans-culottes had asked for a strong government to crush the aristocracy; they never considered the possibility that, in order to do this, it would be forced to discipline the popular movement.

In addition, the political ideals of the sans-culotterie, vaguely defined during the revolutionary insurrections, did not tend to further the interests of liberal democracy as interpreted by the bourgeoisie, but those of popular democracy. Control over their elected representatives, the right of the people to revoke their mandate, certain procedures such as those of voting aloud or *par acclamation*, proved that the sectionary militants had no intention of accepting an empty and formal type of democracy. Their struggle succeeded in giving practical expression to what had originally been only an idea; they saw the Republic as the embodiment of the democratic ideal. For the really politically-minded sans-culotte, liberty and equality had not been offered to the people once and for all in 1789; they were principles which had to be reconquered from day to day—liberty becomes liberation, equality, social acquisition. This was the only way in which the happiness of every citizen (*le bonheur commun*), universally recognized as the aim of society, could be realized. This process cannot be explained simply by the unfolding of events during the Year II: it was a fundamental contradiction between the Parisian sans-culotterie and the bourgeoisie, between sectionary militants and the Revolutionary Government.

From an economic and social point of view, the contradiction was equally insurmountable. Robespierre and many other Montagnards had repeated that the country could not be governed in time of war as in peace, a statement which was not only politically, but economically valid. The Revolutionary Government, equally dependent upon both sides, was forced to arbitrate between the conflicting interests of the *possédants* [men of property], prepared to support the government, and the wage-earners, instrumental in bringing it to power.

It was only with considerable reluctance that the members of the Committee of Public Safety—firm adherents of a liberal economic system—agreed to pursue a policy of controls and fixed prices. It was only the realization that they could not harness the resources of the nation for war without a controlled economy that finally convinced them of its necessity as a temporary measure to be discarded once the war had ended. The revolution which they controlled was still, despite its increasingly democratic character, a bourgeois revolution. As such, it would have been absurd to fix the price of manufactured goods without fixing wages which ultimately decided what their cost price would be. The government found that it had to maintain a certain balance between the owners of business and manufacturing concerns, whose support was indispensable, and the wage-earners.

A controlled economy was also necessary if a complete collapse in the intrinsic value of money was to be avoided. In order to prevent the *assignat* from becoming absolutely worthless, despite the inevitable inflation (the possibility of a complete devaluation of money in the middle of a war was not seriously considered), the government was forced to impose a maximum on wages as well as on manufactured goods. If it had agreed to a rise in wages, this would inevitably have led to a rise in the price of supplies vital to the war effort, since the government had decided not to interfere in private ownership or profits —a policy which can only be explained in the light of a bourgeois revolution. The Committee of Public Safety accepted price-fixing as a means of realizing a policy of national defence financed by the State without releasing an "infernal" spiral in prices, profits and wages which would, in turn, have resulted in uncontrollable inflation—the *assignat* would have been ruined and the Revolutionary Government swept from power.

This policy depended upon the continuation of the alliance between the Montagnards and the sans-culotterie, and, although it adversely affected the interests of the bourgeoisie—even the jacobin bourgeoisie —by restricting economic freedom and placing a ceiling on profits, the latter, at least, were prepared to play their part in the defence of the Revolution and accepted the dictatorship of the Committees. But, apart from war supplies bought by the State and fodder requisitioned from the peasantry, craftsmen and shopkeepers—Jacobins included—evaded the provisions of the maximum. A conflict with the wage-earners was inevitable.

The sans-culottes, suffering from the effects of inflation and the shortage of food supplies, still looked at the problem from the standpoint of a relationship between wages and prices as they had done under the *ancien régime*. Their campaign for price-controls and requisitioning does not reflect their concern for national defence so much as their interest in providing themselves and their families with sufficient food. As for the workers, they were naturally anxious to take advantage of the relative shortage of labour to demand higher wages without bothering to consider the effect upon prices. From the autumn to the spring of the Year II, when the sans-culottes were in control of the capital, or, at least, feared by the Convention, they were successful in these demands: the Hébertist Commune, disregarding the law, refused to intervene. The government decided that it was time to act.

After Germinal, the Revolutionary Government reviewed the problem of the declining profits of manufacturing concerns, caught between the maximum on the one hand and an illegal rise in wages on the other. Numerous decrees by the Committee of Public Safety authorized a rise in the price of goods compared with the scale fixed by the maximum of Ventôse, despite the law. But these higher prices would have had no real effect if wages had continued to rise. The result was the decree of the Robespierrist Commune on 5 Thermidor enforcing the *maximum des salaires*. Although this decree was only to be introduced in the capital, the Committee of Public Safety—in view of the approaching harvest—had asked the districts to decree what amounted to a similar drop in wages for agricultural workers as early as Prairial. By depriving the wage-earners of the advantage which they had so recently acquired, the Commune appeared to be departing from the mediatory policy which had previously been adopted by the government. The controlled economy of the Year II, which was not based upon class differences, became unbalanced: after Thermidor, the whole structure collapsed.

It is clear that in a fundamentally bourgeois society the system of arbitration introduced by the Committee of Public Safety would be bound to favour the *possédant* class more than the wage-earners; the former being in a position to compensate for losses sustained as a result of price-fixing by producing for a private market. If it had been at all possible, the Robespierrists would probably have been only too happy to redress the balance. There can be little doubt that artisans and shopkeepers would have been less hard on the consumer if, assured of an adequate supply of raw material and food supplies, their sales guaranteed them a reasonable profit. *Compagnons* [journeymen] and artisans had always maintained that, in order to safeguard their right to live, prices should bear a direct relationship to wages: they might well have resigned themselves to the maximum if only they could have been sure of receiving the basic necessities of life.

But the Revolutionary Government simply did not have the means of regulating the law of supply and demand for manufactured goods and vital food supplies: production methods and transport facilities had not yet been modernized by the capitalist concentration, rationalization, and mechanization of industry. The government had to work within the framework of an outmoded economic structure; war further aggravated the problem of keeping the nation supplied. Insurmountable

difficulties arose when the economic system of the Year II was introduced to meet the demand for livestock and farm produce. The interests of the peasantry had also to be taken into consideration. Even the
regular supply of bread was affected by inadequate means of transport,
coupled with the absence of any form of concentration in the milling
trade—one of the problems which capitalism would eventually solve.

The Revolutionary Government decided, therefore, that the best it
could do in these circumstances was to keep the population of Paris
supplied with bread, without going so far as to organize rationing on a
national basis. As for the rest, local authorities and consumers had to
make what arrangements they could to see that producers and merchants observed the provisions of the maximum. Requisitioning was
reserved solely for the benefit of the army. The Parisian sans-culottes,
discovering that this arrangement did not appear to be working in
their favour, demanded a rise in wages and resorted to strike action:
the Committees, faithful to the tradition of the *ancien régime*, declared
such action to be illegal. Thus, at the root of the fundamental contradiction which had arisen between the Revolutionary Government and
the popular movement responsible for bringing it to power, lay the
failure of an artisanat economy to adapt itself to the demands of a
full-scale national war.

The contradictions peculiar to the Parisian sans-culotterie were equally
as important in explaining the collapse of the system of the Year II as
the conflicts which divided the Revolutionary Government and the
popular movement.

There was a social contradiction between the Jacobins, drawn
almost exclusively from the ranks of the lower, middle, and even the
upper bourgeoisie, and the sans-culottes, if we accept Petion's description of the latter as day-labourers and *compagnons de métiers*. But it
would be wrong to identify the sans-culotte with the wage-earner,
despite the fact that wage-earners formed the largest section of the sans-
culotterie. The reality is far more complex. The sans-culotterie did not
constitute a class, nor was the sans-culotte movement based on class
differences. Craftsmen, shopkeepers and merchants, *compagnons* and
day-labourers joined with a bourgeois minority to form a coalition but
there was still an underlying conflict between craftsmen and merchants,
enjoying a profit derived from the private ownership of the means of
production, and *compagnons* and day-labourers, entirely dependent
upon their wages.

The application of the maximum brought this contradiction into
the open. Craftsmen and shopkeepers agreed that it was a sound and
reasonable policy to force the peasantry to feed the population of the
towns; but they protested immediately the provisions of the maximum

began to affect their own interests. *Compagnons* reacted in much the same way. By creating a shortage of labour, the *levée en masse* [mass recruitment of men and materiel] and the civil war led to a rise in wages: if producers and "middlemen" refused to observe price-fixing, why should the workers offer themselves as victims? The demands of the revolutionary struggle had welded the unity of the Parisian sans-culotterie and momentarily pushed the conflict of interests into the background: there was no question, however, of suppressing them altogether.

Differences in social outlook complicated the problem even further. The contradictions within the ranks of the sans-culotterie were not simply those which separated the *possédants* and producers from the salaried workers. Amongst the latter we find, in particular, those who belonged to the clerical and teaching professions, who, because of their way of life, regarded themselves as bourgeois, not to be identified with the *bas-peuple* [lower classes], even if they embraced the same cause. On the other hand, many citizens recognized as being members of the bourgeoisie described themselves as "sans-culotte" and acted as such.

The sans-culottes, recruited from so many different levels of society, could not, therefore, have been really conscious of belonging to a certain class. Although they were generally hostile to the new methods of production, it was not always from the same motives—the craftsman was afraid of being reduced to the status of a wage-earner; the *compagnon* detested the monopolist because he held him responsible for the rising cost of living. As for the *compagnons* alone, it would be anachronistic to speak of them as being class-conscious, since their mentality was still conditioned by the world of the craftsman in which they lived and worked. The capitalist concentration of industry, by bringing them into daily contact through the factory, had not yet created the mentality which would awaken the feeling of class solidarity.

However, if class-consciousness cannot be attributed to the sans-culotterie as a body, it is possible to detect a certain awareness of class amongst the wage-earners. Entirely dependent upon their employers, they regarded themselves as a distinct social group, not only because of the manual nature of their work and their place in the system of production, but also on account of the clothes which they wore, the food they ate, their pastimes, social habits and, in particular, their living accommodation. The fact that they were mostly uneducated—education being reserved solely for citizens privileged by birth and wealth—also tended to distinguish them from their fellow citizens, creating a feeling of inferiority and, sometimes, of powerlessness amongst the lower classes. Militant sans-culottes frequently reveal their hostility towards *hommes-à-talent* [talented men], but, by raising themselves to the same level, longed to play a decisive part in controlling their destiny.

Composed of diverse elements, not constituting a class and, therefore, devoid of class-consciousness, the Parisian sans-culotterie, despite a few hesitant attempts to co-ordinate their activity, lacked a really effective weapon of political action—a strictly disciplined party which could only have been created by a drastic purge followed by recruitment on a class basis. This was equally true of the Revolutionary Government, since the Jacobins themselves were not representative of any one social class. The entire régime of the Year II rested upon an abstract conception of political democracy which largely explains its weakness. The consequences of this were particularly disastrous for the popular movement.

Although there were many militants who tried to discipline the general assemblies and popular societies, leading figures in a number of the Sections aggravated the situation by disputing power amongst themselves, occasionally by abusing it when they eventually succeeded in gaining control. As for the mass of the sans-culotterie, apart from hatred of the aristocracy and the summary methods envisaged for dealing with the problem—chiefly massacre—they do not appear to have been gifted with any degree of political insight: they were simply waiting to receive the benefits which the Revolution would inevitably bring. They campaigned for the maximum, not so much in order to defend the *assignat* and guarantee the production of war supplies, but because they believed that price-controls would help to maintain their standard of living. When they realized that, in many respects, a controlled economy did not meet this requirement, they abandoned it in favour of a new policy. Would the sans-culottes have agreed to drop their demand for higher wages if—an untenable hypothesis—*possédants* and producers had agreed to respect the provisions of the maximum by accepting a margin of profit which the Revolutionary Government considered to be reasonable. The possibility appears to be extremely remote. The war made certain sacrifices inevitable—one of them was that no section of the community should try and profit from the circumstances it created in order to further its own particular interests.

From this point of view, the 9 Thermidor was, indeed, a *journée de dupes* [day of fools] for the sans-culottes. Disillusioned by the effect of the maximum, discontented with the Revolutionary Government, they failed to realize that its collapse would also involve their own ruin. Ten months later, their resistance weakened by the effects of famine and the high cost of living, realizing at last what they had lost, they demanded a return to a controlled economy, rose in insurrection for the last time only to be completely crushed and swept from the stage of history.

The internal contradictions of the sans-culotterie, however, do not entirely explain the collapse of the popular movement: its gradual disintegration was inscribed in the dialectical march of history itself. The indirect attacks of the Committees and the consolidation of the Revolutionary Government, the drama of Germinal and the feeling of deception which followed, only partly explain its weakness. It was, in fact, inevitable that the popular movement should have lost momentum: its development, its very success, only strengthened those factors which finally contributed to its defeat.

There was, in the first place, a reason of a biological nature. Most of the militants had been actively engaged in the revolutionary struggle since 14 July 1789; they had participated in every insurrection. Since 10 August 1792, they had redoubled their activity. But the enthusiasm and excitement of the great *journées* involved a certain expenditure of nervous energy which, after the victory, increased the tension and strain involved in the daily life of the militant. Five years of revolution had drained the physical resources of the sectionary personnel who provided the cadres of the popular movement. It was only natural that this physical exhaustion which, at different times, forced many of the leading figures of the Revolution—Robespierre himself in Messidor —to retire momentarily from the political scene, should not also have affected the militants always in the thick of the battle. Robespierre had predicted that as the war dragged on, the people would begin to "show signs of apathy." This apathy communicated itself to the popular movement, depriving it of its vigour and initial enthusiasm.

There was also a psychological reason arising out of the events of the Year II. The end of the civil war, the halt to the invasion, and, finally, the realization of victory, led to an understandable relaxation of tension. This was true of the population as a whole, although the relief felt by the bourgeoisie cannot be explained by the end of the Terror alone—there was also the prospect of an end to the economic policy of controls and fixed prices, as well as the return of administrative and governmental authority into the hands of the *notables*. The people were anxious to reap the benefits of all their effort. The opening of a register in the Section de la Montagne for new adherents to the Constitution cannot be regarded simply as a political manoeuvre: in the eyes of the militants, the *Acte constitutionnel* of June 1793 was the symbol of social democracy; they had continuously campaigned for the right to receive public relief and the right to instruction. But the majority of the people were primarily concerned with their right to subsist. Since victory was at last in sight, they expected, if not exactly abundance, then, at least, less difficulty in being provided with food as well as a guaranteed daily supply of bread. In fact, victory led to the demobilization of the popular movement.

The Parisian sans-culotterie were also weakened from month to month by the dialectical effect of the war effort. The conscription of 300,000 men, the recruitment for the Vendée, then for the Eure, the *levée en masse* and the creation of the Revolutionary Army, deprived the Sections of a considerable number of the youngest, most active, often the most conscientious and enthusiastic patriots who regarded the defence of the nation as their first civic duty. In order to assess the vitality of the popular movement, an exact calculation of the number of men who enlisted for the various campaigns would clearly be of the greatest possible advantage. But, if we cannot attempt a general study, we can, at least, gain some idea of the significance of the loss of human energy suffered by the Parisian Sections in 1793. In the Section des Piques, which had 3,540 voters aged 21 and over in the Year II, 233 volunteers enrolled for the Vendée from 3 to 17 May 1793 alone— mainly sans-culottes in the prime of life. The lists of citizens capable of carrying arms drawn up by the Sections underline this sapping of the armed strength of the Sections: men of over 50 and, occasionally, of 60 years of age represent a large proportion of the companies formed. Out of the 3,231 men in the Section de Quatre-Vingt-Douze, 767 (23.7 per cent.) were over 50 years of age. In the Section des Arcis, the companies totalled 2,986 men "of whom, a quarter would have to be subtracted" of men aged over 60. The popular movement grew old as a result of these successive enrolments: the inevitable effect on the revolutionary enthusiasm and combative keenness of the Parisian masses can readily be appreciated.

Finally, the dialectical effect of success led to a gradual disintegration of the framework of the popular movement. Many of the sectionary militants, even if they were not motivated by ambition alone, regarded an official position as the legitimate reward for their militant activity. The stability of the popular movement largely depended upon the satisfaction of these personal interests which happened to coincide with the need for purging the various committees. But, in such cases, success breeds a new conformity, as the example of the *commissaires révolutionnaires* illustrates. At first, their revolutionary ardour had distinguished them from the other members of the political organizations of the Sections. But since they had been recruited chiefly from the lowest social ranks of the sans-culotterie, it became necessary, even for the success of the Revolution, for them to be paid a salary. The fear of losing their position, just as much as the strengthening of the Revolutionary Government, soon turned them into willing instruments of the central power. Throughout the Year II, many of the militants were transformed into salaried civil servants as a result of this process, which was not only a necessary outcome of the internal evolution of the sans-culotterie, but also of the intensification of the class struggle within France and on her frontiers. The really politically-minded elements of the sans-culotterie became part of the administrative machinery of the State; the sectionary organizations suffered a corresponding loss of political activity, allowance having been made for the accumulated demands of national defence. At the same time, the democratic ideal was being weakened in the Sections, the process of bureaucratization gradually paralysing the critical spirit and activity of the masses. The eventual outcome was a relaxation of the control exercised by the popular movement over the Revolutionary Government which became increasingly authoritarian in character. This bureaucratic encroachment deprived the sans-culottes of many of the channels through which the popular movement had operated.

These various considerations—which have a far wider application than to the events of the Year II—account for the weakening of the popular movement, and clearly precipitated its collapse.

It would be wrong, however, to draw up a purely negative balance sheet of the popular movement in the Year II. Doubtless it was impossible for it to attain its particular objective—the egalitarian and popular republic towards which the sans-culottes were moving without any clearly defined programme—prevailing circumstances as well as its own contradictions raised far too many obstacles. Nevertheless, the popular movement has still contributed towards historical progress by its decisive intervention in support of the bourgeois revolution.

Without the Parisian sans-culotterie, the bourgeoisie could not have triumphed in so radical a fashion. From 1789 to the Year II, the sans-culottes were used as an effective weapon of revolutionary combat and national defence. In 1793, the popular movement made possible the installation of the Revolutionary Government and, consequently, the defeat of the counter-revolution in France and the allied coalition in Europe. It was the Thermidoreans who really benefited from this victory; and if they failed to use their advantage to secure peace, it was because the decision to abandon a controlled economy, added to the demoralization of the troops totally deprived of supplies, paralysed the army and gave the enemy the necessary time to prepare new campaigns. This contrast helps us to appreciate the work of the Revolutionary Government as well as the importance of the popular movement of the Year II.

If we widen the perspective, its intervention in the course of history does not appear to be less significant. The success of the popular movement during the summer of 1793 led to the organization of the Terror which struck such an irreparable blow to the old social order. The upper bourgeoisie of the *ancien régime,* founded on commercial capital and linked in some ways with the old social and political system of the feudal aristocracy, failed to survive the upheaval. In the Year II, the shopkeeper and craftsman element of the sans-culotterie, its leading members drawn from the ranks of the small independent producers (this is proved by the analysis of the Parisian *comités révolutionnaires*), became the most effective weapon in the struggle for the destruction of outmoded methods of production and the social relationships founded upon them. Thermidor was, in fact, the signal for an economic as well as a political reaction; for, by this time, the Terror had cleared the way for the introduction of new relationships of production. In the capitalist society born of the Revolution, industry was destined to dominate commerce: the function of commercial capital, against which the sans-culottes had fought so bitterly in the Year II, would be subordinated henceforth to the sole productive form of capital—industrial capital.

As for the sans-culottes themselves, the economic evolution would eventually lead to a new division of their ranks. Of the small and fairly substantial producers and merchants who had filled the leading positions in the popular movement from 1793–4, some would succeed and become industrial capitalists, others would be eliminated to swell the ranks of the wage-earners. Many would retain their interest in the workshop and the store. Economic freedom accelerated the concentration of small concerns, transforming the material conditions of social life, but altering, at the same time, the structure of the so-called "popular" classes. Craftsmen and *compagnons* had a dim awareness of the fate which awaited them (for one craftsman who would succeed in industry, how many were destined to fail?), the latter realizing that mechanization would increase the risks of unemployment; the former that capitalist concentration would lead to the closing down of their workshops and transform them into wage-earners. Throughout the nineteenth century, both craftsmen and shopkeepers defended themselves desperately against this threat. It would be interesting to know in this respect, the part played by the proletariat—in the accepted meaning of the word—from the *journées* of 1848 to the Commune of 1871, and that played by the popular classes of the traditional type. This information would enable us to measure the disintegration of the latter faced with the triumph of industrial capitalism and to emphasize by so doing one of the causes for the failure of revolutionary attempts in the nineteenth century.

Thus, as we are reminded of the dramatic character of class struggles in the Year II by an examination of their ultimate consequences, so we are able to distinguish more clearly the original characteristics of the national history of contemporary France.

Jeffry Kaplow

3

The Culture of Poverty in Paris on the Eve of the Revolution

At the very beginning of the investigation, it is necessary to find a word to describe the European masses before the coming of the twin revolutions, the French and Industrial, that have contributed so much to the making of the modern world. "Proletariat" is clearly anachronistic; "wage-earners" is inadequate in a society where cash wages were far from being the most common form of payment for labor. "Working class" is too much identified with nineteenth century developments and, what is worse, conjures up an image of a homogeneous group that does not conform to eighteenth century realities. "Laboring poor" is by far the best, for it emphasizes two primary facts about the people with whom we are concerned; first, that, to one extent or another, they earned their living by doing manual labor, and, second, that they were being continuously impoverished, as Professor Labrousse has shown. The category has several virtues as a tool of historical analysis. It is large enough to take account of the complexities of eighteenth century social conditions, stressing the mobility and social intercourse that existed, albeit on a diminishing scale, between the master artisans and shopkeepers, their apprentices and journeymen on the one hand, and the domestics, beggars, criminals and floating elements in the population, on the other. *Classes laborieuses* and *classes dangereuses* lived side by side and recruited their personnel from one another. They did in fact form a whole, whom contemporaries called *"les classes inférieures."* If we look toward the future, we see that the French Revolution was to bring about a temporary split in their ranks by politicizing those among them who became the sans-culottes, and that the Industrial Revolution was to complete this division on other bases by allowing some of the laboring poor to become petty capitalists, while forcing the majority to become proletarians or to fall further still into the nether-world of the lumpenproletariat. In sum, the use of the concept of the laboring poor enables us to come close to the reality of eighteenth century Paris and to watch the disaggregation of that reality with the passage of time.

What part of the population belonged to the laboring poor? On the basis of information found in marriage contracts, Furet estimates that in certain quarters, such as the Faubourg Saint Antoine, the figure may have been as high as 90 per cent in 1750–1755. Léon Cahen counts 100,000 *"salariés"* in a population of approximately 550,000 at the same date. If a substantial part of these 100,000 are counted as heads of families, then we may conclude, however tentatively, that at least 50 per cent of the total urban population belonged to this category.

For years historians tended to regard the activities of the laboring poor, and particularly of the sans-culottes during the Revolution, as the result of manipulation by their "social betters." It is only in relatively recent years that we have, by stages, come to recognize the often autonomous nature of their action. We have even so tried to explain that action in terms of response to the stimulus of bread shortages and high prices, almost exclusively. This is not sufficient. While I have no doubt that the laboring poor believed with Brecht that one ought "first feed the face and then tell right from wrong," it is clear that we cannot allow the matter to rest there. Man does not live by bread alone, and lack of bread does not necessarily make a man a revolutionary. The entire experience of the eighteenth century bread riot bears witness to the fact. And even in 1789, we hear an unemployed and starving *découpeuse en gaze* (textile worker) say: "Le roi est bon; s'il savoit combien nous sommes malheureux, il ne nous laisseroit pas languir" [The king is good; if he knew how miserable we were, he would not allow us to languish]. . . . She had six children, and her husband made 18 sous a day, for an annual wage of about 252 livres—assuming that he could find work at least 280 out of 365 days a year. In 1790, a year of more or less normal prices, the Comité de Mendicité of the Constituent Assembly estimated that a family of five needed a strict minimum of 435 livres a year in order to subsist. In other words, we have here a case of absolute indigence accompanied by protestations of loyalty to the monarchy and, by inference, to the established order. It is highly unlikely that this particular woman went out to storm the Bastille, but it is altogether possible that her next door neighbor did just that. But then what drives one man to revolution, while another man in similar circumstances remains passive, if bread no longer appears as the crucial variable? The answer must be derived from the study, first, of the material life of the poor, not only at moments of crisis but over a span of normal years, and, second, of the values peculiar to them. Although it is difficult to separate the two, it is with the latter that I would like to deal at this time.

I am convinced that a culture of poverty did in fact exist in eighteenth century cities, and that it consisted of a great deal more than getting drunk on gin or cheap wine. To be sure, this culture of poverty is not the same as that which has been brought to our attention by contemporary social scientists and commentators. Although the two cultures may have points in common, the very principle of historical specificity makes it impossible to read twentieth century observations back into our period. We cannot reason by analogy, and our task is made still more difficult by the limited amount of source material at our disposal, given the tendency of the poor to be inarticulate. Still the potential results are such that a study of the culture of poverty is worth a try. Commenting on a trip to Paris made in 1774, an English observer wrote:

The French are really a contented race of mortals;—precluded almost from the possibility of adventure, the low Parisian leads a gentle, humble life, nor envies the greatness he can never obtain; but either wonders delightedly, or diverts himself philosophically with the sight of splendours which seldom fail to excite serious envy in an Englishman, and sometimes occasion even suicide, from disappointed hopes, which never could take root in the heart of these unaspiring people. . . . Emulation, ambition, avarice, however, must in all arbitrary governments be confined to the great; the other set of mortals, for there are none there of middling rank, live, as it should seem, like eunuchs in a seraglio; feel themselves irrevocably doomed to promote the pleasures of their superiors, nor even dream of fighting for enjoyments from which an irremediable boundary divides them. They see at the beginning of their lives how that life must necessarily end, and trot with a quiet, contented, and unaltered pace down their long, straight, and shaded avenue. . . .

The avenue that led through life to an obscure grave was neither so long, nor so shaded from misfortune as Mrs. Piozzi indicates, but her observation is nonetheless substantially correct. The situation of the Paris poor was a static one. The channels of mobility were narrow and becoming more so as the century went on. A properly trained journeyman had less hope than ever before of becoming a master, while the unskilled new arrival from the country, come to make his fortune in the great city, was lucky to get even the lowest sort of menial work, and as often as not was forced to rely on public charity or to resort to beggary. There was no way out, and no place to hide.

To the misery imposed on the poor by their means of making a living was added the power of death, personally experienced on an every day basis in the eighteenth century—above all in the urban setting. Only a full scale study employing the methods of differential demography can tell the whole story. Here it is sufficient to note that in the years around 1770 infant mortality (before the age of one year) stood at 233 per thousand. In a group of 1000 persons born in a given year, 449 would be dead ten years later, and fewer than 300 would reach the age of 50, which is to say that fewer than 300 would expect to see the birth of grandchildren. These figures given for France as a whole would most certainly be higher in the case of the urban poor. Is there any wonder then that they developed a sense of futility, that they lost whatever dynamism they may once have had—and I am thinking here in individual terms, of the young men who set out to make their way in the world only to be ground down by defeat into despair. Their attitude towards death itself is characterized mainly by acceptance. "Mourning and consternation" were indeed present, but death was implacable, and there was nothing to be done but to accept the cold comfort offered by the maxim *"Mort saisit sans exception"* [Death spares no one]. Because they had never been able to control their destinies, the very thought of someday exercising such control was foreign to the poor at this time. Babies kept coming and children kept dying, prices went up, real wages went down, it was the way of the world, not to be questioned.

There is still more. In a society characterized by hereditary legal inequality, there are what we may call the ordinary discriminations, privileges having to do with taxation, justice, access to careers, precedence, etc., which, in theory at least, affect equally all persons not lucky enough to have been born noble. In reality, however, to be rich was a good thing, then no less than now. Money, if it could not buy honor—and it sometimes could and did just that—made the lack of it tolerable. The poor man lacked this resource. He lived with his family in a miserably furnished narrow little room devoid of material comfort. The single room and lone bed that often constituted his total patrimony completely deprived him of privacy, and even the sexual act became a public one. It is possible that he did not feel this deprivation, for privacy is very much a bourgeois value, and there is no evidence to show that the poor had accepted it. Still, this was not a state of things calculated to give the poor a sense of self-esteem.

When a poor man ventured out of his hovel, he came up against the dominant behavior patterns of society, to which he had not the means to conform, and his dignity suffered from this confrontation. His clothing was generally second hand and therefore out of fashion. The food he ate was limited in variety as it was in quantity. The lack of public transportation reenforced his sense of inferiority by making him conscious that he could only walk, while others rode. The places he went for entertainment, like the guinguettes [popular taverns] in the suburbs where the drink was cheaper than in the city proper, were frequented by his own kind. And lest it be argued that the tendency of several social classes to live together in the same building was an effective counterweight to this kind of isolation, it should be pointed out that the anonymity of the urban apartment dweller, reenforced by vertical segregation, worked against any real mixing of the classes. Tenants might meet on the stairway, but their acquaintance probably stopped there. The poor man saw just enough of another kind of life to know that he was excluded from it.

Behind all this was a message the poor could not fail to perceive. They were different and condemned to remain so, not because they individually lacked character or personal qualities that would enable them to adapt to, and advance within, given situations, as the later theorists of Social Darwinism had it, but because they were born as a group to play a specific role, from which there was no escape. When, on a rare occasion, a poor man sought to establish himself in a role for which he was not thought to be suited, the barriers were raised in a more explicit manner. In 1781, the Parlement of Paris annulled the election of an agricultural day laborer as vestryman in the parish church of suburban Chaillot because "des gens d'une profession vile, ou des journaliers, qui gagnent leur vie par des moyens qui sont la preuve de leur indigence" [persons of vile, i.e., lowly, professions or day laborers, who earn their living by means that are proof of their indigence] were not eligible for this position.

Even death did not put an end to the indignities to which the poor were subject. A funeral, of whatever class, appears to have been a costly affair, and attempts to raise the price might provoke the poor to display their anger. There was also the refusal of the clergy and pallbearers to do their duty, unless properly rewarded. In June, 1781, a poor parishioner of Saint Sulpice, having somehow come up with enough money to buy a coffin for his late wife, still lacked funds to pay the pallbearers. Service was refused him, and he had finally to employ six poor women to transport the body from his home to the church. This was the kind of thing to which the poor were particularly sensitive, for they were Christians and concerned about the welfare of their immortal souls, whether or not they were assiduous in their attendance at mass. They showed their annoyance at this particular incident by treating the local clergy, whom they held responsible for the pallbearers' loutish behavior, to a steady stream of abuse when they dared to appear in the streets at the head of another, presumably well paid, procession. The poor, who left little or no trace of their existence behind them, could not even be buried properly. If relatives or friends did not pay for the burial, their bodies were thrown into the common pits of the Cemetery of the Holy Innocents near the Halles, and not much care was taken to record their names. This was the ultimate indignity, a kind of deprivation of identity.

Under these conditions, the poor had no alternative but to accept their situation, and this they did in a very particular way. Forced into misery by society, they reacted by seeking to make the best of that misery, rather than to do away with it. The poor turned inwards to form their own community with its own values and norms of behavior. The community was at once a cushion against the harsh realities of their daily lives and a barrier against full participation in the world at large. Although feelings of frustration no doubt remained quite strong at the individual level, the culture as a whole was characterized by the growth of a psychology of acceptance. And as that psychology was passed down across the generations from parents to children, it made it impossible for the group to develop self-esteem and class consciousness, and thereby to engage in political action.

The first characteristic of the withdrawal from the larger community is the distrust and/or the reluctance to make use of certain major institutions. The hatred of hospitals by the poor is proverbial and was due not alone to the miserable conditions that prevailed there and to the fact that such a large percentage of those who entered never came out again. The hospital was also looked upon as a trap for the unfortunate poor, a kind of Malthusian instrument for keeping the population down. The mode of administration of charity was notably hard-hearted ouside as well as in the hospitals, and the poor resented it. How often they made their resentment known is another matter, but I know of at least one police ordinance forbidding the poor "to injure and mistreat the Sisters of Charity of the parishes of Paris while receiving alms from them. . . ."

On the question of the poor man's attitude to the courts and the judicial system, our evidence is as yet very sparse. But the little we do have, in the form of interrogations of accused criminals, indicates a fear of authority, together with a strong penchant for litigation and the apparently contradictory tendency to apply to judicial or police officers for redress of even the most minor insults. But there can be no doubt as to the poor's lack of friendliness to the police, who were strongly suspected, not without reason, of persecuting the poor in order to fill their own pockets. It was common knowledge that Paris was full of police spies recruited from every walk of life. A bounty was paid for the capture of beggars, and this led to real abuses, much multiplied in the minds of poor men who did not regard beggary as crime. Any rumor concerning the police was readily accepted as true. In May, 1750, a report that police were kidnapping young boys, whose blood was to be used to bathe a princess suffering from a horrible disease, led to a series of riots in which several persons lost their lives.

One institution that escaped the fear and distrust bred by poverty was the Church, notwithstanding hatred of ecclesiastical functionaries and sharp reactions to the abuse of their authority. Although we may think of the poor as having been more superstitious than religious, they remained deeply attached to their own highly syncretic brand of Catholicism. This allegiance is not easily measured by the percentage of persons who went to mass on Sundays or took communion at Easter, as the Canon Law required. I would attach very limited significance to the decrease in church attendance that may have taken place in our period. Nor would I think that the failure to regard Sunday as a day of rest indicated a state of creeping atheism, despite the fears of the royal government and the censure of English ladies raised in the sabbatarian tradition. The fact remains that the laboring poor believed in the community of saints, the use of the sacraments and the exercise of religious devotion. One reason for this is certainly the enormous availability of religion. There was always some church or other to which a visit would secure an indulgence. Special retreats for workers both male and female were held regularly. And of course there were the 29 obligatory holy days each year. Whatever the reason, the poor still relied on Catholicism for comfort and hope and protested bitterly when they thought they might be deprived of its ministrations.

The Parisian poor, one might say, had a superstitious need to believe —what is of relatively little importance. This is not the place to detail all their vagaries, but the examples run the gamut from ghosts to elixirs of life and youth to faith healing. Such beliefs were not the monopoly of the poor. They carried credulity to extreme limits, because it gave them comfort and because they were not restrained by rigorous habits of thought. It was possible for them to believe a self-styled prophetess, Dame Sainte Catherine, when she claimed in 1779 that she was to be the mother of the new messiah. And once again, that the wife of de Barentin, first president of the Cour des Aides, had given birth to "un abrisseau reconnu pour un groseiller quoique sans groseille, mais chargé . . . de cerises. Ce monstre d'une espèce toute nouvelle n'avoit rien de la forme humaine et étoit absolument inanimé. Cet accouchement singulier n'avoit pu que causer beaucoup de chagrin à toute la famille" [a bush recognized to be a gooseberry bush although without gooseberries, but loaded . . . with cherries. This monster of an entirely new species had nothing of the human form about it and was absolutely inanimate. This singular birth could only cause great sadness for the whole family].

This credulity might trouble the enforcement of public order, but it was not likely to serve as a vehicle for revolutionary propaganda. Rumor, which is the handmaiden of belief, might lead to violence, but generally of the Church and King variety. That is clearly what the authorities had in mind when they ordered the arrest of a certain La Vallée d'Arancy in 1778. He had imagined the existence of a plot

against the royal family. He lived in a house occupied by 40 representatives of the "bas peuple," told his story to them, but was not thought
by them to be crazy. The danger was evident.

In the culture of poverty as it exists today, slum dwellers are aware of
the socially dominant values, although they reject them as a code of
behavior. This is what social workers, in their somewhat condescend-
ing vocabulary, call characteriological difficulties. Was this equally
true in eighteenth century Paris, where communications were still in a
primitive state and there were no mass media to be used for the purposes of manipulating public opinion?

On the one hand, as has already been shown, they did meet representatives of other classes in the course of their work, and the gossip
mill may have—no doubt did—keep them abreast of what was going
on in a limited portion of the outside world, the rest of the city and,
just possibly, the rest of France. On the other hand, the poor were
intensely parochial, often working, marrying and dying in the neighborhood where they were born. What I am suggesting here, without in
any way being able to prove it, is that the community of which the
domiciled poor were a part (and the floating poor as well, but only in
so far as they carried their community with them by travelling in
groups) guaranteed them a certain set of roots, a place in the shadow,
if not in the sun. At the same time, that community protected its
members by keeping them out of constant and direct contact with
the pressures of the dominant culture. The poor man may thus have
been spared some part of the personality conflict he would otherwise
have experienced, had he known the full meaning of his inability to
conform.

There is a great deal that we do not know—and may never know,
given the state of the sources—about the culture of poverty in the
eighteenth century, mainly those matters concerning personal habits
and family organization. If we look once again at contemporary
cultures, we are tempted to ask questions about, for example, marriage
and the status of women, the place of the child and paternal authority.
Was there a high rate of common law marriage, or did the prohibition
of the Church serve as an effective counterweight to whatever temp-
tations may have existed in this domain? Were there many illegitimate
children? Did the fact that a large number of women worked, along
with their husbands, to support their families have a positive influence
on their status? Were children cherished, or did the fact that so many
of them died so young and that those who survived were a burden on
the limited resources of their parents diminish the value placed on
children and childhood, as Ariès suggests? The large number of children abandoned to the Foundling Hospital—six to seven thousand a

year in the 1770s—indicates that he was right. And Restif de la Bretonne tells us that it was very common for young working men and women to live separately from their families. Firm conclusions on these matters will have to await the gathering of evidence, but it can be stated here and now that the answers are likely to vary among groups to be distinguished within the general category of the laboring poor. A gild artisan may very well have had a set of attitudes not shared by members of the floating population.

The reaction to insults already cited indicates that the poor shared a strong sense of honor. Honor and its defense may even have served as a surrogate for the material goods of which the poor were deprived. It is possible that as a poor man grew older and more certain that this situation would never change, he sought comfort in the demand for respect and esteem due his paternal authority. The example of many fathers of apparently modest circumstances who ask for a royal order to lock up an erring son in Bicêtre would give weight to this hypothesis. What actions were seen as constituting dishonorable behavior, and more specifically breaches of family honor, it is as yet impossible to say. The answer may well be: anything the father thought wrong. In any case, the makings of acute generational conflict are evident.

The Paris poor lived surrounded by violence. It was the socially approved violence of a society based on principles of inequality, best symbolized by the Dickensian image of the driver running down those who dared to get in the way of his coach-and-four. It was also the socially disapproved violence of the professional criminal, with whom the poor lived at close quarters. But though they sometimes identified with criminals—they turned out in crowds to watch executions less on account of bloodthirstiness than out of sympathy for him who was about to die, and nothing made them happier than a last minute pardon—they were not themselves notably violent. There was a great deal of amateur crime, but it rarely involved physical harm to the victim. As the poor worked hard, so they swore hard and they played hard. In that sense their language was both violent and extremely pungent. When they went out for amusement, they tended to be loud and boisterous, whether dancing in the guinguettes at the Porcherons or staging a charivari—what middle western Americans call a chiveree —under the windows of a newly married couple. They wanted instant gratification at the moment, and devil take the future. Why bother about a future that was likely to be as drab and uninviting as the present? So they drank on a Sunday until the money ran out; they quarrelled, fought, and made up when the sun went down. And the only dire result of all this was that some men did not show up for work on Monday. I have no desire to paint a falsely idyllic picture, but it remains true that the poor were not depraved because they were deprived.

The poor were set off from the rest of society by so many differences of clothing, diet, working and living conditions, not to mention language, that they could not fail to develop some sense of themselves as belonging to a special community, that of the bottom dogs. They knew that they were different from, and less fortunate than, the nobles and bourgeois, no doubt lumped together in their minds in the single category of men one called Monsieur. This sense of difference, which takes into account only the most obvious phenomena of social life, is perfectly compatible with a sense of inferiority, a psychology of acceptance and deferential behavior in general, although it may as well serve to create feelings of suspicion and even contempt towards those outside the group. It is very different from class consciousness which, by definition, involves an identification of the individual with an entity having positive attributes. Corollary to class consciousness (as it develops amongst those deprived of power in a society) are notions of oppression and the need for change. The bourgeois of 1789 were class conscious, and thus were able to make a revolution. The laboring poor, by contrast, had not yet developed to the same point, hence they could, in the first instance, serve only as a *force d'appoint* [an additional force]. This should not surprise us. In a very real sense, this group consciousness corresponded to the social situation in which they found themselves. The laboring poor did not constitute a single class, but rather a melange of producers and merchants, skilled and unskilled, sedentary and nomadic. The positive identifications open to them, with a craft, a province or an occupational group, were always within the group, never encompassing the whole. They were divisive rather than unifying. Only later, with the coming of modern industrial society, were conditions for the development of a unitary class consciousness created.

This said, it should be remembered that the laboring poor were neither foolish nor blind. They were capable of resentment and anger, even of identifying the representatives of authority as the agents of their ills. We know the violence of their response to the *pacte de famine* [the accusations made against Louis XV and other government figures in the 1760s] and to bread shortages and high prices in general, to militia recruitment and police brutality. While in the main they blamed the king's ministers for their misfortunes, they could be driven to curse the monarch himself. At the death of Louis XV, a popular jingle was heard all over Paris:

> Here lies Louis the Do-nothing
> He gave us paper money at birth
> War as he grew up
> Famine as he grew old
> And the Plague when he died.

But this remained personal criticism, rather than a call for the destruction of the monarchy. When Louis XVI ascended the throne, he was acclaimed a worthy successor to King Henri IV of glorious memory—although one wit wrote:

> That Henri is reborn, I'm willing to say
> But before I'm sure, I'll see the chicken in the pot.

The poor were not capable of sustaining their anger, because they did not—could not—place it in a larger context.

I submit that they were incapable of thinking in larger terms, incapable of transforming their dislike for a man or set of men into a critique of society not only because they were poor, overworked, underfed, lacking education and opportunities, but because all of these disabilities had let them into the blind alley of the culture of poverty. Once there, they came to feel themselves helpless, dependent and inferior. They responded to pressures only in terms of that culture. They were caught in a vicious circle, and they could not break out until someone showed them the way. The idea that it was possible, not to say legitimate, to challenge the established order pointed out the direction to follow, and it was provided in 1789 by the revolutionary bourgeoisie. The bourgeois, however consciously, used the laboring poor as their shock troops, and the laboring poor, at least in part shaken out of their lethargy, soon began to pursue a program of their own. It was a program full of contradictions both in its means and its ends, and it would never be more than partially realized. It was, however, the beginning of a new struggle and a new tradition. At last the laboring poor had the chance to prove what Marivaux had said of them forty years earlier, that they were "beaucoup plus peuple et beaucoup moins canaille" [much more people and much less rabble] than was generally believed.

II/THE INDUSTRIAL REVOLUTION

BETWEEN 1760 and 1830, Great Britain underwent an industrial revolution that was to become the prototype for all the others that came to pass in nineteenth-century Europe. The quantity of goods produced increased enormously, more than keeping pace with the spectacular population explosion that started around 1750. More important still, the quality of the productive process was completely transformed. Power machinery took the place of human and animal muscle. Workshops gave way to factories. Artisans and yeoman farmers were replaced by large-scale entrepreneurs, and a new working class, an industrial proletariat, emerged to run the machines. All of this was accomplished under capitalist conditions, and it was industrialization that made possible the maturation of the capitalist mode of production, its conditioning of every area—economic, political, social, and intellectual—of human activity. Finally, what distinguishes the industrial revolution from every earlier period of economic growth is its irreversibility; henceforth, there would be no turning back.

The history of the industrial revolution raises an enormous number of questions, not the least of which is whether the word "revolution" is, in this connection, justified. Historians of a conservative (that is, antisocialist) persuasion have not limited themselves to casting doubt upon particular statements of Marxist political economy, for instance the hypothesis that the removal of the traditional peasantry from the land was a necessary prerequisite to capitalist industrialization because it was, at one and the same time, a means of accumulating investment capital and of creating a legally free, but economically dependent, labor force. They have gone considerably further to create a new catechism, whose parts we may label continuity, convergence, and consensus.

Now, if one wishes to denigrate the new, nothing is more tactically desirable than to show that, besides its negative features, it isn't really as new as all that. The man who forgets to return his neighbor's lawnmower, when asked to give it back has been known to reply that (1) he never borrowed it, (2) he returned it a long time ago, and (3) it didn't work well anyway. This procedure has often been applied to the Renaissance by partisans of the Middle Ages. To be sure, the matter here is somewhat different, for the historians who stress that there was no industrial revolution, only a continuous, predictable economic development, are not necessarily themselves adversaries of industrial society. Quite the contrary, they may be all for it, even tending to find suspect the "bleeding hearts" who, in their view, pay too much attention to the horrors of the dark satanic mills. Their insistence on continuity, however, allows them to minimize the disruption in the lives of the worker participants occasioned by the process of industrialization. Yet there can hardly be a greater change in a man's life than the one he experiences in having to become accustomed to a factory whistle after years of hard, but less regimented, labor.

The continuity hypothesis is not fully comprehensible without reference to the second term of the triad. The idea of convergence amounts to simply this: All societies go through the same stages of economic development, regardless of their social systems: from the traditional to the mature, to the "age of high mass-consumption," having in the interim "taken off" and become airborne. In this formulation, societies resemble unidentified flying objects more than organized groups of human beings. Now, convergence theory is inadequate in several respects. First, it isolates the economic from the sociological, which not even a high level of academic abstraction can justify. It is like trying to cook the white meat of the chicken, while leaving the dark meat raw. This can be done, but only at the price of tearing the bird apart. Second, convergence theory is abusive in its use of terms like "traditional" (or "preindustrial") society, in that it would ignore the specifics of concrete historical development and, above all, the political economic configuration of the society in which industrialization takes place. The unstated assumption is that all men wish to (or have to) "modernize." In so doing, some men have chosen "inefficient," not to say unfortunate, means, like communism. But we may take heart. Perverse though these men may be, the logic of development will lead them inexorably back to the straight and narrow path, no matter what the political mishaps along the way. In the end, it is no surprise to learn that the gate opens onto some species of reformist capitalism. The emphasis is placed on consensual agreement in place of conflict, which is made to appear wrong and counterproductive.

No method of historical analysis is ever entirely innocent, just as there is no value-free social science, especially when it is so directly relevant to contemporary problems. In reality, "continuity, convergence, and consensus" is the "children, church and kitchen" (*Kinder, Kirche und Küche*) of the third world. Like the latter expression used by the Nazis to define the ideal role of women, our triad is an ideological expression of advanced capitalism's desire to take charge of economic development for its own purposes. W. W. Rostow, whose work is most representative of this school of thought, has taught at the Massachusetts Institute of Technology but is no doubt better known for his activity as advisor to President Johnson. Although it is lese-majesty not to accept his prescriptions, some voices have been raised in dissent. Notable among them are Paul Baran, late professor of economics at Stanford University, and Eric J. Hobsbawm of the University of London, whose Marxist analysis of Rostow's shortcomings is reprinted here.

Dissenting historians seem to have a habit of associating themselves with the victims of history—and this is as it should be, so long as that association is not marked by silly sentimentalism. Marxists, who know that men make their own history, are concerned with the totality of historical change, and not least of all with the activity of the masses in the process. Nothing could be more natural or more proper than that they should refuse the easy optimism of those who would write off or ignore the human suffering that qualitative leaps into the future so often involve. It is all well and good to state that omelets cannot be made without breaking eggs, but, as radicals know only too well from their own experience, human beings are not eggs.

In the following section I reprint the debate between Hobsbawm and R. M. Hartwell of the University of Oxford on the standard of living of the British worker between 1790 and 1840. The confrontation permits us to learn many things about the historian's craft, not least of all that objectivity (but not respect for the ascertained facts) is a chimera, and that arguments are useless unless both parties have decided to use the same words to mean the same things. When all is said and done, neither Hobsbawm nor Hartwell wants to stand or fall on his evidence concerning real wages in this period. The question is a different one, and has to do with the texture of life in the presence of alienation. The workers were alienacted in the proper sense of the term, that is, increasingly divorced from control over the productive process, from the product of their labor and from self. This would remain true, even if it could be shown (which is not yet the case) that they had never had it so good. The workers felt both material and moral deprivation and, while we would not want to fall into the trap of seeing history through the eyes and limited consciousness of contemporaries, the fact is itself important, more important no doubt than the objective truth as statistically measured, for, in the final analysis, the standard of living is a subjective category.

In a still more fundamental sense, Hobsbawm and Hartwell cannot agree on the meaning of progress, because of their ideological differences. For the former, it is the fact of exploitation that counts (not because he compares factory life to some imagined golden age in the past, but rather, I would suggest, because he has an image of what the future should hold and an idea of how it is to be brought about); for the latter, industrialism makes social engineering, piecemeal reform, possible, which is a good thing and about all we may legitimately expect.

The last selection reprinted here is from E. P. Thompson's *The Making of the English Working Class*. Since its publication in 1964, it has become an acknowledged classic on the proletarian and artisan culture of the England of the industrial revolution. With mastery of historical technique and an extraordinary sympathy for his characters, Thompson has set out to analyze the response of working men to the new discipline of factory labor and all that went with it. He has also taken it as his task to rescue the laboring poor from what he terms the "enormous condescension of posterity." How admirably he succeeds is, I think, self-evident. The source of his success is a contemporaneity and a commitment that enable him to integrate the particular evidence of the past into the framework of still-unanswered questions about the future. Who has a better definition of the historian's role?

W. W. Rostow

4

The Five
Stages of Growth

It is possible to identify all societies, in their economic dimensions, as lying within one of five categories: the traditional society, the preconditions for take-off, the take-off, the drive to maturity, and the age of high mass-consumption.

THE TRADITIONAL SOCIETY

First, the traditional society. A traditional society is one whose structure is developed within limited production functions, based on pre-Newtonian science and technology, and on pre-Newtonian attitudes towards the physical world. Newton is here used as a symbol for that watershed in history when men came widely to believe that the external world was subject to a few knowable laws, and was systematically capable of productive manipulation.

The conception of the traditional society is, however, in no sense static; and it would not exclude increases in output. Acreage could be expanded; some *ad hoc* technical innovations, often highly productive innovations, could be introduced in trade, industry and agriculture; productivity could rise with, for example, the improvement of irrigation works or the discovery and diffusion of a new crop. But the central fact about the traditional society was that a ceiling existed on the level of attainable output per head. This ceiling resulted from the fact that the potentialities which flow from modern science and technology were either not available or not regularly and systematically applied.

Both in the longer past and in recent times the story of traditional societies was thus a story of endless change. The area and volume of trade within them and between them fluctuated, for example, with the degree of political and social turbulence, the efficiency of central rule, the upkeep of the roads. Population—and, within limits, the level of life—rose and fell not only with the sequence of the harvests, but with the incidence of war and of plague. Varying degrees of manufacture

53

developed; but, as in agriculture, the level of productivity was limited by the inaccessibility of modern science, its applications, and its frame of mind.

Generally speaking, these societies, because of the limitation on productivity, had to devote a very high proportion of their resources to agriculture; and flowing from the agricultural system there was a hierarchical social structure, with relatively narrow scope—but some scope —for vertical mobility. Family and clan connexions played a large role in social organization. The value system of these societies was generally geared to what might be called a long-run fatalism; that is, the assumption that the range of possibilities open to one's grandchildren would be just about what it had been for one's grandparents. But this long-run fatalism by no means excluded the short-run option that, within a considerable range, it was possible and legitimate for the individual to strive to improve his lot, within his lifetime. In Chinese villages, for example, there was an endless struggle to acquire or to avoid losing land, yielding a situation where land rarely remained within the same family for a century.

Although central political rule—in one form or another—often existed in traditional societies, transcending the relatively self-sufficient regions, the centre of gravity of political power generally lay in the regions, in the hands of those who owned or controlled the land. The landowner maintained fluctuating but usually profound influence over such central political power as existed, backed by its entourage of civil servants and soldiers, imbued with attitudes and controlled by interests transcending the regions.

In terms of history then, with the phrase "traditional society" we are grouping the whole pre-Newtonian world: the dynasties in China; the civilization of the Middle East and the Mediterranean; the world of medieval Europe. And to them we add the post-Newtonian societies which, for a time, remained untouched or unmoved by man's new capability for regularly manipulating his environment to his economic advantage.

To place these infinitely various, changing societies in a single category, on the ground that they all shared a ceiling on the productivity of their economic techniques, is to say very little indeed. But we are, after all, merely clearing the way in order to get at the subject of this book; that is, the post-traditional societies, in which each of the major characteristics of the traditional society was altered in such ways as to permit regular growth: its politics, social structure, and (to a degree) its values, as well as its economy.

THE PRECONDITIONS FOR TAKE-OFF

The second stage of growth embraces societies in the process of transition; that is, the period when the preconditions for take-off are developed; for it takes time to transform a traditional society in the ways necessary for it to exploit the fruits of modern science, to fend off diminishing returns, and thus to enjoy the blessings and choices opened up by the march of compound interest.

The preconditions for take-off were initially developed, in a clearly marked way, in Western Europe of the late seventeenth and early eighteenth centuries as the insights of modern science began to be translated into new production functions in both agriculture and industry, in a setting given dynamism by the lateral expansion of world markets and the international competition for them. But all that lies behind the break-up of the Middle Ages is relevant to the creation of the preconditions for take-off in Western Europe. Among the Western European states, Britain, favoured by geography, natural resources, trading possibilities, social and political structure, was the first to develop fully the preconditions for take-off.

The more general case in modern history, however, saw the stage of preconditions arise not endogenously but from some external intrusion by more advanced societies. These invasions—literal or figurative—shocked the traditional society and began or hastened its undoing; but they also set in motion ideas and sentiments which initiated the process by which a modern alternative to the traditional society was constructed out of the old culture.

The idea spreads not merely that economic progress is possible, but that economic progress is a necessary condition for some other purpose, judged to be good: be it national dignity, private profit, the general welfare, or a better life for the children. Education, for some at least, broadens and changes to suit the needs of modern economic activity. New types of enterprising men come forward—in the private economy, in government, or both—willing to mobilize savings and to take risks in pursuit of profit or modernization. Banks and other institutions for mobilizing capital appear. Investment increases, notably in transport, communications, and in raw materials which other nations may have an economic interest. The scope of commerce, internal and external, widens. And, here and there, modern manufacturing enterprise appears, using the new methods. But all this activity proceeds at a limited pace within an economy and a society still mainly characterized by traditional low-productivity methods, by the old social structure and values, and by the regionally based political institutions that developed in conjunction with them.

In many recent cases, for example, the traditional society persisted side by side with modern economic activities, conducted for limited economic purposes by a colonial or quasi-colonial power.

Although the period of transition—between the traditional society and the take-off—saw major changes in both the economy itself and in the balance of social values, a decisive feature was often political. Politically, the building of an effective centralized national state—on the basis of coalitions touched with a new nationalism, in opposition to the traditional landed regional interests, the colonial power, or both, was a decisive aspect of the preconditions period; and it was, almost universally, a necessary condition for take-off.

. . .

THE TAKE-OFF

We come now to the great watershed in the life of modern societies: the third stage in this sequence, the take-off. The take-off is the interval when the old blocks and resistances to steady growth are finally overcome. The forces making for economic progress, which yielded limited bursts and enclaves of modern activity, expand and come to dominate the society. Growth becomes its normal condition. Compound interest becomes built, as it were, into its habits and institutional structure.

In Britain and the well-endowed parts of the world populated substantially from Britain (the United States, Canada etc.) the proximate stimulus for take-off was mainly (but not wholly) technological. In the more general case, the take-off awaited not only the build-up of social overhead capital and a surge of technological development in industry and agriculture, but also the emergence to political power of a group prepared to regard the modernization of the economy as serious, high-order political business.

During the take-off, the rate of effective investment and savings may rise from say 5% of the national income to 10% or more; although where heavy social overhead capital investment was required to create the technical preconditions for take-off the investment rate in the preconditions period could be higher than 5%, as, for example, in Canada before the 1890's and Argentina before 1914. In such cases capital imports usually formed a high proportion of total investment in the preconditions period and sometimes even during the take-off itself, as in Russia and Canada during their pre-1914 railway booms.

During the take-off new industries expand rapidly, yielding profits a large proportion of which are reinvested in new plant; and these new industries, in turn, stimulate, through their rapidly expanding requirement for factory workers, the services to support them, and for other manufactured goods, a further expansion in urban areas and in other modern industrial plants. The whole process of expansion in the modern sector yields an increase of income in the hands of those who not only save at high rates but place their savings at the disposal of those engaged in modern sector activities. The new class of entrepreneurs expands; and it directs the enlarging flows of investment in the private sector. The economy exploits hitherto unused natural resources and methods of production.

New techniques spread in agriculture as well as industry, as agriculture is commercialized, and increasing numbers of farmers are prepared to accept the new methods and the deep changes they bring to ways of life. The revolutionary changes in agricultural productivity are an essential condition for successful take-off; for modernization of a society increases radically its bill for agricultural products. In a decade or two both the basic structure of the economy and the social and political structure of the society are transformed in such a way that a steady rate of growth can be, thereafter, regularly sustained.

One can approximately allocate the take-off of Britain to the two decades after 1783; France and the United States to the several decades preceding 1860; Germany, the third quarter of the nineteenth century; Japan, the fourth quarter of the nineteenth century; Russia and Canada the quarter-century or so preceding 1914; while during the 1950's India and China have, in quite different ways, launched their respective take-offs.

THE DRIVE TO MATURITY

After take-off there follows a long interval of sustained if fluctuating progress, as the now regularly growing economy drives to extend modern technology over the whole front of its economic activity. Some 10–20% of the national income is steadily invested, permitting output regularly to outstrip the increase in population. The make-up of the economy changes unceasingly as technique improves, new industries accelerate, older industries level off. The economy finds its place in the international economy: goods formerly imported are produced at home; new import requirements develop, and new export commodities to match them. The society makes such terms as it will with the requirements of modern efficient production, balancing off the new against the older values and institutions, or revising the latter in such ways as to support rather than to retard the growth process.

Some sixty years after take-off begins (say, forty years after the end of take-off) what may be called maturity is generally attained. The economy, focused during the take-off around a relatively narrow complex of industry and technology, has extended its range into more refined and technologically often more complex processes; for example, there may be a shift in focus from the coal, iron, and heavy engineering industries of the railway phase to machine-tools, chemicals, and electrical equipment. This, for example, was the transition through which Germany, Britain, France, and the United States had passed by the end of the nineteenth century or shortly thereafter. But there are other sectoral patterns which have been followed in the sequence from take-off to maturity. . . .

Formally, we can define maturity as the stage in which an economy demonstrates the capacity to move beyond the original industries which powered its take-off and to absorb and to apply efficiently over a very wide range of its resources—if not the whole range—the most advanced fruits of (then) modern technology. This is the stage in which an economy demonstrates that it has the technological and entrepreneurial skills to produce not everything, but anything that it chooses to produce. It may lack (like contemporary Sweden and Switzerland, for example) the raw materials or other supply conditions required to produce a given type of output economically; but its dependence is a matter of economic choice or political priority rather than a technological or institutional necessity.

Historically, it would appear that something like sixty years was required to move a society from the beginning of take-off to maturity. Analytically the explanation for some such interval may lie in the powerful arithmetic of compound interest applied to the capital stock, combined with the broader consequences for a society's ability to absorb modern technology of three successive generations living under a regime where growth is the normal condition. But, clearly, no dogmatism is justified about the exact length of the interval from take-off to maturity.

THE AGE OF HIGH MASS-CONSUMPTION

We come now to the age of high mass-consumption, where, in time, the leading sectors shift towards durable consumers' goods and services: a phase from which Americans are beginning to emerge; whose not unequivocal joys Western Europe and Japan are beginning energetically to probe; and with which Soviet society is engaged in an uneasy flirtation.

As societies achieved maturity in the twentieth century two things happened: real income per head rose to a point where a large number of persons gained a command over consumption which transcended basic food, shelter, and clothing; and the structure of the working force changed in ways which increased not only the proportion of urban to total population, but also the proportion of the population working in offices or in skilled factory jobs—aware of and anxious to acquire the consumption fruits of a mature economy.

In addition to these economic changes, the society ceased to accept the further extension of modern technology as an overriding objective. It is in this post-maturity stage, for example, that, through the political process, Western societies have chosen to allocate increased resources to social welfare and security. The emergence of the welfare state is one manifestation of a society's moving beyond technical maturity; but it is also at this stage that resources tend increasingly to be directed to the production of consumers' durables and to the diffusion of services on a mass basis, if consumers' sovereignty reigns. The sewing-machine, the bicycle, and then the various electric-powered house gadgets were gradually diffused. Historically, however, the decisive element has been the cheap mass automobile with its quite revolutionary effects—social as well as economic—on the life and expectations of society.

For the United States, the turning point was, perhaps, Henry Ford's moving assembly line of 1913–1914; but it was in the 1920's, and again in the post-war decade, 1946–56, that this stage of growth was pressed to, virtually, its logical conclusion. In the 1950's Western Europe and Japan appear to have fully entered this phase, accounting substantially for a momentum in their economies quite unexpected in the immediate post-war years. The Soviet Union is technically ready for this stage, and, by every sign, its citizens hunger for it; but Communist leaders face difficult political and social problems of adjustment if this stage is launched.

· · ·

COMMUNISM: A DISEASE OF THE TRANSITION

On the other hand, Communism as it is—a great fact of history—cannot be disposed of merely by revealing its nature, its deceptions, and its dilemmas. To identify the errors in Marxism and to demonstrate the un-Marxist character of Communism is not a very important achievement. The fact is that Communism as a technique of power is a formidable force. Although it was an un-Marxist insight, it was a correct insight of Lenin's that power could, under certain circumstances, be seized and held by a purposeful minority prepared to use a secret police. Although it was an un-Marxist insight, it was a correct insight that societies in the transition from traditional to modern status are peculiarly vulnerable to such a seizure of power.

It is here, in fact, that Communism is likely to find its place in history. Recall [that] the preconditions period is . . . a situation in which the society has acquired a considerable stock of social overhead capital and modern know-how, but is bedevilled not merely by the conflict between the residual traditional elements and those who would modernize its structure, but bedevilled as well by conflicts among those who would move forward, but who cannot decide which of the three roads to take, and who lack the coherence and organization to move decisively forward in any sustained direction.

It is in such a setting of political and social confusion, before the take-off is achieved and consolidated politically and socially as well as economically, that the seizure of power by Communist conspiracy is easiest; and it is in such a setting that a centralized dictatorship may supply an essential technical precondition for take-off and a sustained drive to maturity: an effective modern state organization.

Remember, for example, what it was in Communism that attracted the Chinese intellectuals after the First World War. It was not its Marxist strain; for the Chinese Communists were—and have remained —indifferent Marxists. It was not the Communist economic performance; for the Russian economy was in poor shape in the early 1920's. The Chinese intellectuals were drawn by Lenin's technique of organization as a means to unify and control a vast, deeply divided country. Both the Kuomintang and the Chinese Communists set themselves up on the Leninist model; and this was understandable in a transitional nation without an effective central government, dominated, in fact, by regional warlords. (Incidentally, if the First World War had not occurred—or had occurred a decade later—Russia would almost certainly have made a successful transition to modernization and rendered itself invulnerable to Communism. Communism gripped Russia very nearly at the end of the phase when it was likely to be vulnerable to the kind of crisis which confronted it in 1917.)

Communism is by no means the only form of effective state organization that can consolidate the preconditions in the transition of a traditional society, launch a take-off, and drive a society to technological maturity. But it may be one way in which this difficult job can be done, if—and this still remains to be seen—if it can solve the problem of agricultural output in the take-off decades. Communism takes its place, then, beside the regime of the Meiji Restoration in Japan, and Ataturk's Turkey, for example, as one peculiarly inhumane form of political organization capable of launching and sustaining the growth process in societies where the preconditions period did not yield a substantial and enterprising commercial middle class and an adequate political consensus among the leaders of the society. It is a kind of disease which can befall a transitional society if it fails to organize effectively those elements within it which are prepared to get on with the job of modernization.

For those who would prefer to see the aspiring societies of the world not follow this particular road to modernization—in Asia, the Middle East, Africa, and Latin America—the Communist technique for mobilizing power and resources poses a formidable problem, almost certainly what historians will judge the central challenge of our time; that is, the challenge of creating, in association with the non-Communist politicians and peoples of the preconditions and early take-off areas, a partnership which will see them through into sustained growth on a political and social basis which keeps open the possibilities of progressive, democratic development.

Paul Baran and E. J. Hobsbawm

5

The Stages
of Economic Growth

On the jacket of W. W. Rostow's *The Stages of Economic Growth: A Non-Communist Manifesto* [first edition, 1960], the publisher advertises the product in these terms: "This book is a generalization from the whole span of modern history. It gives an account of economic growth based on a dynamic theory of production and interpreted in terms of actual societies. It helps to explain historical changes and to predict major political and economic trends; and it provides the significant links between economic and non-economic behavior which Karl Marx failed to discern." The author's own sales-pitch is equally strident: "The stages are not merely descriptive. They are not merely a way of generalizing factual observations about the sequence of development of modern societies. They have an inner logic and continuity. They have an analytical bone-structure rooted in a dynamic theory of production" (pp. 12 f.). And the reason for this enthusiasm is not only the light which the new theory is supposed to shed upon the process of economic and social evolution but also its alleged power to dispose once and for all of the Marxian dragon with which so many others have done battle but failed to slay. The reader is urged to "note the similarities between his (Marx's) analysis and the stages of growth; and the differences between the two systems of thought, stage by stage."

We propose to accept this invitation and to carry out the comparison which Professor Rostow suggests. In what follows the first section will deal with the stages-of-growth scheme's contribution to the theory of economic development. The second section will attempt to answer the question whether Marxian thought is capable of surviving this newest assault.

Such attention as Professor Rostow's writings have hitherto been able to command in the literature on economic development has been based upon some of his earlier empirical studies. His theoretical contributions have been meager—in fact, largely confined to various types of classification. Does his latest effort significantly change this picture?

Professor Rostow advances three propositions. First, he insists that the problem of growth is a historical one which must be considered within a framework of a historical periodization. Second, he emphasizes —and this is perhaps his most notable point—that economic growth is not a continuous and smooth but a discontinuous and dialectical process which pivots on a sudden revolutionary transformation, the "take-off into self-sustained growth." Third, he stresses a particular aspect of this discontinuity of economic growth: that it proceeds not by a balanced development of all sectors of the economy, but by successive leaps forward of the economy's "leading sectors."

These are undoubtedly valuable insights, although it can hardly be said that they are new or that they originate with Professor Rostow. That theories of growth must be historical was perhaps the first discovery of political economy; it has merely been forgotten in the century or so in which economic growth was almost wholly neglected in academic economics, except for the Marxists and those who, like the Germans and Schumpeter, accepted much of the Marxist *Fragestellung* [way of posing the problem] on the subject. The "take-off" is merely another name for the "industrial revolution" which was the basic analytic concept of modern economic history from the days of Engels to those of Mantoux until smothered by the gradualist criticism of Clapham, Ashton, and others between the two wars. The argument for uneven development is equally old. It was advanced by Marx, developed by Lenin, and underlies the Schumpeter-Kondratiev analysis of 19th century economic development.[1] To be sure, the rediscovery of old truths is a most creditable accomplishment—particularly in contemporary "behavioral sciences" where apparently any nonsense goes as long as it has never been said before—though not one calling in itself for a major ovation.

But when we come to consider Professor Rostow's other achievements in the field of the theory of growth, the weaknesses are all too obvious. The first and most serious is that his theory of "stages" actually tells us nothing except that there are stages. The four other stages are implicit in the "take-off," and add nothing to it. Given a "take-off" there must obviously be a stage before it, but when the conditions for economic growth are not present, another when the pre-conditions for the "take-off" exist, and yet another following it when "an economy demonstrates that it has the technological and entrepreneurial skills to produce not everything, but anything it wants" (which is Rostow's definition of the

---

[1] Cf. also A. F. Burns, *Production Trends in the United States since 1870,* New York 1934.

stage of "maturity"), and yet another when it has acquired the capacity to produce everything it wants (p. 10).[2] Indeed, there is no departure ("take-off") of any kind—in the history of nature, of societies or of individuals—which cannot be thought of as being preceded and followed by a number of "stages." If one has a penchant for symmetry one only has to make sure that the total number of stages—the "take-off" included—should be uneven.

Thus once we have one corner, we have the entire Pentagon. One weakness of this procedure is, of course, that analysis must remain confined to its area. Accordingly, the Rostovian stage theory, despite its comprehensive historic and sociological claims reduces economic growth to a single pattern. Any and every country, whatever its other characteristics, is classifiable only in respect to its position on the stepladder, the middle rung of which is the "take-off." This gives the Rostovian stages an air of spurious generality—they appear to apply to any and all economies, to the USSR as to the USA, to China as to Brazil—which, as we shall see, is not without its ideological implications, though it overlooks the obvious fact that, however universal the technical problems of economic growth may be, different social types of economic organization can, or must, solve them in very different ways.

Yet even within its extremely narrow limits the Rostovian theory can neither explain nor predict without introducing considerations that are completely irrelevant to the stage schema. It simply fails to specify any mechanism of evolution which links the different stages. There is no particular reason why the "traditional" society should turn into a society breeding the "preconditions" of the "take-off." Rostow's account merely summarizes what these preconditions must be,[3] and repeats a version of that "classical answer" the inadequacy of which has long been evident: a combination of the "discovery and rediscovery of regions beyond Western Europe" and the "developing of modern scientific knowledge and attitudes" (p. 31). Here is the *deus cum machina.* Nor is there any reason within the Rostovian stages why the "precon-

---

[2] This stage Rostow misnames "the age of high mass consumption" for both by the logical requirements of his schema and by his own observations on the subject (pp. 73–74) what characterizes it is not fundamentally mass consumption (which is only one of the alternative uses to which resources can be put by society) but *abundance.* This error in nomenclature is by no means trivial; it is associated with Rostow's misleading treatment of the current stage of the United States' economic development, when *armaments* rather than mass consumption represent the economy's "leading sector."

[3] And this not with any great perspicacity. Thus one would suppose that agricultural change creates the preconditions of industrialization not merely by supplying "expanded food, expanded markets, and an expanded supply of loanable funds to the modern sector" (p. 24) but also—and perhaps decisively—an expanded labor force for it.

ditions" should lead to the "take-off" to maturity, as is indeed evidenced by Rostow's own difficulty in discovering, except long *ex post facto*, whether a "take-off" has taken place or not.[4] In fact the Rostovian "take-off" concept has no predictive value. Similarly, when it comes to analyzing the "inner structure" of the take-off or of any other stage, the Rostovian theory subsides into statements of the type that "things can happen in any one of a very large number of different ways," which constitute a rather limited contribution to knowledge.[5]

Such explanations and predictions as Rostow attempts are therefore little more than verbiage which has no connection with his stages theory or indeed with any theory of economic and social evolution, being generally based on what might be charitably called coffeehouse sociology and political speculation. The nearest he actually comes to an attempt at an explanation of *why* economic growth takes place is his emphasis on the importance of "reactive nationalism" and the crucial role of "an inherently competitive system of power" in which states are historically enmeshed.[6] The explanation tends to be circular—when a country has economic growth it is evidence of reactive nationalism[7]—as well as open-ended: when an obviously nationalist country does *not* initiate a take-off, it is because "nationalism can be turned in any one of several directions" (p. 29). Moreover, even this type of explanation is crippled by Rostow's refusal to admit the profit motive into his analysis, a refusal not concealed by an occasional parenthetical remark granting

---

[4] Cf. the hesitations reflected in the footnotes to his table of "take-offs" (p. 38) and his inability to decide "whether the take-off period will, in fact, be successful in the six contemporary economies attempting take-off" (p. 44) as well as his failure to cope with the phenomenon of relapse after apparent take-offs. However critics, and especially statisticians, should resist the easy temptation Rostow thus provides to reject the entire concept of economic development by industrial revolution.

[5] For example: "Perhaps the most important thing to be said about the behavior of these variables in historical cases of take-off is that they have assumed many different forms. There is no single pattern. The rate and productivity of investment can rise, and the consequences of this rise can be diffused into a self-reinforcing general growth process by many different technical and economic routes, under the aegis of many different political, social and cultural settings, driven along by a wide variety of human motivations" (p. 46). Or, we may add, they may not rise, and may not be diffused . . .

[6] "The general case is of a society modernizing itself in a nationalist reaction to intrusion or the threat of intrusion from more advanced powers abroad" (p. 34).

[7] Cf. pp. 34–35 where the attempt is made, half-heartedly, to assimilate the pioneer industrialization of Britain to this pattern on no other grounds than that otherwise it would not fit the "general case." Admittedly, if a theory of economic evolution cannot explain the case which needs explaining most, namely the very first "take-off" in history, it is little more than scrap paper, though Professor Rostow does not seem too keenly aware of this. Cf. p. 27.

its existence.[8] Still, weak as it is, the explanation of economic growth by nationalism and the logic of international rivalry is the closest Rostow comes to an analysis of economic development as distinct from relabelling and classifying it.

And this is not very close. For in addition to an incapacity to answer relevant questions, Professor Rostow shows an astonishing lack of ability for even recognizing their existence or their import. Thus one of the crucial problems which faces both the theorist and would-be planner of economic development under capitalist conditions is that "the criteria for private profit-maximization do not necessarily converge with the criteria for an optimum rate and pattern of growth in various sectors," indeed, that under pre-industrial conditions or in underdeveloped areas it can be shown that they are more likely than not to diverge. The statesman or economic administrator of a backward country knows that a century of western capitalism has failed to transfer any country across the gap which separates the advanced from the backward economies. He also knows that profit-oriented private investment can be relied on to build his country's tourist hotels but not its steelworks. Consequently he has increasingly taken to imitating the Soviet method of achieving economic growth, which does not suffer from this disadvantage, rather than relying on the 19th-century European or American method which does. Rostow neither explains any of these facts which determine the actual problem of economic development in underdeveloped areas, nor does he even seem aware of them beyond the casual mention already quoted. Conversely, the historian must explain why, in spite of this divergence, or lack of convergence, a limited number of countries around the North Atlantic in the 18th and 19th centuries actually managed to industrialize on a capitalist basis. Rostow appears equally oblivious of this problem.

This obtuseness is not accidental. Indeed, the nature of Professor Rostow's approach makes it impossible for him to solve such problems, and difficult even to realize their existence. For if we argue that the main motor of economic change was at no time "profit-maximization (in the sense of) economic advantage," we can hardly deal with, let alone answer questions which arise from the fact that all economic development between the "traditional" society and the appearance of the USSR was actually *capitalist* development and which calls therefore for an analysis of the specific characteristics of *capitalism*. If we abstract from everything that separates "eighteenth century Britain

---

[8] Cf. on p. 28 "The merchant has always been present, seeking in modernization not only the removal of obstacles to enlarged markets and profits, but also the high status denied him," but especially the remarkably contorted pages on colonialism (pp. 108–112).

and Khrushchev's Russia; Meiji Japan and Mao's China; Bismarck's Germany and Nasser's Egypt," we shall be unable to explain why Nasser's Egypt finds Khrushchev's Russia a more useful guide to economic development than eighteenth century Britain. If we are anxious to minimize the element of economic advantage in the relation between advanced and dependent (colonial) economics, we shall be unable to say anything useful about problems which arise out of the fact that dependent economies are dependent.

Why, it may be asked, should a man adopt a theoretical approach so obviously defective and indeed self-defeating? At least one plausible answer may be suggested. Professor Rostow, is, on his own admission, primarily concerned not with arriving at a theory of economic development, but with writing a "non-communist manifesto." Unlike other and wiser—we shall not say abler—scholars with similar objectives, he has chosen to abandon not merely Marx's conclusions and his arguments, but even the basic posing of the problem of economic development as Marx saw it. It was, as we have tried to show, an unwise decision, for the Marxian questions are fundamental to any attempt at an understanding of the process of economic development. What is required is at least an *understanding* of Marx's questions. To that level Professor Rostow has yet to rise.

An examination of the principal tenets of Rostow's theory of economic growth—if it can be at all said that such a *theory* is advanced in his book—thus reveals nothing that can be considered an addition to our knowledge of the history of economic development or an enrichment of our understanding of the processes involved. But Rostow offers something much more ambitious than "merely" a new theory of economic growth. He also proposes "a comprehensive, realistic and soundly based alternative to Marx's theory of how societies evolve." Let us examine this latest effort to put Marx into the waste basket. Since, however, it is neither possible nor would it be rewarding to trace all the misconceptions and misrepresentations of Marxian thought which Rostow has managed to compress in a few pages, we will have to limit ourselves to two problems which Rostow himself considers to be central to his Manifesto.

The first relates to the nature of the engine which propells economic, social, and political evolution in the course of history. To this fundamental question, historical materialism provides a comprehensive and sophisticated answer. Far be it from us to seek to emulate Rostow in the claim that this answer supplies pat solutions to all problems raised by the complex events and patterns of history. What historical materialism does claim is to have discovered an indispensable *approach* to the understanding of historical constellations and to have focused attention on the nature of the principal energies responsible for their emergence, transformation, and disappearance. To put it in a nutshell: these energies are to be traced back to the always present tension between the degree of development of the forces of production on one side, and the prevailing relations of production on the other. To be sure, neither "forces of production" nor "relations of production" are simple notions. The former encompasses the existing state of rationality, science, and technology, the mode of organization of production and the degree of development of man himself, that "most important productive force of all" (Marx). The latter refers to the mode of appropriation of the products of human labor, the social condition under which production takes place, the principles of distribution, the modes of thought, the ideology, the *Weltanschauung* which constitute the "general ether" (Marx) within which society functions at any given time. The conflict between the two—sometimes dormant and sometimes active—is due to a fundamental difference in the "laws of motion" of forces and relations of production respectively. The forces of production tend to be highly dynamic. Driven by man's quest for a better life, by the growth and expansion of human knowledge and rationality, by increasing population, the forces of production tend continually to gain in strength, in depth and in scope. The relations of production on the other hand tend to be sticky, conservative. Prevailing systems of appropriation and social organization, and political institutions favor some classes and discriminate against, frustrate, oppress other classes. They give rise to vested interests. Modes of thought freeze and display a tenacity and longevity giving rise to what is sometimes referred to as "cultural lags." When the forward movement of the forces of production becomes stymied by the deadweight of dominant interests and the shackles of dominant thought, one or the other has to yield. And since a dominant class never willingly relinquishes its time-honored privileges (partly for reasons of self-interest and partly because its own horizon is more or less narrowly circumscribed by the prevailing ideology sanctifying those very privileges), the clash tends to become violent. This is not to say that obsolete, retrograde relations of production are *always* burst asunder and swept away by revolutions. Depending on the circumstances prevailing in each individual case, the process unfolds in a wide variety of ways. Violent upheavals "from below" and relatively peaceful transformations "from above" are as much within the range of possibilities as periods of protracted stagnation in which the political, ideological, and social power of the ruling classes is strong enough to prevent the emergence of new forms of economic and social organization, to block or to slow a country's economic development.

Marx's historical materialism insists, however, that the development of the forces of production has thus far been *the* commanding aspect of the historical process. Whatever may have been its vicissitudes, whatever may have been the setbacks and interruptions that it has suffered in the course of history, in the long run it has tended to overcome all obstacles, and to conquer all political, social and ideological structures subordinating them to its requirements. This struggle between the forces of production and the relations of production proceeds unevenly. Dramatic conquests are less frequent than long periods of siege in which victories remain elusive, imperfect, and impermanent. Different countries display different patterns which depend on their size, location, the strength and cohesion of their ruling classes, the courage, determination and leadership of the underprivileged; on the measure of foreign influence and support to which both or either are exposed; on the pervasiveness and power of the dominant ideologies (e.g. religion). Moreover, the course taken by this struggle and its outcome differ greatly from period to period. Under conditions of capitalism's competitive youth they were different from what they have become in the age of imperialism; in the presence of a powerful socialist sector of the world, they are not the same as they were or would have been in its absence. No bloodless schema of 5 (or 3 or 7) "stages" can do justice to the multitude and variety of economic, technological, political, and ideological configurations generated by this never-ceasing battle between the forces and relations of production. What Marx and Engels and Lenin taught those whose ambition it was to learn rather than to make careers by "refuting" is that these historical configurations cannot be dealt with by "a generalization from the whole span of modern history," but have to be studied *concretely*, with full account taken of the wealth of factors and forces that participate in the shaping of any particular historical case.

To forestall a possible misunderstanding: the foregoing is not intended to advocate renunciation of theory in favor of plodding empiricism. Rather it suggests the necessity of an interpenetration of theory and concrete observation, of empirical research illuminated by rational theory, of theoretical work which draws its life blood from historical study. Consider for instance any one of the many existing underdeveloped countries. Pigeonholing it in one of Rostow's "stages" does not bring us any closer to an understanding of the country's economic and social condition or give us a clue to the country's developmental possibilities and prospects. What is required for that is as accurate as possible an assessment of the social and political forces in the country pressing for change and for development (the economic condition and the stratification of the peasantry, its political traditions and its ideological make-up, the economic and social status, internal differentiation and political aspirations of the bourgeoisie, the extent of its tie-up with foreign interests and the degree of monopoly prevailing in its national business, the closeness of its connection with the landowning interests and the measure of its participation in the existing government; the living and working conditions and the level of class consciousness of labor and its political and organizational strength). Nor is this by any means the entire job. On the other side of the fence are the groups, institutions, relations, and ideologies seeking to preserve the *status quo*, obstructing efforts directed towards its overturn. There are wealthy land-owners and/or rich peasants; there is a segment of the capitalist class firmly entrenched in monopolistic positions and allied with other privileged groups in society; there is a government bureaucracy interwoven with and resting upon the military establishment; there are foreign investors supported by their respective national governments and working hand in hand with their native retainers. Only a thorough historical-materialist analysis, piercing the ideological fog maintained by the dominant coalition of interests and destroying the fetishes continually produced and reproduced by those concerned with the preservation of the *status quo*, only such historical-materialist analysis can hope to disentangle the snarl of tendencies and counter-tendencies, forces, influences, convictions and opinions, drives and resistances which account for the pattern of economic and social development. And it is to this *Marxist* undertaking that Professor Rostow offers us his alternative: to assign the country in question to one of his "stages," and then to speculate on the "two possibilities" with which that country is confronted: it will either move on to the next "stage"— or it won't. And if it should move to the next "stage," it will again face two possibilities: it will either stay there for a while, or it will slide back again.

We may now turn briefly to Professor Rostow's other sally against Marx by which he seeks to provide "significant links between economic and non-economic behavior which Karl Marx failed to discern." This enterprise, he apparently feels, will deliver the "coup de grâce" to Marxian thought, "for," he assures us "it is absolutely essential to Marxism that it is over property that men fight and die." What Karl Marx—"a lonely man, profoundly isolated from his fellows"—did not discern, but Professor Rostow does, is the following: "Man . . . seeks not merely economic advantage, but also power, leisure, adventure, continuity of experience and security . . . in short, net human behavior is . . . not an act of maximizing, but . . . an act of balancing alternative and often conflicting human objectives." "This notion of balance among alternatives," Professor Rostow observes, "is, of course, more complex and difficult than a simple maximization proposition; and it does not lead to a series of rigid, inevitable stages of history." We submit that this "notion" may well be "complex and difficult" but that it is also singularly devoid of any ascertainable content. It is remarkable how

Professor Rostow, after having constructed a strawman bearing no resemblance to Marxism finds it beyond his powers to vanquish even such a "hand-picked" enemy.

Indeed—to put it bluntly—the whole argument is too helpless to serve even as a starting point for a serious discussion. Even a passing acquaintance with the most important writings of Marx, Engels, and more recent Marxist writers is all that is required to realize the irrelevance of Rostow's caricature of Marxism. Far from asserting that "history is uniquely determined by economic forces," and far from ignoring the "significant links between economic and non-economic behavior," the theory of historical materialism advanced by Marx and his followers is nothing if not a powerful effort to explore the manifold, and historically changing connections between the development of the forces and relations of production and the evolution of the consciousness, emotions, and ideologies of men. So much so that the Marxian theory of ideology has served as the point of departure and as a guide to an entire discipline known under the name of "sociology of knowledge," with all analytical history of religion, literature, art and science deriving its inspiration from the same source. Marx's theory of alienation anticipating much of the subsequent development of social psychology, is in the center of modern study and criticism of culture. Marx's political theory has served as a conceptual basis for most that is valuable in modern European and American historical scholarship. And *The Eighteenth Brumaire of Louis Bonaparte*—to name only one unsurpassed gem of historical and sociological study—still shines as a model of a comprehensive and penetrating analysis of the "significant links between economic and non-economic behavior" in one particular historical case.

But all this escapes Mr. Rostow who is not only incapable of contributing anything to the discussion of the relevant problems but even fails to comprehend the context within which they arise. For the problem of the "links between economic and non-economic behavior," or for that matter of the explanation of any human activity, economic or other, is not and never has been whether or not man "balances alternatives" or "adheres to the principle of maximization" (which terms, incidentally, if they mean anything at all, amount to exactly the same), no more than there is meaning to the question whether man does or does not have "freedom of will." No one in his right mind—Marxist, mechanical materialist, or idealist—has ever denied that men make choices, exercise their wills, balance alternatives, or, for that matter, move their legs when they walk. The problem is and always has been to discover what determines the nature of the alternatives that are available to men, what accounts for the nature of the goals which they set themselves in different periods of historical development, what makes them will what they will in various societies at various times. To this fundamental question there have been several answers. The theologian's solution has been that all human acts and decisions are governed by the omnipotent and inscrutable will of God. The idealist who substituted the human spirit for the Deity arrives at a very similar position, unable as he is to explain what accounts for the actions and transactions of the spirit. The adherents of "psychologism" view human activity as an emanation of the human psyche itself an aspect of an eternally constant human nature.[9] The historical materialist considers human actions and motivations to be complex results of a dialectical interaction of biotic and social processes, the latter continually propelled by the dynamism of the forces and relations of production as well as by the ideological evolutions deriving from them and influencing them in turn. Professor Rostow, however, has the simplest solution of all: he does not know what the answer is, nor does he appear to care. Anything can happen: man moves hither and thither, balancing alternatives, making choices, striving for power, engaged in maximization of who knows what. And this is the new, original, unprecedented "theory" which makes good what Karl Marx failed to discern.

We owe the reader an apology. Taken by itself Rostow's Manifesto does not call for a lengthy review. If we have undertaken to write one nevertheless, it is because of considerations from the realm of the sociology of knowledge. His is an important document. It demonstrates in a particularly striking way the low estate to which Western social thought has declined in the current era of the cold war.

---

[9] For a somewhat more extensive discussion of this Cf. Paul A. Baran, *Marxism and Psychoanalysis*, Monthly Review Press, New York 1960.

E. J. Hobsbawm and R. M. Hartwell

6

The Standard of Living during the Industrial Revolution: A Discussion

PART I BY E. J. HOBSBAWM

The debate on the British people's standard of living in the early industrial period, which had for some time been dormant, was revived in the later 1950's and has continued briskly ever since. To be more precise, what had established itself as a virtual academic orthodoxy in Britain, the optimistic view associated with Sir John Clapham and T. S. Ashton, was sharply challenged, and a number of students have since attempted to rebut or to come to terms with this challenge. The debate has perhaps continued long enough for one of the challengers to survey the battlefield, which is less confused than a casual reading of the relevant literature might suggest. This is the object of the present article.

The first point which should be clearly established, for it is in danger of being obscured, is that the traditional Clapham-Ashton view has been dislodged almost without resistance. That view was perfectly plain. It argued that the living standards of most of the British labouring population, so far from declining or even remaining stable, improved *substantially* in the period roughly describable as "the first half of the 19th century." By "living standards" the proponents of this view understood mainly real income, though they also considered a number of other factors. They believed that this improvement in real income could be statistically demonstrated (and not merely inferred) by some form or other of real wage index. In view of what they believed to be a demonstrable and substantial increase in real wages, they therefore held that the traditional case for a deterioration in labour conditions, which rested largely on non-quantitative evidence, must fall to the ground. There was nothing tentative about these claims. "Wages," Clapham stated, "had risen markedly." "In 1831," said Ashton (while admitting that in the '30s and '40s wages were lower than might have been expected), "the cost of living was 11% higher than in 1790, but over this span of time urban real wages had increased by 43%." The deteriorationist view was flatly described as "a legend."

This brash view is now dead. Even Dr. Hartwell, the most militant, though not the most expert, proponent of amelioration, appears to agree that Clapham must be exiled among the "extremists." Less committed observers who survey the trend of the discussion have abandoned the optimistic view in its hitherto prevalent form entirely, while not thereby committing themselves to the pessimistic one: "The conclusions to be drawn, therefore, from the evidence on food consumption are by no means clearly defined: but their general tenor is to suggest rising living standards towards the end of the eighteenth century and less certain progress or decline thereafter."

I would not wish to quarrel with such caution. If the view that there was substantial improvement is no longer tenable in the present state of the evidence, the opposite view that there was substantial, or any, deterioration, has not been firmly established; nor indeed was it the purpose of anyone engaged in this phase of the debate to do so. The object was rather to eliminate "Claphamism" and thereby to show that the onus of proving that the gloomy and traditional views were wrong, continues to rest squarely on the optimists. The case for some deterioration is plausible for the period from the middle 1790's to the early or middle 1840's, but in the absence of some evidence which might well upset it (for instance, figures for per capita meat consumption in the provinces analogous to those we have for London), it remains no more than plausible. Very possibly the absence of evidence will never allow us to settle the matter conclusively, and the argument that real incomes remained roughly stable will commend itself as the most acceptable formula. What is untenable at present is the view that there was substantial improvement, if the word "substantial" is to have the same meaning before the middle 1840's as after.

The debate since 1957 has produced amazingly little in the way of new evidence. It is therefore relatively easy to summarize the state of the question in a few propositions. They are as follows:

1. We cannot at present derive a satisfactory and representative real wage index for our period. The attempt to do so has been for the moment abandoned by the chief proponents of the Clapham school and even Dr. Hartwell makes no serious effort to revive it. Consequently the view that real wages rose markedly during our period is not now based on reliable evidence.

2. The most fruitful way of getting at real wages is probably through the study of actual consumption; certainly this is least likely to lead

to contestable results. The sources for such evidence are defective and may raise methodological difficulties. Incomplete though these data are at present, they are compatible with a slight decrease, possibly with a slight increase, but not before the middle of the 1840's (if we omit short-term fluctuations) with a marked and obvious increase. Dr. Hartwell's cursory and ill-informed discussion has not changed this situation in the slightest.

3. Chronic and cyclical unemployment, though at present only inter-mittently measurable, was almost certainly extremely high, and in times of crisis catastrophic. Few would doubt that it was much higher than in the period after the middle forties, but its effect on real wages, though plainly serious, remains to be investigated. As usual, the optimists (notably Hartwell) continue to neglect it entirely, though sources for local unemployment, analogous to those quoted in my earlier article, await the interested researcher. It may be worth illus-trating the effect by the turnover figures for 50 Salford shopkeepers which fell as follows between 1839—not an exceptionally brilliant year—and 1841—a disastrous one:

	1839	1841
13 provision dealers	£70,700	£47,300
14 butchers	27,800	17,200
10 grocers	63,800	43,300
13 drapers, etc.	35,400	22,300

Evidently no discussion which neglects unemployment can claim to be taken seriously.

4. While it is agreed on all hands that some sections of the popula-tion suffered while others improved their condition, the inadequacy of our occupational and income statistics does not allow us to estimate the size of the respective groups with any confidence. Such data as we possess at present are indeterminate. While a number of estimates are possible, the uncertainty of the assumptions which have to be made in order to construct them, makes it improbable that a conclusive answer can be found along these lines. However, no particular presumption exists in favour of an optimistic interpretation.

5. An optimistic presumption, however, appears to derive from certain global calculations such as those of the general trend of the national income, and it is on these that the optimistic case now seems, in the main, to rest. The argument is that, if we can rely on contem-porary estimates, the rise in national income was so large that personal real incomes per capita must on average have risen also, which in turn is believed to imply that the real incomes of most people must have risen. In fact, this argument is a return to the reasoning of the con-temporary liberal statisticians and economists (Porter, McCulloch *et*

al.), whose case for the improvement of the condition of the people rested, as has been shown, much less on hard evidence than on the inability to believe that an expansion of wealth and productive capacity so vast as that which was taking place in Britain, could fail to produce a rise in the standard of living of the labouring poor.

The difficulty about this argument is threefold. In the first place, like any indirect argument, it must yield to the facts. It is inconclusive, so long as the direct evidence about the standard of living does not permit us to know whether it rose sharply, and valueless if the direct evidence shows that the standard did not rise. It cannot be too often repeated that the debate, in the form which Clapham gave it, will be settled, if at all, not on the basis of presumption about what may have happened or general reasoning about what ought to have happened, but *only* on the basis of direct evidence. In the second place the argument itself rests entirely on a further hitherto unverified, at present unverifiable and somewhat improbable assumption, namely that "an increase in per capita income (was) accompanied by a more equal income distribution." Most of the space devoted by Hartwell to this topic is in fact filled by attempts to establish this second assumption, in the face of the (in the view of most students of industrialization) more plausible contrary assumption that the early stages of industrialization are likely to make the distribution of the national income *less* even, to allow for larger savings and more investments. It is perhaps worth observing, in passing, that the proponent of this argument is obliged to show not merely that the share of the labourers in the national income rose, but that within the labouring poor also its distribution did not become less even. For it is entirely possible for the total share of wages to rise while only a minority of labourers actually improve their real income. However, though arguments are plentiful, facts are scarce, and Hartwell's actual *evidence* for an increasing evenness of income distribution in this period is too negligible to be worth consideration. The third difficulty about the national income argument is also that of all arguments which incline us favourably to a certain view without being able to establish it. They are vulnerable to contrary presumptions which, while equally unable to establish themselves conclusively, point in the opposite direction. And there is a mountain-range of contemporary evidence and argument which does so.

The above summary represents not an extremist position, but almost certainly one which would today (apart from some of the present author's stylistic formulations) command general agreement more nearly than any other except sheer agnosticism. It amounts to the assertion that no certainty in this field is as yet possible, but that the hypothesis of a marked or substantial rise in the standard of living of most Britons between the early 1790's and the early 1840's is, as things stand, an extremely improbable one. The dates, however, are important. Chronological neatness leads us to talk loosely of periods such as 1800–1850. In fact, however, the debate is entirely about what happened in a period which ended, by common consent, some time between 1842 and 1845. After that there is no dispute about the fact of an improvement in the standard of living, and indeed this absence of dispute has meant that the subsequent period has been rather neglected by researchers. The fact that the 1840's divide between two entirely different trend-periods, has led to confusion in the past, e.g. in the debate about whether they should be called the "hungry forties." (The layman may be surprised to find that there is such a debate about the decade which contains the Irish Famine; but English historians are often parochial.) What is worse, it has tempted careless historians to use evidence from the period after 1843–4 to throw light on the trend of the period before this turning-point. It must therefore be very firmly pointed out that this procedure is illegitimate.

At this point one might conclude the survey of the debate. However, as the debate will no doubt continue, it may be as well to consider what sort of evidence will be needed to re-establish the optimistic case, now that the onus of proof once again rests on the optimists, and what sort will be inadequate.

Their first obstacle is the mountain of contemporary opinion, non-quantitative evidence and—as has recently been shown, hitherto neglected quantitative evidence—which cannot be overlooked. Unless it can be levelled or reduced to a hillock, the path of the optimist must be presumed to lead steeply uphill.

Now attempts to lighten the traditional gloom have been made first and foremost by discrediting the contemporary observers and (unless optimistic) theorists. It is true that Dr. Hartwell has denied that there was a prevalence of gloomy contemporaries or, at a later period, of gloomy historians. But this will not do. That there was a predominance of informed opinion inclined to, or implying, a dark interpretation of working-class conditions at that time—however *nuancée*—is admitted even by Professor Ashton. That most of the historians between Marx and Clapham saw the Industrial Revolution as a "bleak age" for the labouring classes, is not in fact denied at all. As to whether the future would grow darker or rosier, there was genuinely even debate even in the 1830's and 1840's, and probably a predominance of optimism. Here, plainly, the optimists had the better case, for after all conditions did improve after the middle 1840's. But the improvement came later, and its most powerful chroniclers, like Giffen and the Fabians, often made their case by contrasting the heights scaled in the later century with the rock-bottom of the early industrial period.

The most obvious way of discrediting the pessimistic contemporaries is by claiming that they approached the subject not as disinterested inquirers, but with a marked bias; in general an anti-capitalist bias. It is perhaps characteristic that the equally marked bias of the meliorists, even when it leads—as in McCulloch's case—to striking perversions of fact, even if so plainly stated and unsupported by anything but rhetoric as with Macaulay, has not attracted the same criticism. Now in fact the accusation is wrong. Whatever their motives, enthusiastic supporters of liberalism collected material of the darkest hue, and Engels used them for preference as his sources in the vain attempt to escape the accusation. The most horror-stricken accounts of Manchester come from foreign liberals like de Tocqueville and Free Traders like Faucher. But whether true or not, the charge is irrelevant and the deductions from it wrong.

Whatever the motives which drove men to inquire into social conditions, their findings stand or fall by the normal criteria of evidence and argument. The fact that Royal Commissions were in those days means for achieving rather than for adjourning reform no more invalidates the findings of the blue books than Porter's obvious bias in favour of British capitalism invalidates the *Progress of the Nation*. Whether any source is true or if true, representative, is a matter for ordinary scrutiny. As it happens Engels' own book has been exhaustively scrutinized by two hostile editors anxious to prove its factual unreliability. Their failure to convict him of more than a handful of slips merely confirms the respect in which this remarkable piece of work has long been held. One would not claim that all contemporary sources stand up to cross-examination so successfully, but the exercise at any rate shows that partisanship need not *a priori* tell against a source.

The mass of contemporary evidence thus remains to block the road of the meliorist scholar. It can be unblocked only by the explosive charge of contrary evidence, strong, positive and relevant, as that adduced by the rearguard optimists is not, even when it dates from the right period. It will not do to base arguments about the standard of living of the labouring poor on the rise of small as against large income-tax payers or fundholders, unless we can prove (what is very unlikely) that the rich are a representative sample of the poor. If one thing is clear about the statistics of savings banks, which have been hopefully explored by meliorists ever since the early nineteenth century, it is that in our period the social composition of their depositors was highly untypical so that, for instance, "they afford no accurate test of the amount of existing misery in times of commercial depression."

They carry no serious weight, especially when used in a purely rhetorical manner.

It is equally inadmissible to argue that the feeble efforts of government in the period up to the early 1840's had much serious effect on the living-standards and working conditions of the labouring poor. Admittedly the Factories Act of 1833, though confined to a narrow sector of industrial work—in effect to women and children in textile mills—marked a genuine advance on the completely negligible legislation before this date, and was not rendered wholly inoperative by the reluctance of employers, many male workers and the law, to apply it or by the impossibility of effective inspection. But nobody not making an *a priori* case for amelioration would seriously care to rest a heavy weight of argument on its efficacy before the early 1840's, still less on the Mines Act of 1842, whose single inspector Engels rightly omitted to record, since that inspector himself, a year after the completion of Engels' book, commented on the Act's ineffectiveness.

As for the rest of social and public health legislation in the period under discussion, it is best forgotten. The Truck Act of 1831 was largely a dead letter. Sanitary legislation can hardly be said to have begun in the early forties, and such improvement as had taken place, almost certainly lagged behind the even more rapid rise in urban population, as is of course demonstrated by the increasing frequency of urban epidemics. As the Select Committee on the Health of Towns wrote in 1840: "It cannot be denied that considerable attention has been directed to sewerage and drainage within the last twelve years, and that great improvements have been effected during that period, still the want of any general system of operation and the defective powers possessed by the commissioners . . . (both in London and the provinces) . . . have altogether prevented the extension and construction of sewers upon a scale commensurate with the increase of population." And though the chief cities actually began to do something in the middle forties—Manchester after 1844, Glasgow in the last years before 1854 ("and then only a beginning"), Birmingham in the later fifties—the optimist is well advised to steer clear of sanitary improvement before the later forties at the very earliest, if he wishes to be taken seriously.

Such feeble props can hardly hold up the case for "the rising standard of living." The case remains to be made. For it must be repeated, and in the face of criticism flatly repeated, that economic theory of whatever brand, gives us no *a priori* presumption in favour of a significant improvement of the standard of living in the period of early industrialization, and a slight presumption against it. The most usual historical case is, in Pollard's words, that of "pressure on consumption and material standards of living of the mass of the population, at a time when it is forced to adapt itself to major social changes." The onus of establishing a different state of affairs continues to rest on the meliorists.

A final and more defensive argument on the optimistic side remains to be considered, for the frank admission of defeat implicit in the view that capitalism did not cause deterioration, because this occurs in all industrial revolutions, hardly requires comment. It has been argued that, while conditions in the early nineteenth century were bad, and possibly not improving, they were better than in the eighteenth century, which the anti-optimists have persistently idealized. Hence the case for improvement stands.

This is admitttedly to call in the unknown to justify the half-known, for we know much less about eighteenth-century standards than we do about those of the period after 1790. Certainly we know too little to settle the argument in quantitative terms. Yet we do know enough to reject certain common contentions of the optimists, or rather to suggest that these express hope rather than research or even thought. These contentions are that urban conditions were better, or at any rate no worse, in the early nineteenth century than in the eighteenth, and that factory work was greatly superior to eighteenth-century domestic work.

Nobody doubts that rookeries as bad as those of the nineteenth century can be cited from the eighteenth. The issue is not whether "slums and adulteration were peculiar products of industrialization" but whether there was more of both in 1840 than in 1780. And of course there was. It is not only likely, but we actually know it. The issue is not whether in some unquantifiable sense "rural life was naturally better than town life." It is also, among other things, why the labourers of Wiltshire, hardly a pampered group, had on average something like twice the life-expectancy at birth of the labourers of Manchester and Liverpool, a comparison which is the staple of sanitary reformers' arguments in the 1840's and 1850's. If it is objected that the superiority of rural health was not new, then it may be pointed out with equal legitimacy that the proportion of the urbanized was now much greater.

The problem of domestic industry and its exploitation and oppression is slightly more complex, for the optimists' view here is based not on simple error or omission, but on misconception. There can be little doubt that where the two coexisted in the nineteenth century, factory work was generally far more materially attractive, at least after the decline of domestic industry set in. The optimists' mistake here is to contrast an eighteenth century identified with "domestic work" with a nineteenth identified with "factory work." But this is wrong. The

Industrial Revolution did not merely replace cottage or slum work-shop by factory, but multiplied *both* domestic industry and factories; the former either in direct dependence on the latter (as in cotton weaving), or in the rapidly expanding branches of production as yet quite untouched by the factory (as in the garment industry), or in industries whose scale remained small even when they adopted new power. It also eventually killed off many of the expanded domestic industries it had created. The fate of these vastly expanded and then sacrificed domestic branches is therefore just as much part of the social impact of the industrial revolution as the fate of the factory popula-tion. It is entirely illegitimate to reject the half-million and more handloom weavers of 1830 or the army of seamstresses as survivals from pre-industrialism. But for the Industrial Revolution most of them would not have been there, or at any rate their life would have been very different.

Moreover, domestic industry in this new phase was—at least after its early boom—probably much less attractive than before the revolution, even setting aside extreme cases such as the slow strangulation of the handloom weavers. Thus in Sheffield grinders' disease was "scarcely known" towards the end of the eighteenth century, but in 1842 it affected 34 per cent of all razor grinders (and between 50 and 100 per cent of all above the age of 30); a natural consequence of expanding the volume of production without adequate corresponding alterations in working and living conditions. It is therefore plain that neither an optimistic nor a gloomy case can rest on a comparison of factory and outworkers *at the same time*; yet optimists still continue to make such comparisons.

The question how social conditions in the period of the "take-off" and after compared with those before the industrial revolution must, in the present state of our knowledge, still be left open. All that can be said is that hitherto the attempts to bring it into the optimistic argument have been more marked by a desire to prove preconceived notions than by careful research.

However, to compare the pre-industrial with the industrial age in purely quantitative terms is to play Lear without the King. For the debate between the optimists and the pessimists has been sociological as much as economic. Engels' own case in favour of the eighteenth century, for instance, was not merely that the standard of living of the cottagers was "much better than that of the factory workers today," which is debatable, but that they lived in a far more secure, psycho-logically satisfactory and fuller community, though at the cost, which he freely admitted, of ignorance and stagnation. The crux of the Hammonds' argument was not simply that the early industrial age was poor, but that it was bleak. In other words, poverty and dirt *alone* are not the issue. The change from one way of life to another is equally at stake. But while the careful student of poverty can only say that the case for deterioration, while not implausible, cannot be proved, though that against a marked improvement is extremely strong, the sociological argument for deterioration is far more powerful.

Now this argument has been virtually absent from the debate since Clapham apparently worsted the Hammonds a generation ago, and recent anti-Claphamites have deliberately not stressed it, for they have rightly chosen to fight the Claphamites on their own chosen ground of quantitative indices. If the Claphamites were right, the non-quantitative arguments became irrelevant or at any rate secondary. The labouring poor might have been subjectively disturbed or unhappy, but at all events they wept all the way to their increasingly large Sunday dinners. Consequently the most effective way of controverting them was to show that there was no reason to believe that the Sunday dinners were becoming larger, and the case would be even stronger if the anti-Claphamites deliberately refrained from bringing in those non-quantitative considerations which the optimists had (mistakenly) dismissed as sentimental and misleading. But this does not mean that these considerations were ever unimportant. And now that the original Claphamite assault has been repulsed, it is time to say firmly that the attempt to dismiss the qualitative and sociological case against early industrialism must also be regarded as unsuccessful.

In fact no such attempt was really made. For the sociology of industrialization implicit in most of the meliorist arguments is extremely primitive. It is barely more advanced than that of Peacock's "Steam Intellect Society," and greatly inferior to, say, Engels'. We need hardly comment on extreme examples such as Chaloner and Henderson's remark that "in the 1840's much hardship among workers was due to secondary or self-induced poverty, the result of excessive and feckless expenditure on drink, gambling and tobacco." The more moderate tendency, which merely holds that some people had one view about the social effects of industrialization, some another, is equally futile. For we now know quite enough about the immense human strains imposed by the process of sudden and large-scale social transformation to state firmly that its eventual—or even its immediate—material benefits cannot be used to offset these strains, and that those who underestimate mass unhappiness or disturbance merely because they can see no adequate reason for it, are unqualified to talk about the subject.

This is not the place to pursue the sociology of British industrialization, which has fortunately once again begun to attract attention. It is enough to remind ourselves that the extraordinary depth, desperation and bitterness of the social discontent in this period (which the optimists have been entirely unable to explain) is at least a partial measure of the stresses to which the labouring poor were exposed. And it is enough to remind ourselves also that the unquantifiable and spiritual sense of loss they felt had a very real basis. The Suffolk farm-labourers, whose village used to be famous for its football in 1810 when custom still gave them a field in which, at certain seasons, they had the *right* to play games, had "somehow or other" lost that right, and the field was now under the plough. Now they had no village green or common for active sports. Only "of late they have introduced a little cricketing; and two or three of the farmers have *very kindly allowed* (my *italics*) them to play in their fields." Are we to omit both the loss and the change in their status from a realistic consideration of the effects of agrarian change on the English labourers of whom the traveller observed not only that they were "severely straitened in their means of living" but also that they were "servile" and "broken-spirited"? Are we to overlook the decline and fall of the self-confident, coherent, educated and cultured pre-industrial mechanics and domestic workers—the Gloucestershire weavers, of whom in 1840 only 15 per cent could neither read nor write, while of the rioters arrested in the manufacturing areas of Lancashire, Cheshire and Staffordshire in 1842 55 per cent could not read and write even "imperfectly"; the community of Dunfermline weavers, destroyed in the 1830's, with its Trades-man's Library, savings' bank, Mechanics' Institute, Literary and Scientific Club, Drawing Academy, missionary meetings, temperance leagues and infant schools, its Florists' Society and literary magazine (the *Dunfermline Gasometer*)—as well as its republican, jacobin and chartist puritanism and Swedenborgian and other heresies?

The fact that the employers and governing classes of the time utterly failed to understand what (apart from sheer poverty) might be troubling the labouring poor, was no doubt historically inevitable, though it also made the impact of the change more catastrophic. But there is no similar excuse for the modern historian who denies that the coming of industrialism and urbanization meant a "depersonaliza-tion" of human relations, or who argues simply that "the breaking up of old social relationships was a liberating and stimulating experi-ence," or who honestly believes that the social discontent of the period was due to the fact that "although the standard of living was rising, it was not rising quickly, and the individual was only aware that his wages were meagre and not sufficient to satisfy his wants." To admit the social stresses of industrialization is not to deny their inevitability (though they could, of course, have been minimized); nor even, in the long run, to reject the price paid for progress. Not to admit their reality and gravity is to make any understanding of history impossible.

As is often the case, the poets saw things which the vulgar economists did not, and those who stammered their sense that the world was upside down were sometimes more correct than those who formulated their ideas lucidly. Charles Dickens, whose criticism of Coketown (a city which fully satisfied the Gradgrinds and Bounderbys) was not merely that its inhabitants were poor and economically insecure, but that it was *inhuman,* expressed the anguish of a generation more profoundly than those who might merely have observed, with justice, that its drains were defective and something ought to be done about it. The historian forgets at his peril that the problem of the social impact of the industrial revolution is not whether men live by white or brown bread, no meat or roast beef; even though it can be shown that in our period it did not actually give them any extra roast beef. It is also, that men do not live by bread alone.

PART II BY R. M. HARTWELL

In my two articles on the standard of living during the Industrial Revolution, which Dr. Hobsbawm now criticizes, I was concerned both with surveying the literature of the controversy, and also with analysing the available evidence to see if conclusions could be made. The conclusions I came to were, first, the controversy has been confused by arguments about values and by people talking about different things as though they were talking about the same thing, and second, that there had been "an upward trend in living standards during the Industrial Revolution" and that "the standard of living of the mass of the people of England was improving . . . slowly during the war, more quickly after 1815, and rapidly after 1840." This conclusion I modified by stressing that the standard of living was *not* high and was not rising fast *before* the forties, and also that there was "dire poverty" and "cyclical and technological unemployment of a most distressing character." I emphasized also that increasing real income was no measure of "ultimate well-being" and that the period of the Industrial Revolution was one of political discontent and social upheaval—but also that it was a period of increasing opportunity for working-class men and women. To this "extreme" view I still hold, and it may be compared with the latest conclusions of Dr. Hobsbawm, which seem mild enough—consumption figures "are compatible with a slight decrease, possibly with a slight increase," the case for deterioration "while not implausible, cannot be proved," "the view that there was substantial, or any, deterioration has not yet been firmly established," "the argument that real incomes remained roughly stable will commend itself as the most acceptable formula"—but which are established in such a fashion as to create an impression of pessimism, quite apart from the grand final conclusion that, whatever can be said about material standards, "the sociological argument for deterioration is far more powerful." Indeed, Dr. Hobsbawm's convictions show not so much in his mild conclusions as in the fervour with which he defends Engels and attacks the optimists.

Dr. Hobsbawm's discussion is "to survey the battlefield." The military metaphor reflects Dr. Hobsbawm's idea of how historical controversy should be conducted; when he is a combatant, he believes in total war. And so he spends much time attacking the expertise and the evidence of the historians with whom he does not agree. Thus, the optimists (J. H. Clapham, T. S. Ashton, etc.) are "committed" to an "*a priori* case for amelioration" and have "a desire to prove preconceived notions"; their sources and evidence are "suspect for their optimist bias," "irrelevant," "anachronistic," "feeble props," "too negligible," "highly untypical"; their analysis and conclusions are "brash" (about Ashton and Clapham!), "unqualified," "implausible," "improbable," "frivolous," "careless," "cursory," "ill-informed," "inconclusive," "unsupported," "illegitimate," "futile," "not now based on reliable evidence," "carry no serious weight," "purely rhetorical," "striking perversions of fact." At the same time as he batters the opposition with pejorative adjectives, Dr. Hobsbawm *assumes* victory and righteousness; he assumes the optimists and their sources are wrong, until they prove the pessimists wrong: "the onus of proving the gloomy and traditional views are wrong, continues to rest squarely on the optimists." As part of the assumption of being right, Dr. Hobsbawm posits time and time again an alleged generally acceptable "conventional view"—"the traditional case for deterioration in labour conditions"—and imputes agreement with his interpretation of history by the majority of good men: "few would doubt," "common consent," "a predominance of informed opinion," "the mass of contemporary evidence," "general agreement," etc. He tries also to discredit the optimists by attributing to them statements they have never made and views they have never held. This is done partly by stating optimist generalizations in an extreme form by using unreasonable adjectives and adverbs which, if they were removed, would leave reasonable, or at least debatable, propositions. As Dr. Hobsbawm states them, however, they are convenient "aunt sallies" for him to demolish; for example, "the hypothesis of a *marked* or *substantial* rise in the standard of living . . . is . . . an extremely improbable one," or "the view that real wages rose *markedly* during our period is not now based on reliable evidence" (italics mine). In this way Dr. Hobsbawm ascribes to J. H. Clapham and T. S. Ashton an extreme view and claims in consequence that it is a point now "clearly established . . . that the traditional Clapham-Ashton view has been dislodged without resistance." But J. H. Clapham had already "modified" his original non-extreme position in the 1939 Preface to the second edition of his history: "I did not mean that everything was getting better. I only meant that recent historians have too often, in my opinion, stressed the worsenings and slurred over or ignored the bettering."

More directly, however, Dr. Hobsbawm misquotes or misrepresents the optimists. Thus, for example, my article on "The Rising Standard of Living in England, 1800–1850" is misused. For example, Dr. Hobsbawm chooses from the sentence—"Generally, as historical analyses of economic development have shown, an increase in per capita income has been accompanied by a more equal income distribution" (with a footnote reference to Kuznets)—only the following—"an increase in per capita income [was] accompanied by a more equal income distribution" (Dr. Hobsbawm's "was")—turning a general into a specific statement, and implying that I was referring only to England during the Industrial Revolution. There are many other examples, but I do not want here to catalogue all Dr. Hobsbawm's misrepresentations. Nor do I want to discuss the methodological and ethical problems of writing history in this fashion. Nevertheless it is necessary to have some knowledge of Dr. Hobsbawm's methods to make the understanding of his history possible.

Dr. Hobsbawm claims that "we cannot at present derive a satisfactory and representative real wage index for our period," and that the lack of such an index makes the use of wage-price data "not now . . . reliable" for generalizations about the course of real wages. On the contrary, as Phyllis Deane and W. A. Cole point out, "For the nineteenth century there is a vast amount of miscellaneous material in average wages and wage rates. This was thoroughly worked over by Bowley and Wood. . . . It would still be possible to strengthen and fill out their results with raw material relating to other years and other industries, but it seems unlikely that the additional data would modify the long-term trends which emerge from their studies." There are a number of price indices—Jevons, Sauerbeck, Silberling, Kondratieff, Rousseaux, Schumpeter, and Gayer, Rostow and Schwartz—and also a number of wage series—Wood, Bowley, Tucker, Kondratieff, Phelps-Brown and Hopkins, and Gayer, Rostow and Schwartz—in addition to a great deal of wage data in industrial histories. Here is a large body of statistics, the result of much detailed research, that cannot simply be assumed away because generalizations from them are inconvenient for Dr. Hobsbawm. Gayer, Rostow and Schwartz, for example, concluded from their statistics that "the most striking single fact concerning labour in the second period (1815–1850) is that money wages declined, in net, very slightly; less even than food prices and much less than other retail goods." Similarly, Deane and Cole have generalized more recently about working-class standards of living that "there was a negligible improvement in the Napoleonic war years, an upward trend in the immediate post-war years (though this may have been outweighed by post-war unemployment), an unprecedently rapid improvement in the second quarter (which might also be modified on the basis of unemployment data) and an indisputable rise in the third and fourth quarters." It is because of such figures that J. L. Hammond long ago conceded that: "Let us take it that so far as statistics can measure material improvement there was improvement," and moved on to a consideration of higher and unmeasurable deteriorations.

The inverse movements of money wages and prices after 1815 is important also for two other reasons: (i) the phenomenon is powerful evidence against a monetary interpretation of the price decline, and, since trade unions were not yet powerful enough to exercise a significant monopolistic pressure on the supply side of the labour market, the rising tendency in real wages must have been associated with the increased productivity of labour; (ii) the phenomenon is also powerful evidence that labour competition (even with increasing population and Irish immigration), technological and structural unemployment, and the trade cycle—factors on the supply side of the labour market which could have led to a lowering of wages—were more than offset, in determining the price of labour, by a sustained and increasing demand for labour that kept up money wages when all other prices were falling.

Unemployment is certainly relevant in considering standards of living, and except for technological unemployment (which I discussed in some detail in my previous article), I have not dealt with it adequately. Nor has Dr. Hobsbawm, who suggests, however, that chronic cyclical unemployment, although a short-term phenomenon, more than offset any long-term gains from rising real wages. But why, then, did not money wages fall in the period of falling prices? In any case, cyclical unemployment can only be relevant, in comparing real wages over different long periods, if the intensity of the cycle varies greatly in the different periods. There was a cycle in the eighteenth century, and again after 1850, but it has not yet been proved that the cycle between 1800 and 1850 was responsible, *proportionately*, for more unemployment than the cycles before 1800 or after 1850. "Few would doubt," writes Dr. Hobsbawm, "that it [unemployment] was much higher than in the period after the middle forties." The onus of proof, in this case, surely rests with Dr. Hobsbawm?

Dr. Hobsbawm's chosen period ends conveniently after the depression of 1842, of which he is so fond. Anything about the period after 1845 he dismisses as being irrelevant, irrelevant because "the debate is entirely about what happened in a period which ended, *by common consent*, some time between 1842 and 1845" (italics mine), "What is worse," he continues, "it has tempted careless historians to use evidence from the period after 1843–4 to throw light on the trend of the period before this turning-point." In so far as there are recognizable trend periods in the nineteenth century, the turning point is either 1848–9 (marking the trough of the downswing after the boom of 1844–5), or 1850–1 (marking the end of the long period of falling prices). Thus, the one detailed, indeed massive volume on trends and cycles in this period, that of Gayer, Rostow and Schwartz, uses the years 1815 to 1850 as a trend period. 1850 or 1851 is also the terminal date accepted by W. T. Layton, by J. R. T. Hughes, and by Phyllis Deane and W. A. Cole. Indeed, if there are any events that "by common consent" mark the end of an era and the beginning of a new, they are the gold discoveries of 1849–51 and the Great Exhibition of 1851. What is important, in considering the relevance of what happened after 1845 (Dr. Hobsbawm's turning point), is *the rate of change* at which the standard of living was improving thereafter, and *the absolute level* (compared with 1800) reached in the early fifties. If there was stability, or decline, in real wages up to 1845 (as Dr. Hobsbawm claims), and if (as the evidence warrants, and even as Dr. Hobsbawm seems to admit) the standard of living in the early fifties was *substantially* above that of 1800 (and I would agree with J. H. Clapham that it was at least 40 per cent higher), then the whole of the improvement must have come in five, or at most ten years. If this is not plausible (and I think it is not), Dr. Hobsbawm has either to discredit the evidence of this later period (for example, evidence from G. R. Porter, 1847; T. Tooke and W. Newmarch, 1848–1856; Report of Commissioners on Smithfield Market, 1850; H. Mayhew, 1851; B. Poole, 1852; "The Commissariat of London," 1854; and G. Dodd, 1856), or else has to allow that real wages had been improving over a longer period. Moreover, there is no indication in the multitude of wage indices of a spectacular rise in real wages after 1845. And so the relevance of the sources that establish a real-wage level in the early fifties that was well above that of 1800 now becomes obvious; they prove that this standard of life could only have been achieved over a period longer than the ten years after 1845.

Dr. Hobsbawm claims—although a reading of J. H. Clapham and T. S. Ashton, and even of Hartwell, will show the claim to be quite untrue—that the optimist case rests "in the main" on "certain global calculations such as those of the general trend of the national income," which he cannot accept. "In the first place," Dr. Hobsbawm writes, "like any indirect argument, it must yield to the facts." Second, "the argument itself rests entirely on a further hitherto unverified, at present unverifiable and somewhat improbable assumption, namely that 'an increase in per capita income [was] accompanied by a more equal income distribution.' " Third, the argument is "vulnerable to contrary presumptions which, while equally unable to establish themselves conclusively, point in the opposite direction." Dr. Hobsbawm's basic assumption here is that "global calculations" are a *different* kind and a *less reliable* kind of historical fact than what he calls "direct evidence." But global calculations surely are aggregates of "the facts," of "the direct evidence," as Dr. Hobsbawm understands them. Moreover, these aggregates—of national income, population, industrial production, trade, public finance and capital accumulation—*all* point to an increasing per capita real income, and are *not* vulnerable, as Dr. Hobsbawm claims, "to contrary presumptions."

However, Dr. Hobsbawm is right to stress, as I did, the importance of knowing the trend in distribution in order to interpret the aggregate statistics. Dr. Hobsbawm now claims (i) that any improvement in income distribution is "unverified" and "improbable," (ii) that "economic theory of whatever brand gives us no *a priori* presumption in favour of a *significant improvement* in the standard of living in the period of early industrialisation" (italics mine), and (iii) that real wages were kept down "to allow for larger savings and more investment." I have already produced some "direct evidence"—from taxation returns, from the changing structure of employment (the shift from lower to higher paid employment), from social legislation (the trend, in spite of Dr. Hobsbawm, was towards protection and improvement), and from public finance (for example, the repeal of the beer duty in 1830, which, as J. H. Clapham pointed out, added £1 per annum to the average household)—that income distribution was improving. In any case, such was the rate of increase of national income, that stability, or even a slight worsening of distribution, would still have left the worker better off in 1840 than in 1800. But the argument here is also deductive: the application of generalizations about growth and income that have been derived by the economists from theory and from the study of time series over a long period and from a large number of countries. The relevant generalizations are: (i) generally, there has been over secular periods the simultaneous rise, at similar rates of growth, of income and its components (consumption and investment); (ii) generally, rises in national savings rates have been the response to secular rises in per capita income; (iii) the share of wages in national income over secular periods has generally been constant in the earlier decades of growth, and thereafter an increasing proportion of national income; (iv) economic development over a long period has generally been accompanied by a more equal income distribution, although, as E. H. Phelps-Brown has emphasized, "the changes in real wages due to distributive shifts have been very small compared with those associated with the movements of productivity." These generalizations certainly apply to England *after* 1850, when more accurate statistics allow the measurement of the relevant indices. In the period *before* 1850, when real national income, capital accumulation and productivity were all rising faster than population, it is reasonable to assume also that the standard of living of the workers was rising.

Against this assumption one might argue, as Dr. Hobsbawm does, and "globally" on this occasion, that investment during the Industrial Revolution was of such magnitude that average consumption was not only curtailed but reduced. But the one detailed attempt to estimate capital accumulation over this period, by Phyllis Deane and W. A. Cole, concludes: "In the early stages of the Industrial Revolution the level of capital formation—measured as a percentage of national income—rose only slowly. At this period, covering the last quarter of the eighteenth century and the first quarter of the nineteenth, savings were being used more productively and a large portion of the new developments were taking place in industries with a relatively low ratio of capital to income." The upward shift in the rate of capital accumulation—from the 5 or 6 per cent of 1780 to the 10 per cent of 1860—took place between 1830 and 1860 rather than in the earlier period. In any case, although it is obvious, as the theory of income determination demonstrates, that in the short run increased savings implies reduced consumption, we are here considering a period of at least half a century during which the productivity of investment, because of technical progress and improved industrial organization, was high, and when the real cost of most investment, until the railways in the forties, was relatively low.

There is also the problem of what happened to the goods produced. Increasing home demand had been of paramount importance in stimulating the beginnings of industrialization in the eighteenth century; increasing real wages during the Industrial Revolution provided the large and increasing market without which the goods of the new technology could not have been sold. Certainly it was not foreign demand that sustained continued industrialization. Indeed, during the period of rapid economic growth after 1815 "the home market seems to have responded more rapidly than the overseas trade, and United Kingdom domestic exports averaged 10 per cent or less of national income for most of the first half of the nineteenth century."

Dr. Hobsbawm twice claims that the eighteenth century is "unknown" and that "in the present state of our knowledge," comparisons with the nineteenth century "must . . . still [be] left open." Elsewhere, however, he still posits a golden age, and, in comparison with the earlier period describes how the labouring poor of the Industrial Revolution felt an "unquantifiable and spiritual sense of loss," and how "the self-confident, coherent, educated and cultured pre-industrial mechanics and domestic workers" declined and fell (in spite of agreeing also with Engels that the pre-industrial workers lived in "ignorance and stagnation"). But the researches of Mrs. M. D. George, Miss D. Marshall and the Webbs reveal a pre-industrial society that was static and sordid, with the labouring poor on subsistence wages and periodically decimated by cycles, plagues and famines. What Dr. Hobsbawm has to prove is that living conditions in the eighteenth century were *better* than in the early nineteenth, not, as we all know, that conditions during the Industrial Revolution were bad. Again, it proves very little that life-expectation was higher in the country than in the cities of the Industrial Revolution; it was also higher in the eighteenth century, and it is still higher to-day. What Dr. Hobsbawm has to explain away is that average life-expectancy increased between 1780 and 1840, *during* the Industrial Revolution. In the most detailed examination yet made of the decline in mortality during and after the Industrial Revolution T. McKeown and R. G. Record conclude that "the main reason for the rise in population in the late eighteenth and early nineteenth centuries was an improvement in economic and social conditions."

But perhaps the whole debate is irrelevant? In his final paragraphs Dr. Hobsbawm argues that, although the case for deterioration of material standards "while not implausible, cannot be proved" (a disarming concession after so much argument) "the sociological argument for deterioration is far more powerful." The claim is accompanied by the usual accusations that the optimists have neglected sociological problems, that they "underestimate mass unhappiness as disturbance merely because they can see no adequate reason for it, and are unqualified to talk about the subject." As with the debate on material standards, Dr. Hobsbawm has *commenced* what might become a new debate with a thoroughly gloomy picture, claiming that the social effects of industrialization were all evil. On the relationship of material progress (or deterioration) to social progress (or deterioration), and even on the precise nature of social deterioration, he is more vague, using such phrases as "spiritual sense of loss," "loss and change in status," "immense human strains," and "the extraordinary depth, desperation and bitterness of the social discontent"; and Dr. Hobsbawm's only excursions into social theory to explain these alleged conditions are, on the one hand, to claim the *"inevitability"* (italics mine) of "the social stresses of industrialization," and, on the other, to generalize, not very originally, that "men do not live by bread alone." This debate on the dynamics of social change cannot be concluded here, but some *specific* social gains of this period might be mentioned to offset in the minds of more impressionable readers the pessimism of Dr. Hobsbawm: (i) the increasing social and economic independence of women, (ii) the reduction in child labour, (iii) the growth of friendly societies, trade unions, savings' banks, mechanics' institutes and co-operative societies, (iv) the growth of literacy (more of the population could read and write in 1850 than in 1800), and (v) the changing character of social disorder, which, as F. C. Mather recently demonstrated, was much less brutish and destructive in the 1840's than in the 1780's. The Marxist doctrine of social and economic evolution cannot be protected for ever, even by Dr. Hobsbawm, from that misfortune, long ago foreseen by Herbert Spencer, of being "a deduction killed by a fact." And in this case, the facts are legion.

Edward Thompson

7

The Making of
the English Working Class

COMMUNITY

Leisure and Personal Relations
                              The Methodist revival of the war
years mediated the work-discipline of industrialism. It was also, in some
part, a reflex of despair among the working population. Methodism
and Utilitarianism, taken together, make up the dominant ideology
of the Industrial Revolution. But in Methodism we see only the
clearest expression of processes at work within a whole society. Many
of its features were reproduced in the evangelical movement in all the
churches, and in the social teaching of some Utilitarians and Deists.
Hannah More held quite as strongly as Wesley to the view that it was
a "fundamental error to consider children as innocent beings," rather
than as beings of "a corrupt nature and evil dispositions." And in the
Sundays schools which were promoted by the Church of England in
many villages in the 1790s and 1800s we find exactly the same emphasis (although sometimes with a more paternalist tone) upon discipline
and repression as we have noted in the schools of Stockport or Halifax.
Their function is uniformly described as being to cherish in the children of the poor "a spirit of industry, economy, and piety"; Sunday
school teachers at Caistor (Lincs) were instructed to—

. . . tame the ferocity of their unsubdued passions—to repress the
excessive rudeness of their manners—to chasten the disgusting and
demoralizing obscenity of their language—to subdue the stubborn
rebellion of their wills—to render them honest, obedient, courteous,
industrious, submissive, and orderly. . . .

The pressures towards discipline and order extended from the factory,
on one hand, the Sunday school, on the other, into every aspect of
life: leisure, personal relationships, speech, manners. Alongside the
disciplinary agencies of the mills, churches, schools, and magistrates
and military, quasi-official agencies were set up for the enforcement
of orderly moral conduct. It was Pitt's moral lieutenant, Wilberforce,

93

who combined the ethos of Methodism with the unction of the Establishment, and who was most active between 1790 and 1810 in this cause. In 1797 he expounded at length "the grand law of subordination," and laid down articles for the management of the poor:

. . . that their more lowly path has been allotted to them by the hand of God; that it is their part faithfully to discharge its duties and contentedly to bear its inconveniences; that the present state of things is very short; that the objects, about which worldly men conflict so eagerly, are not worth the contest.

By 1809 he was satisfied that overt Jacobinism was no longer a danger; but in every manifestation of moral indiscipline he saw the danger of Jacobin revival. "We are alive to the political offence," he wrote, "but to the moral crime we seem utterly insensible."

In this he was too modest, since his own Society for the Suppression of Vice had clocked up 623 successful prosecutions for breaking the Sabbath laws in 1801 and 1802 alone. But his conviction as to the intimate correlation between moral levity and political sedition among the lower classes is characteristic of his class. Prosecutions for drunken and lewd behaviour increased; Blake's old enemy, Bishop Watson of Llandaff, preached a sermon in 1804 in which he found the rôle of the common informer to be "a noble Design . . . both in a religious and in a political Point of View." The amusements of the poor were preached and legislated against until even the most innocuous were regarded in a lurid light. The Society for the Suppression of Vice extended its sphere of interference to "two-penny hops, gingerbread fairs, and obscene pictures." Nude sea bathers were persecuted as if they were forerunners of tumbrils and guillotine. "With regard to adultery," wrote John Bowdler darkly, "as it was punished capitally by the Jewish law, some think it ought to be so . . . among us." The Evangelicals exhorted the upper classes to reform their own manners as an example to the poor. In "Society" itself the post-revolutionary years saw "an increased reserve of manner . . . fatal to conviviality and humour."

The process of social discipline was not uncontested. The attempt of Dr. Bowdler's supporters to carry new legislation for the imprisonment of adulterers foundered in the House of Commons; unlike penalties imposed upon common Sabbath-breakers, vagrants, tinkers, stage-dancers and tumblers, ballad-singers, free-thinkers and naked bathers, legislation against adultery was open to objection in that it might discriminate against the amusement of the rich as well as of the poor. And other attempts to interfere with the leisure of the people were thrown out by the House of Commons, on slender majorities made up of one part *laissez faire* inertia, one part Foxite defence of the liberty of the subject, and one part traditional Tory tolerance for "bread and circuses" and dislike for Methodistical "fanaticism." (An irony of the time was the defence by the War Minister, Windham, of bull-baiting against both Evangelicals and reformers—a defence which led to the cry going up, from Satan's strongholds, of "Windham and Liberty!")

But if the disciplinarians lost a few legislative skirmishes, they won the battle of the Industrial Revolution; and in the process the "Irish" temperament often attributed to the 18th-century English poor in town and countryside was translated into the methodical way of life of industrial capitalism. In the countryside this can be seen most clearly in the triumph of the money-economy over the casual, "uneconomic" rhythms of peasant semi-subsistence. In the industrial areas it can be seen in the extension of the discipline of the factory bell or clock from working to leisure hours, from the working-day to the Sabbath, and in the assault upon "Cobbler's Monday" and traditional holidays and fairs.

Although the economic functions of the 18th-century fair were still of great importance—annual "hirings," horse and cattle fairs, sale of miscellaneous commodities—we should not forget their equal importance in the cultural life of the poor. Still, in the early years of the Industrial Revolution, the working man's year was made up of cycles of hardship and short commons, puctuated with "feast" days when drink and meat were more plentiful, luxuries like apples and ribbons were bought for the children, dancing, courtship, convivial visiting and sports took place. Until late in the 19th century there was still a network of fairs held throughout the country (many of which authority tried in vain to limit or proscribe), at which a fraternity of pedlars, card-sharpers, real or pretended gipsies, ballad-mongers and hawkers were in attendance. A Northumberland diarist of 1750 describes Whit Monday:

. . . went to Carton Sports—a Saddle, bridle, whip, etc. all to be Gallopt for. . . . Abundance of young men and women diverted themselves with the game or pastime here that they call Losing their Suppers . . . And after all they ended their recreation with Carrouzing at the Ale-houses and ye men Kissing and toying away most of the night with their Mistresses. . . .

Three weeks later there was the Lebberston Sport—"a Copper Pan was play'd for at Quoites . . . there was also a Dove neatly deckt and adorned with Ribbons of divers colours and other fine Trappings which was danced for by the Country Girls. . . ." In 1783 a Bolton

magistrate complained that—at a time when oatmeal was selling at
two guineas a load—

. . . there was so little appearance of want in this township that one
evening I met a very large procession of young men and women with
fiddles, garlands, and other ostentation of rural finery, dancing Morris
dances in the highway to celebrate an idle anniversary, or, what they
had been pleased to call for a year or two, a fair at a paltry thatched
alehouse upon the neighbouring common.

It is tempting to explain the decline of old sports and festivals
simply in terms of the displacement of "rural" by "urban" values.
But this is misleading. The more robust entertainments, whether in
their ugly form of animal baiting and pugilism, or in more convivial
festivities, were as often, or more often, to be found in the 18th century in London or the great towns as in the countryside. They continued into the 19th century with a vigour which recalls both the
unruly traditions of the London apprentices of Tudor times, and also
the very large proportion of 19th-century Londoners who were immigrants from the village. The greatest festival of all was Bartholomew
Fair, with its menageries, pickpockets, pantomimes of Harlequin and
Faustus, card sharpers, plays, exhibitions of wild men and of horse-
manship. In 1825 the *Trades Newspaper* complained:

For weeks previous it is denounced from the pulpit and the press, and
stories are raked up of apprentices led away from the paths of honesty,
of ruined maids of all-work, of broken heads and brawlings. . . .

In the previous decade the authorities had feared that the Fair would
become "the general rendezvous for sedition and the signal for
insurrection."

On the other hand, the Industrial Revolution, which drained the
countryside of some of its industries and destroyed the balance between
rural and urban life, created also in our own minds an image of rural
isolation and "idiocy." The urban culture of 18th-century England
was more "rural" (in its customary connotations), while the rural culture was more rich, than we often suppose. "It is a great error to
suppose," Cobbett insisted, "that people are rendered stupid by
remaining always in the same place." And most of the new industrial
towns did not so much displace the countryside as grow *over* it. The
most common industrial configuration of the early 19th century was a
commercial or manufacturing centre which served as the hub for a
circle of straggling industrial villages. As the villages became suburbs,
and the farmlands were covered over with brick, so the great conurba-
tions of the late 19th century were formed.

But there was nothing in this process so violent as to enforce a disruption of older traditions. In south Lancashire, the Potteries, the West Riding and the Black Country local customs, superstitions, and dialect were neither severed nor transplanted: the village or small town craftsman grew into the industrial worker. Bamford has testified in his *Early Days* to the vigour of tradition in Lancashire weaving villages at the turn of the century. There were the tales of witches, boggarts, "fyerin"; the furious pugilism and the cock-fighting; the customs, such as "pace-egging" (at Easter) or "Riding the Black Lad"; the holidays with their traditional celebrations—Christmas, Shrove-Tide, "Cymbalin Sunday," and "Rushbearing" in August when morris dancers were to be found in Middleton, Oldham or Rochdale:

> My new shoon they are so good,
> I cou'd doance morrice if I wou'd;
> An' if hat an' sark be drest,
> I will doance morrice wi' the best.

Or there was "Mischief-neet," on May 1st, when lads would leave signs on the doorsteps of the village women:

A gorse bush indicated a woman notoriously immodest; and a holly bush, one loved in secret; a tup's horn intimated that man or woman was faithless to marriage; a branch of sapling, truth in love; and a sprig of birch, a pretty girl.

We may set beside Bamford's picture of the 1790s Joseph Lawson's reminiscences of a "backward" clothing village in the West Riding—Pudsey—in the 1820s, with the old and new ways of life at a moment of transition. The houses were scattered "as if they had sprung up from seeds dropped unawares," the roads unlighted and unflagged, the groups of houses approached by crooked folds and passages. Rooms are low, windows small without sashes:

There is dense ignorance of sanitary science. A doctor comes into a house where there is fever, and he knocks a pane of glass out with his stick, his first dose of medicine being fresh air.

Most of the houses are without ovens but have a "bakstone" for baking. The stone floors are sanded, furniture is plain and sparse: "in some houses there is an oaken chest or kist—a family heirloom, or a small cupboard fastened up in a corner, and a delfcase for pots and plates." Water is scarce, and on wash-days queues of twenty or thirty may form at the wells. Coal and candles are dear, and in the winter neighbours gather to share each other's fires. Baking and brewing are done at home; white bread and meat are regarded as luxuries: "oat-cake, brown bread, porridge pudding, skimmed milk, potatoes, and home-brewed beer, which they always call 'drink,' are the principal articles of food."

The sparse routine is broken by occasional "tides" or feasts, when "a bit of beef" is bought, and all go to the fair, where gingerbread, fruit, and toys are sold, there are peep-shows of the Battle of Waterloo, Punch and Judy shows, gambling stalls, swings; and a customary "love market," where the young men court the girls with "tidings" of brandy-snaps and nuts. Very few of the working people can read well enough to read a newspaper; although papers are taken (and read aloud) at the blacksmith's, the barber's and several public houses. Much of the news still comes by way of broadsheet vendors and street singers. Old superstitions are a living source of terror to old and young. There are ghosts at Jumble's Well, Bailey Gallows, Boggard Lane; parents commonly discipline their children by shutting them "in cellars and other dark places for the black boggards to take them." "Another most serious and mischievous superstition, everywhere prevalent, was the belief that when any child died, it was the will of the Lord that it should be so." Sanitary reformers were regarded as "Infidels." Dog-fighting and cock-fighting were common; and it was also common at feast-times "to see several rings formed, in which men stripped to their bare skin would fight sometimes by the hour together, till the combatants were not recognisable. . . ." Drunkenness was rife, especially at holidays and on "Cobbler's Monday," which was kept by weavers and burlers as well as cobblers. But there were plenty of less violent pastimes: knur and spell, "duck knop," and football through the streets. The village was clannish within, and a closed community to outsiders from only two or three miles distant. Some very old traditions survived, such as "Riding the Steng," whereby if a man was known to ill-use his wife, or a woman was thought to be lewd, a straw effigy would be carried through the streets by a hooting crowd, and then burnt by the offender's door.

So far from extinguishing local traditions, it is possible that the early years of the Industrial Revolution saw a growth in provincial pride and self-consciousness. South Lancashire and the West Riding were not rural wildernesses before 1780; they had been centres of domestic industry for two centuries. As the new factory discipline encroached upon the handworker's way of life, and as the Corporation and Coronation Streets were built over Yep-fowd and Frogg Hole and T'Hollins, so self-consciousness was sharpened by loss, and a quasi-nationalist sentiment mingles with class feeling in the culture of the industrial workers (new machines versus old customs, London tyranny or "foreign" capital against the local clothier, Irish labour undercutting the native weaver). George Condy, a leading publicist of the 10 Hour Movement, wrote a foreword to Roby's *Traditions of Lancashire* (1830); Bamford was only one among a score of plebeian authors who followed in the steps of the 18th-century "Tim Bobbin," in celebrating and idealising local customs and dialect.

But this was a conscious resistance to the passing of an old way of life, and it was frequently associated with political Radicalism. As important in this passing as the simple physical loss of commons and "playgrounds," was the loss of leisure in which to play and the repression of playful impulses. The Puritan teachings of Bunyan or Baxter were transmitted in their entirety by Wesley: "Avoid all lightness, as you would avoid hell-fire; and trifling, as you would cursing and swearing. Touch no woman. . . ." Card-playing, coloured dresses, personal ornaments, the theatre—all came under Methodist prohibition. Tracts were written against "profane" songs and dancing; literature and arts which had no devotional bearing were profoundly suspect; the dreadful "Victorian" Sabbath began to extend its oppression even before Victoria's birth.

A characteristic tract shows the extent of Methodist determination to uproot pre-industrial traditions from the manufacturing districts. It had been noted at a Sheffield Quarterly Meeting in 1799 that some members were not "altogether free from conforming to the custom of *visiting* or *receiving visits*, at the *annual Feast*." Such feasts, known variously as "Wakes" (Derbyshire and Staffordshire), "Rushbearing" (Lancashire) and "Revels" (west of England) might in origin have been permisssible but had become "dreadfully prostituted to the most diabolical purposes." Time was spent in "eating and drinking intemperately; talking prophanely, or at least unprofitably; in laughing and jesting, fornication and adultery. . . ." The least participation was "fellowship with the unfruitful works of darkness." Money was wasted by the poor which might have been saved; many contracted debts. Methodists who mixed in such festivities were exposed to the worldly ways of the unconverted—backsliding was a common result. They should refuse to entertain even friends and relatives (from among the unconverted) who might call; and if such visitors could not be turned from the door they should be entertained only by Bible-reading, holy discourse and hymn-singing:

Oh, Brethren, what are we doing! There is death in the pot. The plague is begun. Wrath is gone forth against fruitless professors. The slumbers of sin are upon us. . . .

Other customary survivals, such as meat and drink at the funeral "wake," came in for equal condemnation. Even the visiting of relatives on a normal Sabbath day could not be condoned, unless in cases of sudden sickness.[1]

The warmth of the argument suggests that in many places, like Bamford's Middleton, the struggle between the old way of life and the new discipline was sharp and protracted. And Lawson's account of Pudsey shows the "chapel folk" as a group set *apart* from the community by their sombre manners. There were many who were brought up in devout families who reacted strongly against their upbringing, as did William Lovett:

. . . being obliged to frequent a place of worship three times of a Sunday, strictly prohibited all books but the Bible and Prayer Book, and not being allowed to enjoy a walk, unless to chapel . . . are sufficient to account for those boyish feelings. My poor mother . . . thought that the great power that has formed the numerous gay, sportive, singing things of earth and air, must above all things be gratified with the solemn faces, prim clothes, and half-sleepy demeanour of human beings; and that true religion consists in listening to the reiterated story of man's fall. . . .

To many men in the post-war generation, such as Lovett, it seemed that it was the Methodists who were uncouth and backward. And this reminds us of the extreme difficulty in generalising as to the moral tone and manners of working-class communities during the Industrial Revolution. It is clear that between 1780 and 1830 important changes took place. The "average" English working man became more disciplined, more subject to the productive tempo of "the clock," more reserved and methodical, less violent and less spontaneous. Traditional sports were displaced by more sedentary hobbies:

The Athletic exercises of Quoits, Wrestling, Foot-ball, Prison-bars and Shooting with the Long-bow are become obsolete . . . they are now Pigeon-fanciers, Canary-breeders and Tulip-growers—

or so a Lancashire writer complained in 1823. Francis Place often commented upon a change, which he saw in terms of a growth in self-respect and an elevation in "the character of the working-man." "Look even to Lancashire," he wrote a month after Peterloo:

---

[1] The Wakes were important kinship occasions, when the townsfolk visited their kin in the country, and "the married daughter came to her former home with her children." Howitt, who described them as "a short pause in the otherwise ever-going machinery of servitude," recounted how old people in the villages, when asked about their sons and daughters in the towns, would say: "Well, well, we shall see them at the wake." Even the disciplinary Wedgewood was defeated by the Wakes, which "must be observ'd though the World was to end with them."

Within a few years a stranger walking through their towns was "touted," i.e. hooted, and an "outcomling" was sometimes pelted with stones. "Lancashire brute" was the common and appropriate appellation. Until very lately it would have been dangerous to have assembled 500 of them on any occasion. Bakers and butchers would at the least have been plundered. Now 100,000 people may be collected together and no riot ensue. . . .

It is here that evaluation becomes most difficult. While many contemporary writers, from Cobbett to Engels, lamented the passing of old English customs, it is foolish to see the matter only in idyllic terms. These customs were not all harmless or quaint.

In the first decades of the 19th century, cases of wife-selling were reported from places as widely scattered as Colne, Plymouth, Sheffield, and Smithfield Market; indeed, where the wife admitted that she had been unfaithful, this was held in folklore to be the husband's *right*— "many people in the country" (said one husband who had offered his wife in the Plymouth cattle-market) "told him he could do it."[2] The unmarried mother, punished in a Bridewell, and perhaps repudiated by the parish in which she was entitled to relief, had little reason to admire "merrie England." The passing of Gin Lane, Tyburn Fair, orgiastic drunkenness, animal sexuality, and mortal combat for prize-money in iron-studded clogs, calls for no lament. However repressive and disabling the work-discipline of Methodism, the Industrial Revolution could not have taken place without *some* work-discipline, and, in whatever form, the conflict between old and new ways must inevitably have been painful.

But the alignments for and against traditional "amusements" are so complex as to defy analysis. For example, it is often supposed that the old-fashioned Tory squire looked with tolerance upon old customs, or actively defended them against attack. There is evidence that, in the rural counties, this was sometimes the case. But these same squires were notorious for the vindictive measures which they employed in the defence of their game. The nearer they dwelled to the manufacturing centres, the more jealous they were of their privacy and privileges. For the daughters of Sheffield cutlers there was to be no gathering of nuts in May (the streets were posted with warning notices threatening the prosecution of nutters):

The great ones of the Nation [complained a pamphleteer in 1812] have claimed . . . all the Hares, Partridges, Woodcocks, Moor Game, &c, &c.,

---

[2] Several of the cases suggest that the practice was not always barbarous, but could be a popular form of divorce, with the consent of the wife. She was "purchased" for a token sum by her lover; and the transaction in the open market legitimised the exchange in popular lore. No other form of divorce was available.

to say nothing of fish; and at length they are beginning to turn their attention to the common hasel Nut.

Or, to take another example, while the Methodist and Evangelical assault upon the Sunday amusements of the poor seems often to have been motivated by officious bigotry, or by the desire to find some dramatic occasion for an encounter with Satan, more complex issues were sometimes involved. In the Newcastle area in the Thirties a sharp contest was fought by the Evangelicals of all denominations to suppress the practice of "Sunday hirings" in the summer, where the farmers obtained their harvest labour at fairs, to which labourers were attracted by gaming stalls, racing, and much liquor. Some of the trade unionists supported the Evangelicals, while on the side of the Sunday fairs were Chartists, farmers, hucksters, bookies, and publicans.

It is by no means clear that the change in the deportment of working men can be so far attributed to the influence of Wesleyan teaching, as historians of Methodism have tended to assume. Undoubtedly the evangelical movement generally, and the Sunday school in particular, contributed greatly to the Puritan character-structure of the 19th-century artisan, even when (like Lovett) he repudiated the narrowness of his upbringing and became a free-thinker. It is right to see the Methodist chapel at Todmorden, built on the site of the old bull-ring, as emblematic of this change. But the evidence is often presented in too one-sided a manner. If some old superstitions perished, hysterical illusions of new kinds multiplied. Wesley himself perpetuated ignorant and barbaric superstitions: bibliomancy, belief in possession by the devil, and medical remedies as dangerous or cruel as any known to the 18th century. . . Moreover, beneath the bigoted exterior of the evangelical tradesman or artisan, colder and meaner forms of witch-hunting and obscuranticism might linger; fatalism towards child mortality, violent intolerance of "atheists" and free-thinkers.

Indeed, between old superstitition and new bigotry, it is proper to be cautious when meeting the claims of the Evangelicals to have been an agency of intellectual enlightenment. We have already noted the tendency of the Methodists to harden into a sect, to keep their members apart from the contagion of the unconverted, and to regard themselves as being in a state of civil war with the ale-house and the denizens of Satan's strongholds. Where the Methodists were a minority group within a community, attitudes hardened on both sides; professions of virtue and declamations against sin reveal less about actual manners than they do about the rancour of hostilities. Moreover, the air of the early 19th century is thick with assertions and counter-assertions, especially where the values of handworkers and factory workers were in conflict, or those of the opponents and defenders of child labour. Critics of the factory system saw it as destructive of family life and constantly indicted the mills as centres of the grossest sexual immorality; the coarse language and independent manners of Lancashire mill-girls shocked many witnesses. Gaskell contrasted the idyllic innocence of the domestic workers, whose youth was spent in a pagan freedom which entailed the obligation of marriage only if conception took place, with the febrile promiscuity of the factory where some of the employers enacted scenes with the mill-girls which—

put to blush the lascivious Saturnalia of the Romans, the rites of the Pagoda girls of India, and the Harem life of the most voluptuous Ottoman.

Such colorful accounts were, not unnaturally, resented not only by the employers but by the factory workers themselves. They pointed out that the illegitimacy rate in many rural districts compared unfavourably with that in mill-towns. In many mills the greatest propriety was enforced. If there were "Ottomans" among the mill-owners, there were also paternalists who dismissed any girl detected in a moral lapse.

The discussion is unrewarding, not because of the paucity of evidence as to family life and sexual behaviour, but because the evidence tells us so little about essential relations between parents and children, or between men and women. The Churches undoubtedly won converts from among those who had witnessed the suffering brought upon children by drunken or feckless parents. But there is no evidence that a repressive sexual code and patriarchal family relations brought enhancement of either happiness or of love. Even animalism might be preferable to cold and guilty sexuality; while, as sexual conduct in the early 19th century became more inhibited and secretive, so also, in the great towns, prostitution grew. Nor can we assume any direct correlation between church membership, or even the forms of marriage, and family loyalties. Mayhew was to discover that groups like the costermongers, among whom paganism and concubinage were customary, showed as much mutual loyalty as professing Christians.

Working people discovered in the Industrial Revolution a moral rhetoric which was authentic and deeply expressive of their collective grievances and aspirations, but which seems stilted and inadequate when applied to personal relations. But there is plenty of evidence as to the heroic family loyalties which sustained many people in these years. And there is evidence also as to a minority of men and women, in the main Radicals and free-thinkers, who consciously sought for a comradeship and equality unknown among working people in the 18th century. William Lovett, the cabinet-maker, whose engagement was broken off for a year because his fiancée (a lady's maid) found him heretical on doctrinal points; and who, after his marriage, shared with her his self-education, "reading and explaining to her the various subjects that came before us," may be taken as an example.

It is here that it is most difficult to draw a balance. On the one hand, the claim that the Industrial Revolution raised the status of women would seem to have little meaning when set beside the record of excessive hours of labour, cramped housing, excessive child-bearing and terrifying rates of child mortality. On the other hand, the abundant opportunities for female employment in the textile districts gave to women the status of independent wage-earners. The spinster or the widow was freed from dependence upon relatives or upon parish relief. Even the unmarried mother might be able, through the laxness of "moral discipline" in many mills, to achieve an independence unknown before. In the largest silk-mills at Macclesfield, righteous employers prided themselves upon dismissing girls who made a single "false step." A witness who contrasted this with the easier-going manners of Manchester came up with observations disturbing to the moralist:

I find it very generally . . . the case, that where the mills and factories are nearly free from mothers of illegitimate children, there the streets are infested with prostitutes; and on the contrary, where the girls are permitted to return to their work, after giving birth to a child, there the streets are kept comparatively clear of those unhappy beings.

The period reveals many such paradoxes. The war years saw a surfeit of sermonising and admonitory tracts limiting or refuting claims to women's rights which were associated with "Jacobinism." Women's subordination in marriage was dictated in the bleakest terms. "The Christian scriptures," declared Paley, enjoin upon the wife an obedience in marriage "in terms so peremptory and absolute, that it seems to extend to everything not criminal, or not entirely inconsistent with the women's happiness." But the same years see also a stubborn minority tradition, in the main among professional people and radical artisans in the great cities, which set forward claims more far-reaching than any known before the French Revolution. The claims made in the 1790s by Mary Wollstonecraft, William Blake and Thomas Spence were never wholly abandoned; they recur, not only in Shelley's circle, but also in the Radical publications of the post-war years. They were voiced, self-deprecatingly, in the Black Dwarf; more stridently in Richard Carlile's publications; most powerfully by Anna Wheeler and William Thompson and in the Owenite movement. But it was in the textile districts that the changing economic status of women gave rise to the earliest widespread participation by working women in political and social agitation. In the last years of the 18th century female benefit societies and female Methodist classes may have given experience and self-confidence—the claim of women to act as local preachers was a persistent Wesleyan "heresy." But the war years, with their increased demand for labour not only in the spinning-mills but also at the hand-loom, accelerated the process. In 1818 and 1819 the first Female Reform Societies were founded, in Blackburn, Preston, Bolton, Manchester, Ashton-under-Lyne. Samuel Bamford's account—if we may credit it—suggests a sudden leap forward in consciousness. At a meeting in the Saddleworth district on the Lancashire-Yorkshire border.

I, in the course of an address, insisted on the right, and the propriety also, of females who were present at such assemblages voting by a show of hand for or against the resolutions. This was a new idea; and the women, who attended numerously on that bleak ridge, were mightily pleased with it. The men being nothing dissentient, when the resolution was put the women held up their hands amid much laughter; and ever from that time females voted with the men at the Radical meetings. . . . It became the practice, female political unions were formed, with their chairwomen, committees, and other officials; and from us the practice was soon borrowed . . . [by] religious and charitable institutions.

(In Newcastle, at the same time, one of Jabez Bunting's correspondents was lamenting the default of the "pious sisterhood" who were embroidering reform banners.) The twenty years between 1815 and 1835 see also the first indications of independent trade union action among women workers. John Wade, commenting upon a strike of 1,500 female card-setters in the West Riding in 1835, pointed the moral: "Alarmists may view these indications of female independence as more menacing to established institutions than the 'education of the lower orders.'"

But there is a paradox of feeling even in this advance. The Radicalism of northern working women was compounded of nostalgia for lost status and the assertion of new-found rights. According to conventions which were deeply felt, the woman's status turned upon her success as a housewife in the family economy, in domestic management and forethought, baking and brewing, cleanliness and child-care. The new independence, in the mill or full-time at the loom, which made new claims possible, was felt simultaneously as a loss in status and in personal independence. Women became more dependent upon the employer or labour market, and they looked back to a "golden" past in which home earnings from spinning, poultry, and the like, could be gained around their own door. In good times the domestic economy, like the peasant economy, supported a way of life centred upon the home, in which inner whims and compulsions were more obvious than external discipline. Each stage in industrial differentiation and specialisation struck also at the family economy, disturbing customary relations between man and wife, parents and children, and differentiating more sharply between "work" and "life." It was to be a full hundred years before this differentiation was to bring returns, in the form of labour-saving devices, back into the working woman's home. Meanwhile, the family was roughly torn apart each morning by the factory bell, and the mother who was also a wage-earner often felt herself to have the worst of both the domestic and the industrial worlds.

"Once we could have welcomed you, by spreading before you a board of English hospitality, furnished by our industry," the Female Reformers of Bolton addressed William Cobbett in 1819: "Once, we could have greeted you, with roseate countenances of English females. . . . We could have presented to your view our Cottages, vieing for cleanliness and arrangement with the Palace of our King." The Female Reformers of Blackburn took up the same theme—their houses "robbed of all their ornaments," their beds "torn away . . . by the relentless hand of the unfeeling tax-gatherer" so that "borough-mongering tyrants" might repose on "beds of down" while their families lay on straw. Above all, they appealed on behalf of their children: "we are daily cut to the heart to see them greedily devour the coarse food that some would scarcely give to their swine." It was natural that they should respond to Cobbett, who was soon to consolidate their support with his *Cottage Economy*, and also to Oastler, with his emphasis upon "the home." Neither Cobbett nor Oastler gave the least support to the notion of women's suffrage, nor did the Female Reform Societies raise the demand on their own account. Their rôle was confined to giving moral support to the men, making banners and caps of liberty which were presented with ceremony at reform demonstrations, passing resolutions and addresses, and swelling the numbers at meetings. But even these forms of participation called forth the abuse of their opponents. The "petticoat reformers" of Manchester were described in the *Courier* as "degraded females," guilty of "the worst prostitution of the sex, the prostitution of the heart," "deserting their station" and putting off the "sacred characters" of wife and mother "for turbulent vices of sedition and impiety." Whatever his views on women's suffrage, Cobbett had no second thoughts about coming to the Female Reformers' aid:

Just as if women were made for nothing but to cook oat-meal and to sweep a room! Just as if women had no minds! Just as if Hannah Moore and the Tract Gentry had reduced the women of England to a level with the Negresses of Africa! Just as if England had never had a queen. . . .

The Rituals of Mutuality

Again and again the "passing of old England" evades analysis. We may see the lines of change more clearly if we recall that the Industrial Revolution was not a settled social context but a phase of transition between two ways of life. And we must see, not one "typical" community (Middleton or Pudsey), but many different communities co-existing with each other. In south-east Lancashire alone there were to be found, within a few miles of each other, the cosmopolitan city of Manchester upon which migrants converged from every point in the kingdom; pit-villages (like the Duke of Bridgewater's collieries) emerging from semi-feudalism; paternal model villages (like Turton); new mill-towns (like Bolton); and older weaving hamlets. In all of these communities there were a number of converging influences at work, all making towards discipline and the growth in working-class consciousness.

The working-class community of the early 19th century was the product, neither of paternalism nor of Methodism, but in a high degree of conscious working-class endeavour. In Manchester or New-castle the traditions of the trade union and the friendly society, with their emphasis upon self-discipline and community purpose, reach far back into the 18th century. Rules which survive of the Manchester small-ware weavers in the 1750s show already meticulous attention to procedure and to institutional etiquette. The committee members must sit in a certain order. The doors must be kept locked. There are careful regulations for the safe-keeping of the "box." Members are reminded that "Intemperance, Animosity and Profaneness are the Pest and Vermin that gnaw out the very Vitals of all Society."

If we consider this Society, not as a Company of Men met to regale themselves with Ale and Tobacco, and talk indifferently on all Subjects: but rather as a Society sitting to Protect the Rights and Privileges of a Trade by which some hundreds of People . . . subsist . . . how awkward does it look to see its Members jumbled promiscuously one amongst another, talking indifferently on all Subjects. . . .

"Decency and Regularity" are the watchwords; it is even hoped that when "Gentlemen and Magistrates" observe such order "they will rather revere than punish such a Society."

This represents the code of the self-respecting artisan, although the hope that such sobriety would win the favour of the authorities was to be largely disappointed. It was in a similar school that such men as Hardy and Place received their education in London. But as the Industrial Revolution advanced, it was this code (sometimes in the form of model rules) which was extended to ever-wider sections of working people. Small tradesmen, artisans, labourers—all sought to insure themselves against sickness, unemployment, or funeral expenses[3] through membership of "box clubs" or friendly societies. But the discipline essential for the safe-keeping of funds, the orderly conduct of meetings and the determination of disputed cases, involved an effort of self-rule as great as the new disciplines of work. An examination of rules and orders of friendly societies in existence in Newcastle and district during the Napoleonic Wars gives us a list of fines and penalties more exacting than those of a Bolton cotton-master. A General Society imposed fines for any member "reflecting upon" another member in receipt of sick money, being drunk on the Sabbath, striking another, "calling one another bye-names," coming in the clubroom in liquor, taking God's name in vain. The Brotherhood of Maltsters added fines for drunkenness at *any* time, or for failure to attend the funerals of brothers or of their wives. The Glass-Makers (founded as early as 1755) added fines for failure in attending meetings, or for those who refused to take their turn in the rota of officers; for failing to keep silence when ordered, speaking together, answering back the steward, betting in the club, or (a common rule) disclosing secrets outside the society. Further,

Persons that are infamous, of ill character, quarrelsome, or disorderly, shall not be admitted into this society. . . . No Pitman, Collier, Sinker, or Waterman to be admitted . . .

The Watermen, not to be outdone, added a rule excluding from benefits any brother sick through "any illness got by lying with an unclean woman, or is clap't or pox'd." Brothers were to be fined for ridiculing or provoking each other to passion. The Unanimous Society was to cut off benefits if any member in receipt of sick money was found "in ale-houses, gaming, or drunk." To maintain its unanimity there were fines for members proposing "discourse or dispute upon political or ecclesiastical matters, or government and governors." The Friendly

---

[3] Working-people attached an exceptional valuation to the ceremony of funeral. A pauper funeral was the ultimate social disgrace. And ceremony bulked large in folk-lore, and preoccupied dying men. "I could wish," wrote a condemned Luddite, "for John Rawson, John Roberts, and John Roper to be my bearers; dear wife, choose the other three thyself": *The Surprising . . . History of "General Ludd"* (Nottingham, n.d.), p. 239.

Society of All Trades had a rule similar to "huffing" in draughts; there was a fine "if any member has an opportunity of fining his brother, and does not." The Cordwainers added fines for calling for drink or tobacco without leave of the stewards. The House-Carpenters and Joiners added a prohibition of "disloyal sentiments" or "political songs."

It is possible that some of these rules, such as the prohibition of political discourse and songs, should be taken with a pinch of salt. While some of these societies were select sick-clubs of as few as twenty or thirty artisans, meeting at an inn, others were probably covers for trade union activity; while at Newcastle, as at Sheffield, it is possible that after the Two Acts the formation of friendly societies was used as a cover for Jacobin organisation. (A "company" friendly society, in 1816, bore testimony to "the loyal, patriotic, and peaceable regulations" of many Newcastle societies, but complained that these regulations were often insufficient to prevent "warm debate and violent language.") The authorities were deeply suspicious of the societies during the war years, and one of the purposes of the rules was to secure registration with the local magistrates. But anyone familiar with procedure and etiquette in some trade unions and working-men's clubs today will recognise the origin of still-extant practices in several of the rules. Taken together, they indicate an attainment of self-discipline and a diffusion of experience of a truly impressive order.

Estimates of friendly society membership suggest 648,000 in 1793, 704,350 in 1803, 925,429 in 1815. Although registration with the magistrates, under the first Friendly Society Act of 1793, made possible the protection of funds at law in the event of defaulting officers, a large but unknown number of clubs failed to register, either through hostility to the authorities, parochial inertia, or through a deep secretiveness which, Dr. Holland found, was still strong enough to baffle his enquiries in Sheffield in the early 1840s. Nearly all societies before 1815 bore a strictly local and self-governing character, and they combined the functions of sick insurance with convivial club nights and annual "outings" or feasts. An observer in 1805 witnessed near Matlock—

. . . about fifty women preceded by a solitary fiddler playing a merry tune. This was a female benefit society, who had been to hear a sermon at Eyam, and were going to dine together, a luxury which our female benefit society at Sheffield does not indulge in, having tea only, and generally singing, dancing, smoking, and negus.

Few of the members of friendly societies had a higher social status than that of clerks or small tradesmen; most were artisans. The fact that each brother had funds deposited in the society made for stability in membership and watchful participation in self-government. They had almost no middle-class membership and, while some employers looked upon them favourably, their actual conduct left little room for paternalist control. Failures owing to actuarial inexperience were common; defaulting officers not infrequent. Diffused through every part of the country, they were (often heart-breaking) schools of experience.

In the very secretiveness of the friendly society, and in its opaqueness under upper-class scrutiny, we have authentic evidence of the growth of independent working-class culture and institutions. This was the sub-culture out of which the less stable trade unions grew, and in which trade union officers were trained. Union rules, in many cases, were more elaborate versions of the same code of conduct as the sick club. Sometimes, as in the case of the Woolcombers, this was supplemented by the procedures of secret masonic orders:

> Strangers, the design of all our Lodges is love and unity,
> With self-protection founded on the laws of equity,
> And when you have our mystic rights gone through,
> Our secrets all will be disclosed to you.

After the 1790s, under the impact of the Jacobin agitation, the preambles to friendly society rules assume a new resonance; one of the strangest consequences of the language of "social man" of the philosophical Enlightenment is its reproduction in the rules of obscure clubs meeting in the taverns or "hush-shops" of industrial England. On Tyneside "Social" and "Philanthropic" societies expressed their aspirations in terms which ranged from throw-away phrases—"a sure, lasting, and loving society," "to promote friendship and true Christian charity," "man was not born for himself alone"—to more thundering philosophical affirmations:

> Man, by the construction of his body, and the disposition of his mind, is a creature formed for society. . . .
> We, the members of this society, taking it into our serious consideration, that man is formed a social being . . . in continual need of mutual assistance and support; and having interwoven in our constitutions those humane and sympathetic affections which we always feel at the distress of any of our fellow creatures. . . .

The friendly societies, found in so many diverse communities, were a unifying cultural influence. Although for financial and legal reasons they were slow to federate themselves, they facilitated regional and national trade union federation. Their language of "social man" also made [a contribution] towards the growth in working-class consciousness. It joined the language of Christian charity and the slumbering imagery of "brotherhood" in the Methodist (and Moravian) tradition with the social affirmations of Owenite socialism. Many early Owenite societies and stores prefaced their rules with the line from Isiah (XLI, 6): "They helped every one his neighbour; and every one said to his brother, be of good courage." By the 1830s there were in circulation a score of friendly society or trade union hymns and songs which elaborated this theme.

Mr. Raymond Williams has suggested that "the crucial distinguishing element in English life since the Industrial Revolution is ... between alternative ideas of the nature of social relationship." As contrasted with middle-class ideas of individualism or (at their best) of service, "what is properly meant by 'working-class culture' ... is the basic collective idea, and the institutions, manners, habits of thought, and intentions which proceed from this." Friendly societies did not "proceed from" an idea; both the ideas and the institutions arose in response to certain common experiences. But the distinction is important. In the simple cellular structure of the friendly society, with its workaday ethos of mutual aid, we can see many features which were reproduced in more sophisticated and complex forms in trade unions, co-operatives, Hampden Clubs, Political Unions, and Chartist lodges. At the same time the societies can be seen as crystallising an ethos of mutuality very much more widely diffused in the "dense" and "concrete" particulars of the personal relations of working people, at home and at work. Every kind of witness in the first half of the 19th century—clergymen, factory inspectors, Radical publicists—remarked upon the extent of mutual aid in the poorest districts. In times of emergency, unemployment, strikes, sickness, childbirth, then it was the poor who "helped every one his neighbour." Twenty years after Place's comment on the change in Lancashire manners, Cooke Taylor was astounded at the way in which Lancashire working men bore "the extreme of wretchedness,"

with a high tone of moral dignity, a marked sense of propriety, a decency, cleanliness, and order . . . which do not merit the intense suffering I have witnessed. I was beholding the gradual immolation of the noblest and most valuable population that ever existed in this country or in any other under heaven.

"Nearly all the distressed operatives whom I met north of Manchester . . . had a thorough horror of being forced to receive parish relief."

It is an error to see this as the *only* effective "working-class" ethic. The "aristocratic" aspirations of artisans and mechanics, the values of "self-help," or criminality and demoralisation, were equally widely dispersed. The conflict between alternative ways of life was fought out, not just between the middle and working classes, but within working-class communities themselves. But by the early years of the 19th century it is possible to say that collectivist values are dominant in many industrial communities; there is a definite moral code, with sanctions against the blackleg, the "tools" of the employer or the unneighbourly, and with an intolerance towards the eccentric or individualist. Collectivist values are consciously held and are propagated in political theory, trade union ceremonial, moral rhetoric. It is, indeed, this collective self-consciousness, with its corresponding theory, institutions, discipline, and community values which distinguishes the 19th-century *working class* from the 18th-century *mob*.

Political Radicalism and Owenism both drew upon and enriched this "basic collectivist idea." Francis Place may well have been right when he attributed the changed behaviour of Lancashire crowds in 1819 to the advance of political consciousness "spreading over the face of the country ever since the Constitutional and Corresponding Societies became active in 1792":

Now 100,000 people may be collected together and no riot ensue, and why? . . . The people have an object, the pursuit of which gives them importance in their own eyes, elevates them in their own opinion, and thus it is that the very individuals who would have been the leaders of the riot are the keepers of the peace.

Another observer attributed the changes in Lancashire to the influence both of Cobbett and of the Sunday schools and noted a "general and radical change" in the character of the labouring classes:

The poor, when suffering and dissatisfied, no longer make a riot, but hold a meeting—instead of attacking their neighbors, they arraign the Ministry.

This growth in self-respect and political consciousness was one real gain of the Industrial Revolution. It dispelled some forms of superstition and of deference, and made certain kinds of oppression no longer tolerable. We can find abundant testimony as to the steady growth of the ethos of mutuality in the strength and ceremonial pride of the unions and trades clubs which emerged from quasi-legality when the Combination Acts were repealed. During the Bradford wool-comber's strike of 1825 we find that in Newcastle, where the friendly society was so well rooted, the unions contributing to the Bradford funds included smiths, mill-wrights, joiners, shoemakers, morocco leather dressers, cabinet-makers, shipwrights, sawyers, tailors, woolcombers, hatters, tanners, weavers, potters and miners. Moreover, there is a sense in which the friendly society helped to pick up and carry into the trade union movement the love of ceremony and the high sense of status of the craftsman's guild. These traditions, indeed, still had a remarkable vigour in the early 19th century, in some of the old Chartered Companies or Guilds of the masters and of master-craftsmen, whose periodical ceremonies expressed the pride of both the masters and of their journeymen in "the Trade." In 1802, for example, there was a great jubilee celebration of the Preston "Guilds." In a week of processions and exhibitions, in which the nobility, gentry, merchants, shopkeepers, and manufacturers all took part, the journeymen were given a prominent place:

The Wool-Combers and Cotton Workers . . . were preceded by twenty-four young blooming handsome women, each bearing a branch of the cotton tree, then followed a spinning machine borne on men's shoulders, and afterwards a loom drawn on a sledge, each with work-people busily employed at them. . . .

At Bradford, on the eve of the great strike of 1825, the woolcombers' feast of Bishop Blaize was celebrated with extraordinary splendour:

Herald, bearing a flag.
Twenty-four Woolstaplers on horseback, each horse caparisoned
with a fleece.
Thirty-eight Worsted-Spinners and Manufacturers on horseback,
in white stuff waiscoats, with each a sliver of wool over his shoulder
and a white stuff sash: the horses' necks covered with nets made of
thick yarn

And so on until we reach:

BISHOP BLAIZE
Shepherd and Shepherdess.
Shepherd-Swains.
One hundred and sixty Woolsorters on horseback, with ornamented
caps and various coloured slivers.
Thirty Comb-makers.
Charcoal Burners.
Combers' Colours.
Band.
Four hundred and seventy Wool-combers, with wool wigs, &c.
Band.
Forty Dyers, with red cockades, blue aprons, and crossed slivers
of red and blue.

After the great strike such a ceremony could not be repeated.

This passage from the old outlook of "the Trade" to the duality of the masters' organisations, on the one hand, and the trade unions on the other, takes us into the central experience of the Industrial Revolution. But the friendly society and trade union, not less than the organisations of the masters, sought to maintain the ceremonial and the pride of the older tradition; indeed, since the artisans (or, as they still are called, *tradesmen*) felt themselves to be the *producers* upon whose skill the masters were parasitic, they emphasised the tradition the more. With the repeal of the Combination Acts their banners moved openly through the streets. In London, in 1825, the Thames Ship Caulkers Union (founded in 1794) displayed its mottos: "Main et Coeur," "Vigeur, Verité, Concorde, Depêche," which reveal the pride of the medieval craft. The Ropemakers Union proceeded with a white banner on which was portrayed a swarm of bees around a hive: "Sons of Industry! Union gives Strength." (At the houses of masters who had granted them an increase, they stopped and gave a salute.) John Gast's Thames Shipwrights Provident Union, the pacemaker of the London "trades," outdid all with a blue silk banner: "Hearts of Oak Protect the Aged," a handsome ship drawn by six bay horses, three postilions in blue jackets, a band, the Committee, the members with more banners and flags, and delegations representing the trade from Shields, Sunderland, and Newcastle. The members wore blue rosettes and sprigs of oak, and in the ship were old shipwrights who lived in the union's almshouses at Stepney. At Nantwich in 1832 the shoemakers maintained all the sense of status of the artisan's craft union, with their banner, "full set of secret order regalia, surplices, trimmed aprons ...and a crown and robes for King Crispin." In 1833 the King rode on horseback through the town attended by train-bearers, officers with the "Dispensation, the Bible, a large pair of gloves, and also beautiful specimens of ladies' and gents' boots and shoes":

Nearly 500 joined in the procession, each one wearing a white apron neatly trimmed. The rear was brought up by a shopmate in full tramping order, his kit packed on his back, and walking-stick in hand.

No single explanation will suffice to account for the evident alteration in manner of the working people. Nor should we exaggerate the degree of change. Drunkenness and uproar still often surged through the streets. But it is true that working men often appear most sober and disciplined, in the twenty years after the Wars, when most in earnest to assert their rights. Thus we cannot accept the thesis that sobriety was the consequence only, or even mainly, of the Evangelical propaganda. And we may see this, also, if we turn the coin over and look at the reverse. By 1830 not only the Established Church but also the Methodist revival was meeting sharp opposition in most working-class centers from free-thinkers, Owenities, and non-denominational Christians. In London, Birmingham, south-east Lancashire, Newcastle, Leeds and other cities the Deist adherents of Carlile or Owen had an enormous following. The Methodists had consolidated their position, but they tended increasingly to represent tradesmen and privileged groups of workers, and to be morally isolated from working-class community life. Some old centres of revivalism had relapsed into "heathenism." In Newcastle's Sandgate, once "as noted for praying as for tippling, for psalm-singing as for swearing," the Methodists had lost any following among the poor by the 1840s. In parts of Lancashire weaving communities as well as factory operatives became largely detached from the chapels and were swept up in the current of Owenism and free-thought:

If it had not been for Sunday schools, society would have been in a horrible state before this time. . . . Infidelity is growing amazingly. . . . The writings of Carlile and Taylor and other infidels are more read than the Bible or any other book. . . . I have seen weeks after weeks the weavers assembled in a room, that would contain 400 people, to applaud the people who asserted and argued that there was no God. . . . I have gone into the cottages around the chapel where I worship, I have found 20 men assembled reading infidel publications. . . .

Owenite and secular movements often took fire "like whins on the common," as revivalism had done before.

Engels, writing from his Lancashire experience in 1844, claimed that "the workers are not religious, and do not attend church," with the exception of the Irish, "a few elderly people, and the half-bourgeois, the overlookers, foremen, and the like." "Among the masses there prevails almost universally a total indifference to religion, or at the utmost, some trace of Deism. . . ." Engels weakened his case by overstating it; but Dodd quoted a Stockport factory where nine out of ten did not attend any church, while Cooke Taylor, in 1842, was astonished at the vigour and knowledge of the Scriptures shown by Lancashire working men who contested Christian orthodoxies. "If I thought that the Lord was the cause of all the misery I see around me," one such man told a Methodist preacher, "I would quit his service, and say he was not the Lord I took him for." Similarly, in Newcastle in the Chartist years thousands of artisans and engineers were convinced free-thinkers. In one works employing 200 "there are not more than six or seven who attend a place of worship." "The working classes," said one working-man, are gathering knowledge, and the more they gather, the wider becomes the breach between them and the different sects. It is not because they are ignorant of the Bible. I revere the Bible myself . . . and when I look into it . . . I find that the prophets stood between the oppressor and oppressed, and denounced the wrong doer, however rich and powerful. . . . When the preachers go back to the old book, I for one will go back to hear them, but not till then. . . .

The Sunday schools were bringing an unexpected harvest.

The weakening hold of the churches by no means indicated any erosion of the self-respect and discipline of class. On the contrary, Manchester and Newcastle, with their long tradition of industrial and political organisation, were notable in the Chartist years for the discipline of their massive demonstrations. Where the citizens and shopkeepers had once been thrown into alarm when the "terrible and savage pitmen" entered Newcastle in any force, it now became necessary for the coal-owners to scour the slums of the city for "candy-men" or rag-collectors to evict the striking miners. In 1838 and 1839 tens of thousands of artisans, miners and labourers marched week after week in good order through the streets, often passing within a few feet of the military, and avoiding all provocation. "Our people had been well taught," one of their leaders recalled, "that it was not riot we wanted, but revolution."

. . .

Myriads of Eternity

If we can now see more clearly many of the elements which made up the working-class communities of the early 19th century, a definitive answer to the "standard-of-living" controversy must still evade us. For beneath the word "standard" we must always find judgements of value as well as questions of fact. Values, we hope to have shown, are not "imponderables" which the historian may safely dismiss with the reflection that, since they are not amenable to measurement, anyone's opinion is as good as anyone else's. They are, on the contrary, those questions of human satisfaction, and of the direction of social change, which the historian ought to ponder if history is to claim a position among the significant humanities.

The historian, or the historical sociologist, must in fact be concerned with judgements of value in two forms. In the first instance, he is concerned with the values *actually held* by those who lived through the Industrial Revolution. The old and newer modes of production each supported distinct kinds of community with characteristic ways of life. Alternative conventions and notions of human satisfaction were in conflict with each other, and there is no shortage of evidence if we wish to study the ensuing tensions.

In the second instance, he is concerned with making some judgement of value upon the whole process entailed in the Industrial Revolution, of which we ourselves are an end-product. It is our own involvement which makes judgement difficult. And yet we are helped towards a certain detachment, both by the "romantic" critique of industrialism which stems from one part of the experience, and by the record of tenacious resistance by which hand-loom weaver, artisan or village craftsman confronted this experience and held fast to an alternative culture. As we see them change, so we see how we became what we are. We understand more clearly what was lost, what was driven "underground," what is still unresolved.

Any evaluation of the quality of life must entail an assessment of the total life-experience, the manifold satisfactions or deprivations, cultural as well as material, of the people concerned. From such a standpoint, the older "cataclysmic" view of the Industrial Revolution must still be accepted. During the years between 1780 and 1840 the people of Britain suffered an experience of immiseration, even if it is possible to show a small statistical improvement in material conditions. When Sir Charles Snow tells us that "with singular unanimity . . . the poor have walked off the land into the factories as fast as the factories could take them," we must reply, with Dr. Leavis, that the "actual history" of the "full human problem [was] incomparably and poignantly more complex than that." Some were lured from the countryside by the glitter and promise of wages of the industrial town; but the old village economy was crumbling at their backs. They moved less by their own will than at the dictate of external compulsions which they could not question: the enclosures, the Wars, the Poor Laws, the decline of rural industries, the counter-revolutionary stance of their rulers.

The process of industrialisation is necessarily painful. It must involve the erosion of traditional patterns of life. But it was carried through with exceptional violence in Britain. It was unrelieved by any sense of national participation in communal effort, such as is found in countries undergoing a national revolution. Its ideology was that of the masters alone. Its messianic prophet was Dr. Andrew Ure, who saw the factory system as "the great minister of civilization to the terraqueous globe," diffusing "the life-blood of science and religion to myriads . . . still lying 'in the region and shadow of death.' " But those who served it did not *feel* this to be so, any more than those "myriads" who were served. The experience of immiseration came upon them in a hundred different forms; for the field labourer, the loss of his common rights and the vestiges of village democracy; for

the artisan, the loss of his craftsman's status; for the weaver, the loss
of livelihood and of independence; for the child, the loss of work
and play in the home; for many groups of workers whose real earnings improved, the loss of security, leisure and the deterioration of the
urban environment. R. M. Martin, who gave evidence before the Hand-
Loom Weavers' Committee of 1834, and who had returned to England
after an absence from Europe of ten years, was struck by the evidence
of physical and spiritual deterioration:

I have observed it not only in the manufacturing but also in agricultural communities in this country; they seem to have lost their anima-
tion, their vivacity, their field games and their village sports; they
have become a sordid, discontented, miserable, anxious, struggling
people, without health, or gaiety, or happiness.

It is misleading to search for explanations in what Professor Ashton
has rightly described as "tedious" phrases,—man's "divorce" from
"nature" or "the soil." After the "Last Labourers' Revolt," the Wiltshire field labourers—who were close enough to "nature"—were far
worse degraded than the Lancashire mill girls. This violence was
done to *human* nature. From one standpoint, it may be seen as the
outcome of the pursuit of profit, when the cupidity of the owners of
the means of production was freed from old sanctions and had not
yet been subjected to new means of social control. In this sense we
may still read it, as Marx did, as the violence of the capitalist class.
From another standpoint, it may be seen as a violent technological
differentiation between work and life.

It is neither poverty nor disease but work itself which casts the
blackest shadow over the years of the Industrial Revolution. It is
Blake, himself a craftsman by training, who gives us the experience:

Then left the sons of Urizen the plow & harrow, the loom,
The hammer & the chisel & the rule & compasses . . .
And all the arts of life they chang'd into the arts of death.
The hour glass contemn'd because its simple workmanship
Was as the workmanship of the plowman & the water wheel
That raises water into Cisterns, broken & burn'd in fire
Because its workmanship was like the workmanship of the shepherds
And in their stead intricate wheels invented, Wheel without wheel,
To perplex youth in their outgoings & to bind to labours
Of day & night the myriads of Eternity, that they might file
And polish brass & iron hour after hour, laborious workmanship,
Kept ignorant of the use that they might spend the days of wisdom
In sorrowful drudgery to obtain a scanty pittance of bread,

In ignorance to view a small portion & think that All,
And call it demonstration, blind to all the simple rules of life.

These "myriads of eternity" seem at times to have been sealed in their work like a tomb. Their best efforts, over a lifetime, and supported by their own friendly societies, could scarcely ensure them that to which so high a popular value was attached—a "Decent Funeral." New skills were arising, old satisfactions persisted, but over all we feel the general pressure of long hours of unsatisfying labour under severe discipline for alien purposes. This was at the source of that "ugliness" which, D. H. Lawrence wrote, "betrayed the spirit of man in the nineteenth century." After all other impressions fade, this one remains; together with that of the loss of any felt cohesion in the community, save that which the working people, in antagonism to their labour and to their masters, built for themselves.

III/THE REVOLUTION OF 1848 IN FRANCE

A SPECTER is haunting Europe, the specter of communism." The year was 1848, and Marx's declaration in the *Communist Manifesto* was neither idle boasting nor a gratuitous statement of intent. It corresponded to reality insofar as it meant (1) that for the first time the nascent proletariat all over the continent was beginning to organize for the pursuit of its own revolutionary purposes, and (2) that the proletariat had already taken a hand in every major revolution, although they were primarily bourgeois-democratic in nature.

There was still unfinished business on the Continent in 1848—the bourgeois revolution itself. In that year, it was made, more or less successfully and in accordance with special national circumstances, in practically every European state. Only England was in the end spared a violent upheaval, but not without a good deal of fear and trembling on the part of the ruling class. And a combination of reform acts to extend the franchise to holders of nonreal property, Corn Law repeal to ensure an adequate cheap bread supply, and workers' blood as an antidote to militancy (in less spectacular, but not necessarily smaller doses than was customary across the Channel) accomplished the same result. In Germany, the bourgeoisie showed itself too weak to seize power. The revolution was defeated, and the so-called Prussian road to capitalist society and national unity (that is, an alliance between the bourgeoisie, the Junker aristocracy, and the Prussian state) was opened. In Russia, there was as yet no bourgeoisie capable of revolutionary activity because of the low level of capitalist development and the maintenance of feudal relationships on the land. Nor was there, after the defeat of the young officers who organized the Decembrist Revolt against Nicholas I in 1825, any surrogate body ready to do the job for them. Among the subject peoples of Central Europe, the revolutions were equally abortive, although in every case they were the starting point of long-term political change.

Only in France was the bourgeois republic successfully, if temporarily, established. The Revolution of February 1848 was an uprising of certain elements of the bourgeoisie against others, notably bankers and financial speculators, who had exercised a monopoly of power during the reign of Louis Philippe but had done nothing to promote the economic development of the country as a whole. At the same time, workers and peasants, particularly hard hit by the crisis that had begun with the bad harvest of 1846, demanded political rights and social reform of an extensive nature, such as the guarantee of the right to work at a decent wage. Socially conscious Romantic intellectuals also joined in this revolt against Prime Minister Guizot's celebrated reply to those who complained against the July Monarchy. "Get rich," he had counseled them.

The monarchy literally crumbled under this combined attack, and its place was taken by a weak, indecisive provisional government essentially bourgeois in nature and almost as insensitive to popular demands as its predecessor. The failure of the victors of February to satisfy the working class brought on the June Revolution, drowned in blood by General Cavaignac. Thereafter, the story is one of constant moving to the right, with the conservative bourgeois once again getting the upper hand over disorganized workers and a peasantry increasingly scared of a rumored socialization of their precious small holdings. The development of the situation favored the election of Louis Napoleon to the presidency of the Republic in 1849 and further allowed him to carry out the coup d'état of December 2, 1851, that created the Second Empire.

It was under these conditions that Marx was moved to write his celebrated pamphlet *The Eighteenth Brumaire of Louis Bonaparte*, from which the following selection is taken. The first line sets the tone of the entire work: "Hegel remarks somewhere that all facts and personages of great importance in world history occur, as it were, twice. He forgot to add: the first time as tragedy, the second as farce." Even the title is ironic, because it is the date in the revolutionary calendar on which the real Napoleon took power in 1799. Napoleon the Little, as Victor Hugo called him, was the comic transposition of his genial uncle.

To speak of a bourgeois revolution is only the beginning of analysis. Marx asked: Who among the bourgeoisie rebelled and why? Why should the republic have been their rallying cry when monarchy no longer was synonymous with feudal reaction? And why did the republic die at the hands of a man on horseback, a charlatan not in himself to be taken seriously? He found the answer in the class relationships that had evolved from the conquests of the Revolution of 1789—a bourgeoisie that wanted to get on with the business of making money, a small-holding peasantry frightened for the security of its property, a working class increasingly restive. Louis Napoleon freed the bourgeoisie from political cares, while favoring their commercial and industrial ambitions. For the moment, they were willing to accept this as the price of economic development—until 1870, when defeat in war and a variety of other offenses against their interests and dignity caused them to look elsewhere for a solution to the vital problem of maintaining law, order, and exploitation.

Bonapartism has become a fairly common phenomenon in the twentieth century. The world is full of caudillos and fathers of their country who appear, on the surface, to operate independently of the classes upon which their power is based. Fascism often, though not always, takes a Bonapartist form, insofar as it relies on the figure of the charismatic leader as a principle of organization. For the understanding of regimes of personal power, whether or not fascist in content, from de Gaulle to Franco to Papa Doc, the example of Louis Napoleon is not without interest. The question raised concerns the relationship of the state apparatus to the ruling class, one of the most important for both historical study and contemporary action. Our concepts here need strengthening, for recent experience has shown that it is too simple by far to believe that the relationship operates in one direction only, that is, by the ruling class transmitting its orders to the bureaucrats and political leaders.

In 1848, beneath the tinseled splendor of Haussmann and Offenbach's Paris, the reality was grim enough. And no one suffered more than the new working class then in the process of formation. This no doubt would have been inevitable, no matter what the regime, so long as the mode of production remained capitalist, and industrialization the order of the day. The character of

Louis Napoleon is not at issue here, despite all the ink spilled by biographers and historians in debating that very question. Infinitely more significant is the suffering of the laboring poor themselves in enabling us to understand their conditions of work and life and what these meant for the future development of consciousness and action.

Louis Chevalier, professor at the Collège de France and a leading demographic historian, writes of the misery, violence, and death prevailing among Parisian workers between 1815 and 1848, and thinks it proper to stress a kind of biological foundation to social history. He argues that class warfare had so differentiated the chief contestants from one another both physically and mentally that they had become, as it were, two opposed races. The hypothesis is attractive and certainly has the merit of underlining an aspect of the problem hitherto much neglected. One caveat: It would be wrong, I think, to make of "race" (in this restricted sense) a precondition, a foundation of class. The former does not happen before the latter; both are aspects of a single process. Race, like population, becomes meaningful only when inserted into the framework of class.

Karl Marx

8

The Eighteenth Brumaire
of Louis Bonaparte

Hegel remarks somewhere that all facts and personages of great importance in world history occur, as it were, twice. He forgot to add: the first time as tragedy, the second as farce. Caussidière for Danton, Louis Blanc for Robespierre, the *Montagne* of 1848 to 1851 for the *Montagne* of 1793 to 1795, the Nephew for the Uncle. And the same caricature occurs in the circumstances attending the second edition of the eighteenth Brumaire!

Men make their own history, but they do not make it just as they please; they do not make it under circumstances chosen by themselves, but under circumstances directly encountered, given and transmitted from the past. The tradition of all the dead generations weighs like a nightmare on the brain of the living. And just when they seem engaged in revolutionising themselves and things, in creating something that has never yet existed, precisely in such periods of revolutionary crisis they anxiously conjure up the spirits of the past to their service and borrow from them names, battle cries and costumes in order to present the new scene of world history in this time-honoured disguise and this borrowed language. Thus Luther donned the mask of the Apostle Paul, the Revolution of 1789 to 1814 draped itself alternately as the Roman republic and the Roman empire, and the Revolution of 1848 knew nothing better to do than to parody, now 1789, now the revolutionary tradition of 1793 to 1795. In like manner a beginner who has learnt a new language always translates it back into his mother tongue, but he has assimilated the spirit of the new language and can freely express himself in it only when he finds his way in it without recalling the old and forgets his native tongue in the use of the new.

Consideration of this conjuring up of the dead of world history reveals at once a salient difference. Camille Desmoulins, Danton, Robespierre, Saint-Just, Napoleon, the heroes as well as the parties and the masses of the old French Revolution, performed the task of their time in Roman costume and with Roman phrases, the task of unchaining and setting up modern *bourgeois* society. The first ones knocked the feudal basis to pieces and mowed off the feudal heads which had grown on it. The other created inside France the conditions under which alone free competition could be developed, parcelled landed property exploited and the unchained industrial productive power of the nation employed; and beyond the French borders he everywhere swept the feudal institutions away, so far as was necessary to furnish bourgeois society in France with a suitable up-to-date environment on the European Continent. The new social formation once established, the antediluvian Colossi disappeared and with them resurrected Romanity—the Brutuses, Gracchi, Publicolas, the tribunes, the senators, and Caesar himself. Bourgeois society in its sober reality had begotten its true interpreters and mouthpieces in the Says, Cousins, Royer-Collards, Benjamin Constants and Guizots; its real military leaders sat behind the office desks, and the hogheaded Louis XVIII was its political chief. Wholly absorbed in the production of wealth and in peaceful competitive struggle, it no longer comprehended that ghosts from the days of Rome had watched over its cradle. But unheroic as bourgeois society is, it nevertheless took heroism, sacrifice, terror, civil war and battles of peoples to bring it into being. And in the classically austere traditions of the Roman republic its gladiators found the ideals and the art forms, the self-deceptions that they needed in order to conceal from themselves the bourgeois limitations of the content of their struggles and to keep their enthusiasm on the high plane of the great historical tragedy. Similarly, at another stage of development, a century earlier, Cromwell and the English people had borrowed speech, passions and illusions from the Old Testament for their bourgeois revolution. When the real aim had been achieved, when the bourgeois transformation of English society had been accomplished, Locke supplanted Habakkuk.

Thus the awakening of the dead in those revolutions served the purpose of glorifying the new struggles, not of parodying the old; of magnifying the given task in imagination, not of fleeing from its solution in reality; of finding once more the spirit of revolution, not of making its ghost walk about again.

From 1848 to 1851 only the ghost of the old revolution walked about, from Marrast, the *républicain en gants jaunes* [republican in yellow gloves], who disguised himself as the old Bailly, down to the adventurer, who hides his commonplace repulsive features under the iron death mask of Napoleon. An entire people, which had imagined that by means of a revolution it had imparted to itself an accelerated power of motion, suddenly finds itself set back into a defunct epoch and, in order that no doubt as to the relapse may be possible, the old dates arise again, the old chronology, the old names, the old edicts, which had long become a subject of antiquarian erudition, and the old minions of the law, who had seemed long decayed. The nation feels like that mad Englishman in Bedlam who fancies that he lives in the times of the ancient Pharaohs and daily bemoans the hard labour that he must perform in the Ethiopian mines as a gold digger, immured in this subterranean prison, a dimly burning lamp fastened to his head, the overseer of the slaves behind him with a long whip, and at the exits a confused welter of barbarian mercenaries, who understand neither the forced labourers in the mines nor one another, since they speak no common language. "And all this is expected of me," sighs the mad Englishman, "of me, a freeborn Briton, in order to make gold for the old Pharaohs." "In order to pay the debts of the Bonaparte family," sighs the French nation. The Englishman, so long as he was in his right mind, could not get rid of the fixed idea of making gold. The French, so long as they were engaged in revolution, could not get rid of the memory of Napoleon, as the election of December 10 proved. They hankered to return from the perils of revolution to the flesh-pots of Egypt, and December 2, 1851, was the answer. They have not only a caricature of the old Napoleon, they have the old Napoleon himself, caricatured as he must appear in the middle of the nineteenth century.

The social revolution of the nineteenth century cannot draw its poetry from the past, but only from the future. It cannot begin with itself before it has stripped off all superstition in regard to the past. Earlier revolutions required recollections of past world history in order to drug themselves concerning their own content. In order to arrive at its own content, the revolution of the nineteenth century must let the dead bury their dead. There the phrase went beyond the content; here the content goes beyond the phrase.

The February Revolution was a surprise attack, a *taking* of the old society *unawares*, and the people proclaimed this unexpected *stroke* as a deed of world importance, ushering in a new epoch. On December 2 the February Revolution is conjured away by a card-sharper's trick, and what seems overthrown is no longer the monarchy but the liberal concessions that were wrung from it by centuries of struggle. Instead of *society* having conquered a new content for itself, it seems that the *state* only returned to its oldest form, to the shamelessly simple domination of the sabre and the cowl. This is the answer to the *coup de main* [unexpected stroke] of February 1848, given by the *coup de tête* [rash act] of December 1851. Easy come, easy go. Meanwhile the interval of time has not passed by unused. During the years 1848 to 1851 French society has made up, and that by an abbreviated because revolutionary method, for the studies and experiences which, in a regular, so to speak, textbook course of development, would have had to precede the February Revolution, if it was to be more than a ruffling of the surface. Society now seems to have fallen back behind its point of departure; it has in truth first to create for itself the revolutionary point of departure, the situation, the relations, the conditions under which alone modern revolution becomes serious.

Bourgeois revolutions, like those of the nineteenth century, storm swiftly from success to success; their dramatic effects outdo each other; men and things seem set in sparkling brilliants; ecstasy is the everyday spirit; but they are short-lived; soon they have attained their zenith, and a long crapulent depression lays hold of society before it learns soberly to assimilate the results of its storm-and-stress period. On the other hand, proletarian revolutions, like those of the nineteenth century, criticise themselves constantly, interrupt themselves continually in their own course, come back to the apparently accomplished in order to begin it afresh, deride with unmerciful thoroughness the inadequacies, weaknesses and paltrinesses of their first attempts, seem to throw down their adversary only in order that he may draw new strength from the earth and rise again, more gigantic, before them, recoil ever and anon from the indefinite prodigiousness of their own aims, until a situation has been created which makes all turning back impossible, and the conditions themselves cry out:

Hic Rhodus, hic salta!
Here is the rose, here dance!

For the rest, every fairly competent observer, even if he had not followed the course of French development step by step, must have had a presentiment that an unheard-of fiasco was in store for the revolution. It was enough to hear the self-complacent howl of victory with which Messieurs the Democrats congratulated each other on the expected gracious consequences of the second Sunday in May 1852. In their minds the second Sunday in May 1852 had become a fixed idea, a dogma, like the day on which Christ should reappear and the millennium begin, in the minds of the Chiliasts. As ever, weakness had taken refuge in a belief in miracles, fancied the enemy overcome when he was only conjured away in imagination, and it lost all understanding of the present in a passive glorification of the future that was in store for it and of the deeds it had in petto [in secret] but which it merely did not want to carry out as yet. Those heroes who seek to disprove their demonstrated incapacity by mutually offering each other their sympathy and getting together in a crowd had tied up their bundles, collected their laurel wreaths in advance and were just then engaged in discounting on the exchange market the republics *in partibus* for which they had already providently organised the government personnel with all the calm of their unassuming disposition. December 2 struck them like a thunderbolt from a clear sky, and the peoples that in periods of pusillanimous depression gladly let their inward apprehension be drowned out by the loudest bawlers will perchance have convinced themselves that the times are past when the cackle of geese could save the Capitol.

The Constitution, the National Assembly, the dynastic parties, the blue and the red republicans, the heroes of Africa, the thunder from the platform, the sheet lightning of the daily press, the entire literature, the political names and the intellectual reputations, the civil law and the penal code, the *liberté, égalité, fraternité* and the second Sunday in May 1852—all has vanished like a phantasmagoria before the spell of a man whom even his enemies do not make out to be a magician. Universal suffrage seems to have survived only for a moment, in order that with its own hand it may make its last will and testament before the eyes of all the world and declare in the name of the people itself: All that exists deserves to perish.[1]

It is not enough to say, as the French do, that their nation was taken unawares. A nation and a woman are not forgiven the unguarded hour in which the first adventurer that came along could violate them. The riddle is not solved by such turns of speech, but merely formulated differently. It remains to be explained how a nation of thirty-six millions can be surprised and delivered unresisting into captivity by three swindlers.

Let us recapitulate in general outline the phases that the French Revolution went through from February 24, 1848, to December 1851.

Three main periods are unmistakable: *the February period*; May 4, 1848, to May 28, 1849: *the period of the constitution of the republic, or of the Constituent National Assembly*; May 28, 1849, to December 2, 1851: *the period of the constitutional republic or of the Legislative National Assembly.*

The *first period*, from February 24, or the overthrow of Louis Philippe, to May 4, 1848, the meeting of the Constituent Assembly, the *February period* proper, may be described as the *prologue* to the revolution. Its character was officially expressed in the fact that the government improvised by it itself declared that it was *provisional* and, like the government, everything that was mooted, attempted or enunciated during this period proclaimed itself to be only *provisional*.

---

[1] Mephistopheles in Goethe's *Faust*. [Unless otherwise noted, the footnotes in this selection are from the 1969 edition of Marx's *Selected Works*, published by Foreign Languages Publishing House, Moscow.—*Ed.*]

Nothing and nobody ventured to lay claim to the right of existence and of real action. All the elements that had prepared or determined the revolution, the dynastic opposition, the republican bourgeoisie, the democratic-republican petty bourgeoisie and the social-democratic workers, provisionally found their place in the February *government*.

It could not be otherwise. The February days originally intended an electoral reform, by which the circle of the politically privileged among the possessing class itself was to be widened and the exclusive domination of the aristocracy of finance overthrown. When it came to the actual conflict, however, when the people mounted the barricades, the National Guard maintained a passive attitude, the army offered no serious resistance and the monarchy ran away, the republic appeared to be a matter of course. Every party construed it in its own way. Having secured it arms in hand, the proletariat impressed its stamp upon it and proclaimed it to be a *social republic*. There was thus indicated the general content of the modern revolution, a content which was in most singular contradiction to everything that, with the material available, with the degree of education attained by the masses, under the given circumstances and relations, could be immediately realised in practice. On the other hand, the claims of all the remaining elements that had collaborated in the February Revolution were recognised by the lion's share that they obtained in the government. In no period do we, therefore, find a more confused mixture of high-flown phrases and actual uncertainty and clumsiness, of more enthusiastic striving for innovation and more deeply-rooted domination of the old routine, of more apparent harmony of the whole of society and more profound estrangement of its elements. While the Paris proletariat still revelled in the vision of the wide prospects that had opened before it and indulged in seriously-meant discussions on social problems, the old powers of society had grouped themselves, assembled, reflected and found unexpected support in the mass of the nation, the peasants and petty bourgeois, who all at once stormed on to the political stage, after the barriers of the July monarchy had fallen.

The *second period*, from May 4, 1848, to the end of May 1849, is the period of the *constitution, the foundation, of the bourgeois republic*. Directly after the February days not only had the dynastic opposition been surprised by the republicans and the republicans by the Socialists, but all France by Paris. The National Assembly, which met on May 4, 1848, had emerged from the national elections and represented the nation. It was a living protest against the pretensions of the February days and was to reduce the results of the revolution to the bourgeois scale. In vain the Paris proletariat, which immediately grasped the character of this National Assembly, attempted on May 15, a few days after it met, forcibly to negate its existence, to dissolve it, to disintegrate again into its constituent parts the organic form in which the proletariat was threatened by the reacting spirit of the nation. As is known, May 15 had no other result save that of removing Blanqui and his comrades, that is, the real leaders of the proletarian party, from the public stage for the entire duration of the cycle we are considering.

The *bourgeois monarchy* of Louis Philippe can be followed only by a *bourgeois republic,* that is to say, whereas a limited section of the bourgeoisie ruled in the name of the king, the whole of the bourgeoisie will now rule on behalf of the people. The demands of the Paris proletariat are utopian nonsense, to which an end must be put. To this declaration of the Constituent National Assembly the Paris proletariat replied with the *June Insurrection,* the most colossal event in the history of European civil wars. The bourgeois republic triumphed. On its side stood the aristocracy of finance, the industrial bourgeoisie, the middle class, the petty bourgeois, the army, the *lumpenproletariat* organised as the Mobile Guard, the intellectual lights, the clergy and the rural population. On the side of the Paris proletariat stood none but itself. More than three thousand insurgents were butchered after the victory, and fifteen thousand were transported without trial. With this defeat the proletariat passes into the *background* of the revolutionary stage. It attempts to press forward again on every occasion, as soon as the movement appears to make a fresh start, but with ever decreased expenditure of strength and always slighter results. As soon as one of the social strata situated above it gets into revolutionary ferment, the proletariat enters into an alliance with it and so shares all the defeats that the different parties suffer, one after another. But these subsequent blows become the weaker, the greater the surface of society over which they are distributed. The more important leaders of the proletariat in the Assembly and in the press successively fall victims to the courts, and ever more equivocal figures come to head it. In part it throws itself into *doctrinaire experiments, exchange banks and workers' associations, hence into a movement in which it renounces the revolutionising of the old world by means of the latter's own great, combined resources, and seeks, rather, to achieve its salvation behind society's back, in private fashion, within its limited conditions of existence, and hence necessarily suffers shipwreck.* It seems to be unable to rediscover revolutionary greatness in itself or to win new energy from the connections newly entered into, until *all classes* with which it contended in June themselves lie prostrate beside it. But at least it succumbs with the honours of the great, world-historic struggle; not only France, but all Europe trembles at the June earthquake, while the ensuing defeats of the upper classes are so cheaply bought that they require barefaced exaggeration by the victorious party to be able to pass for events at all, and become the more ignominious the further the defeated party is removed from the proletarian party.

The defeat of the June insurgents, to be sure, had now prepared, had levelled the ground on which the bourgeois republic could be founded and built up, but it had shown at the same time that in Europe the questions at issue are other than that of "republic or monarchy." It had revealed that here *bourgeois republic* signifies the unlimited despotism of one class over other classes. It had proved that in countries with an old civilisation, with a developed formation of classes, with modern conditions of production and with an intellectual consciousness in which all traditional ideas have been dissolved by the work of centuries, *the republic* signifies *in general only the political form of revolution of bourgeois society* and not its *conservative form of life,* as, for example, in the United States of North America, where, though classes already exist, they have not yet become fixed, but continually change and interchange their elements in constant flux, where the modern means of production, instead of coinciding with a stagnant surplus population, rather compensate for the relative deficiency of heads and hands, and where, finally, the feverish, youthful movement of material production, which has to make a new world its own, has left neither time nor opportunity for abolishing the old spirit world.

During the June days all classes and parties had united in the *party of Order* against the proletarian class as the *party of Anarchy,* of socialism, of communism. They had "saved" society from *"the enemies of society."* They had given out the watchwords of the old society, *"property, family, religion, order,"* to their army as passwords and had proclaimed to the counter-revolutionary crusaders: "By this sign thou shall conquer!" From that moment, as soon as one of the numerous parties which had gathered under this sign against the June insurgents seeks to hold the revolutionary battlefield in its own class interest, it goes down before the cry: "Property, family, religion, order." Society is saved just as often as the circle of its rulers contracts, as a more exclusive interest is maintained against a wider one. Every demand of the simplest bourgeois financial reform, of the most ordinary liberalism, of the most formal republicanism, of the most shallow democracy, is simultaneously castigated as an "attempt on society" and stigmatised as "socialism." And, finally, the high priests of "the religion of order" themselves are driven with kicks from their Pythian tripods, hauled out of their beds in the darkness of night, put in prison-vans, thrown into dungeons or sent into exile; their temple is razed to the ground, their mouths are sealed, their pens broken, their law torn to pieces in the name of religion, of property, of the family, of order. Bourgeois fanatics for order are shot down on their balconies by mobs of drunken soldiers, their domestic sanctuaries profaned, their houses bombarded for amusement—in the name of property, of the family, of religion and of order. Finally, the scum of bourgeois society forms the *holy phalanx of order* and the hero Crapulinski[2] installs himself in the Tuileries as the *"saviour of society."*

.   .   .

"C'est le triomphe complet et définitif du Socialisme" [This is the complete and final triumph of socialism]! Thus Guizot characterised December 2. But if the overthrow of the parliamentary republic contains within itself the germ of the triumph of the proletarian revolution, its immediate and palpable result was *the victory of Bonaparte over parliament, of the executive power over the legislative power, of force without phrases over the force of phrases.* In parliament the nation made its general will the law, that is, it made the law of the ruling class its general will. Before the executive power it renounces all will of its own and submits to the superior command of an alien will, to authority. The executive power, in contrast to the legislative power, expresses the heteronomy of a nation, in contrast to its autonomy. France, therefore, seems to have escaped the despotism of a class only to fall back beneath the despotism of an individual, and, what is more, beneath the authority of an individual without authority. The struggle seems to be settled in such a way that all classes, equally impotent and equally mute, fall on their knees before the rifle butt.

But the revolution is thoroughgoing. It is still journeying through purgatory. It does its work methodically. By December 2, 1851, it had completed one half of its preparatory work; it is now completing the other half. First it perfected the parliamentary power, in order to be able to overthrow it. Now that it has attained this, it perfects the *executive power,* reduces it to its purest expression, isolates it, sets it up against itself as the sole target, in order to concentrate all its forces of destruction against it. And when it has done this second half of its preliminary work, Europe will leap from its seat and exultantly exclaim: Well grubbed, old mole![3]

This executive power with its enormous bureaucratic and military organisation, with its ingenious state machinery, embracing wide strata, with a host of officials numbering half a million, besides an army of another half million, this appalling parasitic body, which enmeshes the body of French society like a net and chokes all its pores, sprang up in the days of the absolute monarchy, with the decay

---

[2] Louis Bonaparte.

[3] Shakespeare, *Hamlet,* Act I, Scene V.

of the feudal system, which it helped to hasten. The seignorial privileges of the landowners and towns became transformed into so many attributes of the state power, the feudal dignitaries into paid officials and the motley pattern of conflicting mediaeval plenary powers into the regulated plan of a state authority whose work is divided and centralised as in a factory. The first French Revolution, with its task of breaking all separate local, territorial, urban and provincial powers in order to create the civil unity of the nation, was bound to develop what the absolute monarchy had begun: centralisation, but at the same time the extent, the attributes and the agents of governmental power. Napoleon perfected this state machinery. The Legitimist monarchy and the July monarchy added nothing but a greater division of labour, growing in the same measure as the division of labour within bourgeois society created new groups of interests, and, therefore, new material for state administration. Every *common* interest was straightway severed from society, counterposed to it as a higher, *general* interest, snatched from the activity of society's members themselves and made an object of government activity, from a bridge, a schoolhouse and the communal property of a village community to the railways, the national wealth and the national university of France. Finally, in its struggle against the revolution, the parliamentary republic found itself compelled to strengthen, along with the repressive measures, the resources and centralisation of governmental power. All revolutions perfected this machine instead of smashing it. The parties that contended in turn for domination regarded the possession of this huge state edifice as the principal spoils of the victor.

But under the absolute monarchy, during the first Revolution, under Napoleon, bureaucracy was only the means of preparing the class rule of the bourgeoisie. Under the Restoration, under Louis Philippe, under the parliamentary republic, it was the instrument of the ruling class, however much it strove for power of its own.

Only under the second Bonaparte does the state seem to have made itself completely independent. As against civil society, the state machine has consolidated its position so thoroughly that the chief of the Society of December 10 suffices for its head, an adventurer blown in from abroad, raised on the shield by a drunken soldiery, which he has bought with liquor and sausages, and which he must continually ply with sausage anew. Hence the downcast despair, the feeling of most dreadful humiliation and degradation that oppresses the breast of France and makes her catch her breath. She feels dishonoured.

And yet the state power is not suspended in mid air. Bonaparte represents a class, and the most numerous class of French society at that, the *small-holding [Parzellen] peasants*.

Just as the Bourbons were the dynasty of big landed property and just as the Orleans were the dynasty of money, so the Bonapartes are the dynasty of the peasants, that is, the mass of the French people. Not the Bonaparte who submitted to the bourgeois parliament, but the Bonaparte who dispersed the bourgeois parliament is the chosen of the peasantry. For three years the towns had succeeded in falsifying the meaning of the election of December 10 and in cheating the peasants out of the restoration of the empire. The election of December 10, 1848, has been consummated only by the *coup d'état* of December 2, 1851.

The small-holding peasants form a vast mass, the members of which live in similar conditions but without entering into manifold relations with one another. Their mode of production isolates them from one another instead of bringing them into mutual intercourse. The isolation is increased by France's bad means of communication and by the poverty of the peasants. Their field of production, the small holding, admits of no division of labour in its cultivation, no application of science and, therefore, no diversity of development, no variety of talent, no wealth of social relationships. Each individual peasant family is almost self-sufficient; it itself directly produces the major part of its consumption and thus acquires its means of life more through exchange with nature than in intercourse with society. A small holding, a peasant and his family; alongside them another small holding, another peasant and another family. A few score of these make up a village, and a few score of villages make up a Department. In this way, the great mass of the French nation is formed by simple addition of homologous magnitudes, much as potatoes in a sack form a sack of potatoes. In so far as millions of families live under economic conditions of existence that separate their mode of life, their interests and their culture from those of the other classes, and put them in hostile opposition to the latter, they form a class. In so far as there is merely a local interconnection among these small-holding peasants, and the identity of their interests begets no community, no national bond and no political organisation among them, they do not form a class. They are consequently incapable of enforcing their class interests in their own name, whether through a parliament or through a convention. They cannot represent themselves, they must be represented. Their representative must at the same time appear as their master, as an authority over them, as an unlimited governmental power that protects them against the other classes and sends them rain and sunshine from above. The political influence of the small-holding peasants, therefore, finds its final expression in the executive power subordinating society to itself.

Historical tradition gave rise to the belief of the French peasants in the miracle that a man named Napoleon would bring all the glory back to them. And an individual turned up who gives himself out as the man because he bears the name of Napoleon, in consequence of the *Code Napoléon,* which lays down that *la recherche de la paternité est interdite* [inquiry into paternity is forbidden]. After a vagabondage of twenty years and after a series of grotesque adventures, the legend finds fulfilment and the man becomes Emperor of the French. The fixed idea of the Nephew was realised, because it coincided with the fixed idea of the most numerous class of the French people.

But, it may be objected, what about the peasant risings in half of France, the raids on the peasants by the army, the mass incarceration and transportation of peasants?

Since Louis XIV, France has experienced no similar persecution of the peasants "on account of demagogic practices."

But let there be no misunderstanding. The Bonaparte dynasty represents not the revolutionary, but the conservative peasant; not the peasant that strikes out beyond the condition of his social existence, the small holding, but rather the peasant who wants to consolidate this holding, not the country folk who, linked up with the towns, want to overthrow the old order through their own energies, but on the contrary those who, in stupefied seclusion within this old order, want to see themselves and their small holdings saved and favoured by the ghost of the empire. It represents not the enlightenment, but the superstition of the peasant; not his judgement, but his prejudice; not his future, but his past; not his modern Cévennes, but his modern Vendée.

The three years' rigorous rule of the parliamentary republic had freed a part of the French peasants from the Napoleonic illusion and had revolutionised them, even if only superficially; but the bourgeoisie violently repressed them, as often as they set themselves in motion. Under the parliamentary republic the modern and the traditional consciousness of the French peasant contended for mastery. This progress took the form of an incessant struggle between the schoolmasters and the priests. The bourgeoisie struck down the schoolmasters. For the first time the peasants made efforts to behave independently in the face of the activity of the government. This was shown in the continual conflict between the *maires* [mayors] and the prefects. The bourgeoisie deposed the *maires.* Finally, during the period of the parliamentary republic, the peasants of different localities rose against their own offspring, the army. The bourgeoisie punished them with states of siege and punitive expeditions. And this same bourgeoisie now cries out about the stupidity of the masses, the vile multitude, that has betrayed it to Bonaparte. It has itself forcibly strengthened the empire sentiments [*Imperialismus*] of the peasant class, it conserved the conditions that form the birthplace of this peasant religion. The bourgeoisie, to be sure, is bound to fear the stupidity of the masses as long as they remain conservative, and the insight of the masses as soon as they become revolutionary.

In the risings after the *coup d'état,* a part of the French peasants protested, arms in hand, against their own vote of December 10, 1848. The school they had gone through since 1848 had sharpened their wits. But they had made themselves over to the underworld of history; history held them to their word, and the majority was still so prejudiced that in precisely the reddest Departments the peasant population voted openly for Bonaparte. In its view, the National Assembly had hindered his progress. He had now merely broken the fetters that the towns had imposed on the will of the countryside. In some parts the peasants even entertained the grotesque notion of a convention side by side with Napoleon.

After the first revolution had transformed the peasants from semi-villeins into freeholders, Napoleon confirmed and regulated the conditions on which they could exploit undisturbed the soil of France which had only just fallen to their lot and slake their youthful passion for property. But what is now causing the ruin of the French peasant is his small holding itself, the division of the land, the form of property which Napoleon consolidated in France. It is precisely the material conditions which made the feudal peasant a small-holding peasant and Napoleon an emperor. Two generations have sufficed to produce the inevitable result: progressive deterioration of agriculture, progressive indebtedness of the agriculturist. The "Napoleonic" form of property, which at the beginning of the nineteenth century was the condition for the liberation and enrichment of the French country folk, has developed in the course of this century into the law of their enslavement and pauperisation. And precisely this law is the first of the *"idées napoléoniennes"* [Napoleonic ideas] which the second Bonaparte has to uphold. If he still shares with the peasants the illusion that the cause of their ruin is to be sought, not in this small-holding property itself, but outside it, in the influence of secondary circumstances, his experiments will burst like soap bubbles when they come in contact with the relations of production.

The economic development of small-holding property has radically changed the relation of the peasants to the other classes of society. Under Napoleon, the fragmentation of the land in the countryside supplemented free competition and the beginning of big industry in the towns. The peasant class was the ubiquitous protest against the landed aristocracy which had just been overthrown. The roots that small-holding property struck in French soil deprived feudalism of all nutriment. Its landmarks formed the natural fortification of the bourgeoisie against any surprise attack on the part of its old overlords. But in the course of the nineteenth century the feudal lords were replaced by urban usurers; the feudal obligation that went with the land was replaced by the mortgage; aristocratic landed property was replaced by bourgeois capital. The small holding of the peasant is now only the pretext that allows the capitalist to draw profits, interest and rent from the soil, while leaving it to the tiller of the soil himself to see how he can extract his wages. The mortgage debt burdening the soil of France imposes on the French peasantry payment of an amount of interest equal to the annual interest on the entire British national debt. Small-holding property, in this enslavement by capital to which its development inevitably pushes forward, has transformed the mass of the French nation into troglodytes. Sixteen million peasants (including women and children) dwell in hovels, a large number of which have but one opening, others only two and the most favoured only three. And windows are to a house what the five senses are to the head. The bourgeois order, which at the beginning of the century set the state to stand guard over the newly arisen small holding and manured it with laurels, has become a vampire that sucks out its blood and brains and throws them into the alchemistic cauldron of capital. The *Code Napoléon* is now nothing but a *codex* of distraints, forced sales and compulsory auctions. To the four million (including children, etc.) officially recognised paupers, vagabonds, criminals and prostitutes in France must be added five million who hover on the margin of existence and either have their haunts in the countryside itself or, with their rags and their children, continually desert the countryside for the towns and the towns for the countryside. The interests of the peasants, therefore, are no longer, as under Napoleon, in accord with, but in opposition to the interests of the bourgeoisie, to capital. Hence the peasants find their natural ally and leader in the *urban proletariat,* whose task is the overthrow of the bourgeois order. But *strong and unlimited government*—and this is the second *"idée napoléonienne,"* which the second Napoleon has to carry out—is called upon to defend this "material" order by force. This *"ordre matériel"* also serves as the catchword in all of Bonaparte's proclamations against the rebellious peasants.

Besides the mortgage which capital imposes on it, the small holding is burdened by taxes. Taxes are the source of life for the bureaucracy, the army, the priests and the court, in short, for the whole apparatus of the executive power. Strong government and heavy taxes are identical. By its very nature, small-holding property forms a suitable basis for an all-powerful and innumerable bureaucracy. It creates a uniform level of relationships and persons over the whole surface of the land. Hence it also permits of uniform action from a supreme centre on all points of this uniform mass. It annihilates the aristocratic intermediate grades between the mass of the people and the state power. On all sides, therefore, it calls forth the direct interference of this state power and the interposition of its immediate organs. Finally, it produces an unemployed surplus population for which there is no place either on the land or in the towns, and which accordingly reaches out for state offices as a sort of respectable alms, and provokes the creation of state posts. By the new markets which he opened at the point of the bayonet, by the plundering of the Continent, Napoleon repaid the compulsory taxes with interest. These taxes were a spur to the industry of the peasant, whereas now they rob his industry of its last resources and complete his inability to resist pauperism. And an enormous bureaucracy, well-gallooned and well-fed, is the *"idée napoléonienne"* which is most congenial of all to the second Bonaparte. How could it be otherwise, seeing that alongside the actual classes of society he is forced to create an artificial caste, for which the maintenance of his regime becomes a bread-and-butter question? Accordingly, one of his first financial operations was the raising of officials' salaries to their old level and the creation of new sinecures.

Another *"idée napoléonienne"* is the domination of the *priests* as an instrument of government. But while in its accord with society, in its dependence on natural forces and its submission to the authority which protected it from above, the small holding that had newly come into being was naturally religious, the small holding that is ruined by debts, at odds with society and authority, and driven beyond its own limitations naturally becomes irreligious. Heaven was quite a pleasing accession to the narrow strip of land just won, more particularly as it makes the weather; it becomes an insult as soon as it is thrust forward as substitute for the small holding. The priest then appears as only the anointed bloodhound of the earthly police—another *"idée napoléonienne."* On the next occasion, the expedition against Rome will take place in France itself, but in a sense opposite to that of M. de Montalembert.

Lastly, the culminating point of the *"idées napoléoniennes"* is the preponderance of the *army*. The army was the *point d'honneur* [matter of honor] of the small-holding peasants, it was they themselves transformed into heroes, defending their new possessions against the outer world, glorifying their recently won nationhood, plundering and revolutionising the world. The uniform was their own state dress; war was their poetry; the small holding, extended and rounded off in imagination, was their fatherland, and patriotism the ideal form of the sense of property. But the enemies against whom the French peasant has now to defend his property are not the Cossacks; they are the *huissiers* [bailiffs] and the tax collectors. The small holding lies no longer in the so-called fatherland, but in the register of mortgages. The army itself is no longer the flower of the peasant youth; it is the swamp-flower of the peasant *lumpenproletariat*. It consists in large measure of *remplaçants*, of substitutes, just as the second Bonaparte is himself only a *remplaçant*, the substitute for Napoleon. It now performs its deeds of valour by hounding the peasants in masses like chamois, by doing *gendarme* duty, and if the internal contradictions of his system chase the chief of the Society of December 10 over the French border, his army, after some acts of brigandage, will reap, not laurels, but thrashings.

One sees: *all "idées napoléoniennes" are ideas of the undeveloped small holding in the freshness of its youth*; for the small holding that has outlived its day they are an absurdity. They are only the hallucinations of its death struggle, words that are transformed into phrases, spirits transformed into ghosts. But the parody of the empire [*des Imperialismus*] was necessary to free the mass of the French nation from the weight of tradition and to work out in pure form the opposition between the state power and society. With the progressive undermining of small-holding property, the state structure erected upon it collapses. The centralisation of the state that modern society requires arises only on the ruins of the military-bureaucratic government machinery which was forged in opposition to feudalism.[4]

The condition of the French peasants provides us with the answer to the riddle of the *general elections of December 20 and 21*, which bore the second Bonaparte up Mount Sinai, not to receive laws, but to give them.

Manifestly, the bourgeoisie had now no choice but to elect Bonaparte. When the puritans at the Council of Constance complained of the dissolute lives of the popes and wailed about the necessity of moral reform, Cardinal Pierre d'Ailly thundered at them: "Only the devil in person can still save the Catholic Church, and you ask for angels." In like manner, after the *coup d'état*, the French bourgeoisie cried: Only the chief of the Society of December 10 can still save bourgeois society! Only theft can still save property; only perjury, religion; bastardy, the family; disorder, order!

As the executive authority which has made itself an independent power, Bonaparte feels it to be his mission to safeguard "bourgeois order." But the strength of this bourgeois order lies in the middle

---

[4] In the 1852 edition this paragraph ended with the following lines, which Marx omitted in the 1869 edition: "The demolition of the state machine will not endanger centralisation. Bureaucracy is only the low and brutal form of a centralisation that is still afflicted with its opposite, with feudalism. When he is disappointed in the Napoleonic Restoration, the French peasant will part with his belief in his small holding, the entire state edifice erected on this small holding will fall to the ground and *the proletarian revolution will obtain that chorus without which its solo song becomes a swan song in all peasant countries*."

class. He looks on himself, therefore, as the representative of the middle class and issues decrees in this sense. Nevertheless, he is somebody solely due to the fact that he has broken the political power of this middle class and daily breaks it anew. Consequently, he looks on himself as the adversary of the political and literary power of the middle class. But by protecting its material power, he generates its political power anew. The cause must accordingly be kept alive; but the effect, where it manifests itself, must be done away with. But this cannot pass off without slight confusions of cause and effect, since in their interaction both lose their distinguishing features. New decrees that obliterate the border line. As against the bourgeoisie, Bonaparte looks on himself, at the same time, as the representative of the peasants and of the people in general, who wants to make the lower classes of the people happy within the frame of bourgeois society. New decrees that cheat the "True Socialists" of their statecraft in advance. But, above all, Bonaparte looks on himself as the chief of the Society of December 10, as the representative of the *lumpenproletariat* to which he himself, his entourage, his government and his army belong, and whose prime consideration is to benefit itself and draw California lottery prizes from the state treasury. And he vindicates his position as chief of the Society of December 10 with decrees, without decrees and despite decrees.

This contradictory task of the man explains the contradictions of his government, the confused groping about which seeks now to win, now to humiliate first one class and then another and arrays all of them uniformly against him, whose practical uncertainty forms a highly comical contrast to the imperious, categorical style of the government decrees, a style which is faithfully copied from the Uncle.

Industry and trade, hence the business affairs of the middle class, are to prosper in hothouse fashion under the strong government. The grant of innumerable railway concessions. But the Bonapartist *lumpenproletariat* is to enrich itself. The initiated play *tripotage* [hanky-panky] on the *bourse* [Paris stock exchange] with the railway concessions. But no capital is forthcoming for the railways. Obligation of the Bank to make advances on railway shares. But, at the same time, the Bank is to be exploited for personal ends and therefore must be cajoled. Release of the Bank from the obligation to publish its report weekly. Leonine agreement of the Bank with the government. The people are to be given employment. Initiation of public works. But the public works increase the obligations of the people in respect of taxes. Hence reduction of the taxes by an onslaught on the *rentiers*, by conversion of the five per cent bonds to four-and-a-half per cent. But, once more, the middle class must receive a *douceur* [sop]. Therefore doubling of the wine tax for the people, who buy it *en détail* [retail], and halving of the wine tax for the middle class, who drink it *en gros* [wholesale]. Dissolution of the actual workers' associations, but promises of miracles of association in the future. The peasants are to be helped. Mortgage banks that expedite their getting into debt and accelerate the concentration of property. But these banks are to be used to make money out of the confiscated estates of the House of Orleans. No capitalist wants to agree to this condition, which is not in the decree, and the mortgage bank remains a mere decree, etc., etc.

Bonaparte would like to appear as the patriarchal benefactor of all classes. But he cannot give to one class without taking from another. Just as at the time of the Fronde it was said of the Duke of Guise that he was the most *obligeant* man in France because he had turned all his estates into his partisans' obligations to him, so Bonaparte would fain be the most *obligeant* man in France and turn all the property, all the labour of France into a personal obligation to himself. He would like to steal the whole of France in order to be able to make a present of her to France or, rather, in order to be able to buy France anew with French money, for as the chief of the Society of December 10 he must needs buy what ought to belong to him. And all the state institutions, the Senate, the Council of State, the legislative body, the Legion of Honour, the soldiers' medals, the washhouses, the public works, the railways, the *état-major* [General Staff] of the National Guard to the exclusion of privates, and the confiscated estates of the House of Orleans—all become parts of the institution of purchase. Every place in the army and in the government machine becomes a means of purchase. But the most important feature of this process, whereby France is taken in order to give to her, is the percentages that find their way into the pockets of the head and the members of the Society of December 10 during the turnover. The witticism with which Countess L., the mistress of M. de Morny, characterised the confiscation of the Orleans estates: *"C'est le premier vol[5] de l'aigle"* [It is the first flight (theft) of the eagle] is applicable to every flight of this *eagle* [that is, Napoleon], which is more like a *raven*. He himself and his adherents call out to one another daily like that Italian Carthusian admonishing the miser who, with boastful display, counted up the goods on which he could yet live for years to come. *"Tu fai conto sopra i beni, bisogna prima far il conto sopra gli anni."*[6] Lest they make a mistake in the years, they count the minutes. A bunch of blokes push their way forward to the court, into the ministries, to the head of the administration and the army, a crowd of the best of whom it must be said that no one knows whence he comes, a noisy, disrepu-

---

5 *Vol* means flight and theft. [Note by Marx]

6 "Thou countest thy goods, thou shouldst first count thy years." [Note by Marx]

table, rapacious bohème that crawls into gallooned coats with the same grotesque dignity as the high dignitaries of Soulouque. One can visualise clearly this upper stratum of the Society of December 10, if one reflects that *Véron-Crevel*[7] is its preacher of morals and *Granier de Cassagnac* its thinker. When Guizot, at the time of his ministry, utilised this Granier on a hole-and-corner newspaper against the dynastic opposition, he used to boast of him with the quip: *"C'est le roi des drôles,"* "he is the king of buffoons." One would do wrong to recall the Regency or Louis XV in connection with Louis Bonaparte's court and clique. For "often already, France has experienced a government of mistresses; but never before a government of *hommes entretenus* [kept men]."[8]

Driven by the contradictory demands of his situation and being at the same time, like a conjurer, under the necessity of keeping the public gaze fixed on himself, as Napoleon's substitute, by springing constant surprises, that is to say, under the necessity of executing a *coup d'état en miniature* every day, Bonaparte throws the entire bourgeois economy into confusion, violates everything that seemed inviolable to the Revolution of 1848, makes some tolerant of revolution, others desirous of revolution, and produces actual anarchy in the name of order, while at the same time stripping its halo from the entire state machine, profanes it and makes it at once loathsome and ridiculous. The cult of the Holy Tunic of Treves he duplicates at Paris in the cult of the Napoleonic imperial mantle. But when the imperial mantle finally falls on the shoulders of Louis Bonaparte, the bronze statue of Napoleon will crash from the top of the Vendôme Column.

---

[7] In his work, *Cousine Bette,* Balzac delineates the thoroughly dissolute Parisian philistine in Crevel, a character which he draws after the model of Dr. Véron, the proprietor of the *Constitutionnel.* [Note by Marx]

[8] The words quoted are those of Madame Girardin. [Note by Marx]

Louis Chevalier

9

Violence and the
Working Class in Paris,
1815–1848

JOURNEYMEN'S VIOLENCE

At certain periods, and particularly during the first ten years of the Restoration, in certain trades and certain neighborhoods of the capital, workers' violence took a form that was definitely foreign to city life, and extended to the heart of the city journeymen's conflicts, which were definitely provincial and rural in nature. These workers' clashes, which broke out on certain evenings on the Ile Saint Louis, near La Grève, in Saint-Denis or at the gates, filling the city jails with ordinarily conscientious, hard-working, well-behaved workers, were only the urban expression of conflicts between journeymen's societies which were on the rise at that time. Describing those years, Agricol Perdiguier wrote: "The journeymen's societies were armed enemies, rival societies."

The Parisian conflicts were purely rural in the sense that they took place there as elsewhere along the traditional itinerary of the *tour de France*,[1] which is one long battle; they took place at work sites, at inns, along roads, and so on. They occurred particularly in certain places, the sites of ancient and memorable episodes, which seemed constantly to engender violence and to stir up conflict. They clung to the unavoidable crossroads, to the obligatory river crossings—for example, at Nantes, where with the help of a little white wine, violence was endemic; at Blois, which in 1827 witnessed the great battle that inspired George Sand's description of the struggle between the *gavots* and the *drilles*; in the countryside of the Midi which, according to Perdiguier, "was the scene of virtual warfare between workers." Paris was also prey

---

[1] After their apprenticeship years, journeymen undertook to travel around the country, stopping in various cities to work and to further perfect their skills. This period was known as the *tour de France.—Ed.*

to such group violence because it was one of the main crossroads of the *tour de France*.

This violence was also purely of a journeyman nature because it corresponded to traditions of struggle that were not those of the city. The combat technique was different: It involved the use of bare fists, a pure confrontation between two physical forces. The only weapons were the fist, the cane, and the club. Perdiguier writes:

> In those days, the journeymen, especially the truck-farmers, the blacksmiths, the carpenters, the stonecutters, the shoemakers, the bakers, the tanners, all knew how to wield the club and frequently attacked with this weapon. The soldier had to retreat before the journeyman, his sabre twisted or broken under the club; it was a formidable weapon. After six or seven years of service, the soldier could return to his village as provost or master of arms; the journeyman returned as provost or master of the club. . . .

The technique was also different in that individual fights were the exception, unless the individuals were simply representatives of their respective groups assigned to settle some collective scores. The scenes of action were also different. Some battles took place in the center of the city, near the shops and work sites. "The group spirit which has taken hold of the apprentice hatters, following the example of other workers, often produces deadly results," says the *Journal des Débats* of November 9, 1825. "They are divided into two societies, one known as the *compagnons du devoir* or *les dévorants*, the other as *les bons enfants* or *les droguistes*. On October 7, members of these two journeymen's societies fought with each other and blood was spilt." We also read in the June 16, 1827, issue of the same journal:

> The day before yesterday at about noon the rue des Rosiers and adjacent streets were the scene of many gatherings of hatmakers, known as the *boursiers moireux des bons enfants*. Soon other hatters calling themselves the *compagnons du devoir* came to the spot, and a serious fight began. That evening, the *bons enfants* again attacked the *compagnons du devoir*, who were congregated at their headquarters on the rue de Charonne. There was another fight, with clubs. Twenty workers were arrested and taken to the police station.

Other places, however, were more frequently the scene of confrontations between the old journeymen's societies. These were at some distance from the city, far from the Parisian public, the gendarmes, the busybodies; for example, at the gate of Monceau or near Bercy.

These conflicts were also purely of a journeyman nature in the sense that they resulted from problems of concern only to the rival societies and usually had nothing to do with events in the city. For this reason, they were all the more conspicuous (and also all the more puzzling to the authorities, who merely registered them without any real understanding) when the economic situation was favorable, and neither the condition of the labor market nor the wage rate explains why these workers should have been trying to kill one another. Often, of course, professional interests are at stake:

On May 23, 1833, 50 carpenters armed with so-called journeymen's clubs marched in a body to the market of Sceaux to interrupt the work of their comrades who, it seems, had taken control of a carpenters' company, in violation of the society's statutes. One man was knocked off a wall and was clubbed over the head.

More frequently, the cause of the conflict was some old question of honor, all the more obvious when the times were quiet and the workers had few reasons for discontent. A gendarmerie report states:

On November 5, 1836, a group of carpenters and one of bakers, coming from opposite directions, met on the Neuilly plain to settle an old score between the two societies. There were 500 carpenters against 100 bakers. Three people, sent to negotiate in the name of the bakers, were mistreated in a brutal, cowardly way.

Thus, in the midst of Parisian violence, certain conflicts stand out. Profoundly different from the others, easy to recognize and to identify, they belong to a tradition which is not that of Paris.

PARISIAN VIOLENCE

The journeymen's traditions of violence mingled in Paris with other, specifically Parisian traditions, however, and were transformed, as a result, to the point where they gave rise to behavior that was no longer just that of the journeymen's societies, but simply Parisian, as shown by the spectacle of brutality provided by the working-class population of the capital, regardless of its origin, in the second half of the July Monarchy.

The worker population of Paris was indeed no less brutal than that of the provinces, but in another way.

Urban Violence

They were a violent people, especially in certain trades. In all the descriptions we have of the times, the butchers are associated with scenes of violence, whether at work or in their leisure hours at their favorite entertainment, the animal fights at the Combat Gate, where they were the most faithful customers. But the people as a whole were prone to violence, although in a different way. Theirs was not the muscular violence of the country people, used to long walks, to work in the fields, or to the physical labor of the work sites, but the nervous violence of ill-nourished people who drank too much. It was not the collective, codified, regulated violence of the great journeymen's conflicts that took place in the open air of the fields or outside the gates, but rather the violence of individual vengeance that occurred when coming out of the workshop, at the street corner, at a dance, or during the great days of debauchery of the Courtille which for contemporary writers typifies the habits of the working classes. "To really understand the spirit of the workers of the Faubourg Saint Antoine," writes Luchet, "you must study them on Monday, the day of rest. You must go with them into the taverns of the Place du Trône and see how they settle their differences with their feet."

Foot-Boxing
It is, as a matter of fact, the use of the foot that best characterizes working-class violence in Paris then and now. Foot-boxing (the *savate*) originated, developed, and is still practiced in the slum neighborhoods of Paris and at the gates, especially the Courtille, the worst of all, where it found its first theoretician in the person of Michel Pisseux, an old baker once the terror of the neighborhood. "Foot-boxing," writes Theophile Bautier in *La Presse* of August 17, 1846, "was long considered a nasty form of combat fit only for the pale hoodlum with a puny body, his skin as yellow as an old coin. Indeed, only horrible bandits in overalls full of holes, torn caps, and worn-out shoes were known in earlier times to resort to these sinister and mysterious gestures of the hands, so frightening to the law-abiding citizen, these movements of the feet that caught the patrolman off guard and made him sit down suddenly in the gutter." This "hoodlum's fencing," this "boxing for the Cour des Miracles" is practiced with a low, squatting guard; the hands are only a defensive weapon, forward and open, to push the adversary's face, to give him a "nosebag"; leg work and kicks in the underbelly play the major role.

Although codified by Michel and his pupils, and practiced later by Parisian dandies and the friends of Sue,[2] this slum technique was to

---

[2] The expression "friends of Sue" refers to the characters created by the novelist Eugene Sue in his *Mysteries of Paris,* first published in 1843. This novel, very important for our knowledge of the Parisian workers in this period, was one of the first to reflect the increasing concern of contemporaries over the radical transformation the city was then undergoing.—*Ed.*

continue to reign in the slums and to draw from them its main inspiration. But news items in the press and the court records tell us that this technique was also widely practiced by the workers of Paris.

Although it is clear that the workers' taste for force and violence was not merely a journeyman survival, it is necessary to refer to these urban traditions to understand the transformation of journeyman violence in the Paris environment, to see how it was intensified and then declined.

PARISIAN VIOLENCE AND JOURNEYMEN'S VIOLENCE
The first period—until the end of the crisis that coincides with the first years of the July Monarchy—witnessed the exacerbation of this violence, then its decline and transformation.

The Exacerbation of Journeymen's Violence

The Causes. In Paris the journeymen's societies found themselves in a state of permanent rivalry not only among themselves, but also with the Parisian professional organizations. They rubbed elbows in a limited labor market, on the same work sites, in the same streets, sometimes in the same tenements. Within the great societies themselves, competition between various groups became more intense. Provincial and departmental groupings were splintered by canton and village. Referring to the year 1834, which saw a sharp increase of jealousy and hatred between workers of different groups. Nadaud writes:

First of all, the journeymen doing their *tour de France* continued to get involved in bloody fighting among themselves. And the workers from the Creuse were divided into clans according to their cantons and villages. If by chance they met on the same work site, they would immediately try to beat each other up. Then would begin one of those struggles where the boss is the only winner.

The provincial journeymen's societies themselves became excited by these Parisian conflicts. "If we had behaved like cowards," writes Perdiguier, describing these encounters along the road or in the fields, "they would certainly have known about it in the tenements of Paris; for under no circumstances must an insult to the mason's society go unpunished."

Finally, we must add to the rivalry among societies and among regional or village groups the competition with the Parisian workers—not only at work, but also at rest or play. In this overcrowded city, people lived alongside one another at one another's expense, or at any rate within full view of one another.

We find any number of references to these conflicts and humiliations in the *Mémoires* of Nadaud (1895): the sarcasm of the salesmen in the stores of the rue Saint-Fiacre, laughing aloud when they hear the masons calling their buddies on the nearby scaffolding by the names of their region or their trade; the attitude of passers-by "when they see us gathered in the evening at the doors of our tenements, or covered with plaster on leaving the work site." An even bitterer pill was the refusal of the girls to dance with them at a ball, at the Courtille! The result was the journeymen's violence described by Nadaud or recorded by the police. It broke out during the first years of the July Monarchy and differed from the violence of the preceding or following years. There was violence at work: "His great reputation," writes Nadaud of one of his fellow workers in 1831, "came from his muscular strength. He used to brag that no one could beat him at passing the bricks up the ladder, nor in the hand-to-hand fights that took place after a bet or when the journeymen would play among themselves. We of today can hardly realize to what extent strength was valued in those days." And there was violence at play: "Fights broke out then between Auvergnats and Limousins at the Poissonnière gate on Sunday," writes Nadaud. "The state of mind and the strength of certain customs were such that if workers would return to their tenements from a romp without showing the signs of having been in a good fight, their friends would say that they had not enjoyed themselves. Our manners were rough."

The significance of this violence goes far beyond these brutalities. "Then the masons of the Creuse began to develop a sense of pride and independence that would not permit them to feel inferior to the workers of any other trade." The history of workers' violence, the petty history of fistfights, merges here with the great history of social and political events. Nadaud writes:

At that time there was a great period of dissoluteness in our neighborhood, which lasted for two or three years. The freedom we desired and which the newspaper promised us every day inflamed our minds and—since we had but little education or knowledge—the slightest insult made us kick back like husky mules when they are whipped in the fields. We told each other that we must punish with our fists anyone who expressed a low opinion of the chestnut eaters of Limoges and the Creuse. We went around in bands. The police rarely interfered.

No one who would understand the general history of Paris during these years can afford to ignore this violence. He must give equal attention to those sober workshops where well-behaved workmen (of whom there were not so many) spent their leisure time to create a workers' literature and a workers' press, and to those popular places where workers in far greater numbers came to flex their muscles. The history of the boxing halls *(salles de chausson)* is no less important for social and political history than the history of the workshops where, from September 1830, the *Journal des ouvriers,* the *Artisan,* and *le Peuple* were produced. Physical violence had a political significance. . . . The opening of numerous gymnasiums in the Hotel de Ville and la Cité neighborhoods between 1830 and 1834 reveals a state of mind that traditional history records in other forms. It expresses a new attitude on the part of the working-class population. It is not irrelevant to note that it is of rural origin and will retain the marks of its birth for a long time to come. During the second half of the nineteenth century, the majority of the managers of the gymnasiums were former masons or even builders, and some of them combined the two occupations, construction and wrestling. (It should be added that the technique of rural violence contrasts sharply with the Parisian technique of the *savate.* The *chausson* is a noble sport, and the victory goes to the most skillful and the most loyal. The face and the chest are the only targets, not the underbelly.)

The Decline and Transformation of Journeymen's Violence

Little by little, however, the journeymen's violence, like the journeymen's societies themselves, took on a completely different character in Paris. Just as the journeymen merged into the Parisian working masses, the journeymen's violence became increasingly similar to the proletarian violence mentioned earlier.

"Communities and Communions." Yet what resistance was put up by these groups, in which contemporary sociological analysis would easily recognize the characteristic traits of what are called "communities" and "communions"! What homogeneity and coherence were displayed by these closed circles, planted in the midst of the working-class mass, but distinct from it, and fully defended against it! There were the common origins, not only rural and departmental, but also cantonal and communal. There were the common trades and common careers, developing at the same rhythm for each age category. There were the common traditions of migration, taking place at the same seasons, following the same itinerary, and ending up, if not at the same work sites, at least in the same neighborhoods, the same employment centers, the same cafés, the same dormitories. For example, the Nadauds lived for generations, at 62 rue de la Tisseranderie, which was owned, also for generations, by the same family. There were the common family habits concerning the close association of father and son for work, earnings, and par-

ticularly savings, and also concerning marriage arrangements. "The women who married masons had a strange lot," writes Nadaud. "Today some of them bring their young wives with them, but formerly this was not the custom. Each had to live separately, often to the age of fifty, aside from the intervals of the winter season." And finally, there were the common concerns and common memories. In the dormitories of Paris, the talk was all of the native village and region they had left. "Those who are not married," writes Nadaud, "poke fun at the married men concerning the women they have left behind. Often homesickness forces the older ones to hurry back." Each dormitory was a village lost under the roofs of the tall workers' tenements of the Cité, far from the rest of a hostile Paris and buttressed against it.

The Threatened Groups. During the July Monarchy, these defenses weakened and fell. The reasons for this have often been described, but some of them appear particularly significant. First of all, there was the lowering of the average age of members of the group, and the increasing conflict between the older generation, intolerant guardians of outdated rules, and the youth who had little patience with these strange rituals, these curious ordeals, often cruel and sometimes obscene. Describing the young journeymen arriving in Paris after 1830, Nadaud writes:

There was a group of about twenty young people from the canton of Pontarion or of Saint-Sulpice-les-Champs, very hard-working and polite to each other, who came to Paris after the 1830 Revolution. They were not at all the same type of people as those of the preceding generation. Their conversation was more pleasant, as were their manners and their way of dressing, especially when not at work. Our predecessors had after all grown up under the gloved hand of the nobles and priests brought in by the coalition armies in 1815. . . . The people were kept in complete ignorance and learned little more than the catechism.

The causes connected with the Paris environment, however, are more important. The hold of the city was stronger than in previous periods because the traditional rhythm of the migrations was interrupted. From about 1840, the seasonal migrations diminished and no longer functioned as automatically as they had under the Restoration. This is apparent first of all in the upsetting of the normal pattern of coming and going between Paris and the provinces. It still continued, but it was no longer considered useful, and it was sometimes even felt as a burden. Martin Nadaud's memoirs bring out very well this decadence of an old custom, surviving only on the strength of its past. Now the worker hesitated to take this long trip, which was so tiring and even dangerous. A coach service now linked Paris with the furthest province, but instead of facilitating the old habit of periodically returning, this new means of transportation seems to have made it still more difficult. The trip was expensive, and rather than spend a large part of his savings to undertake it, the provincial preferred to remain in Paris.

The improvement in transportation had another effect: The trip may have been too expensive for the Parisian to return to the province, but it rarely prevented the provincial from going to Paris. In the hope of earning more later, he cheerfully accepted the expense; and since that expense was of little importance in comparison with the ease of the trip to Paris, the movement from the countryside to the city was naturally accentuated. The arrival of these newcomers with every intention of settling in the capital forced the older generation of immigrants to take root as well. The development of railways did the rest. In 1847, out of 9,287 masons, 4,859 were sedentary and 4,428 were mobile; 39 percent had their own homes and 61 percent lived in furnished quarters. "A small number," according to a Chamber of Commerce survey, "return every year to the province, and these are mostly married workers. More often they return only every two or three years, especially when their earnings are particularly good." The 1860 survey still records seasonal returns, but in increasingly smaller numbers.

From the end of the July Monarchy, this change influenced the integration of these immigrants into the Paris environment. The prolonged and then continuous residence of the provincials in Paris led to the formation of a working-class mass that was homogeneous in its composition as well as in its suffering. Until then, Paris was distinguished from other great working-class cities like Lyon, Mulhouse, and Lille by the greater variety of its workers. The building workers formed a group apart from the mass of the labor force; only a small number of immigrants became accustomed to Paris life, and the others returned to their native villages after a few years. The different colonies of immigrants from the Creuse, the Corrèze, the Haute-Vienne, and also those, somewhat less numerous, from the eastern departments never consisted of the same individuals. Around 1840, the new development was not the disappearance of these colonies, for they continued to exist alongside each other in the various neighborhoods. Now, however, they consisted of increasingly stable elements. Natives of Lorraine or Limousin could still be distinguished, alongside the Parisians, but now these people, who returned only rarely to their provinces and lived and died in Paris, became more like genuine Parisians, despite their special traits and customs. Neighborhoods, traditions, speech persisted, but more as signs of loyalty than as a way of life. Paris was still the crossroads of the provinces, but the people of these provinces became less provincial in their habits, and the workers tended to become class-conscious.

There were also causes other than professional ones. The major one was the population expansion, in which the journeymen not only participated, but felt its effects in the same way as other groups. . . . Journeymen's literature of the period . . . blames the city for all the ills of the time. . . . Describing the neighborhood of place Maubert, Nadaud . . . writes:

We found ourselves in the neighborhood of rue Saint Victor, a stone's throw from the place Maubert and the many narrow dirty streets of the area, in a center of ragged children, of women stupefied in stinking bars with their children on their arms or sleeping on the tables or on the floor. These poor little creatures only left this depraved, disgusting, filthy scene to go stealing in the streets, where the police picked them up and packed them off to prison.

In the journeymen's classic descriptions, the mechanisms whereby the city ruined these groups are the same as those we have already mentioned. To as great an extent as the major literary and social works we have studied, these journeymen's writings are genuine documents concerning the influence of the city environment, from the moral and material point of view, on the people. In them we can see how the harsh urban environment succeeded in destroying the group—its rules, its beliefs, its homogeneity, as well as the personal pride that belonging to a community gives each of its members. The general rules governing the life of the Paris workers, and particularly the most underprivileged among them, finally prevailed over the rules of the group: different hiring conditions; different working conditions; different daily living conditions; different habits so far as food, drink, sleep, and pleasure are concerned. In addition to all this, there was a further consequence of settling in Paris: the arrival of the women, and with it not only a complete break with the village, since there was no longer any reason to return there, but also a complete break with what remained of the village in Paris because of the impossibility of bringing the wife to live in the dormitory.

The immigrants were than submerged in a common condition of poverty, an urban poverty that Nadaud describes, speaking of the first and last ten years of the July Monarchy, in a passage that deserves to be quoted, if only to underline the relevance of the economic and biological factors we have already studied:

We saw this poverty at close range in its immense variety, and we were able to compare the poverty of the countryside with that of the city. The latter is much more terrible. It sickens the body and the mind, destroys the body and stifles the morale. It is a slowly applied torture that dulls the sensitivity. In the cities there are no resources when there is no work for the arms of a proletarian, there is no shelter, no clothing, no bread. In his destitution, charity—disdainful, insulting, and too often inadequate—is his only refuge. In Paris I recall seeing the workers crowd around the coffee or potato vendors. Pale-faced, barely covered with a few miserable rags, eating for a penny or two—all these unfortunates encumber the Public Assistance centers. It was the same thing at the beggars' depots and the prisons.

Hunger, sickness, death: these were the main themes of journeymen's poverty, as well as of the poverty of the Parisian workers. And prison awaited them both. Not only did the journeymen's misery become more and more identical with typical Parisian misery, but it also adopted the corresponding behavior: violence. Individual violence assumed forms that are not those of the journeymen—for example, knife brawls, "which are so frequent that it is to be feared that they are becoming part of the customs of the people." The violence also reveals the connection we have often emphasized with criminality. In those days of swift and merciless justice, how many workers were pushed into a criminal situation by the bad luck of a blow or a knife thrust, a dare at work, a drunken brawl or a shove? There was also collective violence, either during typical journeymen's strikes or in the midst of those great social and political upheavals in which the journeymen no longer played a role as such, but were members of a larger community, suffering and rebelling together.

The history of Paris during the Restoration and the July Monarchy, as told successively by historians of political events, historians of workers' struggles, and historians of economic facts can be supplemented by the study of another dimension: that of the crowd. The older descriptions remain valid—electoral struggles, professional conflicts, riots and revolutions, as well as social and political groups and ideas—but they are strongly affected by the demographic considerations presented here . . . which can easily be collected and reorganized. The social and political violence that has been so minutely and so frequently studied is limited to crisis and to special situations. It is complemented by other types of violence that are more continuous, more complex, harsher, involving greater numbers, and taking their sweep, their unity, and their force from the upsurge and weight of the masses. Crises are linked to other crises. Public dramas are reinforced by private, daily dramas that develop independently of them, but accumulate and come to a head in and through them. To this violence the weight of the masses lends a different character and a different meaning. Over and above the class conflicts, and regardless of the increasing class consciousness, there has been a purely Parisian problem over the years: the problem of a population trying to make a place for itself in a hostile environment and—unable to succeed—giving vent to all kinds of hatred and violence. Class struggle, of course, but reinforced by another kind of struggle, which contemporaries themselves describe as one of race, as a conflict between two populations distinct in every respect, but primarily in their very bodies, distinct not only socially, but biologically.

This contemporary view is confirmed by so many facts that the conclusions reached by this history justify larger conclusions concerning not only the biological aspects of the history of Paris throughout these years, but also the biological foundations of social history.

IV/THE RISORGIMENTO

I
T took a long time for Italy to trade its status as a "geographical expression" (Metternich) for nationhood. Fragmentation was maintained by the presence in the peninsula of "foreign" powers like Austria and the papacy, but that presence was in turn made possible only by the class conflicts that divided Italians among themselves. In other words, unity could only be forged by a national front, an alliance between the bourgeoisie, the substantial segments of the peasantry, and the still-limited numbers of urban workers. Only then would they be capable of confronting and defeating the great semi-feudal landlords whose interest it was to keep things as they were.

The process of nationalist struggle and nation-building reached a triple climax in 1848, 1861, and 1870. In 1848, republican revolutions in Venice, Rome, and Naples temporarily defeated the forces of reaction, but the massive Austrian intervention of the following year together with structural weaknesses of the revolutionary movement soon dashed all hopes for knitting the liberated territories into a viable state. Ten years later, the balance of power was altered by Louis Napoleon's defeat of the Austrians at Solferino, and France's willingness to support Piedmontese nationalist ambitions in return for the annexation of Nice and Savoy. In 1861, the combined forces of the Piedmontese monarchy and the popular militia of Garibaldi and his followers made possible the creation of the Kingdom of Italy. But it was not until 1870 when the Second Empire of Louis Napoleon, facing disaster at home, withdrew the troops it had sent to protect the papacy, that the last piece, Rome and the Papal States, was fitted into the puzzle. Italy was at long last united, but the form of the unified society was yet to be decided. What eventually emerged under the leadership of the moderates (bourgeois originally associated with the Piedmontese monarchy under Cavour) was a non-revolutionary state favoring the domination of the North over the South and the development of modern capitalist social relations. This was not, however, the only alternative. It might have been possible for the Party of Action, the most popularly based and radical group among the revolutionary forces, to take a different turn and to organize a Jacobin-type mass movement, which in turn would have guaranteed the creation of a more thoroughgoing bourgeois democratic regime.

It is normal that a country so recently united should be obsessed with this theme in its historical literature. As in the case of the French and their revolution, the viewpoint of an Italian intellectual in regard to the Risorgimento is a good index of his attitude on a whole range of social issues. The identification of a man of the left with Garibaldi goes beyond the myth and the symbolism of the red shirt; it takes on an aura of lost opportunities and the resolve to make them good the next time around. It is indeed what the Italian historian Rosario Romeo calls a "practical political" conception, but is it necessarily therefore ahistorical? In a system of thought that emphasizes the need to tie together theory and practice, this would not seem to be the case.

Antonio Gramsci (1891–1937) was one of the founders of the Italian Communist party in 1921. Imprisoned by the Fascists between 1926 and 1937, he devoted his time to a study of Italian history and Marxist theory. The prison notebooks he kept during this period have become a classic of Italian culture, and it is from them that the following selection is taken. Gramsci was at some pains to demonstrate that Marxist theory could take into account political and ideological forces at work in the real world. He evolved the theory of hegemony as a means of explaining the exercise of class power. In brief, he distinguished between two characteristics of a ruling class: domination and direction. The former was acquired by seizing power, but the latter might already be in existence or, in any case, had to be secured if the kingdom were not to stand on brittle glass. Domination means political control, but direction is the imposition of intellectual and cultural norms as an ideology. Only when a class exercises both simultaneously can it truly be called hegemonic. In regard to the Risorgimento, Gramsci argues that the Action Party never acceded to true hegemony, since the moderates continued to influence and co-opt them. Hence the failure of the Italian movement of unification to take on a more positive (that is, Jacobin) shape.

Gramsci has been sharply challenged by other Italian historians, in particular by Rosario Romeo, whose critique is reprinted here. Romeo argues that Gramsci's political motivation gets in the way of the search for truth, of his appreciation of reality. It is charged that he wanted to apply the French Jacobin model to Italy and that this is an invalid procedure. Furthermore, the agrarian revolution of which Gramsci dreamt was a practical impossibility—and it is a good thing, because it could only have hindered the economic development of the country. The facts of the matter are open to continuing argument; it does seem to me, however, that Gramsci's use of the Jacobin model is perfectly justified by the canons of comparative history, for nowhere does it assume a simple, mechanistic correspondence between France and Italy at a distance of three-quarters of a century. Moreover, granting that economic development was the order of the day, it did not have to take the form it did, nor did the peasantry have to bear the burden. This celebration of the straight and narrow path taken by the Risorgimento tends not only to recount "things as they really were," but to sanctify them. In a way, Romeo's attack parallels the Furet-Richet thesis on the French Revolution (section I) in being a refusal to view the past—or certain events in it—as truly open to inquiry.

Antonio Gramsci

10

The Risorgimento

THE PROBLEM OF POLITICAL LEADERSHIP IN THE
FORMATION AND DEVELOPMENT OF THE NATION
AND THE MODERN STATE IN ITALY

The whole problem of the connection between the various political currents of the Risorgimento—of their relations with each other, and of their relations with the homogeneous or subordinate social groups existing in the various historical sections (or sectors) of the national territory—can be reduced to the following basic factual datum. The Moderates[1] represented a relatively homogeneous social group, and hence their leadership underwent relatively limited oscillations (in any case, subject to an organically progressive line of development); whereas the so-called Action Party[2] did not base itself specifically on any historical class, and the oscillations which its leading organs underwent were resolved, in the last analysis, according to the interests of the Moderates. In other words, the Action

---

[1] The Moderate Party, formally constituted in 1848, had grown out of the neo-Guelph movement (see note 4). Its first document was C. Balbo's *Le speranze d'Italia* (1844), and its ideas inspired the reforms of 1846–47. It stood initially for a confederation of the Italian States, and demanded reforms and written constitutions in each state. It was to some extent eclipsed in 1849, but its influence increased during the ten years from 1849–59, under the leadership of d'Azeglio and Cavour. It abandoned federalism, and was in fact the main instrument, at the level of political institutions, of national unification in 1859–61, and the main beneficiary of the Risorgimento. After Cavour's death in 1861, it became the Right in the Italian parliament, and held power until 1876. [Unless otherwise noted, the footnotes in this selection were added by the translators of the *Prison Notebooks.—Ed.*]

[2] The *Partito d'Azione* was founded by Mazzini in March 1853, after the defeat of the February rising in Milan and the dissolution of the *Associazione Nazionale Italiana*. It was republican, but its ambiguous aims were symbolised by its motto *"Dio e popolo"* (God and the people). After several years of tenuous existence, it was revitalised by Garibaldi's influence in 1859, and played an important role in the organisation of the Sicilian expedition of the Thousand. After the unification of the country, most of its members joined the parliamentary "Left," a minority of the tiny Republican Party.

Party was led historically by the Moderates. The assertion attributed to Victor Emmanuel II that he "had the Action Party in his pocket," or something of the kind, was in practice accurate—not only because of the King's personal contacts with Garibaldi, but because the Action Party was in fact "indirectly" led by Cavour and the King.

The methodological criterion on which our own study must be based is the following: that the supremacy of a social group manifests itself in two ways, as "domination" and as "intellectual and moral leadership." A social group dominates antagonistic groups, which it tends to "liquidate," or to subjugate perhaps even by armed force; it leads kindred and allied groups. A social group can, and indeed must, already exercise "leadership" before winning governmental power (this indeed is one of the principal conditions for the winning of such power); it subsequently becomes dominant when it exercises power, but even if it holds it firmly in its grasp, it must continue to "lead" as well. The Moderates continued to lead the Action Party even after 1870 and 1876, and so-called "transformism"[3] was only the parliamentary expression of this action of intellectual, moral and political hegemony. Indeed one might say that the entire State life of Italy from 1848 onwards has been characterised by transformism—in other words by the formation of an ever more extensive ruling class, within the framework established by the Moderates after 1848 and the collapse of the neo-Guelph[4] and federalist[5] utopias. The formation of this class involved the gradual but continuous absorption, achieved by methods which varied in their effectiveness, of the active elements produced by allied groups—and even of those which came from antagonistic groups

---

[3] *Trasformismo.* This term was used from the 1880s onwards to describe the process whereby the so-called "historic" Left and Right parties which emerged from the Risorgimento tended to converge in terms of programme during the years which followed, until there ceased to be any substantive difference between them— especially after the "Left" came to power under Depretis in 1876 and the latter began to recruit his ministers indiscriminately from both sides of the parliament. The two main parties disintegrated into personal cliques and factions, which characterised Italian parliamentary life until fascism. . . .

[4] Neo-Guelphism was a liberal catholic movement in Italy in the first half of the nineteenth century. The term was coined by its enemies (the Guelphs had been the Papal party in mediaeval and pre-renaissance Italy), but was accepted by its members—who were quite willing to be identified with the pre-renaissance Papacy, which they saw as symbolising Italian unity and independence. Their aim was an Italian federation under the Pope. . . . The movement's ideals were definitively proved illusory when the Risorgimento created a national Italian state under the Piedmont monarchy, and when the Pope refused to come to terms with that state; most of its members in fact then rallied to the monarchy. . . .

[5] There were various federalist tendencies in pre-Risorgimento Italy, in opposition to the unitary concept of the future Italian state held on the one hand by Mazzini and Garibaldi, and on the other by Cavour and the Piedmont monarchy. . . .

and seemed irreconcilably hostile. In this sense political leadership became merely an aspect of the function of domination—in as much as the absorption of the enemies' *élites* means their decapitation, and annihilation often for a very long time. It seems clear from the policies of the Moderates that there can, and indeed must, be hegemonic activity even before the rise to power, and that one should not count only on the material force which power gives in order to exercise an effective leadership. It was precisely the brilliant solution of these problems which made the Risorgimento possible, in the form in which it was achieved (and with its limitations)—as "revolution" without a "revolution," or as "passive revolution." . . .

In what forms, and by what means, did the Moderates succeed in establishing the apparatus (mechanism) of their intellectual, moral and political hegemony? In forms, and by means, which may be called "liberal"—in other words through individual, "molecular," "private" enterprise (i.e. not through a party programme worked out and constituted according to a plan, in advance of the practical and organisational action). However, that was "normal" given the structure and the function of the social groups of which the Moderates were the representatives, the leading stratum, the organic intellectuals.[6]

For the Action Party, the problem presented itself differently, and different systems of organisation should have been adopted. The Moderates were intellectuals already naturally "condensed" by the organic nature of their relation to the social groups whose expression they were. (As far as a whole series of them were concerned, there was realised the identity of the represented and the representative; in other words, the Moderates were a real, organic vanguard of the upper classes, to which economically they belonged. They were intellectuals and political organisers, and at the same time company bosses, rich farmers or estate managers, commercial and industrial entrepreneurs,

---

[6] *Editor's Note:* Gramsci was much concerned with the role of intellectuals in society, and made some fundamental contributions to Marxist thought on this subject. Quintin Hoare and Geoffrey Nowell Smith, the translators of his *Prison Notebooks,* have written: "[In Gramsci's view] the notion of 'the intellectuals' as a distinct social category independent of class is a myth. All men are potentially intellectuals in the sense of having an intellect and using it, but not all are intellectuals by social function. Intellectuals in the functional sense fall into two groups. In the first place there are the 'traditional' professional intellectuals, literary, scientific, and so on, whose position in the interstices of society has a certain inter-class aura about it but derives ultimately from past and present class formations. Secondly, there are the 'organic' intellectuals, the thinking and organising element of a particular fundamental social class. These organic intellectuals are distinguished less by their profession, which may be any job characteristic of their class, than by their function in directing the ideas and aspirations of the class to which they organically belong."

etc.) Given this organic condensation or concentration, the Moderates exercised a powerful attraction "spontaneously," on the whole mass of intellectuals of every degree who existed in the peninsula, in a "diffused," "molecular" state, to provide for the requirements, however rudimentarily satisfied, of education and administration. One may detect here the methodological consistency of a criterion of historico-political research: there does not exist any independent class of intellectuals, but every social group has its own stratum of intellectuals, or tends to form one; however, the intellectuals of the historically (and concretely) progressive class, in the given conditions, exercise such a power of attraction that, in the last analysis, they end up by subjugating the intellectuals of the other social groups; they thereby create a system of solidarity between all the intellectuals, with bonds of a psychological nature (vanity, etc.) and often of a caste character (technico-juridical, corporate, etc.). This phenomenon manifests itself "spontaneously" in the historical periods in which the given social group is really progressive—i.e. really causes the whole society to move forward, not merely satisfying its own existential requirements, but continuously augmenting its cadres for the conquest of ever new spheres of economic and productive activity. As soon as the dominant social group has exhausted its function, the ideological bloc tends to crumble away; then "spontaneity" may be replaced by "constraint" in ever less disguised and indirect forms, culminating in outright police measures and *coups d'état*.

The Action Party not only could not have—given its character—a similar power of attraction, but was itself attracted and influenced: on the one hand, as a result of the atmosphere of intimidation (panic fear of a terror like that of 1793, reinforced by the events in France of 1848–49) which made it hesitate to include in its programme certain popular demands (for instance, agrarian reform); and, on the other, because certain of its leading personalities (Garibaldi) had, even if only desultorily (they wavered), a relationship of personal subordination to the Moderate leaders. For the Action Party to have become an autonomous force and, in the last analysis, for it to have succeeded at the very least in stamping the movement of the Risorgimento with a more markedly popular and democratic character (more than that perhaps it could not have achieved, given the fundamental premisses of the movement itself), it would have had to counterpose to the "empirical" activity of the Moderates (which was empirical only in a manner of speaking, since it corresponded perfectly to the objective) an organic programme of government which would reflect the essential demands of the popular masses, and in the first place of the peasantry. To the "spontaneous" attraction of the Moderates it would have had to counterpose a resistance and a counter-offensive "organised" according to a plan.

As a typical example of spontaneous attraction by the Moderates, one might recall the formation and development of the "liberal-catholic" movement[7] which scared the Papacy so much—partially succeeding in paralysing its movements; demoralising it; in an initial period pushing it too far to the left (with the liberalising measures of Piux IX); in a subsequent period driving it into a more right-wing position than it need have adopted; and in the last analysis being the cause of its isolation in the peninsula and in Europe. The Papacy has since demonstrated that it has learnt its lesson, and has shown itself capable in more recent times of manœuvring brilliantly. Modernism first, and later Popularism,[8] are movements resembling the liberal-catholic movement of the Risorgimento, due in great part to the power of spontaneous attraction exercised on the one hand by the modern historicism of the secular intellectuals of the upper classes, and on the other by the practical movement of the philosophy of praxis.[9] The Papacy combated Modernism as a tendency aimed at reforming the Church and the Catholic religion, but it encouraged Popularism— i.e. the socio-economic basis of Modernism—and today with Pius XI is making it the pivot of its world policies.

---

[7] Liberal catholic movements developed in several European countries—France, Belgium, Italy, England, etc.—in the early and mid-nineteenth century. In Italy they included notably the neo-Guelphs. Their common ideological basis was an acceptance of the main body of bourgeois liberal thought at the time. In Italy, after the blow of the Pope's withdrawal to the Lateran in 1870, liberal catholicism more or less disappeared, but as Gramsci points out it can be seen as a precursor of the "Modernist" movement (see following note).

[8] Modernism was an intellectual movement which developed among catholics in the late nineteenth and early twentieth centuries. Its proclaimed aims were to bring the Church into harmony with the culture and society of the contemporary world— especially with new developments in scientific and sociological thinking. It was condemned by the Papal decree *Lamentabili* and the Encyclical *Pascendi* in 1907. However, via the work notably of Romolo Murri, it was an important ideological ancestor of contemporary Christian Democracy.

The Popular Party was founded by Luigi Sturzo and others in January 1919. Based on social-christian ideas current throughout Europe at the time, it was encouraged initially by the Papacy (as a political movement directed outwards, and not towards reform of the Church itself like Modernism). It grew swiftly— especially in the agricultural areas of North and Central Italy, where it set up "white" unions whose strength among the small peasants often outstripped that of their "red" rivals. After vacillating in its attitude towards fascism between 1921–25, it was suppressed in 1925–26 like the other opposition parties. After the fall of fascism, it re-emerged as the Christian Democrat Party.

[9] i.e. Modernism and Popularism were a result of—and aimed to counteract—the influence of Croce and Gentile on the one hand, and of socialism on the other.

But the Action Party lacked even a concrete programme of government. In essence it was always, more than anything else, an agitational
and propagandist body in the service of the Moderates. The disagreements and internal conflicts of the Action Party, and the tremendous
hatred which Mazzini aroused among the more valiant men of action
(Garibaldi, Felice Orsini,[10] etc.) against himself personally and against
his activities, were caused by the lack of any firm political leadership.
These internal polemics were for the most part as abstract as Mazzini's
preaching, but it is possible to draw useful historical indications from
them. . . . The Action Party was steeped in the traditional rhetoric of
Italian literature. It confused the cultural unity which existed in the
peninsula—confined, however, to a very thin stratum of the population, and polluted by the Vatican's cosmopolitanism—with the political and territorial unity of the great popular masses, who were foreign
to that cultural tradition and who, even supposing that they knew of
its existence, couldn't care less about it. A comparison may be made
between the Jacobins and the Action Party. The Jacobins strove with
determination to ensure a bond between town and country, and they
succeeded triumphantly. Their defeat as a specific party was due to
the fact that at a certain point they came up against the demands of
the Paris workers; but in reality they were perpetuated in another
form by Napoleon, and today, very wretchedly, by the radical-socialists
of Herriot and Daladier.

In French political literature, the necessity of binding the town
(Paris) to the countryside had always been vividly felt and expressed.
It is enough to recall the series of novels by Eugène Sue,[11] very widely
disseminated in Italy too. . . . Sue's novels stress with particular insistence the necessity of having a concern for the peasantry, and of binding it to Paris. And Sue was the popular novelist of the Jacobin
political tradition, and a "primary source" for Herriot and Daladier[12]
from many points of view (Napoleonic legend, anti-clericalism and
anti-Jesuitism, petty bourgeois reformism, penal theories, etc.).

It is true that the Action Party was always implicitly anti-French
by virtue of its Mazzinian ideology but it found in the history of the

---

10 Felice Orsini (1819–58). After participating in the early stages of the Risorgimento
as a follower of Mazzini, he broke with the latter in the mid-50s and made an
attempt in 1858 to assassinate Napoleon III, for which he was executed.

11 Eugène Sue (1804–57) was the author of a series of extremely popular novels of
Paris life published by instalments in the 1840s and 1850s, e.g. *Les Mystères de
Paris* (1842–43), *Le Juif Errant* (1844–45), *Les Sept Péchés Capitaux* (1847–49), *Les
Mystères du Peuple* (1849–57). Set in a popular milieu, they contained a mish-mash
of vaguely humanitarian and democratic ideas. *Les Mystères de Paris* and its ideal-
istic interpreters were savagely lampooned by Marx in *The Holy Family*.

12 French "Radicals" prominent in the twenties and thirties—both were prime
ministers.

peninsula a tradition to which it could go back and attach itself. The history of the mediaeval Communes is rich in relevant experiences: the nascent bourgeoisie seeks allies among the peasant against the Empire and against the local feudalism. (It is true that the question is complicated by the struggle between bourgeoisie and nobles competing for cheap labour. The bourgeoisie needs an abundant supply of labour, which can only be provided by the rural masses—but the nobles want the peasants tied to the soil: flight of the peasants into the cities where the nobles cannot capture them. In any case, even though the situation is different, there is apparent in the development of Communal civilisation the function of the city as a directive element, of the city which deepens the internal conflicts of the countryside and uses them as a politico-military instrument to strike down feudalism.) But the most classic master of the art of politics for the Italian ruling classes, Machiavelli, had also posed the problem—naturally in the terms and with the preoccupations of his time. In his politico-military writings, the need to subordinate the popular masses organically to the ruling strata, so as to create a national militia capable of eliminating the companies of fortune, was quite well understood.

. . .

If one goes deeper into the question, it appears that from many aspects the difference between many members of the Action Party and the Moderates was more one of "temperament" than of an organically political character. The term "Jacobin" has ended up by taking on two meanings: there is the literal meaning, characterised historically, of a particular party in the French Revolution, which conceived of the development of French life in a particular way, with a particular programme, on the basis of particular social forces; and there are also the particular methods of party and government activity which they displayed, characterised by extreme energy, decisiveness and resolution, dependent on a fanatical belief in the virtue of that programme and those methods. In political language the two aspects of Jacobinism were split, and the term "Jacobin" came to be used for a politician who was energetic, resolute and fanatical, because fanatically convinced of the thaumaturgical virtues of his ideas, whatever they might be. This definition stressed the destructive elements derived from hatred of rivals and enemies, more than the constructive one derived from having made the demands of the popular masses one's own; the sectarian element of the clique, of the small group, of unrestrained individualism, more than the national political element. Thus, when one reads that Crispi[13] was a Jacobin, it is in this derogatory sense that

---

13 Francesco Crispi (1818–1901). At first a Sicilian autonomist, he became linked with Mazzini and converted to the aim of a unitary post-Risorgimento Italian state. In 1859 he organised an insurrection in Sicily, and played an important part in

the assertion should be understood. In his programme, Crispi was a Moderate pure and simple. His most noble Jacobin "obsession" was the politico-territorial unity of the country. This principle was always the compass by which he took his direction, not only in the period of the Risorgimento, in the strict sense, but in the succeeding period as well, when he was a member of the government. A man of strong passions, he hated the Moderates as individuals: he saw in them the latecomers, the heroes of the eleventh hour; people who would have made peace with the old régimes if these had become constitutional; people like the Tuscan Moderates, who clung to the Grand Duke's coat-tails, afraid that he might run away. He had little trust in a unity achieved by non-unitarians. Hence he tied himself to the monarchy, which he realised would be resolutely unitarian for dynastic reasons, and embraced the principle of Piedmontese hegemony with an energy and ardour which the very Piedmontese politicians themselves could not match. Cavour had warned that the South should not be dealt with by placing it under martial law: Crispi on the contrary at once established martial law and set up military courts in Sicily after the Fasci movement,[14] and accused the leaders of the Fasci of plotting with England for the secession of Sicily (pseudo-treaty of Bisacquino).[15] He allied himself closely with the Sicilian latifundists, since their fear of the demands of the peasantry made them the stratum most dedicated to unity, at the same time as overall policy was tending to reinforce Nothern industrialism by means of the tariff war against France and customs protectionism. He did not hesitate to plunge the South and the Islands into a terrifying commercial crisis, so long as he was able to reinforce the industry which could give the country a real independence, and which would expand the cadres of the dominant social group: this is the policy of manufacturing the manufacturer. The

---

Garibaldi's expedition of 1860. After the achievement of national unity, he became a parliamentary deputy of the Left. In 1865 he broke with Mazzini and rallied to the monarchy. He was Minister of the Interior and consistent advocate of Italian colonial expansion, notably into Ethiopia. In 1893–94 he repressed the Sicilian Fasci (see following note) with extreme savagery. In many ways he can be seen as a precursor of the nationalist and fascist movements of the twentieth century.

[14] *Fasci dei lavoratori* ("workers' leagues"), led by socialists, spread throughout Sicily in 1892–93. They were basically peasant organisations, and their main aim was the break-up of the big estates and distribution of the land. They had considerable success in securing improved contracts between peasants and landowners in 1893. In 1893–94, under the impact of the economic crisis of that year, the peasantry rose throughout the island, and was repressed with great brutality by Crispi.

[15] It was rumoured that contacts had taken place at Bisacquino, near Palermo, between representatives of the Fasci and the English, with a view to detaching Sicily from Italy and establishing it as an independent state.

government of the Right from 1861 to 1876 had merely, and timidly, created the general external conditions for economic development—rationalisation of the government apparatus, roads, railways, telegraph—and had restored to health the country's finances, over-burdened by the wars of the Risorgimento. The Left had attempted to remedy the hatred aroused among the people by the Right's unilateral fiscalism, but it had only succeeded in acting as a safety-valve: it had continued the policies of the Right with a left-wing personnel and phraseology. Crispi, on the other hand, gave the new Italian society a real heave forward: he was the true man of the new bourgeoisie. His figure, however, is characterised by a disproportion between deeds and words, between the repressions and their objects, between the instrument and the blow delivered; he handled a rusty culverin as if it were a piece of modern artillery. Crispi's colonial policy too is connected with his obsession with unity, and in it he proved able to understand the political innocence of the Mezzogiorno [the area south of Rome]. The southern peasant wanted land, and Crispi, who did not want to (or could not) give it to him in Italy itself, who had no wish to go in for "economic Jacobinism," conjured up the mirage of colonial lands to be exploited. Crispi's imperialism was passionate, oratorical, without any economic or financial basis. Capitalist Europe, rich in resources and arrived at the point at which the rate of profit was beginning to reveal its tendency to fall, had a need to widen the area of expansion of its income-bearing investments; thus, after 1890, the great colonial empires were created. But the still immature Italy not only had no capital to export, but had to have recourse to foreign capital for its own pressing needs. Hence there was lacking any real drive behind Italian imperialism, and it was substituted for by the strong passions of the peasants, blindly intent on possessing land. It was a question of an exigency of internal politics which had to be resolved, and was—by the sidetracking of its solution to infinity. Hence Crispi's policy was opposed by the (northern) capitalists themselves, who would more willingly have seen employed in Italy the huge sums spent in Africa; but in the South Crispi was popular for having created the "myth" of easy land.

Crispi left a profound stamp upon an enormous number of Sicilian intellectuals (these especially, though he influenced all Italian intellectuals, creating the first cells of a national socialism which was later to develop vertiginously).[16] He created that unitarian fanaticism which brought about a permanent atmosphere of suspicion against

---

[16] i.e. the nationalist party, which as Gramsci showed in *Alcuni temi* was effectively founded by ex-socialists and syndicalists (e.g. Corradini, with his concept of the "proletarian nations"), and fascism, which claimed to be a national socialism.

anything which might have the air of separatism. This, however (understandably), did not prevent the Sicilian latifundists from meeting in Palermo in 1920, and pronouncing a literal ultimatum against the government "of Rome," threatening secession; just as it did not prevent several of these latifundists from continuing to keep Spanish nationality, nor from calling on the Madrid government's diplomatic intervention to safeguard their interests, threatened by the agitation of the peasants back from the war. The attitude of the various social groups in the Mezzogiorno from 1919 to 1926 serves to reveal and to emphasise certain weaknesses of the obsessively unitarian approach of Crispi, and to emphasise certain corrections contributed to it by Giolitti. These were very few in reality, since Giolitti essentially kept to the furrow traced by Crispi. For the temperamental Jacobinism of Crispi, Giolitti substituted bureaucratic diligence and continuity; he kept up the "mirage of land" in colonial policy. . . .

Another element in evaluating the real significance of the obsessedly unitary policies of Crispi is the complex of feelings created in the North with regard to the Mezzogiorno. The poverty of the Mezzogiorno was historically "inexplicable" for the popular masses in the North; they did not understand that unity had not taken place on a basis of equality, but as hegemony of the North over the Mezzogiorno in a territorial version of the town-country relationship—in other words, that the North concretely was an "octopus" which enriched itself at the expense of the South, and that its economic-industrial increment was in direct proportion to the impoverishment of the economy and the agriculture of the South. The ordinary man from Northern Italy thought rather that, if the Mezzogiorno made no progress after having been liberated from the fetters which the Bourbon régime placed in the way of a modern development, this meant that the causes of the poverty were not external, to be sought in objective economic and political conditions, but internal, innate in the population of the South—and this all the more since there was a deeply-rooted belief in the great natural wealth of the terrain. There only remained one explanation—the organic incapacity of the inhabitants, their barbarity, their biological inferiority. These already widespread opinions were consolidated and actually theorised by the sociologists of positivism, acquiring the strength of "scientific truth" in a period of superstition about science. Thus a polemic arose between North and South on the subject of race, and about the superiority or inferiority of North and South. Meanwhile, in the North there persisted the belief that the Mezzogiorno was a "ball and chain" for Italy, the conviction that the modern industrial civilisation of Northern Italy would have made greater progress without this "ball and chain," etc. The early years of this century then saw the beginnings of a strong

Southern reaction on this very subject. In the Sardinian Congress of
1911, held under the presidency of General Rugiu, a calculation was
made of how many hundreds of millions had been extorted from
Sardinia in the first fifty years of the unitary State, to the advantage
of the mainland. Then came Salvemini's campaigns—brought to their
culmination in the foundation of *Unità*, but already being waged in
Voce. In Sardinia an autonomist movement started, under the leadership of Umberto Cau, which also had a daily newspaper: *Il Paese*. In
those early years of the century a certain "intellectual bloc"—a "pan-
Italian" one—was created; it was led by B. Croce and Giustino Fortunato, and sought to pose the Southern Question as a national problem
capable of renovating political and parliamentary life. Not simply the
influence of Croce and Fortunato, but their contributions, were to be
seen in every review of the younger generation which had liberal
democratic tendencies and proposed in general to rejuvenate and
deprovincialise national life and culture in all fields—in art, in literature, in politics.

. . .

From this series of observations and analyses of certain elements of
Italian history after unity, certain criteria may be drawn for evaluating
the position of confrontation between the Moderates and the Action
Party, and for investigating the respective political "wisdom" of these
two parties and of the various tendencies which contested the political
and ideological leadership of the latter of them. It is obvious that, in
order to counterpose itself effectively to the Moderates, the Action
Party ought to have allied itself with the rural masses, especially those
in the South, and ought to have been "Jacobin" not only in external
"form," in temperament, but most particularly in socio-economic
content. The binding together of the various rural classes, which was
accomplished in a reactionary bloc by means of the various legitimist-
clerical intellectual strata, could be dissolved, so as to arrive at a new
liberal-national formation, only if support was won from two directions: from the peasant masses, by accepting their elementary demands
and making these an integral part of the new programme of government; and from the intellectuals of the middle and lower strata, by
concentrating them and stressing the themes most capable of interesting them (and the prospect of a new apparatus of government being
formed, with the possibilities of employment which it offered, would
already have been a formidable element of attraction for them—if
that prospect had appeared concrete, because based on the aspirations
of the peasantry).

The relation between these two actions was dialectical and recipro-
cal: the experience of many countries, first and foremost that of France
in the period of the great Revolution, has shown that, if the peasants

move through "spontaneous" impulses, the intellectuals start to waver; and, reciprocally, if a group of intellectuals situates itself on a new basis of concrete pro-peasant policies, it ends up by drawing with it ever more important elements of the masses. However, one may say that, given the dispersal and the isolation of the rural population and hence the difficulty of welding it into solid organisations, it is best to start the movement from the intellectual groups; however, in general, it is the dialectical relation between the two actions which has to be kept in mind. It may also be said that peasant parties in the strict sense of the word are almost impossible to create. The peasant party generally is achieved only as a strong current of opinion, and not in schematic forms of bureaucratic organisation. However, the existence even of only a skeleton organisation is of immense usefulness, both as a selective mechanism, and for controlling the intellectual groups and preventing caste interests from transporting them imperceptibly onto different ground.

These criteria must be kept in mind when studying the personality of Giuseppe Ferrari, who was the Action Party's unheeded "specialist" on agrarian questions. It is also necessary to study closely Ferrari's attitude towards the agricultural labourers [bracciantato], i.e. the landless peasants who live by day-labour. It is on these that he bases a notable part of his ideological positions, for which he is still sought out and read by certain schools of thought. It must be recognised that the problem of the agricultural labourers is an extremely difficult one, and even today very hard to solve. In general, the following criteria must be borne in mind: the agricultural labourers to this day are for the most part simply peasants without land (hence were all the more so in the Risorgimento period) and not the workers of an agricultural industry developed through concentration of capital and the division of labour. Moreover, in the period of the Risorgimento, tied labour [obbligato] was considerably more widespread than casual labour [avventizio]. Their psychology is therefore, with all due exceptions, the same as that of the farmer and the small-holder.

The question was posed in acute form not so much in the Mezzogiorno, where the artisanal character of agricultural labour was too obvious, as in the Po valley where it was more disguised. Even in recent times, however the existence of an acute problem of the agricultural labourers in the Po valley was partly due to extra-economic causes: 1. over-population, which did not find an outlet in emigration as in the South, and was artificially maintained through the policy of public works; 2. policy of the landowners, who did not wish to consolidate the working population into a single class of agricultural labourers and share-croppers [mezzadri]; they alternated sharecropping with leaseholding, utilising this alternation in order to bring about a better selection of privileged sharecroppers who would be their allies: in every congress of landowners from the Po region, there was always a discussion on whether sharecropping or direct tenancy was more advantageous, and it was clear that the choice was made for motives of a socio-political character. During the Risorgimento, the problem of the Po agricultural labourers appeared in the guise of a terrible phenomenon of pauperism. . . .

Ferrari's position is moreover weakened by his "federalism"; especially in his case—living in France as he did—this appeared all the more like a reflection of the national and State interests of France. Proudhon should be recalled, with his pamphlets against Italian unity —combated from the declared standpoint of French State interest and of democracy. In reality, the principal tendencies of French politics were bitterly opposed to Italian unity. To this day the monarchists (Bainville and Co.) "reproach" retrospectively the two Napoleons with having created the "nationalitarian" myth, and with having helped to secure its realisation in Germany and Italy, thus lowering the relative stature of France, which "ought" to be surrounded by a swarm of little states of the Switzerland type in order to be "secure."

Now the Moderates after 1848 formed a national bloc under their own hegemony—influencing the two supreme leaders of the Action Party, Mazzini and Garibaldi, in different ways and to a different extent. They did this precisely under the slogan of "independence and unity," without taking any account of the concrete political content of such generic formulae. How successful the Moderates had been in their intention of diverting attention from the kernel to the husk is demonstrated, among so many other examples, by this expression of Guerrazzi's in a letter to a Sicilian student: "Whatever we desire— whether it is despotism or republic or anything else—let us not seek division among ourselves; with this guiding principle, the world can collapse and we will still find the way again." In any case, Mazzini's entire activity was concretely devoted to a continuous and permanent preaching of unity.

On the subject of Jacobinism and the Action Party, an element to be highlighted is the following: that the Jacobins won their function of "leading" [dirigente] party by a struggle to the death; they literally "imposed" themselves on the French bourgeoisie, leading it into a far more advanced position than the originally strongest bourgeois nuclei would have spontaneously wished to take up, and even far more advanced than that which the historical premises should have permitted—hence the various forms of backlash and the function of Napoleon I. This feature, characteristic of Jacobinism (but before that, also of Cromwell and the "Roundheads") and hence of the entire French Revolution, which consists in (apparently) forcing the situation, in creating irreversible *faits accomplis,* and in a group of extremely energetic and determined men driving the bourgeois forward with kicks in the backside, may be schematized in the following way. The Third Estate was the least homogeneous; it had a very disparate intellectual élite, and a group which was very advanced economically but politically moderate. Events developed along highly interesting lines. The representatives of the Third Estate initially only posed those questions which interested the actual physical members of the social group, their immediate "corporate" interests (corporate in the traditional sense, of the immediate and narrowly selfish interests of a particular category). The precursors of the Revolution were in fact moderate reformers, who shouted very loud but actually demanded very little. Gradually a new élite was selected out which did not concern itself solely with "corporate" reforms, but tended to conceive of the bourgeoisie as the hegemonic group of all the popular forces. This selection occurred through the action of two factors: the resistance of the old social forces, and the international threat. The old forces did not wish to concede anything, and if they did concede anything they did it with the intention of gaining time and preparing a counter-offensive. The Third Estate would have fallen into these successive "pitfalls" without the energetic action of the Jacobins, who opposed every "intermediate" halt in the revolutionary process, and sent to the guillotine not only the elements of the old society which was hard a-dying, but also the revolutionaries of yesterday—today become reactionaries. The Jacobins, consequently, were the only party of the revolution in progress, in as much as they not only represented the immediate needs and aspirations of the actual physical individuals who constituted the French bourgeoisie, but they also represented the revolutionary movement as a whole, as an integral historical development. For they represented future needs as well, and, once again, not only the needs of those particular physical individuals, but also of all the national groups which had to be assimilated to the existing fundamental group. It is necessary to insist, against a tendentious and fundamentally anti-historical school of thought, that the Jacobins were realists of the Machiavelli stamp and not abstract dreamers. They were convinced of the absolute truth of their slogans about equality, fraternity and liberty, and, what is more important, the great popular masses whom the Jacobins stirred up and drew into the struggle were also convinced of their truth. The Jacobins' language, their ideology, their methods of action reflected perfectly the exigencies of the epoch, even if "today," in a different situation and after more than a century of cultural evolution, they may appear "abstract" and "frenetic." . . . The first necessity was to annihilate the enemy forces, or at least to reduce them to impotence in order to make a counter-revolution impossible. The second was to enlarge the cadres of the bourgeoisie as such, and to place the latter at the head of all the national forces; this meant identifying the interests and the requirements common to all the national forces, in order to set these forces in motion and lead them into the struggle, obtaining two results: (a) that of opposing a wider target to the blows of the enemy, i.e. of creating a politico-military relation favourable to the revolution; (b) that of depriving the enemy of every zone of passivity in which it would be possible to enrol Vendée-type armies.[17] Without the agrarian policy of the Jacobins, Paris would have had the Vendée at its very doors. The resistance of the Vendée properly speaking is linked to the national question, which had become envenomed among the peoples of Brittany and in general among those alien to the slogan of the "single and indivisible republic" and to the policy of bureaucratic-military centralisation—a slogan and a policy which the Jacobins could not renounce without committing suicide. The Girondins tried to exploit federalism in order to crush Jacobin Paris, but the provincial troops brought to Paris went over to the revolutionaries. Except for certain marginal areas, where the national (and linguistic) differentiation was very great, the agrarian question proved stronger than aspirations to local autonomy. Rural France accepted the hegemony of Paris; in other words, it understood that in order definitively to destroy the old régime it had to make a bloc with the most advanced elements of the Third Estate, and not with the Girondin moderates. If it is true that the Jacobins "forced" its hand, it is also true that this always occurred in the direction of real historical development. For not only did they organise a bourgeois government, i.e. make the bourgeoisie the dominant class—they did more. They created the bourgeois State, made the bourgeoisie into the leading, hegemonic class of the nation, in other words gave the new State a permanent basis and created the compact modern French nation.

That the Jacobins, despite everything, always remained on bourgeois ground is demonstrated by the events which marked their end, as a party cast in too specific and inflexible a mould, and by the death of Robespierre. Maintaining the Le Chapelier law, they were not willing to concede to the workers the right of combination; as a consequence they had to pass the law of the *maximum*.[18] They thus broke the Paris

---

[17] From 1793–96 royalist priests and landowners fomented peasant guerrilla warfare against the Republic in the Vendée region in western France.

[18] The Le Chapelier law of June 1791 was brought in to dissolve the craft guilds which had survived from the *ancien régime*. Although it was in conception a "progressive" bourgeois measure, it was used throughout the first half of the nineteenth century to ban workers' associations.

The law of the *maximum* fixed a ceiling for food prices and for wages, and drove a wedge between the Jacobins and the workers.

urban bloc: their assault forces, assembled in the Commune, dispersed in disappointment, and Thermidor gained the upper hand. The Revolution had found its widest class limits. The policy of alliances and of permanent revolution had finished by posing new questions which at that time could not be resolved; it had unleashed elemental forces which only a military dictatorship was to succeed in containing.[19]

In the Action Party there was nothing to be found which resembled this Jacobin approach, this inflexible will to become the "leading" [dirigente] party. Naturally one has to allow for the differences: in Italy the struggle manifested itself as a struggle against old treaties and the existing international order, and against a foreign power— Austria—which represented these and upheld them in Italy, occupying a part of the peninsula and controlling the rest. This problem arose in France too, in a certain sense at least, since at a certain point the internal struggle became a national struggle fought at the frontiers. But this only happened after the whole territory had been won for the revolution, and the Jacobins were able to utilise the external threat as a spur to greater energy internally: they well understood that in order to defeat the external foe they had to crush his allies internally, and they did not hesitate to carry out the September massacres.[20] In Italy, although a similar connection, both explicit and implicit, did exist between Austria and at least a segment of the intellectuals, the nobles and the landowners, it was not denounced by the Action Party; or at least it was not denounced with the proper energy and in the most practically effective manner, and it did not become a real political issue. It became transformed "curiously" into a question of greater or lesser patriotic dignity, and subsequently gave rise to a trail of acrimonious and sterile polemics which continued even after 1898.

If in Italy a Jacobin party was not formed, the reasons are to be sought in the economic field, that is to say in the relative weakness of the Italian bourgeoisie and in the different historical climate in Europe after 1815. The limit reached by the Jacobins, in their policy of forced reawakening of French popular energies to be allied with the bourgeoisie, with the Le Chapelier law and that of the *maximum*, appeared in 1848 as a "spectre" which was already threatening—and this was skillfully exploited by Austria, by the old governments and

---

[19] Gramsci is here referring to what he elsewhere terms the "forty-eightist" slogan of "permanent revolution," since it was first put forward by Marx during the 1848 wave of bourgeois revolutions in the belief that these would lead directly to proletarian revolutions. . . .

[20] Between 2 and 5 September 1792, at the insistence notably of Marat, some 1200 royalist prisoners were massacred. They were accused of having by their treachery brought about the defeats suffered by the revolutionary armies prior to the battle of Valmy.

even by Cavour (quite apart from the Pope). The bourgeoisie could not (perhaps) extend its hegemony further over the great popular strata—which it did succeed in embracing in France—(could not for subjective rather than objective reasons); but action directed at the peasantry was certainly always possible. [There were] differences between France, Germany and Italy in the process by which the bourgeoisie took power (and England). It was in France that the process was richest in developments, and in active and positive political elements. In Germany, it evolved in ways which in certain aspects resembled what happened in Italy, and in others what happened in England. In Germany, the movement of 1848 failed as a result of the scanty bourgeois concentration (the Jacobin-type slogan was furnished by the democratic Far Left: "permanent revolution"), and because the question of renewal of the State was intertwined with the national question. The wars of 1864, 1866 and 1870[21] resolved both the national question and, in an intermediate form, the class question: the bourgeoisie obtained economic-industrial power, but the old feudal classes remained as the governing stratum of the political State, with wide corporate privileges in the army, the administration and on the land. Yet at least, if these old classes kept so much importance in Germany and enjoyed so many privileges, they exercised a national function, became the "intellectuals" of the bourgeoisie, with a particular temperament conferred by their caste origin and by tradition. In England, where the bourgeois revolution took place before that in France, we have a similar phenomenon to the German one of fusion between the old and the new—this notwithstanding the extreme energy of the English "Jacobins," i.e. Cromwell's "roundheads." The old aristocracy remained as a governing stratum, with certain privileges, and it too became the intellectual stratum of the English bourgeoisie (it should be added that the English aristocracy has an open structure, and continually renews itself with elements coming from the intellectuals and the bourgeoisie). The explanation given by Antonio Labriola of the fact that the Junkers and Kaiserism continued in power in Germany, despite the great capitalist development, adumbrates the correct explanation: the class relations created by industrial development, with the limits of bourgeois hegemony reached and the position of the progressive classes reversed, have induced the bourgeoisie not to struggle with all its strength against the old régime, but to allow a part of the latter's façade to subsist, behind which it can disguise its own real domination.

These variations in the actual process whereby the same historical development manifests itself in different countries have to be related

---

21 With Denmark, Austria and France respectively.

not only to the differing combinations of internal relations within the
different nations, but also to the differing international relations (international relations are usually underestimated in this kind of research).
The Jacobin spirit, audacious, dauntless, is certainly related to the
hegemony exercised for so long by France in Europe, as well as to the
existence of an urban centre like Paris and to the centralisation attained in France thanks to the absolute monarchy. The Napoleonic
wars on the other hand, intellectually so fertile for the renovation of
Europe, nonetheless through their enormous destruction of manpower
—and these were men taken from among the boldest and most enterprising—weakened not only the militant political energy of France but
that of other nations as well.

International relations were certainly very important in determining
the line of development of the Italian Risorgimento, but they were
exaggerated by the Moderate Party, and by Cavour for party reasons.
Cavour's case is noteworthy in this connection. Before the Quarto[22]
expedition and the crossing of the Straits, he feared Garibaldi's initiative like the devil, because of the international complications which it
might create. He was then himself impelled by the enthusiasm created
by the Thousand in European opinion to the point where he saw as
feasible an immediate new war against Austria. There existed in Cavour a certain professional diplomat's distortion, which led him to see
"too many" difficulties, and induced him into "conspiratorial" exag-
gerations, and into prodigies (which to a considerable extent were
simply tightrope-walking) of subtlety and intrigue. In any case Cavour
acted eminently as a party man. Whether in fact his party represented
the deepest and most durable national interests, even if only in the
sense of the widest extension which could be given to the community
of interests between the bourgeoisie and the popular masses, is another
question.

In examining the political and military leadership imposed on the
national movement before and after 1848, it is necessary to make certain preliminary observations of method and terminology. By military
leadership should be understood not only military leadership in the
strict, technical sense, i.e. with reference to the strategy and the tactics
of the Piedmontese army, or of Garibaldi's troops or of the various
militias improvised in the course of local insurrections (Five Days
of Milan, defense of Venice, defense of the Roman Republic, Palermo
insurrection of 1848, etc.). It should be understood rather in a far
wider sense, and one which is more closely connected with political

---

22 It was at Quarto, near Genoa, that Garibaldi lived prior to the Sicilian expedition, and from there that the expedition set sail.

leadership properly speaking. The essential problem which had to be faced from the military point of view was that of expelling from the peninsula a foreign power, Austria, which had at its disposal one of the largest armies in Europe at that time, and whose supporters in the peninsula itself, moreover, even in Piedmont, were neither few nor weak. Consequently, the military problem was the following: how to succeed in mobilising an insurrectional force which was capable not only of expelling the Austrian army from the peninsula, but of preventing it from being able to come back with a counter-offensive—given the fact that the violent expulsion would endanger the complex structure of the Empire, and hence would galvanise all the forces interested in its cohesion for a reconquest.

Numerous abstract solutions to the problem were presented, all of them contradictory and ineffective. "Italy will go it alone" was the Piedmontese slogan of 1848, but it meant catastrophic defeat. The uncertain, ambiguous, timid and at the same time foolhardy policies of the right-wing Piedmontese parties was the principal reason for the defeat. They were capable only of petty cunning. They were the cause of the withdrawal of the armies of the other Italian States, those of Naples and of Rome, when they showed too early that they wanted Piedmontese expansion and not an Italian confederation. They did not favour, but opposed the volunteer movement. They, in short, wanted the only military victors to be the Piedmontese generals, incapable of commanding in so difficult a war. The absence of a popular policy was disastrous. The Lombard and Venetian peasants enrolled by Austria were one of the most effective instruments for suffocating the Vienna revolution, and hence also that of Italy. For the peasants the movement in Lombardy-Veneto, like the Viennese movement, was an affair of gentlemen and of students. Whereas the Italian national parties ought to have, by their policies, brought about or assisted the dissolution of the Austrian Empire, in fact by their inertia they saw to it that the Italian regiments were one of the best supports for Austrian reaction. In the struggle between Piedmont and Austria, the strategic objective could not be that of destroying the Austrian army and occupying the enemy's territory, for this would have been an unattainable and utopian objective. But it could have been that of dissolving Austria's internal cohesion, and of assisting the liberals to gain power firmly and change the political structure of the Empire into a federalist one, or at least to create within it a prolonged state of internal struggles which would give a breathing-space to the Italian national forces, and permit them to regroup themselves politically and militarily.

Having started the war with the slogan "Italy will go it alone," after the defeat, when the entire undertaking was endangered, an attempt was made to gain French assistance. This occurred precisely at the time when, partly as a result of the reinforcement of Austria, the reactionaries had come to power in France—the enemies of a unitary and strong Italian State, and also of Piedmontese expansion.[23] France did not wish to give Piedmont even an experienced general, and the latter had to turn to the Pole Chrzanowski.

Military leadership was a larger question than the leadership of the army and the working out of the strategic plan which the army was to execute. It included also the politico-insurrectional mobilisation of popular forces who would rise in revolt at the enemy's back and obstruct his movements and logistic services; and the creation of mass auxiliary and reserve forces from which new regiments could be drawn, and which would give to the "technical" army an atmosphere of enthusiasm and ardour.

The policy of popular mobilisation was not carried out even after 1849; indeed stupid quibbles were made about the events of 1849 in order to intimidate the democratic tendencies. The right-wing national policy became involved, during the second period of the Risorgimento, in a search for the assistance of Bonapartist France, and balanced the strength of Austria with the French alliance. The policies of the Right in 1848 delayed the unification of the peninsula by more than two decades.

The uncertainties of political and military leadership, the continual oscillations between despotism and constitutionalism, had their disastrous repercussions within the Piedmontese army too. It may safely be asserted that the more numerous an army is—whether in an absolute sense as a recruited mass, or in a relative sense as a proportion of recruited men to the total population—the more the importance of political leadership increases in comparison with merely technical-military leadership. The combativity of the Piedmontese army was extremely high at the start of the campaign of 1848: the rightists believed that this combativity was an expression of a purely abstract military and dynastic spirit, and began to intrigue to restrain popular freedoms and to tone down expectations of a democratic future. The "morale" of the army fell. Herein lies the entire debate about "fatal Novara." At Novara the army did not want to fight, and therefore was defeated. The "rightists" accused the democrats of having introduced politics into the army and split it: an inept accusation, since constitutionalism precisely "nationalised" the army, made it into an element of general politics, and thereby strengthened it militarily. The accusation is all the more inept in that the army perceives a political change of leadership [or direction], without any need for "splitters," from a host

[23] The Piedmontese under Chrzanowski were defeated by the Austrians at Novara in March 1849. . . .

of little changes—each one of which might seem insignificant and negligible, but which together form a new, asphyxiating atmosphere. Those who are responsible for the splits are consequently those who have altered the political leadership, without foreseeing the military consequences; those who, in other words, have substituted a bad policy for the previous good one—good, because in conformity with its objective. The army is also an "instrument" for a particular end, but it is made up of thinking men and not of robots who can be utilized to the limits of their mechanical and physical cohesion. Even if one can and must, in this case too, speak in terms of what is expedient and appropriate to the objective, it is nevertheless also necessary to add the qualification: in accordance with the nature of the given instrument. If you hit a nail with a wooden mallet with the same strength with which you would hit it with a steel hammer, the nail will go into the mallet instead of into the wall. Correct political leadership is necessary even with an army of professional mercenaries (even in the companies of fortune there was a minimum of political leadership, apart from of a technical-military kind); it is all the more necessary with a national, conscript army. The question becomes even more complex and difficult in wars of position, fought by huge masses who are only able to endure the immense muscular, nervous and psychic strain with the aid of great reserves of moral strength. Only a very skilful political leadership, capable of taking into account the deepest aspirations and feelings of those human masses, can prevent disintegration and defeat.

Military leadership must always be subordinate to political leadership, or in other words the strategic plan must be the military expression of a particular general policy. Naturally, it may be that in a given situation the politicians are inept, while in the army there are leaders who combine military ability with political ability: it was the case with Caesar and with Napoleon. But we have seen how in Napoleon's case the change of policies, combined with the presumption that he had a military instrument which was military in the abstract, brought about his downfall. Even in those cases in which political and military leadership is united in the same person, it is the political moment which must prevail over the military. Caesar's *Commentaries* are a classical example of the exhibition of an intelligent combination of political art and military art: the soldiers saw in Caesar not only a great military leader but especially their political leader, the leader of democracy. It should be recalled how Bismarck, following Clausewitz, maintained the supremacy of the political moment over the military; whereas Wilhelm II, as Ludwig records, scribbled furious notes on a newspaper in which Bismarck's opinion was quoted. Thus the Germans won almost all the battles brilliantly, but lost the war.

There exists a certain tendency to overestimate the contribution of the popular classes to the Risorgimento, stressing especially the phenomenon of volunteers. The most serious and thoughtful things on the subject were written by Ettore Rota in *Nuova Rivista Storica*, in 1928–29. . . . It should be pointed out that the writings of Rota themselves show how the volunteers were viewed with disfavour and sabotaged by the Piedmontese authorities—which precisely confirms their bad politico-military leadership. The Piedmontese government could forcibly enrol soldiers within its own territory in proportion to its population, just as Austria could in its territory and in proportion to an enormously larger population. An all-out war on these terms would always have been disastrous for Piedmont after a certain time. Given the principle that "Italy goes it alone," it was necessary either to accept immediately a confederation with the other Italian States, or to propose territorial unity on such a radically popular basis that the masses would have been induced to rise up against the other governments, and would have constituted volunteer armies who would have hastened to the support of the Piedmontese. But precisely here lay the problem. The right-wing tendencies in Piedmont either did not want auxiliaries, thinking that they could defeat the Austrians with the regular Piedmontese forces alone (and it is incomprehensible how they could have had such presumption), or else would have liked to have been helped for nothing (and here too it is incomprehensible how serious politicians could have asked such an absurdity). In real life, one cannot ask for enthusiasm, spirit of sacrifice, etc. without giving anything in return, even from the subjects of one's own country; all the less can one ask these things of citizens from outside that country, on the basis of a generic and abstract programme and a blind faith in a far-distant government. This was the drama of 1848 and 1849, but it is certainly not fair therefore to despise the Italian people; the responsibility for the disaster should be attributed either to the Moderates or to the Action Party—in other words, in the last analysis, to the immaturity and the scanty effectiveness of the ruling classes.

These observations concerning the deficiencies of political and military leadership in the Risorgimento might be met with a very trivial and threadbare argument: "those men were not demagogues, they did not go in for demagogy." Another very widespread triviality used to parry negative judgements on the strategic abilities of the leaders of the national movement consists in repeating in various ways and forms that the national movement's capacity to act was due to the *merit* of the educated classes *solely*. Where the merit lies is hard to see. The merit of an educated class, because it is its historical function, is to lead the popular masses and develop their progressive elements. If the educated class has not been capable of fulfilling its function, one should speak not of merit but of demerit—in other words, of immaturity and intrinsic weakness. Similarly, it is necessary to be clear about the term, and the concept, of demagogy. Those men in effect were not capable of leading the people, were not capable of arousing their enthusiasm and their passion, if one is to take *demagogy* in its original meaning. Did they at least attain the end which they set themselves? They said that they were aiming at the creation of a modern State in Italy, and they in fact produced a bastard. They aimed at stimulating the formation of an extensive and energetic ruling class, and they did not succeed; at integrating the people into the framework of the new State, and they did not succeed. The paltry political life from 1870 to 1900, the fundamental and endemic rebelliousness of the Italian popular classes, the narrow and stunted existence of a sceptical and cowardly ruling stratum, these are all the consequences of that failure. A consequence of it too is the international position of the new State, lacking effective autonomy because sapped internally by the Papacy and by the sullen passivity of the great mass of the people. In reality, furthermore, the rightists of the Risorgimento were great demagogues. They made the people-nation into an instrument, into an object, they degraded it. And therein lies the greatest and most contemptible demagogy, precisely in the sense which the term has assumed on the lips of the right-wing parties when they polemicise against those of the left—although it has always been the right-wing parties who have shown the worst demagogy, and who have often (like Napoleon III in France) appealed to the dregs of society.

11

Risorgimento and
Capitalism

Gramsci seeks to go beyond the socio-economic doctrinairism of the common Marxist mold into a complete vision of the historical and political relations between the two main powers of the Risorgimento. . . . He discerns in the supremacy of the Moderates the inability of the Action Party to carry out its own politics in a consistently Jacobin way and to incorporate the aims and social problems of the peasants. He conceives of Italian history as dominated by the inability of medieval Italian towns to overcome the conflict with the country, which emerged after the first phase of the antifeudal alliance and which remains at the root of the subsequent history of Italy. The ages-long oppression of the countryside, and the related cosmopolitanism of Italian culture and civilization, the decline in the creative skills of the towns, and the failure of all politics aimed at unifying the country all stem from this conflict. To resolve this nearly thousand-year-old problem, there would have to be an alliance between the workers and the peasants.

We certainly cannot say that there has been an exhaustive discussion of Gramsci's thesis. Almost all of the Marxist historians of the Risorgimento have adopted it as a standard by which to orient their study. But no one, as far as I know, has adequately questioned the serious historical and methodological problems which it implies, not even in the face of the serious objections which were immediately raised. The most authoritative written history, from Croce to Antoni to Chabod, has in fact singled out the common error in all the different forms of Risorgimental revisionism which followed one another, from Oriani to Missiroli to Gobetti. They are all characterized by an appeal to an abstract moral and political ideal, to which they think actual events should have risen, and by the fundamental anachronism of this standard of judgment, which does not stem from the concrete history of the time but from problems which were later posed to the historian. Chabod has emphasized with particular force this anachronism in Gramsci, pointing out the tie between his criticism of the Risorgimento and the problem (which was posed for the Italian Socialists and Communists in the period after the First World War) of coupling the peasant masses, which were largely controlled by the "white" leagues, to the urban proletarian movement.

On the other hand, one must keep in mind that Gramsci's thesis is formulated above all as a criticism of the historical and political consistency of the Action Party and is directed at emphasizing the party's inability to carry out its own battle in a revolution based on a Jacobin alliance of bourgeoisie and peasants; this alone would have permitted it to escape from the "hegemony" of the moderates and realize a "coherent" democratic revolution. But the premise of the whole thesis is the existence of a peasant structure which could be mobilized for a national and democratic revolution, the existence, that is, of an "objective" revolutionary possibility, which the Action Party, unlike the French Jacobins, was unable to exploit, but which was nonetheless real and concrete. It is not necessary to stress all the doubts and reservations which the concept of an "objective" structure, outside the consciousness of men of the time, can and does stir up in the non-Marxist scholar. But it is also true that if we want to realize the unquestioned importance which Gramsci's thesis has assumed in the controversy over the Risorgimento, we must go beyond the mere discussion of principles and seek not only to understand thoroughly the author's thought, within the limitations of his particular methodology, but also to try to translate the results of his analysis into an interpretation valid for other [that is, non-Marxist] viewpoints as well.

Two fundamental questions must be posed, apart from any methodological discussion, with respect to Gramsci's thesis. One has to do with the real possibility of an agrarian revolution, that is, with the existence of a real alternative to the Risorgimento as it was ultimately realized. The other concerns whether this apparent alternative would have had a progressive character in relation to the Risorgimento. This second question is no less important than the first, because Gramsci's criticism of the ruling classes of the Risorgimento focuses precisely on their inability to push through to the very end all the possibilities for progress "objectively" contained in the Italian situation, and above all because an exact statement of the real problems of capitalist and modern development in Italy in the nineteenth century depends on a correct valuation of the meaning of the unsuccessful agrarian revolution.

Now, despite the longer and longer lists of peasant insurrections and uprisings which historians (and not only the Marxist ones) are providing us; despite the unquestioned existence of conditions of great poverty or hardship in a large part of the Italian countryside and the persistence of feudal conditions, particularly in the South; despite the enormous fact of a peasant population of more than fifteen million in 1860, the majority of which were poor farmers, laborers or "wage earners," and despite the plans sometimes put forward to mobilize this mass against the old absolutist regimes, it seems undeniable that an alternative to the Risorgimento remains outside the historical and political reality. This is true not so much because of the tenacious Sanfedism[1] of the country, which perhaps could have been surmounted with a solution to the land problem, but because of the underlying historical conditions in which the Risorgimento was destined to develop. Above all it seems certain that an agrarian and Jacobin revolution in Italy would have provoked an anti-Italian marshalling of the great European powers who were interested in conserving the status quo and who were tied to a vision of civilization and international relations which was profoundly hostile to that kind of subversion. Chabod energetically emphasized the problem of international relations on this question, and Gramsci had already asked himself (and answered negatively) whether a Jacobin type of revolution was possible in Italy in the absence of "international autonomy," when France had been a hegemonic power in Europe for centuries, and he had pointed out the importance of the changed European climate after 1815. But his thought appears particularly confused on this subject, as if he were reluctant to draw all the necessary conclusions from the fact that "the limit (in the shape of the Le Chapelier law and the law of the Maximum) encountered by the Jacobins in pursuing their policy of forcing an allegiance between reawakened French popular energies, and the bourgeoisie, appeared in '48 as an already threatening 'spectre,' cleverly brandished by the old governments and also by Cavour (in addition to the Pope). In Italy the bourgeoisie (perhaps) could no longer extend its hegemony over the vast popular classes, as in France. (It could not do so for subjective, not objective, reasons.) The action on the peasants was, however, certainly always possible." Let us leave aside the "subjective" or "objective" character of the reasons which in nineteenth-century Europe prevented the alliance of the bourgeoisie with the great popular masses, in the sense Gramsci understood. (To do this it would be necessary to pose again the whole question of the relation between bourgeois liberalism and the proletarian movement in that period.) The aversion of all the major powers to an agrarian revolution in Italy is a very "objective" fact. In addition, it is very peculiar that Gramsci

---

[1] Sanfedism refers to the reactionary movement against the French which began in the Parthenopean Republic (Naples) in 1799. Inspired by Cardinal Ruffo, it spread to southern Italy and Sicily where it caused continued harassment to the French revolutionary forces. After 1815 it became a secret society in the Papal States, sanctioned by the government, and it aimed at defending an absolutist, theocratic regime against the Carbonari and other liberals.

asserts the possibility of "action on the peasants" after having denied that bourgeois hegemony could be extended over broad popular masses; it is clear that in reality the two things [action over the peasants and action over the broad masses] are one and the same, it being impossible to shift the question of action to the urban popular classes whom, for that matter, the Action Party succeeded in directing and controlling to a large extent.

Think then of the extreme difficulty of transforming southern Italy into a country of rural democracy and of small landholdings—after what we know about the collection of ground rents in the last century . . . and after the experience of the agrarian reform bureaus had shown how much capital and technical and agrarian resources (which are of decisive importance for increasing productivity of the land and which were entirely non-existent in the last century) would be necessary for the solution of the problem then. It is clear here that only the creation of a rural democracy is being discussed. If one wanted to understand Gramsci's thesis in terms of the kind of support which the Action Party should have given the peasants in the distribution of public lands or in the reform of the old extortionate rent agreements, one would not only distort Gramsci's explicit thought (which hinges on the comparison with the agrarian politics of the French Jacobins), but one would also destroy all interest in the discussion: it is evident that such politics on the part of the Action Party either would have turned into a general insurrection for seizing land or would have had to yield, particularly in the more backward regions, to the survival of old feudal structures. . . .

But it requires more complex argument to assert that the social and economic structure which the Risorgimento realized in Italy represents historically a more backward stage than the one which would have been attained by means of the agrarian revolution. It is precisely this concept which inspires a great deal of the Marxist polemics against the Risorgimento. And it is also in this concept that the "doctrinaire" rather than the practical and political origin of Gramsci's thesis is most clearly revealed. It has already been indicated that Gramsci's thesis originated in the Marxist view of capitalist development which Gramsci applies to Italy, using the French bourgeois revolution as the model. However, we should not undervalue Gramsci's understanding . . . of the agrarian problem in the backward countries of Eastern Europe, where questions of nationalism and anti-feudal revolution seemed closely linked in democratic thought. The problem of capitalist development in Italy can not be identified, however, with either the agrarian revolution in the backward countries of Eastern Europe, which were characterized by extremely weak urban and bourgeois development, or with the development of capitalism in

France, which differs from the analogous Italian process in that expansion of the towns and of urban capitalism were incomparably faster and stronger. From the time of Colbert to the eve of the Revolution, the French industrial and mercantile bourgeoisie had made enormous advances. The Italian situation was very different until after the middle of the nineteenth century. Here industry still had only a negligible importance in the general economic picture of the country. Even commerce, despite its much greater prominence, was also subordinate to agriculture; its function was almost entirely to set in motion the local farm products. Even in Lombardy, the most advanced region, Jacini calculated that six times more was invested in agriculture than in commerce and industry together. And Milan was still a city in the commercial stage of its development. Undoubtedly, huge fortunes of personal property existed in the Italian towns, concentrated in the hands of bankers and entrepreneurial merchants who controlled a large part of the cottage industries in the various regions, particularly in the North. But the importance of those fortunes in the aggregate of the national economy was considerably less in Italy than in France. Therefore in Italy, as late as 1860, the only large scale capitalist phenomena which were capable of inspiring modern forms of productive organization of considerable size, were found in agriculture. In the Po Valley, in the eighteenth and the nineteenth centuries, huge agricultural enterprises developed, characterized by an extensive use of capital and salaried laborers, by the betterment of farming methods, and by the notable increase in technical equipment and in production. Capitalist elements were already being gradually introduced in a large part of the rest of central and northern Italy as well as in those regions dominated by the ancient rent and sharecropping contracts (in themselves precapitalist forms). Here there was always greater participation of the owner in the capital of the enterprise. In the owners' farms the important technical means, cellars, machinery, etc., were centralized and serviced the various sharecroppers' farms. But this diminished the autonomy of the small agricultural unit, which in any case was not sufficient to meet the needs of the new productive techniques which were by then knocking at the door. These were all premonitions of the profound transformation which the sharecropping contract would undergo in the second half of the century as the diffusion of capitalist relations of production increased throughout the country. Even the very important silk industry, which was connected to agriculture and whose exports brought a steady stream of gold to the economy of the Po region, was based largely in the country near the source of the raw materials. However, the work was no longer done in the peasants' homes but was concentrated in the numerous silk factories which had been established on the initiative of the landowners, who often gathered together several dozen workers. These are signs which should be kept clearly in mind in any discussion of capitalist development in Italy.

In fact, the meaning of the peasant revolution hoped for by the Marxists should be studied in the context of the weak development of urban capitalism and the incipient agrarian capitalism. In Italy, in the nineteenth century, the bourgeoisie had already laid its hands on a good part of ecclesiastical property in the Napoleonic era, and the introduction of the Napoleonic code had already cancelled all legal differences between feudal property and bourgeois property. A peasant revolution aimed at winning the land, would have inevitably struck no matter where it took root (but presumably in the north and center of the peninsula), even the most advanced forms in the agrarian economy, thus eliminating the capitalist elements of Italian agriculture and substituting for it a regime of small independent landholders, and in this way stamping on agricultural Italy precisely the features of rural democracy. The eradication of the remaining feudal structures would certainly have accompanied all of this. It would have been an enormously positive event in Italian agricultural relations. But this revolution would have had a very different meaning in the general process of capitalist development in Italy. It is enough to examine the consequences of the French Revolution in the countryside to realize this. If in fact it bettered the conditions of a large stratum of peasants, it is also incontestable that at the same time it blocked the development of capitalism in the French countryside. (The most recent studies have shown that those who benefited most were the rich peasants, and the proportion of laborers who did not own land remained unchanged or diminished slightly; this compels us to greatly revise our view of the effectiveness in such a sense of an agrarian revolution in Italy, which in 1861 had an agrarian population almost equal to that of France in the last decade of the eighteenth century, but had an agricultural surface area half as small and much poorer.) The greatest historian of these problems writes that it is because of the peasant revolution in France that "our [French] agricultural evolution can not glory in the same economic progress as other countries." This is the other side of having saved the French peasant from enclosures and of having guaranteed an evolution which "caused less suffering and was more humane." In fact, the peasants' winning of land in the Revolution did not at all indicate a technical advance in French agriculture. During the entire first half of the nineteenth century it lay in a state of profound stagnation, characterized by very little progress. Only in the second half of the century did the violent development of urban capitalism help pave the way for progress in the country as well, largely subordinating agricultural relations to itself without, however, succeeding in launching agriculture on the path of developed capitalist production. After a stage of more rapid progress in the free-exchange regime inaugurated the Liberal Empire [French Second Empire, 1860–1870]. French agriculture experienced a new period of stagnation with the introduction of protectionism after 1880. There occurred then a true technical regression, of a return to a "kind of pre-agriculture, anachronistically prolonged in the modern era." In our day France still has the problem of an agriculture in which (in 1946) 96.6% of the farms had fewer than three wage earners and occupied 84.2% of the surface area. It has an agriculture in which there are many peasant families who are owners of insufficient property, and who are therefore en route to a demographic decline, to a remuneration for work which is less than the average salary of farm laborers, to an economic Malthusianism, with its various restraints and quotas on production. In French agriculture the penetration of the market economy into the country has reduced personal consumption by 10% for the more well-to-do independent producers and 30–50% for the less fortunate. But capitalism appears more in the form of tribute demanded by the system of distribution and supply to the urban markets than as a force for the promotion of technical progress and agricultural production. It is ultimately an agriculture with its savings mobilized by the banks; thus it has supplied Europe and the world with capital but has not succeeded in equipping itself in an appropriate way and now finds itself with formidable structural problems. These problems are also reflected in urban capitalism itself and have played a basic part in putting France at a clear disadvantage with respect to the more advanced industrial countries.

But the crisis of French agricultural capitalism was in large part met and compensated for by the powerful rise of financial, industrial, and commercial capitalism, which, as we have mentioned, had already reached a high degree of development in the preceding centuries. This is precisely the fundamental condition which was lacking in Italy, and it characterized the whole development of our capitalism as compared to that of the French. If the more advanced agricultural capitalism had been liquidated along with the weak industrial and personal property capitalism, the country would have been blocked in its evolution to a modern country, not only on the level of its economic life but on that of its civil and social relations as well. With the studies we have at this stage, it is very difficult to give a sufficiently precise answer to the questions which are posed about the sources of capitalist accumulation in Italy. Obviously the sources are less varied in Italy than in other countries, since commerce and colonial exploitation have to be excluded, and since the thesis that industrial capital "generates itself" which has been applied to England, has little significance for Italy. Undoubtedly an important source of capitalist accumulation was the policies connected with the foundation and development of the unified state. From the very beginning the nation-state invested huge quantities of forced savings [i.e., taxes, state loans] in the execution of great public works (for example, the construction of the railroads). It favored financial speculation linked to the expansion of the public debt. It also stimulated certain industries with the politics of armament, etc. In the accumulation of capital a conspicuous role should be attributed, as is well-known, to foreign capital, above all French but also English, Swiss, and German. But it should not be forgotten that in general the major amount is always provided by national capital. To a large extent this came from the personal property of the tradesmen or bankers who only later turned to industry. But as we have said, certain agricultural activities on which the first forms of urban capitalism tested were by now largely penetrated by capitalist elements. We have already mentioned, for example, that silk production was to a large extent centralized in factories built in the country during the period of great increase in exports after 1814. ... But it should be kept in mind that agricultural capitalism was one of the principal sources for the accumulation of capital which later flowed into industry. The example of Cavour demonstrates this once more: Starting out as an agricultural capitalist in Leri, Cavour became a merchant in fertilizer and agricultural products; he then passed to financial speculation and to promoting the establishment of industries connected to agriculture, like the *Società del Parco* for the husking of rice or the Rossi and Schiaparelli company of Turin for the manufacture of fertilizers; finally he took an interest in the construction and the supplying of tracks for the first railroads, such as the Torino-Savigliano and the Torino-Genova.

On the other hand, income from property, which was very conspicuous for the entire century and which increased with particular rapidity after 1860, is also one of the important sources of accumulation. This fact is especially notable inasmuch as from 1830 until the first decade of the twentieth century the gross yield of the land increased about two and a half times, while the rent quadrupled due to improvements on the land and the competition among tenant farmers. And all this was taking place in the same area where the real value of agricultural salaries, which were nominally unchanged for a long time, noticeably decreased in the course of the eighteenth and in the first half of the nineteenth century. Thus the income of the poorest groups remained for several decades below the subsistence level (in some instances as much as one third below). This imposed on the agricultural workers a series of very difficult deprivations, which in turn gave rise to a current which affected all of the urban economy, on the one hand stimulating the demand for goods and on the other setting in motion new initiatives for greater expansion. The formation of the capital necessary for the development of industrial production had already taken place in England and France in the sixteenth and seventeenth centuries, in the form of primitive accumulation, with enclosures, colonial commerce, and mercantile policies which supported industry and commerce at the expense of agriculture and which had permitted the great development of manufacturing industries in those countries. This situation came to pass in Italy only in the course of the nineteenth century; until then it had reached only very modest proportions. In Italy, as in France, this capital was basically formed in the countryside, above all at the expense of the poorest peasant groups. But its delayed development and the particular historical conditions of the peninsula give the process of accumulation in Italy a composite character. This character is determined by the importance (next to income from the land) of agricultural profits, which in Italy act as the mainspring of the whole process. The outside pressure of the world capitalist market intervened to accelerate the process, stimulating the development of mercantile production in the country, hastening the differentiation of wealth, and making possible enormous profits on certain agricultural exports. The historical function of the ruling class of the Risorgimento, and of the Moderates at first, is to guarantee the political conditions necessary for the completion of this process, at the peasants' expense, and to guide the income from it toward a modern line of economic development. Such a line was inaugurated with the laissez-faire policy of Cavour and the Right; it was later changed into a conscious policy of industrial development several decades after 1860, when the accumulation of capital from agriculture created the necessary premises for it. Therefore, to the extent that the development of industrial and commercial capitalism in Italy was backward, the consequences of an agrarian revolution would have been more serious; by protecting the peasants against exploitation, it would have swept away the only existing form of capitalism, which was destined to function in the historical conditions in Italy as the essential mechanism for the accumulation and transfer of agricultural incomes to the services of urban and industrial development.

All of this is valid, however, only for the central and northern regions of Italy. Since it is unthinkable that the Action Party could set off the revolution of the peasants in the South without the uprising extending to the North, it must be kept in mind that it was precisely in the North that the "objective" conditions for the establishment of a rural democracy existed, whereas in the South the revolution would probably have encountered unsurmountable obstacles in the extreme backwardness and poverty of southern agriculture, in addition to the excess of peasant population.

On the other hand, one should consider with great reservation the thesis [held by some] that the agricultural revolution, by raising the standard of living of the peasants, would have guaranteed a more extended market for urban industry. With this the agricultural revolution would have set the conditions for its own development, free from the obstacles and contradictions which have always characterized its history in Italy. In fact, it is probable that an increase in the standard of living would have been realized wherever the peasants succeeded in consolidating their possession of the land. But it is also true that, particularly when domestic industry still survives to a great extent, the creation of small peasant landholdings is a very different thing from the formation of a large market for capitalist industry. Marx himself lucidly set forth the conditions essential to the existence of this socio-economic form: "this form of landholding presupposes that the country population has a great numerical preponderance over the urban population, that even if in some way the capitalist mode of production prevails, it is only relatively little developed, so that even in the other branches of production the concentration of capital moves within narrow limits and the breaking up of capital prevails. Because of the very nature of the thing, a prevalent part of the agricultural product must be consumed by its own producers, the peasants, and only the surplus part must enter as merchandise in the trade with the towns." It is precisely through this segregation of the market— which obviously means a limited market for the urban products in the country—that "small landholding creates a class of barbarians which is half out of society and which joins all the roughness of primitive social forms with all the pains and all the poverty of civilized countries. . . . Naturally this does not mean that the agricultural revolution would have definitively stopped capitalist development in Italy. Certainly the capitalist relations of production would have subjected the new land regime to its rule all the same, even if the French example demonstrates that the extent and the efficacy of that subjugation is strictly conditiond by the pre-existing situation. But certainly the agricultural revolution seems to act more as a check than as an impetus in this process, in the particular historical conditions of Italy.

The greatest danger in Gramsci's thesis is that it leads to a seriously distorted perspective of the problem of capitalist development in Italy. This development was certainly critically affected by the backwardness of the country and its insufficient relations with the towns. But the arrested development of the Italian cities, which goes back to the decadence of the centuries following the Middle Ages, no longer permitted the urban ruling classes in the nineteenth century to carry out an antifeudal revolution consistent to the very end and therefore based on an alliance with the peasant masses. The price of that alliance was historically too great in terms of the delay of capitalist development and of the development in a modern and western sense of the whole country. In the historical conditions of Italy at that time, the agrarian revolution would have resulted in the direct opposite of capitalist accumulation at the peasants' expense, which for over a century had been established (to a greater or lesser extent) in a large part of the countryside in the north and center of the peninsula. That is, it would have represented an effort aimed not at strengthening and accelerating the real historical development, but at violently diverting it toward a different and opposite direction. In short, the conquest of power by the bourgeoisie in the Risorgimento largely coincides with the process of primitive accumulation at the expense of the countryside, that is, with a stage of accentuated antagonism between town and country and between the bourgeoisie and the peasantry. In France, however, this stage had already been largely passed by the time of the Revolution; it was for precisely this reason that the bourgeoisie had been able to side with the peasantry against feudal property. In Italy, on the contrary, feudal property partially survived the Risorgimento, and the relations between the new bourgeois world and the old feudal world prevented a revolutionary alliance between the bourgeoisie and the peasantry after 1860. This delayed antifeudal development was a serious liability in the history of Italy. . . .

Lenin distinguished between the "Prussian way" of capitalist development, which is based on compromise between the capitalist bourgeoisie and the feudal elements, and the "American way," which is free of that compromise. This distinction is often cited. It should be remembered that Lenin put Italy in the first category in this respect. Certainly this is not without some validity, even though a methodology of classifications or analogies with other countries is always dangerous. But it is clear that in order to attempt a concrete investigation of these themes in relation to Italian problems, one ought to take as a basis for comparison not the "American way," which was entirely conditioned by the existence of vast lands which were free and available to the peasant farmers and which therefore cannot be applied to Italy, but rather the "French way," in keeping with the logic of the whole Gramscian thesis. Now, as compared with France, the "Prussian way" of capitalism followed in Germany appears incomparably more powerful and expansive, more capable of completely realizing a modern productive system on an industrial base (even if it is undoubtedly less "democratic"; but the problem here is not democracy but the modernity of economic and social forms). If French economic development in the last 150 years is compared with that of the other great industrial countries (Great Britain, Germany, Belgium, the Scandinavian countries, as well as the United States and the Soviet Union), where capitalist progress was not conditioned to so great an extent by the survival of small peasant landholdings, it is clear that France remained behind in many respects.

Only a consideration of the specific problems in Italy's history can show how an agrarian revolution with dramatic guidance could not take on any progressive significance in the nineteenth century. But our commentary is concerned above all with the illegitimacy of the assumption that the French historical development is an "exemplary" model for the development of a modern bourgeois capitalist country. Behind this attitude and the continual comparisons it involves, is a provincial quality that also boasts descent from a certain traditional francophilism of our democratic thought, but which, however, has a disfiguring effect on historical judgment. In reality, contradictions and delaying tactics were, naturally, not lacking in French history. The very takeover of the land by the peasants only resolved, as we have recalled, certain aspects of the "agrarian question." All this is well known to French historians, even the Marxist ones. But in the minds of our Marxists this process assumes the characteristics of absolute perfection, and this does harm to legitimate intelligence and to Italian and French history.

Certainly Gramsci's thesis has a significance which goes way beyond the objective economic and social facts. The agrarian revolution presented itself to the Sardinian writer as a great possibility for resolving the profound contrasts of Italian history, as a powerful instrument for unifying all of Italian society, which would have created a deeper tie between the state and the "national-popular" forces of the culture and the society. But such a revolution could not come to pass in the nineteenth century because it was unfavorable to the expansion of the modern capitalist relations. It could come to pass only to the extent that it succeeded in promoting these relations and, in a certain way, identifying itself with them (but certainly not by making Italy a country of peasants and craftsmen, according to the ideals of petit-bourgeois democracy at the beginning of the nineteenth century). Therefore, can one say in France, where the Revolution even laid the foundations of a great democratic tradition and united the masses to the life of the state more closely than in Italy, that the agrarian revolution really achieved the profound unity of town and country? The great revolutionary crises of the nineteenth century, in 1848 and 1871, show what a profound rift there was between the revolutionary masses of the towns and the tough conservatism of the small landowners who emerged with the Revolution. Marx himself was one of the first to show this. Undoubtedly the rift was present in Italy as well, and was no less deep. This is not amazing when one remembers that it concerned a problem which was a thousand years old, tenaciously rooted in Italian history, and aggravated by the decadence and inertia which had marked that history for so many centuries. It is a problem which other more fortunate nations have resolved, but only through processes which lasted hundreds of years. One can therefore justly doubt that even the revolution which Gramsci hoped for could have brought about that solution. In fact, in Gramsci's thought, the agrarian revolution assumes a significance which is very similar to the determinative and eschatological one which Marxism attributes to the proletarian revolution. In its innermost meaning, in the place which it occupies in the feeling and mind of Gramsci, it ends by being identified with the proletarian revolution. This is an observation which brings us back to the methodological observation of Croce, Antoni, and Chabod on the practical and political character, and therefore basically antihistorical character, of this conception.

On the other hand, one could also discuss the historical-political interpretation of Gramsci: that is, the affirmation that the Action Party was fundamentally "directed" by the Moderates and that Vittorio Emanuele's saying that he had the Action Party "in his pocket" fundamentally corresponded to the truth. In reality, the democratic alternative to the Moderate solution was something politically real in 1860. Between August and September of that year the possibility of Garibaldi's march on Rome to convoke a constituent assembly there, with foreseeable developments of a republican and democratic nature, appeared anything but outside of reality. The recent results of the very accurate study by Mack Smith serve to confirm this thesis.

The task which was set for the men of the Risorgimento on the socioeconomic level and which they resolved in the way most consistent with the conditions of Italy at the time, was to force a strengthening of the urban capitalist economy of the North and the unification of the market, both of which were historically necessary for the subsequent redemption and transformation of the southern countryside. Obviously this was much more the result of the intrinsic development of the new national economics and politics than of conscious political programs. In fact, the ties of so much of Italian moderatism with landowners and agricultural industry constituted a delay to coherent development of national industrialization. But in essence even the old Right made a fundamental contribution to it with the energetic defense of political unity, with the decided free trade policies, and with the construction of the railroads, which gave rise to the unification of the market. And this was so even before the groups directly tied to the new industrial world became stronger with the advent of the Left. Certainly the whole process developed for a long time on a basis of compromise with the semifeudal elements of the old agricultural world, particularly in the South. All of this meant a strengthening of the towns at the expense of the country, a favoring of the North at the expense of the South. In fact, economic inferiority of the South for a certain period appeared, and in some respects still appears, as a historical condition for industrial development of the North. But it is a "temporary" condition (even if it was prolonged for many decades), which was destined to be upset by the internal development of northern industrialism itself. Above all it should not be forgotten that national unity accelerated the rhythm of certain sectors of the southern economy, for example, the increases in agricultural exports from the South after 1860 and the growth of towns such as Bari or Catania. But it is especially important to emphasize that the economic and industrial development of the northern regions laid the foundations for the southern policy, which was timidly begun with special laws in the early years of the century and which took on much greater proportions in the second post-war period. The economic foundations were northern, to the extent that they were strictly linked to the productive capacities and expansion needs of northern industry. The political foundations were southern, to the extent that they were dependent on setting up and realizing a national policy towards the South which only the firm political and moral unification of the country made possible. It was certainly a very twisted and difficult process. Nevertheless, this was the quickest way considering the historical conditions in Italy, to acquire the structure and the characteristics that are proper to a modern country.

A picture of this kind, which tends to integrate the most valid data and insights of Gramscian revisionism into a fundamentally positive appraisal of the unitarian liberal national revolution ... has, moreover, value in providing a general direction for research. The positive appraisal of the Risorgimento which we have learned from liberal histories should now incorporate the results of more recent historical research, which describe the profound transformation which the peninsula underwent after 1860 in political life, in civil relations, in the economy, and in moral life. Such a view must have its ideal center in the revolutionary function of the towns of the North, which acquired greater strength with the passing decades, and whose development conditioned that of the whole country. Naturally it is not a question of giving validity only to histories of banks and industries. ... It is a question of constructing a political and civil history in which the practical and political realizations are equally as important as the growth and modernization of civil consciousness and culture and the establishment of new kinds of values and social relations. And it is not a question of contrasting the history of the ruling classes to that of the subordinate classes, or the history of the North to that of the South, although certainly the history of the ruling classes and of the North are still by far the least well studied (we know more about Caltanissetta than about Milan after 1860!), precisely as a result of the various "revisionisms." Rather it is a question of focusing on all aspects of our national history. Only in this way can the history of the various themes and of the subordinate classes themselves acquire proper meaning. The concrete treatment of these themes would also serve, it seems to me, to give a more precise sense of the complexity and elasticity of the Italian socio-political fabric, which threatens to be entirely lost when the history of the country is totally conceived as a function of an imminent and speculative revolutionary break. In addition it would help to explain certain concepts of fundamental importance such as that of "northern bourgeoisie," which in contemporary histories threaten to acquire an almost mythological character.

V/THE PARIS COMMUNE

A BOOK of historical readings would be more than derelict in its duty if it did not dedicate a chapter to the Paris Commune, the event that marked the opening of the era of proletarian revolution. (The historian, too, has his justified loyalties.)

The Second Empire of Louis Napoleon came to an ignominious end at the battle of Sedan on September 2, 1871. Having manipulated the French government into a war it was only too willing to fight, the Prussians then proceeded to use their military machine, finely honed in the Danish and Austrian wars of 1864 and 1866, to roll over the enemy. The rottenness of the French regime was exposed for all to see in the incompetence of its generals, the weakness of the emperor, and, most important, its failure to secure the support of a national patriotic front. The news of the defeat at Sedan was, at least partially, welcomed with a sigh of relief, and the politicians of the bourgeois opposition lost no time in declaring the Republic on September 4.

The Third Republic was conceived in negation and born in haste. The fundamental idea was to provide some sort of governmental structure to carry on the war and, at the same time, to keep the revolutionary potential of the populace under control. Throughout the late autumn and winter of 1870–1871, Paris lay under siege, while the Government of National Defense and the Assembly, first at Bordeaux and later at Versailles, temporized and negotiated with the Prussians. The problem for the politicians of the bourgeoisie had three aspects: (1) how to contain popular revolution, (2) how to undermine the foundations of the Republic with which most of them were none too happy, and (3) how to lose as little as possible to the Prussians. Furthermore, it would seem that the first and second considerations took precedence over the third.

It was opposition to this inversion of values that first united the people of Paris. While a great part of the bourgeoisie fled far from the madding crowd to safety and comfort outside the city, the other classes remained and tried to survive in the midst of extremely adverse conditions. Paris was suffering from a war of attrition waged by the Prussians but was, even more, insulted by the attitude of its rulers who were more fearful of revolution than of national humiliation. The attempt of the government to deprive the Parisians of the cannon that were their only substantial means of defense against the Prussians led, on March 18, to the proclamation of the Commune. The Parisians now took their destiny into their own hands. For the next two months until the triumph of the Versailles troops and the murder (not always decked out in judicial forms) of thousands of Communards in the Bloody Week at the end of May, Paris would be the arena not only of an energetic defense against civic betrayal, but, even more important for the future, of the first proletarian socialist revolution.

Marx wrote: "Working-class Paris, with its Commune, will be celebrated forever as the glorious forerunner of a new society. The memory of its martyrs is piously guarded in the great heart of the working class. History has already nailed its exterminators to an eternal pillory, and all the prayers of their priests will not succeed in redeeming them." As befits a genius, he then went on to write what still remains the single most lucid explanation of the Commune, in which his excellence of style, as well as the depth of analysis, plays a vital role. How anyone can accuse Marx of economic determinism after reading this is beyond me.

The Commune, for Marx, was the "positive form of the social republic," that is to say, the expression of the desire of the working class to supersede class rule and to destroy state power. It was a working-class government, even if Engels' affirmation that it was a dictatorship of the proletariat is somewhat more dubious. Of course, it may well be that the Commune corresponded more closely to what Marx and Engels had in mind when they spoke of the dictatorship of the proletariat then do more recent experiences. In any case, it was a working-class government with a general line and a set of accomplishments that are truly amazing given the circumstances and the short amount of time it had at its disposal. Equally, it was a government full of hesitations, of failures in both analysis and action. It might have gone further in a whole variety of areas, but it did not. That much must be recognized and explained in the light of the configuration of social forces. It is hardly a reason for condemnation.

But the Commune was something more than the elected representatives of the people. It was the people themselves, with their aspirations, both confused and generous, their exaltation, their spontaneity, and their joy. The people here referred to are not the French historian Jules Michelet's undifferentiated mass of victors of the great Revolution of 1789, but the heirs to June 1848 and the fighters in the intense class struggles of the Second Empire. They are the workers and artisans on the way to becoming a full-fledged proletariat. As was so often the case in France, their expression was political, but their concerns were greater still. They took their desires for realities and staged an assault on heaven.

Utopian hopes, we have seen, play a fundamental part in all revolutionary movements, and in the Commune no less than others. They may be a source of weakness, insofar as they promote a false consciousness and an inability to judge a situation correctly. But the belief in utopia may also give great strength to a revolution, by constantly holding up the image of the perfect, if unattainable, society. If revolution is to be permanent, this is the only way to proceed.

Marx did not by any means exhaust the subject. Every generation wants to write its own history, in the light of its own experience, and to answer new questions. A prime example of this procedure is the selection by the French Marxist philosopher Henri Lefebvre, written in 1965. Lefebvre left the French Communist party in 1956. He is suspicious of the activities of vanguard parties, which he sees as bureaucratized and insufficiently responsive to the needs and desires of the working class. Much influenced by the philosophical formulations of the young Marx concerning alienation and the revolutionary praxis needed to overcome it, Lefebvre looks to the spontaneity of the working class as the source of revolutionary action. More voluntarist than some orthodox (that is, Communist) Marxists, he nonetheless sees the origin of popular revolutionism in the objective circumstances of historical development, in the necessity of class struggle. He does not deny the need to find structured forms for making working-class spontaneity into a viable political weapon, but he wishes to ensure that no sterile party apparatus will choke off this constant stream of initiative in the name of a strategy that will be no more than a cover for the individual interests of a group (or class?) of bureaucratic leaders. The Commune is the model, and in that way lies democracy and the best guarantee of the future of socialism.

Lefebvre's views take on a new significance in the light of the events of May 1968, when all of France stood on the brink of revolution. For three weeks, the country was kept at a standstill by the combined action of students and workers protesting the alienation characteristic of what they termed consumer society. The usually anonymous crowds were now found to be made up of individuals ready to talk to one another—and the talk showed that they wanted change, even if they were not quite sure about either its content or its form. May was the exercise of spontaneity in the absence of political direction—indeed, the major reason for the failure of the movement was the lack of junction between the two. It was also the rebirth of the idea that revolution in an advanced capitalist society is possible. May was the modernization of the myth of the Commune—myth not as fable, but as possibility.

In 1971, the French left and revolutionaries throughout the world celebrated the hundredth anniversary of the Commune. They did so in fragmented groups, inevitably reflecting the present-day alignment of political forces. How sad—and, indeed, unworthy of the heritage—it was to see two separate processions to the cemetery wall where the last Communards were executed. Despite the fragmentation and the internecine strife, the strength of the Commune's example, of history in the service of a political idea, was evident. And that is why nonsocialist historians have been at pains to deny the Commune its socialist character. "Its impetus and raison d'être are to be found in causes which lie outside the domain of socialism. The war with Germany, the events of the siege, disgust with a strongly centralized and incompetent government, were of more decisive significance." So wrote the American historian Edward Mason in 1930, and there are many who still agree with him. But the question is ill-posed, for it is not the causes but the character of the Commune that is at issue. In that regard, Lenin knew better when, on the seventy-third day of the Bolshevik revolution, he explained his joy by saying that his comrades had held power for one day longer than the Commune.

Karl Marx

12

The Civil War
in France

On the dawn of the 18th of March, Paris arose to the thunderburst of "Vive la Commune!" What is the Commune, that sphinx so tantalising to the bourgeois mind?

"The proletarians of Paris," said the Central Committee in its manifesto of the 18th March, "amidst the failures and treasons of the ruling classes, have understood that the hour has struck for them to save the situation by taking into their own hands the direction of public affairs. . . . They have understood that it is their imperious duty and their absolute right to render themselves masters of their own destinies, by seizing upon the governmental power."

But the working class cannot simply lay hold of the ready-made state machinery, and wield it for its own purposes.

The centralised State power, with its ubiquitous organs of standing army, police, bureaucracy, clergy, and judicature—organs wrought after the plan of a systematic and hierarchic division of labour—originates from the days of absolute monarchy, serving nascent middle-class society as a mighty weapon in its struggles against feudalism. Still, its development remained clogged by all manner of mediaeval rubbish, seignorial rights, local privileges, municipal and guild monopolies and provincial constitutions. The gigantic broom of the French Revolution of the eighteenth century swept away all these relics of bygone times, thus clearing simultaneously the social soil of its last hindrances to the superstructure of the modern State edifice raised under the First Empire, itself the offspring of the coalition wars of old semi-feudal Europe against modern France. During the subsequent *régimes* the Government, placed under parliamentary control—that is, under the direct control of the propertied classes—became not only a hotbed of huge national debts and crushing taxes; with its irresistible allurements of place, pelf, and patronage, it became not only the bone of contention between the rival factions and adventurers of the ruling classes; but its political character changed simultaneously with the economic changes of society. At the same pace at which the progress of modern industry developed, widened, intensified the class antagonism between capital and labour, the State power assumed more and more the character of the national power of capital over labour, of a public force organised for social enslavement, of an engine of class despotism. After every revolution marking a progressive phase in the class struggle, the purely repressive character of the State power stands out in bolder and bolder relief. The Revolution of 1830, resulting in the transfer of Government from the landlords to the capitalists, transferred it from the more remote to the more direct antagonists of the working men. The bourgeois Republicans, who, in the name of the Revolution of February, took the State power, used it for the June massacres, in order to convince the working class that "social" republic meant the Republic ensuring their social subjection, and in order to convince the royalist bulk of the bourgeois and landlord class that they might safely leave the cares and emoluments of Government to the bourgeois "Republicans." However, after their one heroic exploit of June, the bourgeois Republicans had, from the front, to fall back to the rear of the "Party of Order"—a combination formed by all the rival fractions and factions of the appropriating class in their now openly declared antagonism to the producing classes. The proper form of their joint-stock Government was the *Parliamentary Republic,* with Louis Bonaparte for its President. Theirs was a *régime* of avowed class terrorism and deliberate insult toward the "vile multitude." If the Parliamentary Republic, as M. Thiers said, "divided them (the different fractions of the ruling class) least," it opened an abyss between that class and the whole body of society outside their spare ranks. The restraints by which their own divisions had under former *régimes* still checked the State power, were removed by their union; and in view of the threatening upheaval of the proletariat, they now used that State power mercilessly and ostentatiously as the national war-engine of capital against labour. In their uninterrupted crusade against the producing masses they were, however, bound not only to invest the executive with continually increased powers of repression, but at the same time to divest their own parliamentary stronghold—the National Assembly—one by one, of all its own means of defence against the Executive. The Executive, in the person of Louis Bonaparte, turned them out. The natural offspring of the "Party-of-Order" Republic was the Second Empire.

The empire, with the *coup d'état* for its certificate of birth, universal suffrage for its sanction, and the sword for its sceptre, professed to rest upon the peasantry, the large mass of producers not directly involved in the struggle of capital and labour. It professed to save the working class by breaking down Parliamentarism, and, with it, the undisguised subserviency of Government to the propertied classes. It professed to save the propertied classes by upholding their economic supremacy over the working class; and, finally, it professed to unite all classes by reviving for all the chimera of national glory. In reality, it was the only form of government possible at a time when the bourgeoisie had already lost, and the working class had not yet acquired, the faculty of ruling the nation. It was acclaimed throughout the world as the saviour of society. Under its sway, bourgeois society, freed from political cares, attained a development unexpected even by itself. Its industry and commerce expanded to colossal dimensions; financial swindling celebrated cosmopolitan orgies; the misery of the masses was set off by a shameless display of gorgeous, meretricious and debased luxury. The State power, apparently soaring high above society, was at the same time itself the greatest scandal of that society and the very hotbed of all its corruptions. Its own rottenness, and the rottenness of the society it had saved, were laid bare by the bayonet of Prussia, herself eagerly bent upon transferring the supreme seat of that *régime* from Paris to Berlin. Imperialism is, at the same time, the most prostitute and the ultimate form of the State power which nascent middle-class society had commenced to elaborate as a means of its own emancipation from feudalism, and which full-grown bourgeois society had finally transformed into a means for the enslavement of labour by capital.

The direct antithesis to the empire was the Commune. The cry of "social republic," with which the revolution of February was ushered in by the Paris proletariat, did but express a vague aspiration after a Republic that was not only to supersede the monarchical form of class-rule, but class-rule itself. The Commune was the positive form of that Republic.

Paris, the central seat of the old governmental power, and, at the same time, the social stronghold of the French working class, had risen in arms against the attempt of Thiers and the Rurals to restore and perpetuate that old governmental power bequeathed to them by the empire. Paris could resist only because, in consequence of the siege, it had got rid of the army, and replaced it by a National Guard, the bulk of which consisted of working men. This fact was now to be transformed into an institution. The first decree of the Commune, therefore, was the suppression of the standing army, and the substitution for it of the armed people.

The Commune was formed of the municipal councillors, chosen by universal suffrage in the various wards of the town, responsible and revocable at short terms. The majority of its members were naturally working men, or acknowledged representatives of the working class. The Commune was to be a working, not a parliamentary, body, executive and legislative at the same time. Instead of continuing to be the agent of the Central Government, the police was at once stripped of its political attributes, and turned into the responsible and at all times revocable agent of the Commune. So were the officials of all other branches of the Administration. From the members of the Commune downwards, the public service had to be done at *workmen's wages*. The vested interests and the representation allowances of the high dignitaries of State disappeared along with the high dignitaries themselves. Public functions ceased to be the private property of the tools of the Central Government. Not only municipal administration, but the whole initiative hitherto exercised by the State was laid into the hands of the Commune.

Having once got rid of the standing army and the police, the physical force elements of the old Government, the Commune was anxious to break the spiritual force of repression, the "parson-power," by the disestablishment and disendowment of all churches as proprietary bodies. The priests were sent back to the recesses of private life, there to feed upon the alms of the faithful in imitation of their predecessors, the Apostles. The whole of the educational institutions were opened to the people gratuitously, and at the same time cleared of all interference of Church and State. Thus, not only was education made accessible to all, but science itself freed from the fetters which class prejudice and governmental force had imposed upon it.

The judicial functionaries were to be divested of that sham independence which had but served to mask their abject subserviency to all succeeding governments to which, in turn, they had taken, and broken, the oaths of allegiance. Like the rest of public servants, magistrates and judges were to be elective, responsible, and revocable.

The Paris Commune was, of course, to serve as a model to all the great industrial centres of France. The communal *régime* once established in Paris and the secondary centres, the old centralised Government would in the provinces, too, have to give way to the self-government of the producers. In a rough sketch of national organisation which the Commune had no time to develop, it states clearly that the Commune was to be the political form of even the smallest country hamlet, and that in the rural districts the standing army was to be replaced by a national militia, with an extremely short term of service. The rural communes of every district were to administer their common affairs by an assembly of delegates in the central town, and these district assemblies were again to send deputies to the National Delegation in Paris, each delegate to be at any time revocable and bound by the *mandat impératif* (formal instructions) of his constituents. The few but important functions which still would remain for a central government were not to be suppressed, as has been intentionally mis-stated, but were to be discharged by Communal, and therefore strictly responsible agents. The unity of the nation was not to be broken, but, on the contrary, to be organised by the Communal Constitution and to become a reality by the destruction of the State power which claimed to be the embodiment of that unity independent of, and superior to, the nation itself, from which it was but a parasitic excrescence. While the merely repressive organs of the old governmental power were to be amputated, its legitimate functions were to be wrested from an authority usurping pre-eminence over society itself, and restored to the responsible agents of society. Instead of deciding once in three or six years which member of the ruling class was to misrepresent the people in Parliament, universal suffrage was to serve the people, constituted in Communes, as individual suffrage serves every other employer in the search for the workmen and managers in his business. And it is well known that companies, like individuals, in matters of real business generally know how to put the right man in the right place, and, if they for once make a mistake, to redress it promptly. On the other hand, nothing could be more foreign to the spirit of the Commune than to supersede universal suffrage by hierarchic investiture.

It is generally the fate of completely new historical creations to be mistaken for the counterpart of older and even defunct forms of social life, to which they may bear a certain likeness. Thus, this new Commune, which breaks the modern State power, has been mistaken for a reproduction of the mediaeval Communes, which first preceded, and afterwards became the substratum of, that very State power. The Communal Constitution has been mistaken for an attempt to break up into a federation of small States, as dreamt of by Montesquieu and the Girondins, that unity of great nations which, if originally brought about by political force, has now become a powerful coefficient of social production. The antagonism of the Commune against the State power has been mistaken for an exaggerated form of the ancient struggle against over-centralisation. Peculiar historical circumstances may have prevented the classical development, as in France, of the bourgeois form of government, and may have allowed, as in England, to complete the great central State organs by corrupt vestries; jobbing councillors, and ferocious poor-law guardians in the towns, and virtually hereditary magistrates in the counties. The Communal Constitution would have restored to the social body all the forces hitherto absorbed by the State parasite feeding upon, and clogging the free movement of, society. By this one act it would have initiated the regeneration of France. The provincial French middle class saw in the Commune an attempt to restore the sway their order had held over the country under Louis Philippe, and which, under Louis Napoleon, was supplanted by the pretended rule of the country over the towns. In reality, the Communal Constitution brought the rural producers under the intellectual lead of the central towns of their districts, and these secured to them, in the working men, the natural trustees of their interests. The very existence of the Commune involvd, as a matter of course, local municipal liberty, but no longer as a check upon the, now superseded, State power. It could only enter into the head of a Bismarck, who, when not engaged in his intrigues of blood and iron, always likes to resume his old trade, so befitting his mental calibre, of contributor to *Kladderadatsch* (the Berlin *Punch*), it could only enter into such a head, to ascribe to the Paris Commune aspirations after that caricature of the old French municipal organisation of 1791, the Prussian municipal constitution which degrades the town governments to mere secondary wheels in the police-machinery of the Prussian State. The Commune made that catchword of bourgeois revolutions, cheap government, a reality, by destroying the two greatest sources of expenditure—the standing army and State functionarism. Its very existence presupposed the non-existence of monarchy, which, in Europe at least, is the normal incumbrance and indispensable cloak of class-rule. It supplied the Republic with the basis of really democratic institutions. But neither cheap Government nor the "true Republic" was its ultimate aim; they were its mere concomitants.

The multiplicity of interpretations to which the Commune has been subjected, and the multiplicity of interests which construed it in their favour, show that it was a thoroughly expansive political form, while all previous forms of government had been emphatically repressive. Its true secret was this. It was essentially a working-class government, the produce of the struggle of the producing against the appropriating class, the political form at last discovered under which to work out the economic emancipation of labour.

Except on this last condition, the Communal Constitution would have been an impossibility and a delusion. The political rule of the producer cannot coexist with the perpetuation of his social slavery. The Commune was therefore to serve as a lever for uprooting the economical foundations upon which rests the existence of classes, and therefore of class-rule. With labour emancipated, every man becomes a working man, and productive labour ceases to be a class attribute.

It is a strange fact. In spite of all the tall talk and all the immense literature, for the last sixty years, about Emancipation of Labour, no sooner do the working men anywhere take the subject into their own hands with a will, than uprises at once all the apologetic phraseology of the mouthpieces of present society with its two poles of Capital and Wages Slavery (the landlord now is but the sleeping partner of the capitalist), as if capitalist society was still in its purest state of virgin innocence, with its antagonisms still undeveloped, with its delusions still unexploded, with its prostitute realities not yet laid bare. The Commune, they exclaim, intends to abolish property, the basis of all civilisation! Yes, gentlemen, the Commune intended to abolish that class-property which makes the labour of the many the wealth of the few. It aimed at the expropriation of the expropriators. It wanted to make individual property a truth by transforming the means of production, land and capital, now chiefly the means of enslaving and exploiting labour, into mere instruments of free and associated labour.—But this is Communism, "impossible" Communism! Why, those members of the ruling classes who are intelligent enough to perceive the impossibility of continuing the present system —and they are many—have become the obtrusive and full-mouthed apostles of co-operative production. If co-operative production is not to remain a sham and a snare; if it is to supersede the Capitalist system; if united co-operative societies are to regulate national production upon a common plan, thus taking it under their own control, and putting an end to the constant anarchy and periodical convulsions which are the fatality of Capitalist production—what else, gentlemen, would it be but Communism, "possible" Communism?

The working class did not expect miracles from the Commune. They have no ready-made utopias to introduce *par décret du peuple* [by the will of the people]. They know that in order to work out their own emancipation, and along with it that higher form to which present society is irresistibly tending by its own economical agencies, they will have to pass through long struggles, through a series of historic processes, transforming circumstances and men. They have no ideals to realize, but to set free the elements of the new society with which old collapsing bourgeois society itself is pregnant. In the full consciousness of their historic mission, and with the heroic resolve to act up to it, the working class can afford to smile at the coarse invective of the gentlemen's gentlemen with the pen and inkhorn, and at the didactic patronage of well-wishing bourgeois-doctrinaires, pouring forth their ignorant platitudes and sectarian crotchets in the oracular tone of scientific infallibility.

When the Paris Commune took the management of the revolution in its own hands; when plain working men for the first time dared to infringe upon the Governmental privilege of their "natural superiors," and, under circumstances of unexampled difficulty, performed their work modestly, conscientiously, and efficiently—performed it at salaries the highest of which barely amounted to one-fifth of what, according to high scientific authority,[1] is the minimum required for a

---

[1] Professor Huxley. [Note to the German editon of 1871; unless otherwise noted, the footnotes in this selection are from the 1970 edition of Marx's *Selected Works,* published by Foreign Languages Publishing House, Moscow.—*Ed.*]

secretary to a certain metropolitan school board—the old world writhed in convulsions of rage at the sight of the Red Flag, the symbol of the Republic of Labour, floating over the Hôtel de Ville.

And yet, this was the first revolution in which the working class was openly acknowledged as the only class capable of social initiative, even by the great bulk of the Paris middle class—shopkeepers, tradesmen, merchants—the wealthy capitalists alone excepted. The Commune had saved them by a sagacious settlement of that ever-recurring cause of dispute among the middle classes themselves—the debtor and creditor accounts. The same portion of the middle class, after they had assisted in putting down the working men's insurrection of June, 1848, had been at once unceremoniously sacrificed to their creditors by the then Constituent Assembly. But this was not their only motive for now rallying round the working class. They felt that there was but one alternative—the Commune, or the Empire—under whatever name it might reappear. The Empire had ruined them economically by the havoc it made of public wealth, by the wholesale financial swindling it fostered, by the props it lent to the artificially accelerated centralisation of capital, and the concomitant expropriation of their own ranks. It had suppressed them politically, it had shocked them morally by its orgies, it had insulted their Voltairianism by handing over the education of their children to the *frères Ignorantins* ["ignorant brothers," that is, the Christian teaching orders], it had revolted their national feeling as Frenchmen by precipitating them headlong into a war which left only one equivalent for the ruins it made—the disappearance of the Empire. In fact, after the exodus from Paris of the high Bonapartist and capitalist *bohême,* the true middle-class Party of Order came out in the shape of the "Union Républicaine," enrolling themselves under the colours of the Commune and defending it against the wilful misconstruction of Thiers. Whether the gratitude of this great body of the middle class will stand the present severe trial, time must show.

The Commune was perfectly right in telling the peasants that "its victory was their only hope." Of all the lies hatched at Versailles and re-echoed by the glorious European penny-a-liner, one of the most tremendous was that the Rurals represented the French peasantry. Think only of the love of the French peasant for the men to whom, after 1815, he had to pay the milliard of indemnity. In the eyes of the French peasant, the very existence of a great landed proprietor is in itself an encroachment on his conquests of 1789. The bourgeois, in 1848, had burdened his plot of land with the additional tax of forty-five cents in the franc; but then he did so in the name of the revolution; while now he had fomented a civil war against the revolution, to shift on to the peasant's shoulders the chief load of the five milliards of indemnity to be paid to the Prussian. The Commune, on the other hand, in one of its first proclamations, declared that the true originators of the war would be made to pay its cost. The Commune would have delivered the peasant of the blood tax—would have given him a cheap government—transformed his present blood-suckers, the notary, advocate, executor, and other judicial vampires, into salaried communal agents, elected by, and responsible to, himself. It would have freed him of the tyranny of the *garde champêtre* [elected official who enforced agriculture laws], the gendarme, and the prefect; would have put enlightenment by the schoolmaster in the place of stultification by the priest. And the French peasant is, above all, a man of reckoning. He would find it extremely reasonable that the pay of the priest, instead of being extorted by the taxgatherer, should only depend upon the spontaneous action of the parishioners' religious instincts. Such were the great immediate boons which the rule of the Commune— and that rule alone—held out to the French peasantry. It is, therefore, quite superfluous here to expatiate upon the more complicated but vital problems which the Commune alone was able, and at the same time compelled, to solve in favour of the peasant, *viz.*, the hypothecary debt, lying like an incubus upon his parcel of soil, the *prolétariat foncier* (the rural proletariat), daily growing upon it, and his expropriation from it enforced, at a more and more rapid rate, by the very development of modern agriculture and the completion of capitalist farming.

The French peasant had elected Louis Bonaparte president of the Republic; but the Party of Order created the Empire. What the French peasant really wants he commenced to show in 1849 and 1850, by opposing his *maire* [mayor] to the Government's prefect, his schoolmaster to the Government's priest, and himself to the Government's gendarme. All the laws made by the Party of Order in January and February, 1850, were avowed measures of repression against the peasant. The peasant was a Bonapartist, because the great Revolution, with all its benefits to him, was, in his eyes, personified in Napoleon. This delusion, rapidly breaking down under the Second Empire (and in its very nature hostile to the Rurals), this prejudice of the past, how could it have withstood the appeal of the Commune to the living interests and urgent wants of the peasantry?

The Rurals—this was, in fact, their chief apprehension—knew that three months' free communication of Communal Paris with the provinces would bring about a general rising of the peasants, and hence their anxiety to establish a police blockade around Paris, so as to stop the spread of the rinderpest.

If the Commune was thus the true representative of all the healthy elements of French society, and therefore the truly national Government, it was, at the same time, as a working men's Government, as the bold champion of the emancipation of labour, emphatically international. Within sight of the Prussian army, that had annexed to Germany two French provinces, the Commune annexed to France the working people all over the world..

The Second Empire had been the jubilee of cosmopolitan blacklegism, the rakes of all countries rushing in at its call for a share in its orgies and in the plunder of the French people. Even at this moment the right hand of Thiers is Ganesco, the foul Wallachian, and his left hand is Markovsky, the Russian spy. The Commune admitted all foreigners to the honour of dying for an immortal cause. Between the foreign war lost by their treason, and the civil war fomented by their conspiracy with the foreign invader, the bourgeoisie had found the time to display their patriotism by organising police-hunts upon the Germans in France. The Commune made a German working man[2] its Minister of Labour. Thiers, the bourgeoisie, the Second Empire, had continually deluded Poland by loud professions of sympathy, while in reality betraying her to, and doing the dirty work of, Russia. The Commune honoured the heroic sons of Poland[3] by placing them at the head of the defenders of Paris. And, to broadly mark the new era of history it was conscious of initiating, under the eyes of the conquering Prussians, on the one side, and of the Bonapartist army, led by Bonapartist generals, on the other, the Commune pulled down that colossal symbol of martial glory, the Vendôme column.

The great social measure of the Commune was its own working existence. Its special measures could but betoken the tendency of a government of the people by the people. Such were the abolition of the nightwork of journeymen bakers; the prohibition, under penalty, of the employers' practice to reduce wages by levying upon their workpeople fines under manifold pretexts—a process in which the employer combines in his own person the parts of legislator, judge, and executor, and filches the money to boot. Another measure of this class was the surrender, to associations of workmen, under reserve of compensation, of all closed workshops and factories, no matter whether the respective capitalists had absconded or preferred to strike work.

The financial measures of the Commune, remarkable for their sagacity and moderation, could only be such as were compatible with the state of a besieged town. Considering the colossal robberies committed upon the city of Paris by the great financial companies and

---

2 Leo Frankel.
3 J. Dabrowski and W. Wróblewski.

contractors, under the protection of Haussmann,[4] the Commune would have had an incomparably better title to confiscate their property than Louis Napoleon had against the Orleans family. The Hohenzollern and the English oligarchs, who both have derived a good deal of their estates from Church plunder, were, of course, greatly shocked at the Commune clearing but 8,000 f. out of secularisation.

While the Versailles Government, as soon as it had recovered some spirit and strength, used the most violent means against the Commune; while it put down the free expression of opinion all over France, even to the forbidding of meetings of delegates from the large towns; while it subjected Versailles and the rest of France to an espionage far surpassing that of the Second Empire; while it burned by its gendarme inquisitors all papers printed at Paris, and sifted all correspondence from and to Paris; while in the National Assembly the most timid attempts to put in a word for Paris were howled down in a manner unknown even to the *Chambre introuvable* of 1816[5]; with the savage warfare of Versailles outside, and its attempts at corruption and conspiracy inside Paris—would the Commune not have shamefully betrayed its trust by affecting to keep up all the decencies and appearances of liberalism as in a time of profound peace? Had the Government of the Commune been akin to that of M. Thiers, there would have been no more occasion to suppress Party-of-Order papers at Paris than there was to suppress Communal papers at Versailles.

It was irritating indeed to the Rurals that at the very same time they declared the return to the church to be the only means of salvation for France, the infidel Commune unearthed the peculiar mysteries of the Picpus nunnery, and of the Church of Saint Laurent. It was a satire upon M. Thiers that, while he showered grand crosses upon the Bonapartist generals in acknowledgement of their mastery in losing battles, signing capitulations, and turning cigarettes at Wilhelmshöhe, the Commune dismissed and arrested its generals whenever they were suspected of neglecting their duties. The expulsion from, and arrest by, the Commune of one of its members[6] who had slipped in under a false name, and had undergone at Lyons six days' imprisonment for simple bankruptcy, was it not a deliberate insult hurled at

---

[4] During the Second Empire, Baron Haussmann was Prefect of the Department of the Seine, that is, of the City of Paris. He introduced a number of changes in the layout of the city for the purpose of facilitating the crushing of workers' insurrections. [Note to the Russian edition of 1905 edited by V. I. Lenin]

[5] This refers to the Parliament elected in the early days of the Restoration which proved to be more conservative than the Bourbon monarchy.—*Ed.*

[6] Blanchet.

the forger, Jules Favre, then still the foreign minister of France, still selling France to Bismarck, and still dictating his orders to that paragon Government of Belgium? But indeed the Commune did not pretend to infallibility, the invariable attribute of all governments of the old stamp. It published its doings and sayings, it initiated the public into all its shortcomings.

In every revolution there intrude, at the side of its true agents, men of a different stamp; some of them survivors of and devotees to past revolutions, without insight into the present movement, but preserving popular influence by their known honesty and courage, or by the sheer force of tradition; others mere bawlers, who, by dint of repeating year after year the same set of stereotyped declamations against the Government of the day, have sneaked into the reputation of revolutionists of the first water. After the 18th of March, some such men did also turn up, and in some cases contrived to play pre-eminent parts. As far as their power went, they hampered the real action of the working class, exactly as men of that sort have hampered the full development of every previous revolution. They are an unavoidable evil: with time they are shaken off; but time was not allowed to the Commune.

Wonderful, indeed, was the change the Commune had wrought in Paris! No longer any trace of the meretricious Paris of the Second Empire. No longer was Paris the rendezvous of British landlords, Irish absentees, American ex-slaveholders and shoddy men, Russian ex-serfowners, and Wallachian boyards. No more corpses at the morgue, no nocturnal burglaries, scarcely any robberies; in fact, for the first time since the days of February, 1848, the streets of Paris were safe, and that without any police of any kind.

"We," said a member of the Commune, "hear no longer of assassination, theft and personal assault; it seems indeed as if the police had dragged along with it to Versailles all its Conservative friends."

The *cocottes* [prostitutes] had refound the scent of their protectors —the absconding men of family, religion, and, above all, of property. In their stead, the real women of Paris showed again at the surface— heroic, noble, and devoted, like the women of antiquity. Working, thinking, fighting, bleeding Paris—almost forgetful, in its incubation of a new society, of the cannibals at its gates—radiant in the enthusiasm of its historic initiative!

Opposed to this new world at Paris, behold the old world at Versailles—that assembly of the ghouls of all defunct *régimes*, Legitimists and Orleanists, eager to feed upon the carcass of the nation—with a tail of antediluvian Republicans, sanctioning, by their presence in the Assembly, the slaveholders' rebellion, relying for the maintenance of their Parliamentary Republic upon the vanity of the senile mountebank at its head, and caricaturing 1789 by holding their ghastly meetings in the *Jeu de Paume*.[7] There it was, this Assembly, the representative of everything dead in France, propped up to the semblance of life by nothing but the swords of the generals of Louis Bonaparte. Paris all truth, Versailles all lie; and that lie vented through the mouth of Thiers.

Thiers tells a deputation of the mayors of the Seine-et-Oise—"You may rely upon my word, which I have *never* broken!"

He tells the Assembly itself that "it was the most freely elected and most Liberal Assembly France ever possessed"; he tells his motley soldiery that it was "the admiration of the world, and the finest army France ever possessed"; he tells the provinces that the bombardment of Paris by him was a myth: "If some cannon-shots have been fired, it is not the deed of the army of Versailles, but of some insurgents trying to make believe that they are fighting, while they dare not show their faces."

He again tells the provinces that "the artillery of Versailles does not bombard Paris, but only cannonades it."

He tells the Archbishop of Paris that the pretended executions and reprisals (!) attributed to the Versailles troops were all moonshine. He tells Paris that he was only anxious "to free it from the hideous tyrants who oppress it," and that, in fact, the Paris of the Commune was "but a handful of criminals."

The Paris of M. Thiers was not the real Paris of the "vile multitude," but a phantom Paris, the Paris of the *francs-fileurs*, the Paris of the Boulevards, male and female—the rich, the capitalist, the gilded, the idle Paris, now thronging with its lackeys, its blacklegs, its literary *bohême*, and its *cocottes* at Versailles, Saint-Denis, Rueil, and Saint-Germain; considering the civil war but an agreeable diversion, eyeing the battle going on through telescopes, counting the rounds of cannon, and swearing by their own honour and that of their prostitutes, that the performance was far better got up than it used to be at the Porte St. Martin. The men who fell were really dead; the cries of the wounded were cries in good earnest; and, besides, the whole thing was so intensely historical.

This is the Paris of M. Thiers, as the emigration of Coblenz was the France of M. de Calonne.

---

[7] *Jeu de Paume*: The tennis court where the National Assembly of 1789 adopted its famous decisions. [Note to the German edition of 1871]

Henri Lefebvre

13

The Commune
and the Nature of Revolution

The Paris Commune? It was first
of all an immense, grandiose festival, one that the Parisian people,
the essence and symbol of the French people and of people in general,
gave themselves and the world. Spring holiday within the city; festival
of the disinherited and of the proletariat; revolutionary festival and
festival of the revolution; total festival, the greatest of modern times.
It unfolded at first in magnificence and joy.

The historic day of March 18, 1871, put an end to the passivity and
resignation that had reigned without weakening the fundamental
forces during the Empire, the war, and even during the siege of Paris.
These forces erupted within a great calm. The Parisian people broke
the dikes and flooded the streets. Brotherly and warm, the masses
enveloped those who should have fought them, the soldiers of the
established power. They disarmed them. The collective hero, the
popular genius, rose up in his youth and native vigor. He conquered
simply because he appeared. Surprised by his victory, he transmuted
it into splendor. He rejoiced; he contemplated his awakening and
transformed its power into beauty. He celebrated his new-found marriage with his conscience, with the palaces and monuments of the city,
and with the power that had escaped him for so long. And it really
was a festival, a long one, which went on from March 18 to March 26
(the elections) and March 28 (proclamation of the Commune) and
beyond with a magnificently organized ceremony and solemnity.

Then, or at the same time, the people rejoiced in their own festival
and changed it into a show. It so happened that they deluded themselves and made a mistake, for their show turned them away from
themselves. Just as in every real festival, pure drama appeared and
came forward. The popular festival apparently changed character. In
reality, it continued: It sank into pain. It is known that Tragedy and
Drama are bloody festivals during which the failure, sacrifice, and
death of the superhuman hero who has defied his destiny occur. Unhap-

piness becomes greatness, and failure leaves a forceful and hopeful lesson in the heart purified of its cowardly fears. Hercules, monster tamer, fights to prevent the poisonous material from covering his body. He tenses all his muscles, but in vain. He prepares the stake. Then comes death and the triumph of destiny and evil, the failure and final holocaust. But the funeral procession has not lost the grandiose sense of the festival. Those who fought to the cry of "Liberty or death" preferred death to capitulation and the certitude of subjugation. They are still fighting, desperately, madly, intrepidly. They then light with their own hands the stake on which they wish to be consumed and disappear. The tragedy ends in a conflagration and a disaster worthy of it. Continuing to the very end and carrying the titanic challenge to its final result, the Parisian people envisaged the end of Paris and wanted to die with what was for them more than scenery and more than a setting: their city, their body.

Thus the festival became drama and tragedy, absolute tragedy, Promethean tragedy played without a trace of a frivolous game; a tragedy in which the protagonist, the chorus, and the public coincide in unique fashion. But the festival contained the drama from the beginning; it recaptured its original meaning: a collective and real festival, a festival lived by and for the people, a colossal one accompanied by voluntary sacrifice of the principal actor during his failure, his tragedy.

Defining the Commune style in this way as both work and act, we do no more than take up Liebknecht's expression on "the horrible and grandiose tragedy of the Commune." Nor will the other aspects of those events be forgotten—neither the antecedents and circumstances nor the relationships among the men, groups, and ideas that entered into the action, nor the requirements of historical analysis and presentation. But it is our wish to show how Paris experienced its revolutionary passion. We will see why and how the scattered and divided city became a community of action; how during the festival the community became communion on the vastest scale then conceivable; how the people acclaimed the reestablishment of the symbols of nonalienated work, the fall of oppressive power, the end of alienation; how they proclaimed the world of work (that is, the work as world and creator of worlds); how during this huge festival something pierced the opaque veils of customary social life through and through, climbed from the depths, crossed the accumulated layers of inertia and obscurity, and came to the light of day and blossomed. How does one explain it? As a basic will to change the world and life as they are and things as they are, as a spontaneity bearing the highest thoughts, as a total revolutionary plan? As a delirious and generalized "all or nothing"? As a vital and absolute bet on the possible and the impossible?

The revolution as act was supposed to coincide with the results of the revolution. There should have been one single leap from blind necessity into the joyous reign of liberty in a great endless festival. At the same time, free labor should have been reborn as a game, the great, the real game with arms, with life and death.

. . .

The study of the revolutionary event, considered as a total phenomenon, has gone on simultaneously in two directions: the full reconstruction and the recounting of it with its singular and original characteristics set in history, and at the same time, the analysis of its elements and conditions. Trying to understand cannot be separated from trying to explain—that is, the search for the causes, reasons, and conditions. We have attempted to grasp the Commune as a unique and exceptional event. We have tried to explain it without reducing it to its antecedents and consequences, without diminishing its greatness by changing it through explanation into a sort of limited, defined, worn-out object.

Thus we have unveiled a myriad of conditions, causes and reasons, each one necessary, none sufficient. First, there are economic conditions. It is obvious that a proletarian revolution presupposes a proletariat, but neither the description of the economic situation nor that of the class relationships at a given moment was sufficient to explain the negativeness of the proletariat, its capacity to contest what existed, a basic capacity in the case of the Commune.

Second, there are historical conditions and causes—the Second Empire and its disintegration, the lost war. These historical causes are not enough to explain the revolutionary explosion; they are not even enough to explain one profound reason for this explosion, the consciousness of the historical moment.

Third, there is the series of causes that have to do specifically with sociology—that is, the crumbling of existing social structures and simultaneously, at the very heart of this destructuring, the rise of new ones that radically reject the old. Sociological research also reveals another line of reasoning: the necessity for a group of more or less homogeneous men (very heterogeneous for the Commune, since it was made up of men of action and ideologists) capable of orienting the spontaneous movement, taking the formation of new structures in hand, and providing an objective and a program. These men must also be able to face the risks of action, to chance history, to bet on the possible and impossible. In a normal democracy, political parties— or the revolutionary party—assume this role. But by definition the political party wants power, whereas the men of the Commune wanted to abolish that power.

We come then to the strictly ideological reasons. On one hand, the current ideological superstructures—representations, symbols, justifying institutional images, culture—must be devalued; on the other hand, a new ideology must give the spontaneous movement a coherent objective. The task was first to focus on the effacement of patriotism, then on the Proudhonian ideology not only as reformism, but also as a radical revolutionary plan both decentralizing and federative, transforming the existing society into a free association of free associations. Attainable or not under existing conditions, the plan was nevertheless total, stimulating, and vital. It pointed to one set of possibilities.

It is clear that the event can be explained neither by a preceding event nor by one single cause or antecedent. The search for a linear development or a more or less mechanical causal chain reaction can satisfy a certain kind of positivist-oriented scientific mind, but it does not render the event in its singularity and originality. We are brought to distinguish causes and reasons. The causes are objective and blind. They act more or less outside the clear consciousness of the historical actors. Reasons, on the other hand, belong to conscience, to subjectivity, to discourse, to ideology.

The ensemble of causes and reasons that we have been able to determine have first and foremost a negative force. The ensemble clears the way for a fundamental spontaneity: It pushes away the weights that are crushing it. It enables the spontaneity to open up in depth and also in its groping and hesitant clumsiness—its slow experience of itself, its hopes, and its at first uncertain aims. In this way, and only in this way, were the Parisian people able to become an articulate community, an explosive communion. Spontaneity in this total phenomenon appears to us simultaneously as condition, cause, and reason: Condition because nothing happens without it, neither movement nor work; cause because it is blind; reason because it is also awareness, the receiving of an ideology and a program. It presupposes the city, the proletariat, the people, and the going beyond of what cuts people up, disperses them, separates them from each other, divides them into separate segments external to one another.

As Lenin said, it is the unique and singular conjunction of objective and subjective elements, of causes and reasons, that composes the revolutionary event. Analysis always risks relegating an essential feature to the shadows: the fact is that it constitutes an indivisible, original, and singular totality—this even though it does not surge forward irrationally, even though it can be compared to other events, and even though it has a general meaning and scope. Such total phenomena, albeit original and attached to singular situations, nevertheless have laws. For example, Lenin's formulation: "They happen when men can and will no longer live as they were living."

The famous Aristotelian causality scheme provides a first and rough

approximation, but then it is necessary to make it concrete, to introduce the negative, and to restore in their totality the four causal orders
by stripping the scheme of its substantialist ontology—in a word, by
making it dialectic. We have been able to distinguish material causes
(the economic situation, the existence of territorial communities—
primarily the city of Paris), formal causes (negatively, the collapse of
the existing forms and structures; positively, the constitution of new
forms and structures), efficient causes (the defeat, the Prussian entry
into Paris, the trial of strength desired by Thiers), and finally, final
causes (the revolutionary plan, the deep hopes of spontaneity and the
aims it set for itself). Nevertheless, this rough scheme does not fully
account for the totality of the situation and even less for the new
totality that develops in the act and revolutionary event, whose failure
puts its attainment off to an undetermined time in the future. As for
the variation method used so often, consciously or not, by historians
("What would have happened if . . . "), at the most, it allows us to
perceive some of the most superficial causes of the failure.

These rough schemes and techniques enable us just to approach
the object of knowledge: the praxis taken as a whole with its internal
contradictions (creative practice and daily practice) and with its
attempts at solution and at going beyond these contradictions. In this
light, history can be represented as a succession of time stops, of stagnation and (relative) equilibrium separated by creative surges, the
revolutions whose contents and meaning the historian as historian
never manages to exhaust. They are the real events. These periods,
creation and calm development, cannot be separated. The latter carry
the seeds sown by the former to maturity. The former are seedlings
in the heart of the latter. Although the historian as such cannot grasp
the whole development, the cooperation of the historian, the sociologist, the economist, the theoretician of ideas, and the psychologist is
tending toward the production of a total history.

.   .   .

In order to summarize the scattered results of our study of the
Commune, we will examine its importance and meaning on various
interrelated levels.

1. The March 18 insurrection and the great days of the Commune
that followed were the opening up of the future and the possible,
without regard for the obstacles and impossibilities that barred the
way. A fundamental spontaneity (not "unconditional," because it has
historical and social conditions in the city and proletariat) removed
the sediment left by centuries: the state, the bureaucracy, the institutions, the dead culture. A volcanic effervescence heaved up the accumulated refuse. In this movement inspired by the negative creative
elements of the existing society—that is, the proletariat—social prac-

tice strove successfully to make itself free, to throw off the burdens that constrained it. It transformed itself in one leap into a community, into a communion within which work, joy, leisure, and the satisfaction of needs—first of all, social needs—would no longer be separable. After economic "progress," man would free himself from the economy itself. Politics and political society would disappear by being resolved in the civil society. The political function as a specialized activity would no longer exist. What was routine would become a perpetual festival. The daily struggle for bread and work would have no more meaning.

The Commune? It was a festival, the greatest of the century and modern times. The coldest analysis brings to light the will of the insurgents to become masters of their life and history not only in political decision making, but also in their daily lives. This is how we understand Marx: "The greatest social measure of the Commune was in its very existence as act. . . . Paris all truth; Versailles all lies."

This total revolutionary act, historically achieved, is sufficient to show that the Marxist thesis of an end of human prehistory, of a cancellation of human alienation, and of the inauguration of a history consciously lived and dominated by men does not, as is often said, have anything to do with eschatology, with an apocalyptic view, a vain utopian construction. This utopia, this alleged myth, became fact and life for a few days. In this sense, the Commune became the very idea of the revolution, understood not as an abstract ideal, but as the concrete idea of liberty. This idea contains the sense of history, or rather man's prehistory insofar as it opens on his real history and the history of his truth.

The experience of the Commune goes much further than a collection of revolutionary vignettes or political lessons. We willingly call it trans-historic, or even poetic, philosophic and ontologic (in the new sense of these terms). The Parisian masses, in coming forward, in breaking out into the streets, opened up the widest horizon. Their disorder enclosed a new order. The bases of sociology emerge, come to the surface, and are visible. The Commune as act anticipated the possible and the impossible so that even the inapplicable plans and decisions that remained intentions, like the federative plan, retain a deep meaning.

2. In the name of the Commune and of the Parisian people's initiatives, including those of the central committee, the Marxist doctrine on the state and politics took shape. In the effervescent confusion, Marx perceived and chose what could be projected toward the future. The seeds of a radical criticism of the state and politics contained in Marx's work since the criticism of the Hegelian state took shape. The historic mission of the proletariat was not only to continue the devel-

opment of the productive forces, but also to reconcile praxis with truth, to realize the truth of social praxis, to put an end to the state and politics. The new type of state created by the working class in power can and must be only a state that is withering away, that is destined to wither away, that is already being superseded, freed of the burdens of a permanent army, bureaucracy, police, established judiciary—in a nutshell, freed of all the state and governmental apparatus set up throughout history in class societies. Consequently, it must be a state more democratic than any other.

The Commune was the conquest of political power by the working class (Marx), but it radically changed the form and meaning of political power by placing the social aspect and the society above politics, by lowering politics and leading it toward its end. Marxist theory is based on the French experience of the Commune, on the ideology of French socialism, and not on that of Lassalle's state socialism in Germany.

"Thanks to the battle waged by Paris, the struggle of the working class against the capitalist class and its state entered a new phase. Whatever the outcome, we have obtained a new point of departure of universal importance," wrote Marx to Kugelmann, April 17, 1871. Let us be sure to stress the terms "universal" and "world historical" used by Marx, terms which show that he envisaged theoretical developments and not a simple inventory of the initiatives of the Parisian people and the working class at the level of political empiricism.

3. We should take Marx and Engels' expression, "Look at the Paris Commune; it was the dictatorship of the proletariat," as a starting point to show what the dictatorship of the proletariat is and also what it is not. In particular, the Commune experience and the formulations of Marx and Engels are essential parts of the case against Stalinism as a deviation from the dictatorship of the proletariat, the theory of which was developed by Marx, Engels, and Lenin precisely on the basis of the Commune. Stalinist historians manage to deform the history of the Commune because they continue to sweep under the rug the real theory of the dictatorship of the proletariat, which is identical with the theory of the withering away of the state, and of a thoroughgoing and fulfilled democracy.

Lenin wrote that the power of the soviets would have the same characteristics as that of the Commune. The source of power is situated "in the initiative coming from below, direct and local, from the popular masses." The police and the army, as institutions separate from and opposed to the people, "are replaced by direct arming of all the people. . . . It is the people in arms who guard public order." Finally, bureaucracy is replaced by direct power of the people, or at least placed under their control. Civil servants "are not only elected, but are also removable," and are reduced to the role of simple representatives.

Many historians, mainly among Marxists, criticized the Commune's incoherence and the evident lack of a political apparatus (party, governmental personnel). We have reason today to believe that the apparatus problem is far more complicated than the open or hidden Stalinists made it out to be. It is thus time to stop considering the Commune as a typical example of a revolutionary primitivism whose errors are to be overcome, and to begin to see it as an enormous negative and positive experience that has not yet yielded all its truths.

4. In the March 18 insurrection and in the Commune until its dramatic end, the heroes and the geniuses were collective. The Commune did not have great leaders. The official "guides" of the 1871 movement—the theoreticians as well as the men of action, the members of the central committee as well as those of the communal council —lacked depth, genius, and even competence. This explains to a certain extent the paradoxical entanglement of successes and failures. Nevertheless, we would do well to remember that even the most spontaneous and "irresponsible" acts are to be claimed for the continuation of the revolutionary movement of our time—for example, the taking over of the great public bodies by men gifted simply with good sense and daily experience; the constant intervention of the rank and file into affairs generally dealt with at the top.

The importance of arming the people was apparent from the beginning of the movement to its end. On the whole, the Parisian people and their delegates did not abdicate the right to impose the common will in favor of specialized detachments—volunteers, elite or shock troops, marching and attack forces. This collective and spontaneous attitude certainly gave rise to difficulties, contradictions, and conflicts. But the exemplary value of general arming of the people has its reverse side: the lack of coordination in military offensives, the fact that the fight against Versailles never brought popular strength to the level of military effectiveness. Nevertheless, it is worthwhile remembering that the Spanish revolution was made in spite of the solid organization of a republican army.

In addition, the Paris Commune was conquered less by strength of arms than by force of habit, a force shaken for a time but then reconstituted by some leaders in the name of their ideology (the bad side of the Proudhonians). That in Paris the Bank of France remained a Versailles enclave, as well as the Stock Exchange, the banks in general, and the State Deposit and Consignment Bank, is astonishing and scandalous to the historian. Other ideological habits were ruinous and contained the seeds of failure: the resurgence of Jacobinism, the memories of '89 (so well denounced by Marx), the defensive and consequently defeatist strategy of the district barricades in memory of 1848, and so on. The men of the Commune obviously are to be criticized for not having dared to respond to the totalitarian terror of the established power by using all their means and arms.

The Commune and its defeat show how the defenders of the old world took advantage of the complicity of the revolutionaries, of those who thought or pretended to think revolution. They clothed the genuine revolutionary creations with old garments that suffocated them. The old, outdated world thus kept its supporting structure— ideology, language, mores, tastes, dubious rites, sacred images, old symbols—even among its enemies. It used them to regain its ground. Gone forever was the fundamental spontaneity, the creative capacity, the thought and action inherent in the revolutionary proletariat and people. The "fifth column" is too often found in the hearts, souls, and minds of the revolutionaries themselves. It is undeniable that in the single ideology which inspired the men of the Commune, the Proudhonian doctrine (Blanquism and Jacobinism were action attitudes more than anything else), reformism, and the revolutionary plan were mixed up in an inextricable confusion and conflict.

The anecdote about the arsonists who came to destroy Notre Dame and met up with the battalion of the Commune artists suggests a subject for particular study. On the one hand, there were men (artists) who were defending a great work of art in the name of permanent esthetic values. On the other hand, there were men who wanted that day to express by their destructive act their total challenge to a society that rejected them. Thus Hercules, symbol of the collective hero, shows his heroic nature—vital, human, and superhuman—by lighting the stake that will consume him.

5. The Commune still represents the only attempt at a revolutionary urbanism, attacking in the field the petrified signs of the old organization, seizing the sources of sociability (at that time the neighborhood or *quartier*), seeing social space in political terms and not believing in the innocence of a monument (demolition of the Vendôme column, occupation of churches by clubs). Those who classify such acts as nihilistic and barbaric then have to admit that they are prepared to keep everything they consider as positive; that is, all the results of history, all the works of the dominant society, all the traditions— everything acquired, including the dead and the immobile.

The mass of acts performed by the Commune allow some particular actions, left unfinished and still in the spontaneous form of intention, to be labeled as atrocities. Historians who restore history, consciously or not, from the viewpoint of a Divine Providence or an underlying determinism (which comes down to almost the same thing) have no trouble in showing the Commune as objectively condemnable. Caught in its own contradictions, it could not rise above them. But it should not be forgotten that for those who lived it, the rising above (*dépassement*) was there, close by, moving, in the movement itself.

The audaciousness and inventiveness of the revolutionary movement in 1871 obviously should not be measured against our epoch, but against the banalities then reigning in cultural, political, moral, and daily life. The revolutionary movement shattered them. If we consider the sum of banalities now in circulation, we can imagine the invention that would result from an analogous explosion in the so-called modern world. This spontaneous explosion is not possible at this time, but there is nothing that relegates it to the realm of absolute impossibility in a more distant future, because the reasons for revolt, discontent, and frustration are accumulating.

The Commune was one moment of a great, continuing fight (although the conditions have changed). As far as "making the unconscious tendencies of the Commune conscious" (Engels), the last word is far from being said. In taking all of Marx's thinking on the Commune, we have seen in it the great attempt at the destruction of hierarchal power, the entirely subversive praxis exposing (in order to destroy) the existing world, and substituting another in its place, a new world, tangible, sensitive, and transparent. It was a unique moment in the total revolution up to now.

6. The initial victory of the Commune announced and prepared the way for the victory of the October revolution, principally by generating structures and forms of organization. At the same time, the failure and crushing of the Commune introduced a long period of revolutionary stagnation (1871–1917), of relatively peaceful development of capitalism and reformism, as well as the failure of the revolutionary movement in advanced industrialized countries, and the shift of the worldwide revolution toward the predominantly agrarian countries—the deflection of history.

If the Commune gave a new international spur to the socialist movement by "annexing the workers of the world to France" (Marx), the great bloodletting nonetheless weakened the French proletariat. It inevitably had trouble bearing a run of great historic defeats (1848, 1871, and, to a certain extent, 1920, not to speak of 1945 and the "liberation"). The Commune thus has a double meaning and a double importance: It is the summation and symbol of the end of one period, and the herald of a new one.

For a long time in France, liberals, leftist Christians, and Stalinists agreed to reduce the Commune's significance. Remembering the "national front," they stressed the Commune's patriotic confusion. They described a fundamental patriotism gradually colored by social considerations. The Commune would be the French people demanding to be well-governed, claiming a "cheap government" by petition and "honest" leaders, and then being driven to despair by the bourgeois, antipatriotic right. These are banalities and positivist platitudes.

We have found infinitely more in the Commune movement: a radical and living protest of what existed, and the plan for a total renovation. Against these restrictive interpretations, we have tried to find the lost greatness of the drama.

In these comments, we have deliberately ignored the objections that are sure to arise, the accusations of extremism, anarchism, and "leftism" (for having justified the spontaneity and some acts generally thought to be errors and crimes); and the accusation of conservative opportunism (for having partially rehabilitated the Proudhonian ideology concerning the plan for decentralization).

7. Moving toward a "positive" politics and history, we can affirm that the Commune saved the Republic and made possible the later development of a relatively advanced bourgeois democracy.

The March 18 insurrection paralyzed the political will of the Versailles Assembly and of its rural monarchist majority (known, moreover, to be divided). In one sense, the Commune made it possible for the tortuous intrigues of Thiers to succeed. He wanted a bourgeois republic and used Paris to neutralize the monarchist right.

During the Commune's agony and in spite of the crushing of the provincial insurrections, the republican movement got hold of itself again. This was evident in the municipal elections and even more in the July 1871 elections: 44 departments gave an enormous majority to the republicans. Even in Paris, and despite the terror, only 4 deputies out of the 21 newly elected were monarchist. Of a hundred new deputies, only one was "legitimist."

During the next few years, the political battle unfolded largely around the Commune, the rehabilitation of the Communards, and the amnesty. The legalists (Clemenceau), the centralist republicans (Gambetta), the conciliators (the Freemasons), and the centrists and opportunists took advantage of the general circumstances (the sacrifice of the Communards), but that is only a minor aspect of the story. The bourgeois republic was first consolidated on January 30, 1875, and then by general elections in February 1876. This initially conservative republic slowly received a certain democratic content.

Most of the measures advocated by the Commune, and for which it is justly honored, could be adopted into a bourgeois democracy. Lenin noted it: In any other normal period of history a bourgeois republic would have easily solved the problems put to the Commune. "When the bourgeoisie refuses to do this, the proletariat solves these same problems by a revolution, and the Commune was one." In fact, the Commune provided and momentarily put into practice the program that the bourgeois democracy had taken more than thirty years to accomplish only partially: separation of church and state, obligatory and secular education, trade union and workers' associations legislation, and labor laws.

Political success for the Communards could have consisted of a reconciliation and compromise with Versailles in speeding up the development of this democratic and social republic. But such a "success" would have hidden the essential; would it not then have been the greatest of failures?

VI/IMPERIALISM

UNTIL the beginning of the twentieth century, imperialism was a word without emotional content, meant to designate the activities of a state engaged in expanding beyond its borders. The period 1870–1914 saw the beginning of a new kind of expansion, with the highly advanced capitalist countries of Western Europe and the United States attempting to control underdeveloped countries by a variety of means, including physical coercion and occupation. This sometimes took the form of colonialism, as in the so-called scramble for Africa, when England, France, and Germany fought one another to divide up the continent. On other occasions, the lands of imperialist exploitation were left nominally independent, for example Cuba and the Latin American republics dominated by the United States.

"Imperialism" has become and remains a burning issue because of the emergence of the third world, the cold war, and the role the concept plays in Marxist theory. Its meaning is subject to constant debate, although it is now clear that it is not identical with colonialism, nor with just any sort of physical takeover of one state, nation, or territory by another. The concept is a historically specific one and applies to the activities of capitalist states at a certain moment of their history.

The Marxist concept of imperialism was first formulated by Nikolai Bukharin in his *The World Economy and Imperialism* (1915) and popularized and extended by Lenin in *Imperialism: The Highest Stage of Capitalism* (1916). Bukharin's book enjoyed a wide vogue in the 1920s, when he played an important role in the Soviet government. His reputation was effectively destroyed when he fell victim to Stalin's purges of 1937. Only recently has his work emerged from obscurity. Lenin, on the other hand, has become the standard authority, much challenged but not yet replaced.

In recent years, a great deal of effort has been expended by Western European and American historians in an attempt to prove that Lenin was wrong. He may have been, but what is important is the means used to demolish his arguments. In my view, the attacks have done little more than obscure the issue. The critics have, by and large, read him incorrectly, as the young English historian Eric Stokes attempts to show in the article reprinted here.

What did Lenin say? First of all, he defined imperialism as the highest stage of capitalism, a moment in the evolution of the capitalist mode of production. It comes into existence when capital, in obedience to the law that causes it to seek the highest rate of profit, spills over national boundaries to find new areas of investment and markets. Imperialism is by no means limited to the exploitation of the third world, but extends to (and may even be centered in) rivalry among imperialist powers in one another's back-yards. It is not permissible to attribute to Lenin an attitude so gross as to be expressed in terms of the "self-interest of the capitalist." If imperialism indeed cannot be "interpreted as the spontaneous expression of the idealism, the chauvinism or the mere energy of a nation" (D. K. Fieldhouse), neither can it be seen as the result of the sum of individual ambitions. There is no conspiracy afoot, nor any occult control of politics. On the contrary, there are classes and men as members of classes moving about within a social formation of a particular mode of production, complexly motivated and acting is complicated ways. To say that imperialism happens in accordance with the laws of capital seeking profit is not to say that all its dimensions are purely economic. There is plenty of room for the play of expansionist ideology and the strategic interests of professional soldiers. But for a Marxist, they alone would not suffice as an explanation.

The failure to understand Lenin's thesis is, at one level, the result of a curious blindness that persists in making of Marxism an economic determinism. Perhaps it is because the critics are unable to abandon positivist patterns of thought and adopt dialectical ones. It seems to me that positivists seek causes (in the sense that a will always lead to b), whereas Marxists adduce conditions (a is a condition in which b becomes possible or even necessary, because men will intervene in the process with a limited, but not negligible, degree of freedom). At another level, the caricature of Lenin's views makes it possible to lump together all extraterritorial expansion under the rubric "imperialism" regardless of historical context (for example, Soviet "imperialism"). This preemption of the term is an excellent propaganda ploy. Furthermore, if imperialism is colonialism, then the United States is not an imperialist power—or only an insignificant one.

The idea is not to make of Lenin a biblical text, but to examine what he actually said, and then to ask whether the Marxist method of analysis applied to this subject has any validity, whatever the errors he may have made. D. K. Fieldhouse of the Institute of Commonwealth Studies, London, in the article reprinted here finds both Marx and Lenin unsatisfactory. I would urge that his criticism is based on a misapprehension of what his adversaries have said. For instance, Lenin maintained that imperialism began as a system about 1900, not 1870, and that the intervening thirty years were a period of transition setting the stage for imperialism proper. But perhaps it is more important to note that Fieldhouse's hostility to Marxist explanations may proceed from his admitted suspicion of all-embracing theories and a tendency to place the emphasis on continuity so common among mainstream historians.

D. K. Fieldhouse

14

Imperialism:
An Historiographical Revision

It is now nearly sixty years since J. A. Hobson published *Imperialism: a Study*, and thereby gave the word the connotation it still generally carries. His conception of the nature of "imperialism" has, indeed, been almost universally accepted and, partly through the expository literature it has generated, may be said to have exercised a significant historical influence. Yet, for all its success, Hobson's argument has always been extremely vulnerable to criticism: and it is therefore surprising that those historians and economists who have argued effectively that his analysis is basically unsound should have received so little attention. The aim of the present article is to draw together some of the more important arguments that have been put forward for and against his thesis, and to suggest that, on balance, the noes have it.

Hobson's own claim to importance and originality lies simply in his having induced British, and subsequently world, opinion to accept his own special definition of the word imperialism. Professor Koebner has already examined the various meanings given to the word before 1902. He has suggested that, as used in England, it had two general connotations in the 1890's, both of which were morally neutral. In one sense, it was being used of those who wished to prevent the existing British settlement colonies from seceding and becoming independent states, and was therefore a conservative factor. In another, and increasingly common, sense, it was being used to indicate an expansionist and "forward" attitude towards problems connected with the future control of the "uncivilized" parts of the world, such as Africa, the Middle East and the Pacific. Salisbury was, in this sense, regarded as an imperialist in accepting the need for Britain to share in the partition of East Africa. Gladstone, in opposing the acquisition of Uganda, was emphatically anti-imperialist, even though he had acquiesced in the need to gain some control over Egypt in 1882. In the eyes of the anti-imperialists the sin of expansionism lay in the waste of money it entailed on armaments, in the cost of colonial governments, and in the danger of international conflicts over intrinsically unimportant territories which it would be wiser to leave alone. As a rule no worse motive was attributed to the imperialists than "jingoism" or excessive concern with Britain's position as a great power.

But, between 1896 and 1902, imperialism, as a word, began to lose its innocence. Koebner has shown that events in South Africa, and particularly the Jameson Raid, gave rise to a suspicion that, here at least, the expansive urge was motivated by something other than a concern for national greatness, by what Harcourt called "stock-jobbing imperialism"—based on the interests of financiers. This was, of course, a special case; and a distinction remained between an honest, even if misguided, imperialism, and the debased variety to be seen on the Rand. Yet the idea now gained ground that South Africa might not, after all, be a special case, but might exhibit in an extreme form a factor inherent in all expansionism. By 1900 radical opinion had moved so far in this direction that the Fifth International Socialist Congress, taught probably by its English delegation, could resolve

[. . . that the development of capitalism leads inevitably to colonial expansion . . . : that the colonial policy of the bourgeoisie has no other aim but to increase the profits of the capitalist class and to maintain the capitalist system. . . .]

Here, in a nutshell, was Hobson's doctrine of "imperialism." But it remained to be seen whether such a dogmatic interpretation would ever command a wide support: and it was essentially his achievement to ensure that, in his own non-Marxist form, it should become the generally accepted theory.

Hobson's *Imperialism* therefore came out at a time when British public opinion, disillusioned by the Boer war, was already profoundly suspicious about the motives behind recent imperial expansion. It was, in fact, a pamphlet for the times, rather than a serious study of the subject; and, like all pamphlets that achieve influence, it owed much of its success to the fact that it expressed a current idea with peculiar clarity, force and conviction. . . . Yet, paradoxically, Hobson was not primarily concerned with imperial problems: and *Imperialism* can only be properly understood on the basis that his interest, then and throughout his life, was with the social and economic problems of Britain. In a sense, this book was primarily a vehicle for publicizing the theory of "underconsumption," which he regarded as his main intellectual achievement, and which he expressed more fully in *The Evolution of Modern Capitalism,* and other works. In brief, the theory, which was an alternative to the Marxist concept of surplus

value as an explanation of poverty, saw excessive investment by the
capitalist, with its concomitant of underconsumption by the wage-
earner, as the root cause of recurrent slumps, of low interest rates, and
of permanent under-employment. Hobson thought there were only
two answers to this problem. The correct one—which would also be
the answer to the "condition of England question"—was to increase
the buying power of the workers by giving them a higher share of the
profits of industry. The wrong one, which was no answer to the social
question, was to invest the surplus capital overseas, where it could
earn a high interest rate, and thus sustain domestic rates of interest,
without benefiting the British worker. And this, he held, was what
Britain had been doing since at least the middle of the nineteenth
century.

To this point the economic theory, though highly vulnerable, has
no apparent relevance to the phenomenon of overseas expansion, that
is, to imperialism. The key to Hobson's theory of "imperialism" lies
in the connexion he makes between the two.

Overproduction in the sense of an excessive manufacturing plant, and
surplus capital which could not find sound investments within the
country, forced Great Britain, Germany, Holland, France to place larger
and larger portions of their economic resources outside the area of their
present political domain, and then stimulate a policy of political expansion so as to take in the new areas.

Thus "imperialism," in the special sense used by Hobson, is an external symptom of a social malady in the metropolitan countries. Without this domestic pressure for investment overseas, there would be no
effective impulse towards the acquisition of new colonies. Conversely,
without colonies, capital would lack an outlet, and domestic rates of
interest would sink. Thus the need to export capital and to make it
politically secure overseas was what Mr. John Strachey has recently
called the "prime mover for the modern imperialist process...." And
"imperialism," on this assumption, is not variously "sound" or "stock-
jobbing"; but, without exception, results from the special economic
interests of the capitalist, and is therefore "economic imperialism."

It is not proposed at this stage to examine Hobson's theory in detail:
but some comment must be made on the logical value of the argument
he uses to demonstrate the historical truth of this hypothesis. Does he,
in fact, supply any evidence to support the claim that colonies were
the product of a demand either for new investment opportunities, or
for security for existing investments? He begins with a straightforward
account of the expansion of the European empires since 1870, printing
a list of territories acquired by Britain, which Lenin, and later Mr.

Strachey, have reproduced. Then, in chapter two, he demonstrates that the expansion of the British empire had been of little apparent value to British trade; that trade with these recent acquisitions was the least valuable part of intra-imperial trade; and that British trade with all colonies was declining in relation to trade with the rest of the world. Clearly, then, "imperialism" was not good for trade. Nor was it good for emigration (which, in any case, he thought unnecessary), since these new tropical colonies were quite unsuited to white settlement. And his conclusion was that

The Imperialism of the last six decades is clearly condemned as a business policy, in that at enormous expense it has procured a small, bad, unsafe increase of markets, and has jeopardised the entire wealth of the nation in arousing the strong resentment of other nations. . . .

How then can a motive be found for this imperial expansion? The motive is to be seen if, alongside the list of territorial acquisitions, is placed a table showing the increase of British overseas investments in the same period. It then becomes obvious that, during the period in which British possessions had increased by 4,754 m. [million] square miles and by a population of 88 millions, British overseas investments had also increased enormously—from £144 m. to £1698 m. between 1862 and 1893 alone. Could there be any doubt that the two sets of figures were intimately connected as cause and effect? Hobson had no doubts about it: "It is not too much to say that the modern foreign policy of Great Britain has been primarily a struggle for profitable markets of investment."

But it is immediately apparent that Hobson had in no sense proved that there was any connexion between the investments made overseas and the territory acquired contemporaneously. His table of investments made no differentiation between the areas in which investment had taken place, beyond such classifications as "Foreign," "Colonial," "U.S.A." and "Various," and, in fact, he assumes quite arbitrarily that the new colonies had attracted a high proportion of the investment called "Foreign" (i.e. before they were annexed) or "Colonial" (subsequent to annexation). This, it will be suggested below, is a basic fault of his theory of "imperialism." Indeed, to put the case bluntly, Hobson performed an intellectual conjuring trick. Convinced of the essential truth of his economic theory, he deceived the eye by the speed of his hand, creating the illusion that, of the two sets of statistics he held up, one was the cause of the other.

It is not possible here to consider the rest of Hobson's *Imperialism*, interesting though it is in relation to related controversies over protection, tariff reform and imperial unity. But two additional points in his main argument must be mentioned because they were intrinsic to his definition of the origins and nature of "imperialist" expansion.

The first of these concerns the relationship between the financial interest and other "imperialists," and is therefore crucial to his theory. He was aware that, contrary to his argument, the obvious driving force of British expansion since 1870 appeared to lie in the explorers, missionaries, engineers, patriotic pressure groups, and empire-minded politicians, all of whom had evident influence, and had demonstrable interests, other than those of investment, in territorial acquisitions. And he was equally aware that if the impulse to expansion could be satisfactorily explained in the old-fashioned terms of their idealism, their ambition, or their concern with the status of Britain as a world power, rather than in terms of the self-interest of the capitalist, his own central thesis would collapse. It was therefore necessary that these men—the Lugards, the Milners, the Johnstons, and the Roseberys—should be shown to be mere puppets—the tools of "imperialism" rather than its authors. Hobson did this by falling back on what may be called the "faceless men" gambit:

Finance manipulates the patriotic forces which politicians, soldiers, philanthropists, and traders generate; the enthusiasm for expansion which issues from these sources, though strong and genuine, is irregular and blind; the financial interest has those qualities of concentration and clear-sighted calculation which are needed to set Imperialism to work. An ambitious statesman, a frontier soldier, an overzealous missionary, a pushing trader, may suggest or even initiate a step of imperial expansion, may assist in educating patriotic public opinion to the urgent need of some fresh advance, but the final determination rests with the financial power.

In this ingenious way Hobson inverted the apparent relationship between the obvious "imperialists" and the investor. Instead of the financier being induced to invest in new possessions, with more or less enthusiasm, once political control has been imposed for other reasons, he becomes the essential influence in the take-over itself. Investment no longer follows the flag: it decides where it is profitable to plant it, and tells the government whether it is to follow the advice of men of action or of ideas in each particular case. Thus, "imperialism" can never be interpreted as the spontaneous expression of the idealism, the chauvinism or the mere energy of a nation. In its practical form it is the expression of the special interests of the financier behind the scenes, who decides whether it is worth his while to allow a dream to become a reality, and who alone will reap the benefits.

This assumption, which has been adopted by most subsequent supporters of Hobson's thesis, will be examined later.

The other essential point in the theory of "imperialism" is the suggestion that the possession of colonies by individual capitalist states results automatically in the exploitation of the indigenous peoples of Africa and Asia. In his long chapter "Imperialism and the Lower Races," which is in many ways one of the most undogmatic and constructive parts of the book, Hobson argued that exploitation, whether by appropriation of land, or by the use of cheap labour—forced or nominally free—in mines, farms and factories, had been a general feature of the colonies of all the European powers. Hobson, in the British humanitarian tradition, thought such exploitation to be both wrong and inexpedient. Economic development was good for undeveloped colonies and for the world as a whole. The danger lay in allowing the financiers to use the political power of the imperial authority for their own purposes; and the solution was for international control of colonies—the germ of the later mandate concept—and patience in allowing normal economic forces to give the natives an inducement to work freely in European enterprises. Sensible as his general attitude was, it is clear that Hobson had thus included in "imperialism" the suggestion that countries possessing colonies were almost certain to exploit them in their own interests; and this argument was to become a staple of later critics of "colonialism."

The theory of "imperialism" as it developed after the publication of Hobson's *Study* continued to be founded on the three main concepts outlined above. Yet, in examining its historiography, it is clear that it was Lenin, writing in 1916, rather than Hobson himself, who gave "imperialism" its dogmatic coherence and much of its eventual influence. It is therefore necessary to consider briefly the extent to which Lenin modified Hobson's ideas.

The greatest difference lies in the first and most important part of the argument; that is, in the nature of the internal pressure in the capitalist countries which forces them to expand their colonial possessions. Hobson had explained this pressure in terms of "underconsumption": but Lenin naturally had a more orthodox theory to hand. Capitalism as a system was approaching the apocalypse Marx had foretold. Competitive capitalism had, in the late nineteenth century, been replaced by "monopoly capitalism," with its characteristic agencies, the cartels, trusts and tariffs. It was no longer dynamic, but anxious only to maintain its profit margins by more intensive exploitation of limited and protected markets. Moreover, the "finance-capitalists"—the banks and trusts—who now largely controlled capital itself, found that, under monopoly conditions, it was more profitable to employ surplus capital abroad than in domestic industry. At home, it could only increase production, lower prices, and raise wages.

Abroad it could give a high interest return without any of these consequences. But, to gain the highest return from overseas investment it was desirable to have some political control over the territory in which the investment was made. This might be in the limited form of a "semi-colony," such as the Argentine. But only in the colony proper could really comprehensive economic and political controls be imposed which would give investments their highest return. The result had been the competition between the great powers to acquire new colonies after 1870, which would continue until the whole uncivilized world had come under imperial rule. Then would follow the inter-imperial wars for the redivision of the empires, leading to proletarian revolutions in the "imperialist" states, the creation of "socialist" states, and so, automatically, to the end of "imperialism."

How much, then, does Lenin's explanation of the force behind "imperialism" differ from that of Hobson? Fundamentally, only in this: that, whereas Hobson used his theory as evidence that social-democratic reform at home was necessary and possible to eliminate the evil of "under-consumption" and therefore make "imperialism" unnecessary, Lenin made "imperialism" the definition of an inherent and unavoidable stage in the growth of capitalist society which could not be "reformed." Hobson was a doctor prescribing a remedy, Lenin a prophet forecasting catastrophe. But, while they disagreed as to the precise causes, both maintained that there existed in the "capitalist" countries a tremendous pressure for overseas investment, and that this was the main factor in producing "imperialist" expansion after 1870.

On Hobson's second point—the control and influence exercised by "finance" over government and over the men who actually carved out the new empires—there is little difference between them. Lenin, if anything, went further, ignoring the theory that in a democratic country like Britain Hobson's "imperialists" found it necessary to corrupt public opinion through the press; and assuming, on the basis of Marxist theory and German experience, that the financial power of the banks and trusts was now so great that governments virtually did as they were told by the "finance-capitalist." Moreover, Lenin rejected entirely the possibility that the drive behind imperialism might have been the natural product of nationalism in international politics. To him as a Marxist such arguments were superficial. The only true explanation must lie in the fundamental economic environment which dictates political interests: and he castigates the unfortunate Kautsky on the grounds that he "detaches the politics of imperialism from its economics. . . ." Economic factors are the root of all features of the "imperialist" state; and even Franco-German competition for Alsace-Lorraine exists "because an essential feature of imperialism is the rivalry between a number of great powers in the striving for hegemony, i.e.

for the conquest of territory, not so much directly for themselves as to weaken the adversary and undermine *his* hegemony." There is no room here for explaining the actions of governments in any terms other than of the economics of "imperialism."

On Hobson's third point, Lenin had little explicit to say. As a Marxist he assumed it to be axiomatic that all workers were exploited by capital; so that a colony would differ from the metropolis only in the fact that the exploiting capitalist was an alien, and colonies merely added to the pool of labour from which he could extract "surplus value."

. . .

The central feature of the theory of "imperialism," by which it must stand or fall, is the assertion that the empires built up after 1870 were not an option but a necessity for the economically advanced states of Europe and America: that these capitalist societies, because of their surplus of domestically produced capital, were forced to export capital to the under-developed regions of the world: and that it was only this investment—prospective or existing—that supplied a motive for the acquisition of new colonies.

Faced with this theory, the historian who does not take its truth for granted is likely to be sceptical on at least three main grounds. First, his instinct is to distrust all-embracing historical formulas which, like the concept of "the rise of the middle class," seek to explain complex developments in terms of a single dominant influence. Again, he is likely to suspect an argument that isolates the imperial expansion of the period after 1870 from all earlier imperial developments if only because he is aware of so many elements of continuity in the history of overseas empires over the past few centuries. But, above all, he must be aware that the theory simply does not appear to fit the facts of the post-1870 period as he knows them. Looking, for example, at Hobson's list of territories acquired by Britain after 1870, it seems, at first sight at least, difficult to believe that any considerable part of them were annexed either because British capitalists had already invested much of their surplus capital there, or because they regarded them as fields for essential future investment. In some cases, perhaps, it seems that a *prima facie* case could be made out on these lines— for Egypt, the Transvaal and Rhodesia, to take Hobson's three main examples. But, even in these, further consideration must arouse doubts. Surely the strategic importance of the Suez Canal was as good a reason for controlling Egypt in 1882 as the preservation of the interests of the bond holders in the Canal Company. Was it really necessary, on purely economic grounds, to annex the Transvaal in 1899 when the British mine-owners were making vast fortunes under

Kruger's government, and had shown themselves so divided over the question of the Jameson Raid and the independence of the Republic? Again, granted that Rhodes and the British South Africa Company had excellent economic reasons for wanting British control over Rhodesia, was their anxiety really due to the pressure of British funds waiting for investment opportunity?

Doubts such as these concerning even the key examples chosen by Hobson inevitably stimulate further examination of his list: and this makes it clear that not even a *prima facie* case could be made out for most of the territories he includes. To take a random selection, it would surely be ludicrous to suggest that Fiji, British New Guinea or Upper Burma were annexed in order to protect large British investments, or even as a field for subsequent investment. In each case secular explanations seem fully to account for their annexation: the chaotic condition of a mixed society in the Pacific, the fears of Australia for her military security, and the frontier problems of India. And even where, as in Malaya, large capital investment did take place after annexation, the time factor must be considered. Were the British investor and the government really so alert to the possible future need for fields for investment? Or did annexation in fact take place for quite other reasons, being followed by investment when new conditions and new possibilities arose which were then totally unforeseen?

Yet, obvious though the weakness of the theory of "imperialism" may seem when applied in specific cases, it is also clear that it would be extremely difficult to invalidate Hobson's model by a process of piecemeal examination. For the adherents of this, as of most comprehensive formulas, could counter, as Mr. Strachey does, by asserting that an analytical explanation of the phenomenon merely supplied "an unaccountable jumble of facts and dates..." or, as Professor Sweezey does, by calling all annexations that do not fit demonstrably into the pattern "protective and anticipatory," or based on "considerations of a strategic nature." That is, they could fight an indefinite rearguard action, retreating, as Mr. Strachey does, on to the ultimate citadel of the historicist, with the assertion that "After all, each of these things [capital exports and colonial annexation] undeniably existed. Only the intentionally blind will deny a connection between them." Moreover, if the theory is false, it should be possible to demonstrate that its premises are false also. And, since the essential premise of "imperialism" is the belief that the drive to acquire colonies after 1870 was the direct and necessary result of the need of the capitalists to export capital, this proposition demands careful examination.

It has been seen that this theory of surplus capital being forced out into the undeveloped world was expressed differently by Hobson and Lenin, and it will be convenient to consider Lenin's theory first. This was, it will be remembered, that the centrifugal force in the capitalist countries was the interest of the monopolistic "finance-capitalists" who stood only to lose by investment at home.

In this the fallacy is immediately obvious. If it was true of any country, it was not true of Britain; for no one could maintain that British capital was then controlled by a few trusts or even cartels. These, of course, did exist in Britain, such as the Salt Union of 1888, the United Alkali Company of 1897, and others in textiles, shipping and steel. But, whatever the desires of their founders, they were in fact small, tentative and generally unsuccessful. British capital, whatever its tendencies, was still "competitive" on Lenin's definition: and he in fact admitted that in Britain "monopoly" must be taken to mean the reduction of the competing enterprises to "a couple of dozen or so." This is hardly a satisfactory explanation of the need to export capital on a vast scale; so, presumably, Britain must have other reasons both for this and for territorial annexation. But, for different reasons, other countries also escape from the formula. Germany was Lenin's main example of the country dominated by trusts: but, as Professor Hancock has pointed out, the age of German cartels came only after about 1900, while the main German grab for colonies had taken place during the previous twenty years. And America, which certainly had vast industrial and financial combinations, proved, in spite of Roosevelt's attempt to create an expansionist movement, to be the least "imperialist" of all the capitalist states. It would therefore seem reasonable to conclude that Lenin's narrow explanation for the export of capital and the concurrent extension of European political control overseas is unacceptable.

Yet, whatever reasons are assigned to it, the fact of vast capital exports from the advanced countries in the period after 1870 remains. Sir G. Paish . . . estimated that British overseas investment had increased between 1871 and 1911 from £785 m. to £3500 m., with a possible margin of error of 10 per cent either way. These figures are necessarily highly speculative; but there is no question that they were extremely large. And it is quite possible, even while rejecting Lenin's doctrinaire explanation, to see in the fact of this investment support for Hobson's theory that the urge to invest was the main cause of imperial expansion. Hence, the important questions must be faced. Was there in fact a vast reservoir of capital, generated (for example) in Britain, which was available for overseas investment? Why was it invested abroad rather than at home? And was it in fact invested in those areas which were annexed as colonies after 1871?

The publication in 1953 of Professor A. K. Cairncross's *Home and Foreign Investment 1870–1913* has made it possible to approach these questions from a new and non-doctrinaire angle. The key to his interpretation lay in his rejection of Hobson's naive model of the British capitalist, embarrassed by an excess of capital, which could not be invested at home because of the "under-consumption" factor, sending it abroad into undeveloped tropical territories where it would produce a high rate of interest. Instead, it is necessary to see that capital exports were not divorced from the economy of Great Britain but were in fact a necessary concomitant of the pattern of British trade and development. It can be shown that in fact the great majority of this capital went to the "new" countries—to the United States, Canada, Argentine, Australasia and South Africa in particular—who were producing the primary materials that the British economy needed, and who had to have capital to expand their production for British consumption. To invest in these countries was therefore, in one sense, to invest in a primary sector of the British economy itself. And the return to Britain was not entirely, or even primarily, in a tribute of money, but in cheap and plentiful raw materials and food.

Moreover, far from weakening the British economy and reducing the living standards of the working class as both Hobson and Lenin thought they did, these capital exports were essential to both. Indeed, Cairncross argues convincingly that, by creating a demand for British products, these investments simultaneously kept up the level of profits at home, kept down the level of unemployment, and maintained wage levels. And, as the rate of overseas investment seems to have been greatest when the terms of trade were against Britain—the 1880's being an exceptional period when special factors in the United States offset the general tendency—Cairncross concludes that "it was foreign investment that pulled Britain out of most depressions before 1914."

Seen, therefore, from the point of view of Britain's part in the world economy, rather than in purely domestic terms, capital exports no longer seem to have been forced out of the British economy by the selfish interests of the capitalists to maintain artificially high interest rates, and become, as Professor Nurkse has described them, "a means whereby a vigorous process of economic growth came to be transmitted from the centre to the outlying areas of the world." That is to say that the force behind the export of capital was the pull exerted by urgent need for capital in the newly-developing countries, who, because of their higher potential productivity and because markets were available for their exports, could afford to pay higher rates of interest than were obtainable in Britain. Yet, important though it was in explaining why the British and European investor chose to send his capital abroad, this differential in rates of interest should not be over-estimated. For the years 1905–9 Lehfeldt calculated the average interest on home, colonial and overseas investments to be 3.61 per cent, 3.94 per cent and 4.97 per cent respectively. But even this to some extent obscures the real facts of the situation. The interest on British consols might be only 2.88 per cent: but rates of over 5 per cent were available on other British stocks, such as railway debentures and industrials. Equally, in railway loans, which were the most popular type of British overseas investment in the years before 1914, the interest rates varied from a mere 3.87 per cent on India railways to 4.7 per cent in foreign railways. In fact it can be said that the British investor did not choose to invest abroad simply to get high interest rates, but, by and large, to get a slightly higher rate than on an equivalent type of stock at home. Above all, if he chose to invest in a British colony, it was not because he expected higher interest, but because he wanted greater security than he would get in an equivalent foreign investment. If he wanted a "risk" investment—diamonds, copper, gold, nitrates, etc.—he went for it wherever the enterprise happened to be situated. But, in proportion to the whole, investments of this type were very small in 1911.

But, for the present argument, the third and most important fact that emerges from the work of Paish, Cairncross and Nurkse is that Hobson was entirely wrong in assuming that any large proportion of British overseas investment went to those undeveloped parts of Africa which were annexed during the "imperialist" grab after 1870. As Professor Nurkse has remarked of Hobson:

Had he tried to do what he did for trade, that is, to show the geographical distribution of overseas investment, he would have found that British capital tended to bypass the primitive tropical economies and flowed mainly to the regions of recent settlement outside as well as inside the British Empire.

And the figures published by Paish in 1911 demonstrate this conclusively. The bulk of British investment then lay in the United States, £688 m., South America, £587 m., Canada, £372 m., Australasia, £380 m., India and Ceylon, £365 m., and South Africa, £351 m. By contrast, West Africa had received only £29 m., the Straits and Malay States, £22 m., and the remaining British possessions, £33 m. These last were, of course, by no means negligible amounts, and indicate clearly that in some at least of the tropical dependencies which had been recently acquired, British finance was finding scope for profit and investment. But this does not make Hobson's thesis any more valid. The sums invested in these tropical areas, whether newly annexed or not, were quite marginal to the total overseas investment, and continued to be relatively very small in the years immediately before 1911. Hence, to maintain that Britain had found it necessary to acquire these territories because of an urgent need for new fields for investment is simply unrealistic: and, with the rejection of this hypothesis, so ingeniously conjured up by Hobson, the whole basis of his theory that "imperialism" was the product of economic necessity collapses.

But to suggest that Hobson and Lenin were mistaken in thinking that the need to export capital from Europe after 1870 was so intense that it made the colonization of most of Africa and the Pacific necessary as fields for investment is merely to throw the question open again. The essential problem remains: on what other grounds is it possible to explain this sudden expansion of European possessions, whose motive force is called imperialism?

. . .

Looking broadly over the four centuries since the early Portuguese discoveries, it may be said that, although European motives for acquiring colonies were extremely complex, they fell into two general categories. First was the specifically economic motive, whose aim was to create a lucrative trade for the metropolitan country. Its typical expression was the trading base or factory, secured by some form of agreement with the local ruler: but, where no commodities already existed for trade, it could result in territorial possessions, like the sugar islands of the Caribbean, or the spice islands of the East; the fur-producing parts of North America, and the silver mines of Peru. The export of capital played no significant part in this economic activity, for Europe had little surplus capital before the nineteenth century, and investment was restricted to the immediate needs of trade itself, of the mines, sugar estates, etc.

By contrast, it is clear that from the earliest days of European expansion the margin between economic and other motives was small, and that many colonies were rather the product of political and military rivalries than of the desire for profit. The mercantile practices followed by all European states were as much concerned with national power as with economic advantage, and tended, as Adam Smith pointed out, to subordinate opulence to the needs of security. Indeed, by the eighteenth century, imperial policies had come to be largely a reflection of European power politics: and the struggle for territorial supremacy in America, India and the strategic bases on the route to the East were the outcome of political rather than of strictly economic competition. Britain's decision to retain Canada rather than Guadaloupe in 1763 may perhaps stand as an example of preference given to a colony offering mainly military security and prestige over one whose value was purely economic.

If, then, a general view of pre-nineteenth century imperial policies shows the complexity of its aims—made still more complicated in the early nineteenth century by the important new element of humanitarianism—it must seem surprising that Hobson should have interpreted post-1870 imperialism in narrowly economic terms, and have ignored the possibility that strictly political impulses may once again have been of major importance. The reason would seem to be that the evolution of imperial practices since about 1815 appeared, at the end of the century, to have constituted a clear break with earlier methods; to have made both the economic and the political criteria of earlier times irrelevant; and thus to have made comparison pointless. With the independence of almost all the American colonies, and the subsequent adoption by Britain—the chief remaining colonial power—of the practices of free trade, the possession of colonies no longer offered any positive economic advantage. The colonial trades were now open to all; bullion-hunting became the function of the individual prospector; and emigration, although it led to new British colonies in Australasia, flowed more naturally into the existing states of the new world. On the political side also, colonies had ceased to play an important part in diplomacy. With the preponderance of Britain as a naval power, and the weakness of most European states, power politics were largely restricted to Britain, France and Russia. As between them competitive aggressiveness was recurrent: but, except briefly in the Pacific, and more frequently in the Near East and on the borders of India, their rivalry did not produce any major competition for new territory. And this seemed to imply that the end of mercantilism had been followed by the end also of political imperialism: which in turn suggested that the renewal of a general international desire for colonies after 1870 must have sprung from some new phenomenon—the unprecedented need to acquire openings for the safe investment of surplus capital.

It is mainly because Hobson's theory of "imperialism" in his own time was based on this theory of discontinuity in nineteenth century history that it must be regarded as fallacious. For there had, in fact, been no break in the continuity of imperial development; merely a short-term variation in the methods used, corresponding with a temporary change in world conditions. In the first place, the extension of the territorial possessions of the three surviving great powers continued intermittently throughout: and the list of British acquisitions between 1840 and 1871 alone bears comparison with those of the following thirty years. On what grounds, in this period of so-called "anti-imperialism," are these to be explained? Obviously no single explanation will serve. Hong Kong stood alone as a trading base with a specifically economic function. Queensland was the result of internal expansion in Australia, British Columbia of rivalry from the United States. But the rest—the Punjab, Sind, Berar, Oudh and Lower Burma on the frontiers of British India; Basutoland, Griqualand and (temporarily) the Transvaal on the Cape frontier; and small areas round existing trading bases in West Africa—stand as evidence that an existing empire will tend always to expand its boundaries. They were not the product of an expansive British policy, but of the need for military security, for administrative efficiency, or for the protection of indigenous peoples on the frontiers of existing colonies. Basically, they demonstrated the fact, familiar in earlier centuries, that colonies which exist in a power vacuum will tend always to expand slowly until they meet with some immovable political or geographical obstacle; and that a metropolitan government can do little more than slow down the speed of movement. For the purpose of the present argument this process may be said to indicate that Hobson needed no new explanation for the bulk of British acquisitions after 1870: for, as has already been pointed out, most of the new colonies on his list differed little in type or situation from those just mentioned—and were indeed mostly the extension of the same colonial frontiers. And, to this extent, late nineteenth century imperialism was merely the continuation of a process which had begun centuries earlier.

At the same time, it must be said that this "contiguous area" theory does not fully cover certain of the new British possessions on Hobson's list. For some of them, like East Africa, were not strictly contiguous to an existing British colony; and others, such as Nigeria or Rhodesia, were clearly annexed too suddenly and on too large a scale to be seen as the product of the domestic needs of Lagos or the Cape. These therefore suggest that some other factor was at work—competition for new colonies on political grounds—which will be considered later.

Again, in the sphere of economic policy, the antithesis between different parts of the nineteenth century was greatly exaggerated and misunderstood by Hobson. The rejection of most of the mercantile devices for stimulating European trade had not meant that trade ceased to be a matter of national concern, or that governments ceased to use political means to support their men of business; the contrast with earlier centuries lay mainly in the methods now used. Hobson seemed to think that free trade had ended "economic imperialism" of the mercantile variety simply because political control was no longer regarded as a prerequisite for economic exploitation of an undeveloped area. But, as Messrs. Gallagher and Robinson have pointed out, "formal" control, as in a colony, was not the only way in which "economic imperialism" could operate; indeed, it now had two complementary features. On its specifically economic side it implied, as always, the control of the economic assets of some other country for the advantage of the metropolitan state. And the essential weapons of the European trader or financier were economic—the demand for his goods, his capital or his credit, and the effectiveness of the organization he built up in a country lacking business organization. The stranglehold he thus obtained differed only in detail from that held in the eighteenth century by British firms in the American colonies, transferred now to the similarly defenceless, though politically independent, states of South America, the Middle and Far East. By the end of the nineteenth century most of the world had been thus brought under the economic control of European, and now also United States, business enterprise: their trade was organized and carried by foreign merchants, their revenues mortgaged to the loans they had received. This indeed was "economic imperialism" in its purest form; cosmopolitan in outlook, unconcerned with political frontiers, showing no interest in the creation of "formal" colonies except where, as in China, the formula of the open door proved otherwise unworkable. Only in the absolute volume of its activity, and in the increasing competition between rivals from newly industrialized countries, did the character of "economic imperialism" change before 1914. And, while it remained thus strictly economic and cosmopolitan, the "division of the world among the international trusts," which Lenin prophesied, remained a possibility.

Yet, even in its classical form, "economic imperialism" required political support from governments at home: and, in view of developments after about 1870, it is important to define the nature of the support it received. Essentially the men of business needed only two things which their own enterprise could not supply: a minimum standard of political security at the periphery, and the solution of the quasi-political problems arising out of their relations with foreign rivals by diplomatic action at the centre. The first need was met by the network of treaties made for them with their client countries which secured equality of opportunity and reasonable tariffs, and was backed up, where necessary, by the use of threats and force. In the environment of the free world economy, these were the equivalents of the commercial monopolies of the mercantile period in that they supplied the political basis for successful business enterprise in undeveloped countries.

Second, and parallel with this, went the constant diplomatic work of the foreign offices of Europe in maintaining the balance between their nationals at the circumference. On the common assumption that it was to the general interest that competition should remain fair, that an artificial monopoly was to the advantage of none, and that such problems must not be allowed to harm international relations, diplomacy sought to settle these disputes without taking refuge in unilateral annexation of the area concerned. In this it was generally successful, where the will to succeed existed: and the Anglo-French condominium of 1906 in the New Hebrides stands as a late example of how such problems could be met.

It is now possible to place the imperialism of the period of Hobson's *Study* in its historical context, and to attempt a definition of the extent to which it differed from that of earlier years. The most obvious fact on which his theory was based was that, by contrast with the preceding half-century, vast areas of the world were quickly brought under European control for the first time: and it is now evident that this cannot be explained in terms of either of the two tendencies operating throughout the earlier nineteenth century. Although the break with the past was not as sharp as Hobson seemed to think, it remains true that many British annexations cannot be explained on the "contiguous area" theory: and the new possessions of France, Italy and Germany were quite definitely in a different category. But neither can these facts be explained on Hobson's theory: for, as has been said, the places now to be taken over had hitherto attracted little capital, and did not attract it in any quantity subsequently. Nor, again, can an explanation be found in the more general theory of "economic imperialism," for these places in the Pacific and in Africa for which the nations now competed were of marginal economic importance; and, on the assumptions of the past fifty years, governments might have been expected to reject demands by their nationals for annexation of territories whose administrative costs would be out of all proportion to their economic value to the nation. In sum, the most obvious facts of the new phase of imperialism cannot be explained as the logical continuation of the recent past, nor in Hobson's terms of a new economic factor. What, then, was the explanation?

An answer is not, of course, hard to find, and indeed emerges clearly from the vast literature now available. With the exception of the supporters of the "imperialism" thesis, the consensus of opinion is very marked. The new factor in imperialism was not something without precedent, certainly not anything uniquely economic, but essentially a throw-back to some of the characteristic attitudes and practices of the eighteenth century. Just as, in the early nineteenth century, the economic interests had demanded effectively that imperial questions should no longer be decided on political grounds, demanding opulence in place of security, so, at the end of the century, the balance was again reversed. The outstanding feature of the new situation was the subordination of economic to political considerations, the preoccupation with national security, military power and prestige.

Again, reasons are not hard to find. The significant fact about the years after 1870 was that Europe became once again an armed camp. The creation of a united Germany, the defeat of Austria and, above all, of France were to dominate European thinking until 1914. Between Germany and France there stood the question of Alsace-Lorraine: and for both the primary consideration was now a system of alliances which would, on the German side, prevent French counter-attack, on the French side, make revenge possible. Inevitably the rest of Europe was drawn into the politics of the balance of power between them; and for all statesmen military strength became once again the criterion of national greatness. Inevitably too this situation, with its similarities to the politics of the eighteenth century, brought in its train a return to many of the attitudes of mercantilism. Emigration to foreign states, instead of being regarded as an economic safety valve, became once again a loss of military or manufacturing man-power; and population statistics became a measure of relative national strength. Protective tariffs came back also, with the primary aim of building up national self-sufficiency and the power to make war.

Under such circumstances it was only to be expected that colonies would be regarded once again as assets in the struggle for power and status: but in fact the attitude of the powers to the imperial question was not at first a simple one. Indeed, it cannot be said that the atti-tudes characteristic of "the imperialism of free trade" were seriously weakened until the mid-1880's; and until then it seemed possible that the colonial question might be kept clear of European politics. This is not in fact surprising. For most of the men who then ruled Europe retained a realistic appreciation of the potential value to their coun-tries of those parts of the world that were available for annexation. Bismarck in particular recognized that, as sources of raw materials, as fields for emigration or as spheres for trade, the areas available in Africa and the Pacific had little to offer Germany, whatever national advantages those with private interests there might claim. At best they might offer naval bases, a strictly limited trade, and bargaining counters for use in diplomacy. It is improbable that Bismarck ever really changed this opinion: and, while he held off, it was unlikely that any other power would feel strong enough to precipitate a rush for new colonies. Even Belgian and French action in the Congo failed to do this; although their ambitions showed the probable trend of future events.

It was, therefore, Bismarck's action in 1884–5, in announcing the formal control by Germany over parts of West and South West Africa, and of New Guinea, that really began the new phase of political imperialism: and it is therefore important to consider his reasons for giving Germany a "colonial policy." Was it, as Miss Townsend has argued, that the pressure of the commercial interest involved in these places, and the arguments of the new colonial party in politics con-vinced him that colonies were an economic necessity to Germany? The answer must be that it was not. In 1884 Bismarck seems to have decided that it was time for him to stop playing the honest broker in the disputes of other powers over their own possessions—such as

Egypt and the Congo—and that, on two counts, both essentially diplomatic, Germany should now stake her own claims to colonies. The first was that it was politically desirable to show France that his recent support for Britain on the Egyptian question did not imply a general hostility towards her, since he was now prepared to take action resented by Britain: the second that Britain should be made to see that German support for her in the colonial field must be repaid by closer co-operation in Europe.

In a narrow sense, then, the race for colonies was the product of diplomacy rather than of any more positive force. Germany set the example by claiming exclusive control over areas in which she had an arguable commercial stake, but no more, as a means of adding a new dimension to her international bargaining power, both in respect of what she had already taken, and of what she might claim in the future. Thereafter the process could not be checked; for, under conditions of political tension, the fear of being left out of the partition of the globe overrode all practical considerations. Perhaps Britain was the only country which showed genuine reluctance to take a share; and this was due both to her immense stake in the continuance of the *status quo* for reasons of trade, and to her continued realism in assessing the substantive value of the lands under dispute. And the fact that she too joined in the competition demonstrated how contagious the new political forces were. Indeed, until the end of the century, imperialism may best be seen as the extension into the periphery of the political struggle in Europe. At the centre the balance was so nicely adjusted that no positive action, no major change in the status or territory of either side was possible. Colonies thus became a means out of the impasse; sources of diplomatic strength, prestige-giving accessions of territory, hope for future economic development. New worlds were being brought into existence in the vain hope that they would maintain or redress the balance of the old.

This analysis of the dynamic force of the new imperialism has been stated in purely political terms. What part was played in it by the many non-political interests with a stake in the new colonies: the traders, the investors, the missionaries, and the speculators? For these were the most vociferous exponents of a "forward" policy in most countries: and to men like Hobson it seemed that their influence, if backed by that of the greater interest of the financier, was decisive in causing the politicians to act.

Again the problem is complex. In general terms the answer would seem to be that, while statesmen were very much aware of the pressure groups—conscious of the domestic political advantage of satisfying their demands, and often themselves sympathetic to the case they put up—they were not now, any more than earlier in the century, ready to undertake the burden of new colonies simply on their account. What made it seem as if these interests were now calling the tune was that the choice facing the statesman was no longer betweeen annexation and the continued independence of the area in question: it was now between action and allowing a rival to step in. Salisbury and Rosebery may well have been convinced by the argument of men like Lugard that, on humanitarian grounds, it would be desirable for Britain to bring law and order to Uganda. But it was the threat of German or French occupation of the key to the Nile and Egypt that decided them to act. Yet if, in the last resort, the decision by Britain or any other country to annex was based on the highest reasons of state, it is also true that the very existence of these hitherto embarrassing pressure groups now became a diplomatic asset, since they were the obvious grounds on which valid claims could be made, an approximation to the principle of effective occupation.

Thus the relative importance of the concrete interests and demands of the various pressure groups, as compared with the political criteria of the statesmen, was the reverse of that assigned to them by Hobson; and, if the word "investment" is taken to cover the whole range of these interests, the point has been well summarized by Professor E. Staley:

Conflicts between the great powers over private investment matters have rarely, almost never, reached a state of dangerous international tension except in cases where the powers have been led into conflict by the pursuit of political policies extraneous to the investment affair itself. The best explanation of these facts runs in terms of the way in which those in charge of foreign policies interpret national advantage. Where investments can be regarded as economic aids to established lines of foreign policy, they are supported most vigorously; investments receive least vigorous backing where they are not in any sense tools of national policy or where they run counter to national policy.[1]

Yet, if the first, and territorially decisive, factor in the imperialism of the post-1870 period was this unemotional, almost cynical, policy of the statesmen, it cannot be said that it was the only new feature, nor, in the long run, the most important one. For by the time Hobson wrote in 1902, those who supported a "forward" policy were no longer

---

[1] E. Staley, *War and the private investor* (Chicago, 1935), pp. 387–8. It remains true, however, that in the aftermath the main, possibly the only, advantage of the new colonies went to these special interests—particularly the soldiers and administrators, to whom they offered careers; the missions, who gained security; and the wide range of concession-hunters and government contractors who swarmed in all the new colonies.

the few diplomatic chess-players, nor even the relatively small pressure groups, but millions of people for whom an empire had become a matter of faith. Indeed, the rise of this imperialist ideology, this belief that colonies were an essential attribute of any great nation, is one of the most astonishing facts of the period. It was, moreover, an international creed, with beliefs that seemed to differ very little from one country to another. Its basic ideas had been clearly expressed as early as 1879 by a German, Treitschke:

Every virile people has established colonial power. . . . All great nations in the fulness of their strength have desired to set their mark upon barbarian lands and those who fail to participate in this great rivalry will play a pitiable role in time to come. The colonizing impulse has become a vital question for every great nation.

By the end of the century, the "imperial idea," as it has significantly been called, after twenty years of propaganda by such groups of enthusiasts as the German *Kolonverein* [Colonial Society] and the British Imperial Federation League, had become dominant. The process of educating the public has now been examined in detail: and it is interesting to see that in each case the historian has found it necessary to deal almost entirely in ideas, rather than in concrete facts. This is no accident. The imperialism of the early twentieth century, although ironically the product of the power politics of the previous two decades, bore little resemblance to the ideas of men like Bismarck and Salisbury. It was the generation of Kaiser Wilhelm II, of Theodore Roosevelt and of Chamberlain (in his later years) that came to adopt for the first time this mystical faith in the value of an empire. Chamberlain's tariff campaign of 1903–5 indicates that such tenuous links as the imperial movement had ever had with precise calculations of economic—and even of political—advantage had now ceased to be of primary importance.

For, by that time, imperialism had been shown to be a delusion. It was already the common experience of all the countries that had taken part in the partition of Africa and the Pacific that, except for the few windfalls, such as gold in West Africa, diamonds in South West Africa, and copper in the Congo and Rhodesia, the new colonies were white elephants: and that only small sectional interests in any country had obtained real benefits from them. Whether German, French, British or Italian, their trade was minute (German trade with her colonies was only ½ per cent of her external trade); their attraction for investors, except in mines, etc., was negligible; they were unsuitable for large-scale emigration, and any economic development that had taken place was usually the result of determined efforts by the European state concerned to create an artificial asset. Moreover, in most cases, the cost of

administration was a dead weight on the imperial power. By 1900 all
these facts were apparent and undeniable. They were constantly
pressed by opponents of colonial expansion in each country; and
Hobson's book consisted primarily of an exposition of these defects.
Yet public opinion was increasingly oblivious to such facts: the possession of colonies had become a sacred cow, a psychological necessity.
While the financiers continued to invest their money, as they had done
in the previous fifty years, in economically sound projects, such as the
Baghdad railway, in the non-tropical settlement colonies and independent countries, and in places like India—remaining true to the
criteria of true "economic imperialism"—the politicians, pressed on
now by a public demand they could not control, even if they had
wanted to, continued, with increasing bellicosity, to scrape the bottom
of the barrel for yet more colonial burdens for the white man to carry.

The reassessment of so abstract a concept as "imperialism," particularly within the present limitations of space, cannot hope to prove or to
disprove anything. At the most it may lead to the suggestion that an
earlier synthesis does not appear to fit the facts. How far can it be said
that the arguments put forward above make necessary a revision of the
theory of "imperialism" which derives from Hobson and Lenin?

The general conclusion would seem to emerge that, as an historical
interpretation of the expansion of European empires between 1870
and 1914, it is unacceptable. As an economic theory it is unsatisfactory
because detailed investigations have shown that the alleged need of the
European investor, monopolist or individual capitalist, to find outlets
for his surplus capital had little or nothing to do with the division of
Africa and the Pacific between the European powers. Again, as a
theory of historical development, which makes this expansion seem to
be a unique phenomenon, capable of being understood only in terms
of the special methodology used by Hobson and Lenin, it ignores both
the continuity of nineteenth century developments, and also its similarity to earlier periods of European imperialism. In most respects,
indeed, there was no break in continuity after 1870. On the political
side, many of the new annexations of territory, particularly those made
by Britain, resulted from the situation of existing possessions: and, on
the economic side, the rapid expansion of European commercial and
financial influence throughout the world—the true "economic imperialism"—did not change its character after 1870; and was no more
likely then than before to have resulted in significant acquisitions of
land. The real break in the continuity of nineteenth century development—the rapid extension of "formal" control over independent
areas of Africa and the East—was a specifically political phenomenon
in origin, the outcome of fears and rivalries within Europe. The com-

petition for colonies, being as characteristic of economically weak countries like Italy as of others which had large resources of capital available for overseas deployment, was indeed more obviously a throwback to the imperialism of the eighteenth century than the characteristic product of nineteenth century capitalism in an advanced phase. And the ideological fervour that became the dominant feature of the imperial movement after about 1890 was the natural outcome of this fevered nationalism, not the artifact of vested economic interests.

Yet, in conclusion, a paradox must be noted. Hobson's analysis of "imperialism" was defective: but the fact that it was defective was probably the result of his having grasped one essential truth about the imperial movement—that it had become irrational. Seeing clearly that the new tropical colonies could not be justified in terms of their economic values to the metropolitan powers—the criterion a nineteenth century rationalist would naturally apply—he was forced back on the theory that they must have been of value to sectional interests at least; and that these had succeeded in hoodwinking a presumably sane public opinion. Seen in this light, Hobson's sinister capitalists and their "parasites" were nothing more than a hypothesis, a *deus ex machina,* to balance an equation between the assumed rationality of mankind and the unreasonableness of imperial policies: and the book was a plea for a return to a sane standard of values.

His mistake, then, was to think that the equation needed such artificial adjustment. For, in the second half of the twentieth century, it can be seen that imperialism owed its popular appeal not to the sinister influence of the capitalists, but to its inherent attractions for the masses. In the new quasi-democratic Europe, the popularity of the imperial idea marked a rejection of the sane morality of the account-book, and the adoption of a creed based on such irrational concepts as racial superiority and the prestige of the nation. Whether we interpret it, as did J. R. Schumpeter in 1919, as a castback to the ideas of the old autocratic monarchies of the *ancien régime,* or as something altogether new—the first of the irrational myths that have dominated the first half of the twentieth century—it is clear that imperialism cannot be explained in simple terms of economic theory and the nature of finance capitalism. In its mature form it can best be described as a sociological phenomenon with roots in political facts: and it can properly be understood only in terms of the same social hysteria that has since given birth to other and more disastrous forms of aggressive nationalism.

15

Late Nineteenth-Century Colonial Expansion and the Attack on the Theory of Economic Imperialism: A Case of Mistaken Identity?

The concept of imperialism which Hobson, Lenin and the combined force of the international socialist movement forged into an *idée fixe* of the twentieth century was roughly handled by Western scholars long before 1945. But since then the attack has grown more precise and its character has altered. Among the first of the post-war historians (writing in English) to attempt the dethronement of imperialism as the demi-urge of the period between 1870 and 1914 was Richard Koebner. He determined on a semantic approach and put the term's linguistic history to rigorous scrutiny. On the philosophical assumption that a term's meaning is to be defined by its actual use and provenance in the political discourse in which it arose, he found that the modern concept of economic imperialism sprang out of a limited, local controversy over the nature of the Boer War. He concluded that it had been illicitly mated with other forms of militarism and economic expansion to spawn a hybrid, mythical monster that had been allowed to sprawl its length over more than half a century of world history.[1]

On the statistical side the work of Cairncross and others has laid bare the lack of apparent connexion between the export of capital and the late nineteenth-century scramble for colonies.[2] Diplomatic historians, with A. J. P. Taylor in the van, have reinforced the earlier monumental study of W. L. Langer, and while rejecting any mono-

[1] Richard Koebner, "The Concept of Economic Imperialism," *Economic History Review*, 2nd ser. II, no. 1 (1949).
[2] A. K. Cairncross, *Home and Foreign Investment, 1870–1913* (1953). The best summary of the literature is to be found in D. K. Fieldhouse. See below.

causal explanation of imperialism have come down heavily in favour of the view that looks upon it as a primarily political phenomenon.[3]

What has distinguished the contribution of Ronald Robinson and John Gallagher is the alteration they have brought about in the character of the attack. Following the prevailing trend of minimizing the strength and compulsiveness of the expansionist forces in Europe in the later nineteenth century they pursue the full logic of the argument and enforce its corollary. If Europe was drawn reluctantly and involuntarily into Africa after 1870 and not propelled by her own internal dynamism, then the initiative for the African Scramble was to be found primarily in the workings of African and not European societies.[4]

The importance of this re-interpretation needs labouring. Historians like Taylor and Hinsley have seen the partition of Africa as the product of chance and inconsequence rather than necessity, but even so it remains for them essentially a safety-valve for European energies. "All the Great Powers except Austria-Hungary found a safe channel for their exuberance outside Europe. They stumbled on this solution by chance, without foresight. . . . The struggle for mastery in Europe was postponed, not abandoned: this alone was the meaning of the 'age of imperialism.' "[5] Robinson and Gallagher will have none of this, because it reproduces old error in new guise. It still regards imperialism as a home-grown European phenomenon springing out of internal developments within European society. The attractiveness of their own interpretation lies in its recognition of the autonomy of Africa's history and in its subtle accommodation to the historiographical revolution of our time. That revolution may briefly if tritely be described as a shift of the locus of historical initiative and decision from the institutional superstructure to the level of local communities and interest groups. While this reverses the ordinary notion of the direction of historical causation, it effects a still more dramatic reversal of stand-point for viewing the historical relation of Europe with other societies. The decisive initiatives are now read as coming from below not above, from African and Asian societies and not from the colonial

---

[3] A. J. P. Taylor, *Germany's First Bid for Colonies*, and *The Struggle for Mastery in Europe*.

[4] J. Gallagher and R. Robinson, "The Partition of Africa," *New Cambridge Modern History*, xi; *Africa and the Victorians* (1961); "The Imperialism of Free Trade," *Economic History Review*, 2nd ser. vi (1953); R. Robinson, "The Official Mind of Imperialism," *Historians in Tropical Africa*, University College of Rhodesia and Nyasaland (Salisbury, 1962).

[5] A. J. P. Taylor, *The Struggle for Mastery in Europe*, p. 256. Cf. F. H. Hinsley, "International Rivalry in the Colonial Sphere, 1869–1885"; *Cambridge History of the British Empire*, iii, 99.

power structure of Europe. In one sense, therefore, Robinson and Gallagher perform an important ground-clearing operation, removing the bogey of imperialism that blocked the historian's vision and rendering intellectually respectable those microcosmic studies of African societies in the colonial period in which history is detected issuing from the grass-roots.

Such a method stands the classical model on its head, or at least appears to do so. But its efficacy depends on a particular set of assumptions concerning the classical model's construction and, as these assumptions are shared by almost all adverse critics of the model, they need to be made explicit. The assumptions are:

1. that imperialism is synonymous with colonialism, that is to say with the extension of Western political control over the non-Western world;
2. that imperialism was generated by pressures produced within Western society;
3. that these pressures manifested themselves first as ideological and political movements in European life;
4. that such pressures were, however, fundamentally economic in origin, and sprang out of the change from industrial capitalism, with its emphasis on simple commodity-exchange relationships with overseas territories, to finance capitalism, with its emphasis on the export of capital to colonial dependencies;
5. that the colonialism appropriate to industrial capitalism was non-monopolistic, pacific, and abstentionist, and the colonialism appropriate to finance capitalism monopolistic, bellicose, and annexationist;
6. that the latter form of colonialism (imperialism) succeeded the former (mid-Victorian anti-imperialism) suddenly, about 1870, and that from 1870 to 1900 or 1914 there ensued the high age of imperialism whose quintessence was the scramble for colonies among the great powers.

It has been the work of Robinson and Gallagher to refute the applicability of this model to British expansion in general and to the European partition and occupation of tropical Africa between 1870 and 1900 in particular. Their method is deliberately polemical. They overturn the model by reversing each one of its assumptions. Imperialism they argue was the product of presssures within overseas and not within Western societies; it was a consequence and not a cause of the African partition; it came at the end and not the beginning of the colonial scramble; it was first and foremost a political phenomenon, originating in nationalist revolutions overseas that generated by reaction corresponding nationalist movements of defiant self-assertion from Europe. It introduced economic motives only as an afterthought. For Hobson, surplus capital forced the European powers "to place larger and larger portions of their economic resources outside the area of their present political domain, and then stimulate a policy of practical expansion, so as to take in the new areas."[6] For Robinson and Gallagher:

So far from commercial expansion requiring the extension of territorial claims, it was the extension of territorial claims which in time required commercial expansion. The arguments of the so-called new imperialism were *ex post facto* justifications of advances, they were not the original reasons for making them!

For them, misconception as to the logical or causal relation between African and European societies necessarily involves an equivalent error of chronology. Imperialism, with its flags and drums, its belligerent ideologies, its redirection of economic effort, its imperial grants-in-aid came—if it came at all—after the completion of the scramble for colonies, at the end of the nineteenth century. On this hypothesis, then, there was no sharp change in direction after 1870; the notion of an abrupt reversal of colonial policy at that time from pacific abstention to belligerent annexation cannot be sustained. If anything British colonial policy between 1870 and 1895 grew more timid, more pacific, couched in terms of preserving existing commercial interests rather than opening paths for new. Salisbury was no Palmerston. He built his African empire defensively, largely as a strategic outwork for the real empire of trade and investment in the East. British policy held to its old course, continuing to devolve authority where it could, assuming it where it had to but, above all things, maintaining free trade.

If all this is true then the theory of economic imperialism is not so much exploded as merely declared irrelevant as an explanation of European colonial expansion between 1870 and 1900. But the theory on any ordinary reckoning has been dealt all but a knockout blow. The *coup de grâce* has been attempted by D. K. Fieldhouse, who drawing together recent critiques isolates what he holds to be the essential tenets of the theory in order to controvert it explicitly:

The central feature of the theory of imperialism by which it must stand or fall, is the assertion that the empires built up after 1870 were not an

---

6 J. A. Hobson, *Imperialism* (1902), p. 80, cited D. K. Fieldhouse, "Imperialism: an Historiographical Revision," *Economic History Review*, XIV, 2 (1961).

option but a necessity for the economically advanced states of Europe and America: that these capitalist societies, because of their surplus of domestically produced capital, were forced to export capital to the under-developed regions of the world: and that it was only this investment—prospective or existing—that supplied a motive for the acquisition of colonies.[7]

So defined, the model is then assailed with all the arguments used by Robinson and Gallagher but now marshalled in a concentrated, direct assault. The model errs at every point, we are told: in the postulate of a sharp change of direction of colonial policy after 1870; in ignoring the fact that capital exports avoided the new colonial territories acquired after 1870; in misdescribing the primary-exporting country, Great Britain, as dominated in 1870 by monopoly finance capitalism and controlled by a few trusts and cartels; in not taking into account that "the age of German cartels came only after about 1900, while the main German grab for colonies had taken place during the previous twenty years."[8] Elsewhere the same writer concludes: "The Theory of Capitalist Imperialism might have been true, but in fact it was not. Sooner or later the sheer volume of the evidence and argument marshalled on the other side will convince the majority that imperialism was not the simple product of advanced capitalism."[9]

What is noticeable in all these versions of the concept of economic imperialism—in that of Fieldhouse no less than that of Robinson and Gallagher—is the conflation of the arguments of Hobson and Lenin into a single model, Fieldhouse going so far as to maintain that the two differed in only minor particulars. But Hobson's influence remains paramount.[10] Indeed it was Hobson who by his almost exclusive attention to British expansion made imperialism synonymous with colonialism. It was Hobson who tabulated British capital exports and British colonial acquisitions in terms of cause and sequence; who in 1902 spoke of his work as analysing "the imperialism of the last three decades," and who directed his main attention to the largest colonial gain of the period, Africa.

Yet it is too easily forgotten that the theory of economic or capitalist imperialism does not stand or fall on the authority of Hobson but of Lenin. A scrutiny of Lenin's principal writings reveals that no error could be more fundamental than to suppose that he was putting for-

---

[7] D. K. Fieldhouse, "Imperialism: an Historiographical Revision," *Economic History Review*, 2nd ser. xiv 2 (1961), 195.

[8] *Idem*, p. 197.

[9] D. K. Fieldhouse, *The Theory of Capitalist Imperialism*, paperback (1967), p. 192.

[10] Fieldhouse, *Economic History Review*, op. cit. p. 193.

ward the same model of imperialism as Hobson. In the vital question of chronology Lenin made it plain that the era of monopoly finance capitalism did *not* coincide with the scramble for colonies between 1870 and 1900 but came after it.

for Europe [he wrote] the time when the new capitalism *definitely* superseded the old can be established with fair precision: it was the beginning of the twentieth century. . . . Thus the beginning of the twentieth century marks the turning point, not only in regard to the growth of monopolies (cartels, syndicates, trusts) . . . but also in regard to the growth of finance capitalism.[11]

Similarly, in its colonialist aspect imperialism did not emerge, according to Lenin, until the "unoccupied" portions of the world had already been divided up into colonial or semi-colonial territories; for imperialism which "in its economic essence . . . is monopoly capitalism" was the struggle for the re-division of the already divided world:

Fourthly [after listing three other sources] monopoly has grown out of colonial policy. To the numerous "old" motives of colonial policy, finance capital has added the struggle for the sources of raw materials, for the export of capital, for "sphere of influence," i.e., for spheres for profitable deals, concessions, monopolist profits and so on, and finally, for economic territory in general. When the colonies of the European powers in Africa, for instance, comprised only one-tenth of that territory (as was the case in 1876), colonial policy was able to develop by methods other than those of monopoly—by the "free grabbing" of territories, so to speak. But when nine-tenths of Africa had been seized (by 1900), when the whole world had been divided up, there was inevitably ushered in the era of monopoly ownership of colonies and, consequently, of particularly intense struggle for the division and re-division of the world.[12]

---

[11] V. I. Lenin, "Imperialism, the Highest Stage of Capitalism," *Collected Works* (Moscow, 1964), xxii, 200.

[12] *Idem*, pp. 299–300. Cf. "Imperialism and the Split in Socialism," October 1961, Lenin, *Works*, xxiii, 111: "Neither Marx nor Engels lived to see the imperialist epoch of world capitalism, which began not earlier than 1896–1900."

Cf. "The Discussion on Self-Determination Summed Up," July 1916, *Works*, xxii, 341–2: ". . . and 1898–1916 (I take the most important landmarks of imperialism as a period: from the Spanish-American imperialist war to the European imperialist war)."

Cf. Lenin to Jivessa Armand, 25 Dec. 1916: *Works*, xxxv, 268. "You have forgotten the main thing—that in 1891 no imperialism existed at all (I have tried to show in my pamphlet that it was born in 1898–1900, not earlier) . . ."

Earlier he had written:

Imperialism is capitalism in that stage of development in which the dominance of monopolies and finance capital has established itself, in which the export of capital has acquired pronounced importance, in which the division of the world [i.e. in terms of markets] among the international trusts has begun, in which the division of all territories of the globe among the biggest capitalist powers has been completed.

The official textbook, *Political Economy*, issued by the Institute of Economics of the Soviet Academy of Sciences in 1957, spells the theory out with still greater clarity:

Premonopoly capitalism, with free competition predominating, attained the apex of its development in the 1860s and 1870s. During the last third of the 19th century there took place the transition from pre-monopoly to monopoly capitalism. Monopoly capitalism finally took shape towards the end of the 19th century and the beginning of the 20th century. Monopoly capitalism or imperialism is the highest stage of capitalism. . . . In the last quarter of the 19th century, in the period of transition to the monopoly stage of capitalism, the map of the world underwent radical changes. All the developed capitalist countries followed the oldest colonial power, Britain, on the road to territorial conquest. . . . Towards the beginning of the 20th century, the division of the world was complete. The colonial policy of the capitalist countries had led to the conquest of all the lands not hitherto occupied by the imperialists. No more "free" lands remained; a situation had been created in which every fresh conquest presupposed wresting territory from its owner. The completion of the division of the world placed on the order of the day the struggle to *re-divide* it. The struggle to re-divide the already divided world is one of the fundamental distinguishing features of monopoly capitalism.[13]

Lenin, it will be noted, envisaged the period from 1870 to 1900 as a transitional period. He postulated, therefore, no sharp discontinuity between the pre- and post-1870 periods. Colonial policy continued by means of the "free grabbing" of territory and remained in a relative sense fundamentally pacific and non-monopolistic.[14] The export of

---

[13] *Political Economy, A Textbook issued by the Institute of Economics of the Academy of Science of the U.S.S.R.* ed. C. P. Dutt and Andrew Rothstein (London [1957]), pp. 279, 296.

[14] Cf. "The Collapse of the Second International," May–June 1915, *Works*, xxi, 225–6. "Let us recall what the passage from the previous and "peaceful" period of capitalism to the present and imperialist period has been based on: free competition has yielded to monopolist combines and the world has been partitioned. Both these facts (and factors) are obviously of world-wide significance: Free Trade and

capital was not the dominant feature of colonial policy, Lenin fully acknowledging that "the export of capital reached enormous dimensions only at the beginning of the 20th century."[15] All the features of the concept of economic imperialism so freely attributed to him by Fieldhouse and others are not applicable to the period before 1900 or so. The neo-Marxist theory of imperialism is an explanation of the world in the twentieth century. Lenin was concerned not to provide a theoretical analysis of the scramble for colonies in the last three decades of the nineteenth century but of the genesis of war in Europe after 1900.[16]

Even so, it can be urged that Lenin blurred the distinction between the pre- and post-1900 periods, that he saw the features of monopoly capitalism already emerging after 1870, and that his reading of the appropriation of colonies in the transitional period was an avowedly economic one. Lenin certainly did go so far as to say:

We saw above that the development of pre-monopoly capitalism, of capitalism in which free competition was predominant, reached its limit in the 1860s and 1870s. We now see that it is *precisely after that period* that the tremendous "boom" in colonial conquests begins, and that the struggle for the territorial division of the world becomes extraordinarily sharp. It is beyond doubt, therefore, that capitalism's transition to the monopoly stage of capitalism, to finance capital is *connected* with the intensification of the struggle for the partition of the world.[17]

But about the details of this connexion Lenin was studiously vague. The high epoch of finance capitalism was clearly not so concerned with the colonial territories proper as with the struggle for the semicolonial countries which still retained nominal political independence —Persia, the Turkish empire, and China. Of the pre-1900 scramble he noted that the main areas of colonial expansion in the transitional period after 1876 were Africa and Polynesia, but his direct references

---

peaceful competition were possible and necessary as long as capital was in a position to enlarge its colonies without hindrance, and seize unoccupied land in Africa, etc., and as long as the concentration of capital was still weak and no monopolist concerns existed, i.e. concerns of a magnitude permitting domination in an entire branch of industry. The appearance and growth of such monopolist concerns, have rendered the free competition of former times *impossible;* they have cut the ground from under its feet, while the partition of the world *compels* the capitalist to go over from peaceful expansion to an armed struggle for the *re-partitioning* of colonies and spheres of influence."

15 "Imperialism," *Works*, XXII, 242.

16 "Imperialism," 1920 Preface, *Works*, XXII, 189–90. Cf. "Preface to N. Bukharin's Pamphlet, Imperialism and the World Economy," December 1915, *Works*, XXII, 103.

17 "Imperialism," *Works*, XXII, 256.

are few. He drew attention to the manner in which France, although roughly equal in size and population with Germany and Japan, had vastly outdistanced them in colonial expansion, acquiring between 1876 and 1914 three times as much colonial territory as the other two combined.

It was not an accident [commented Lenin] that in France it was precisely the extraordinary rapid development of *finance,* and the weakening of industrial capital, that, from the eighties onwards, gave rise to the extreme intensification of annexationist (colonial) policy.[18]

Yet having said this, Lenin did not go on to say that all territorial acquisitions could be directly referred to economic motives. His theory makes allowance for strategic motives, or for economic motives that were largely speculative. With unoccupied territory running out the scramble for the remaining areas also could take on an irrational fervour:

Hence the inevitable striving of finance capital to enlarge its economic territory and even its territory in general . . . finance capital in general strives to seize the largest amount of lands in all places, and by every means, taking into account potential sources of raw materials and fearing to be left behind in the fierce struggle for the last scraps of undivided territory, or for the repartition of those that have been already divided.[19]

Lenin likewise made allowance for ideological or political movements to assist the expansionist forces, acknowledging that "The non-economic superstructure which grows on the basis of finance capital, its politics and its ideology, stimulates the striving for colonial conquest." While room is made for the operation of factors other than the economic, even the economic factor is not given so simple a character as its critics suppose. Lenin did not argue that in the transitional period to imperialism the new urge to find profitable outlets for export capital displaced the old commodity-exchange relationship. It was simply additional to it, so that the safeguarding of trade rather than capital investment could still rank as a prime motive for colonial acquisition.

---

[18] *Idem,* p. 268. But cf. Lenin to Inessa Armand, 19 Jan. 1917: *Works,* xxxv, 273: "1891. The colonial policy of France and Germany was *insignificant.* Italy, Japan, the United States *had no* colonies *at all* (now they have) . . ."

[19] *Works,* xxii, p. 262. Cf. J. Gallagher and R. Robinson, "The Partition of Africa," *New Cambridge Modern History,* xi, 626, "The partition had brought them [European statesmen] to a kind of geopolitical claustrophobia, a feeling that national expansion was running out of world space, and that the great powers of the twentieth century would be those who had filched every nook and cranny of territory left."

And he nowhere claimed that the full force of capitalism was thrown against the colonial areas. Even Hobson did not. Indeed for Hobson the "distinctive feature of modern Imperialism, from the commercial standpoint, is that it adds to our empire tropical and sub-tropical regions with which our trade is small, precarious and unprogressive";[20] and the problem he set himself to answer in his book was how the British nation was "induced to embark on such unsound business."[21] Lenin appears to have adopted Hobson's solution: although not profitable to the metropolitan country as a whole, colonial acquisitions could prove highly profitable to certain "parasitic" elements of capitalism. Lenin, it will be recalled, spoke of finance capital's struggle for "spheres of influence" which he defined as "spheres for profitable deals, concessions, monopolist profits, and so on."

Robinson and Gallagher rightly pour scorn on the notion that economic interests were anything like powerful enough to bring about a historical phenomenon so remarkable as the scramble for Africa, but it is another thing to say they had no place at all, and *sub silentio* they admit their importance. Given monopoly rights and corresponding political authority it was not unreasonable for African chartered companies or Leopold's Congo Association to suppose they were on to a sound speculation, and even where these early hopes were disappointed it would be difficult to show that the principals in these enterprises made serious losses. Robinson and Gallagher freely allow that the economic expansion of British settlers in South Africa had grown almost too powerful under Rhodes for Britain to control, and they have to acknowledge that direct British trading interests in Nigeria had grown to a magnitude sufficient to coerce British statesmen into taking the country under political tutelage in 1885 in order to ward off French and German encroachment. Only in Egypt and East Africa were commercial interests clearly of subordinate importance. The "official mind" may have placed considerations of strategy and security uppermost in its calculations of African policy, but it would be difficult to show that it acted very differently in that part of the world where Robinson and Gallagher regard the British economic state as preponderant, and for whose strategic defence they argue Britain's African policy was shaped. For in Asia political expansion was, in fact, equally determined more by strategic than economic interest, whether in Malaya in the early seventies or Upper Burma in the eighties.[22] The "official mind" had always been cast in this

[20] J. A. Hobson, *Imperialism* (1902 ed.), p. 38.

[21] Ibid. p. 46.

[22] Cf. C. D. Cowan, *Nineteenth Century Malaya* (1961), p. 270.

mould since its conscious emergence in the eighteenth century when government and overseas commerce were finally separated into autonomous agencies. But in Asia, as in Africa, the *agencies* of expansion were essentially economic and provoked the crises that drew the statesmen on to the scene. The interrelationship of economic activities and the workings of the official mind may be more subtle and complex than either of the rival theories seemingly allow,[23] but when freed of the elements of exaggeration Lenin's account of the colonial scramble is not one of narrow economic determinism, nor is Robinson's and Gallagher's one of simple non-economic motivation.

The priority the latter accord to political over economic motives, and to African over European causal initiatives, turns out to be more apparent than real. Although there is a compelling attraction in their argument that local political crises in Africa rather than insistent economic pressures in Europe brought the powers into "the last continent," these local crises on closer examination are seen to have had their origins in the corrosive action of the expanding European economy on indigenous political structures. And this fact they ultimately acknowledge:

All the processes of expansion were reaching their peak. The metropolitan society was putting forth its strongest energies. It was at this climactic point that the social changes in its satellites were quickest and most violent. Hence it was at this time that their relations with the metropolis tended to move into crisis. The colonial communities were breaking off toward full independence; while anti-Western nationalism and social upheaval were estranging the non-European partners of British interests.[24]

In the light of this admission it is difficult to sustain the argument that for "all the hindsight of social scientists, there was no comprehensive cause or purpose behind" the African partition, or to credit that it was a fortuitous freak.[25] In varying measure both Hobson and Lenin had contended that imperialism was no fortuitous phenomenon and that the unbalanced state of the capitalist economy had left the West no option but external expansion. But on a deeper reading of Robinson and Gallagher the fortuitousness they detect in the African scramble lay rather in the unexpectedness of the local political crisis

---

[23] Cf. D. C. M. Platt, *Finance, Trade, Politics in British Policy 1815–1914* (OUP, 1968); "Economic Factors in British Policy during the 'New Imperalism,'" *Past and Present*, no. 39 (April 1968); "The Imperialism of Free Trade: Some Reservations," *Economic History Review*, 2nd ser. xxi, no. 2 (August, 1968).

[24] *Africa and the Victorians*, p. 469.

[25] J. Gallagher and R. E. Robinson, *New Cambridge Modern History*, xi, 593.

in contemporary political consciousness and not in the predisposing causes.[26]

On any final reckoning it may be said that the two authors nowhere commit themselves to a sustained critique of Lenin or Hobson,[27] that they carefully limit themselves to Africa and indeed urge that African empire was acquired to make trade and investment in the East more secure. But in practice their argument is intended to carry farther and to knock both economic and political explanations of imperialism as a phenomenon sharply on the head. They smell a final inconsequence in all tropical empire and nurse a conviction that in the end it was always peripheral to Europe's main concerns:

the gaudy empires spatch-cocked together in Asia and Africa . . . were linked only obliquely to the expansive impulses of Europe. They were not the objects of serious national attention. . . . It would be a gullible historiography which would see such gimcrack creations as necessary functions of the balance of power, or as the highest stage of capitalism.[28]

But how far did orthodox Marxist-Leninist theory regard tropical empire as the highest stage of capitalism? How far indeed did Lenin equate imperialism with colonialism? The spell cast by Hobson's writings and his concentration on British expansion have led most critics writing in English to suppose that in the classical model of economic imperialism the two terms are synonymous. But this is to overlook the other major source of Lenin's theory and to ignore what he said about the other great powers. Imperialism as an expression had a dual origin, and was used equally to describe expansionist militarism on the European continent as overseas colonialism.[29] Rudolf Hilferding's theory of finance capital had carefully kept the two phenomena in balance, and the most cursory reading of the concluding section of this book is enough to demonstrate how almost all the

---

[26] Cf. *Africa and the Victorians*, p. 156: "The Egyptian crisis after 1876 was no accident. Although both French and British misunderstood its character, it was not unusual for European influences in the end to bring about a nationalist reaction and the fall of a collaborating Oriental regime. The internal crisis was worked by the extension of European influence into Egypt since the beginning of the 19th century; and when the insidious effects had come to a head, the occasion of direct European intervention had arisen."

[27] But there are occasional direct references, cf. "The Imperialism of Free Trade," *Economic History Review*, 2nd ser. VI, 1 (1953), 2, 15.

[28] "The Partition of Africa," *New Cambridge Modern History*, XI, 639.

[29] Some of Lenin's earliest uses of the term "imperialism" omit all reference to extra-European colonialism; cf. "The Tasks of Revolutionary Social Democracy in the European War," Aug. 1914, *Works*, XXI (Moscow 1964), 15 ff. and "The European War and International Socialism," Aug-Sept. 1914, *idem*, pp. 20ff.

principal features of imperialism delineated by Lenin were the product not of Hobson's but of Hilferding's fertile brain.[30] In Hilferding are to be found the ideas of the uneven rate of capitalist development;. of the emergence of capitalist monopoly systems organized behind national frontiers but constrained by their internal dynamic to strive constantly for the enlargement of their economic territory; of the multiple forms taken by export capital, of which the acquisition of colonies proper was but one; and of the inevitable provocation of national liberation movements by finance capital in the world that it subjugated. Hilferding drew the distinction between industrial and loan export capital, the former characterizing the powers expanding most rapidly industrially such as Germany and the United States, the latter those older countries like Britain and France in which finance capital had developed further. Similarly, he drew the traits of the three major capitalist complexes, the United States with a large economic territory politically unified, Britain with its empire capable of being drawn increasingly into a tighter economic unity, and Germany denied both these outlets for economic expansion. Here were all the elements of Lenin's holistic interpretation of the age and the world war into which it plunged.

Lenin gave greater precision to Hilferding's notions and backed them with statistical analysis. He did not suppose that finance capital had been chiefly directed to the colonial world as critics like Fieldhouse suggest. Only of England could this be said to be true. The figures he quotes for 1910 show that Great Britain had foreign capital investments exactly twice as large as either France or Germany, of which some 41 per cent was placed in Asia, Africa, and Australia, some 53 per cent in America (including Canada), and the rest in Europe. France had some 23 per cent of her capital investment in the Asia, Africa, Australia category, 11 per cent in America, and some 66 per cent in Europe. Germany with the same amount of capital investment had distributed her investments respectively 20, 29, and 51 per cent. Lenin concluded:

French capital exports are invested mainly in Europe, primarily in Russia. . . . This is mainly *loan* capital, government loans, and not capital invested in industrial undertakings. Unlike British colonial imperialism, French imperialism might be termed usury imperialism. In the case of Germany, we have a third type; colonies are inconsiderable, and German capital invested abroad is divided most evenly between Europe and America.[31]

---

[30] Cf. R. Hilferding, *Das Finanzkapital* (Wien, 1927 edn.), fünfter Abschnitt, "Zur-Wirtschaftspolitik des Finanzkapitals."

[31] "Imperialism," *Works*, xxii, 243.

It was perfectly possible, he conceded, for monopoly capitalism to enlarge its economic territory without resort to political means. "Economic 'annexation' is *fully* achievable with political annexation and is widely practiced."[32] Imperialism in that sense was the division of the world market by trusts, combines, and banking capital. Yet the inherent tendency of imperialism was to violate political independence. Aggressive expansion was not, however, limited to colonial imperialism but extended to continent militarism:

It is not only in newly opened-up countries, but also in the old, that imperialism is leading to annexation, to increased national oppression, and consequently, to increasing resistance. . . .[33]

The characteristic feature of imperialism is precisely that it strives to annex *not only* agrarian territories, but even most highly industrialised regions (German appetite for Belgium; French appetite for Lorraine), because (1) the fact that the world is already divided up obliges those contemplating a *redivision* to reach out for *every kind* of territory, and (2) an essential feature of imperialism is the rivalry between several Great Powers in the striving for hegemony, i.e. for the conquest of territory, not so much directly for themselves, as to weaken the adversary and undermine his hegemony. . . .[34]

Bukharin specifically nailed common misconceptions on this point in his work on *Imperialism and World Economy*, to which Lenin gave his blessing and contributed a preface in 1915:

None the less, it is customary to reduce imperialism to colonial conquests alone. This entirely erroneous conception formerly found some justification in the fact that the bourgeoisie, following the line of least resistance, tended to widen its territory by the seizure of free lands that offered little resistance. Now, however, the time has come for fundamental redivision. Just as trusts competing with one another within the boundaries of a state first grow at the expense of "third persons," of outsiders, and only after having destroyed the intermediary groupings, thrust themselves against one another with particular ferocity, so the competitive struggle between state capitalist trusts first expresses itself in a struggle for free lands, for the *jus primi occupantis* [the right of the first occupant], then it stages a redivision of colonies, and finally when the struggle becomes more intense, even the territory of the home country is drawn into the process of redivision.[35]

---

[32] "A Caricature of Marxism and Imperialist Economism," Aug.-Oct. 1916; *Works*, XXIII, 44.

[33] "Imperialism, the Highest Stage of Capitalism," *Works*, XXII, 297.

[34] *Idem*, pp. 268–9.

[35] N. Bukharin, *Imperialism and World Economy* (London, Martin Lawrence, n.d.), p. 121.

As always, Lenin's line of argument was shaped by tactical exigencies, and his writing was slanted to condemn the errors of "reformism" and "social democrat opportunism" symbolized for him in the person of "the renegade Kautsky." Kautsky had defined imperialism as "merely a system of foreign policy" with the implication that it was an adventitious excrescence of capitalism, a policy that lay within the range of conscious choice and not an inherent necessity.[36] Lenin was concerned, of course, to represent imperialism as an inescapable stage of capitalism, bringing the capitalist powers into ever more violent conflict, rather than a mere external policy towards undeveloped territories where the powers could come to an agreement without resorting to war. Imperialism became in his eyes, therefore, a fundamental economic condition rather than simply a form of external policy, and this is no doubt the reason why he chose to borrow Hilferding's title "Finance Capital: the Latest Stage of Capitalism," but changed it significantly into "Imperialism: the Latest Stage of Capitalism."[37] Yet even in terms of external policy Kautsky's interpretation had to be condemned. Lenin's insistence that imperialism strove not merely for the annexation of agrarian territories but also highly industrialized regions was directed against Kautsky's definition that imperialism was "a product of highly developed industrial capitalism," and consisted "in the striving of every industrial capitalist nation to subjugate and annex ever larger agrarian territories."[38]

As Winslow has said, this tended to mean that for Kautsky imperialism was "merely another term for colonialism."[39] Lenin read the same error into the theory of Rosa Luxemburg who had vehemently espoused the principle of imperialism as a stage rather than policy, but had gone to the extreme conclusion that capitalism had no other outlet for expansion than continuous invasion of the non-capitalist sectors of the world economy. For her, imperialism was "the political expression of the accumulation of capital in its competitive struggle for what remains still open of the non-capitalist environment."[40] This was in effect to shift the centre of gravity to the colonial frontier with a vengeance, and incurred Lenin's disapproval for what he considered, in her biographer's words, her "whole attempt to transport the prob-

---

[36] "A Caricature of Marxism and Imperialist Economism"; *Collected Works*, XXIII, 42.

[37] This was Lenin's first title, changed later on to *"Imperialism, the Highest Stage of Capitalism."*

[38] "Imperialism. . . ," *Works*, XXII, 297. Cf. "Imperialism and the Split in Socialism," Oct. 1916; *Works*, XXIII, 107.

[39] E. M. Winslow, *The Pattern of Imperialism* (New York, 1948), p. 155.

[40] Rosa Luxemburg, *The Accumulation of Capital* (1963, paperback), p. 446.

lems of imperialism into foreign and colonial territories—instead of leaving them at home where they belonged."[41] He smelled in it a new heresy which he dubbed "imperialist economism," under which lurked his old enemy, Legal Marxism, tricked out in new clothes. Its false doctrine taught that capitalism, in its latest form of imperialism, should be allowed to pursue its brutal but progressive rôle unimpeded, while social democracy eschewed political action and concentrated on trade unionism, syndicalism, and the mass strike. Lenin, of course, stood for political action by a small conspirational party ready to exploit all forms of discontent, even though reactionary. The most potent of these was the nationalism of subject peoples, which "imperialist economism" scouted as diverting the working-class movement to the service of reactionary bourgeois causes. Rosa Luxemburg argued that the erection of a Polish national state was meaningless in the days of large-scale economic concentration and the hegemony of finance capital in the advanced states, since imperialism in these forms rendered political independence a sham.[42] But Lenin regarded the teaching as covert chauvinism which by exporting imperialism to the colonies and semi-colonies allowed the German Social Democrat movement conveniently to ignore imperialist annexation like Alsace and Lorraine.

For him the vital practical importance of the theorizing on imperialism was its relevance for the "national and colonial question," as his writings and letters immediately before and after the composition of his celebrated tract on imperialism make evident. He sought to embrace the phenomena of national liberation movements both in Europe and the semi-colonial and colonial world within a single explanation. The age of industrial capitalism with simple commodity exchange promoted the creation of the bourgeois democratic state in Europe. Monopoly capitalism (or imperialism) on the other hand saw the end of nationalism as a progressive force at home, while its essentially oppressive character provoked national and democratic movements abroad. But the term imperialism had to be stretched in the process, and Lenin is often found slipping into the popular usage whereby it denoted merely an external policy "predatory and oppressive towards other peoples."[43] National liberation movements like that for American independence were clearly far older than the age of

---

41 J. P. Nettl, *Rosa Luxemburg* (1966), II, 533.

42 Cf. "The Junius Pamphlet" and "The Discussion on Self-Determination Summed Up," *Works*, XXII. "A Caricature of Marxism and Imperialist Economism," *Works*, XXIII.

43 "The Question of Peace," July-Aug. 1915, *Works*, XXI, 290.

imperialism, and Lenin could speak of the Seven Years War between Britain and France for colonies as an imperialist war, "which is possible on the basis of slavery and primitive capitalism as well as on the basis of modern highly developed capitalism."[44] Russian imperialism presented even trickier problems since tsarism was basically a precapitalist form of absolutism. He acknowledged that what he called "military and feudal imperialism" was still predominant and characterized the oppression exerted by 70 million Great Russians over 100 million European people. But the policy of tsarism towards Persia, Manchuria and Mongolia (with presumably the backing of foreign finance capital) he saw in contrast as "capitalist imperialism of the latest type."[45] The combination of the two types was reflected in Russia's relations with France and Britain which had resulted in an "alliance of tsarist imperialism and advanced capitalist European imperialism, which is based on their common oppression of a number of nations."[46] The paradoxical character of Russian imperialism had one important advantage from the revolutionary viewpoint. Its contradictions were sharper; from this notion was later to be developed the theory that the chain of imperialism tended to break at its weakest link.

These refinements apart, Lenin was left with a clear doctrine. The world could be divided into three camps: the advanced capitalist countries of Western Europe and the United States, whose progressive bourgeois national movements had come to an end long ago, and oppression of other nations both at home and in the colonies had taken their place; secondly, Eastern Europe comprising Austria, the Balkans and particularly Russia, where it was "the twentieth century that particularly developed the bourgeois-democratic national movements and intensified the national struggle"; and thirdly, the semi-colonial countries like China, Persia and Turkey, and all the colonies where "the bourgeois-democratic movements have hardly begun, or have still a long way to go."[47] He had no doubt as to where the impact of imperialism had been most intense; it was in the second group. Capitalism had been able to develop much faster and more freely among the subject nationalities of Eastern Europe than among the semi-colonial and colonial countries, and consequently had gen-

---

[44] "The Junius Pamphlet," July 1916, *Works*, xxii, 310.

[45] "Socialism and War," July-Aug. 1915, *Works*, xxi, 306.

[46] "The Discussion on Self-Determination Summed Up," July 1916, *Works*, xxii, 342.

[47] "The Socialist Revolution and the Right of Nations to Self-Determination," Feb.-March 1916, *Works*, xxii, 150–1.

erated "greater resistance to national oppression and annexations."[48] There could in his eyes be no comparison in the relative importance of the national liberation movements in Europe and the colonial world:

Social Democracy, we read in the Polish theses . . . "must utilise the struggle of the young colonial bourgeoisie against Europe Imperialism *in order to sharpen the revolutionary crisis in Europe. . . .*" Is it not clear that it is least of all permissible to contrast Europe to the colonies in *this* respect? The struggle of the oppressed nations *in Europe,* a struggle going all the way to insurrection and street fighting, capable of breaking down the iron discipline of the army and martial law, will "sharpen the revolutionary crisis in Europe" to an infinitely greater degree than a much more developed rebellion in a remote colony. A blow delivered against the power of the English imperialist bourgeoisie by a rebellion in Ireland is a hundred times more significant politically than a blow of equal force delivered in Asia or in Africa.[49]

Lenin was not prepared to shift the centre of gravity of capitalist imperialism outside Europe to the colonial frontier. But his teaching did not become widely known until after the Bolshevik victory when it was understandable that it should have been misinterpreted. For by then a theory devised to explain the World War and the revolutionary possibilities in Europe had to be turned to meet a totally different situation, the defence of "socialism in one country" against a potentially hostile capitalist West. Lenin's Eastern European group of countries which he envisaged as the storm centre of imperialism in 1916 had now dropped out of the picture; and imperialism increasingly connoted the oppression of the colonial and semi-colonial world by the advanced capitalist powers. In these terms it came to be understood by the post-First War generation who fell under the influence of Marxism, and whose conception of imperialism—especially that of Anglo-American writers—had been powerfully coloured by Hobson's book. For men like Leonard Woolf or Maurice Dobb it was axiomatic that imperialism meant colonialism.[50] Lenin appeared to lend substance to the idea in 1920 when at the second congress of the Comintern he made a bid for the support of the revolutionary forces among

---

[48] "The Discussion on Self-Determinaion Summed Up," July 1916, *Works,* XXII, 338: ". . . capitalism is undoubtedly developing the productive forces more vigorously, rapidly and independently in Poland, Finland, the Ukraine and Alsace than in India, Turkestan, Egypt and other straightforward colonies."

[49] "The Discussion on Self-Determination Summed Up," July 1916, *Works,* XXII, 356–7.

[50] Leonard Woolf, *Empire and Commerce in Africa* (1920), pp. 22 ff. Maurice Dobb, chap. VII, "Imperialism" in *Political Economy and Capitalism* (1937).

"the toilers of the East." The Draft Theses on the National and Colonial Questions and the Report of the subsequent Commission gave notice that Lenin was prepared to contemplate espousing even peasant movements in the colonial areas, and in a flight of oratory he could predict that Britain's back would be broken not on the banks of the Thames but on the Yangtse, the Ganges, and the Nile.

Even if this mirrored a fading of the hope that the internal contradictions of imperialist capitalism would produce immediate proletarian revolution in the West, it did not mean that the epicentre of imperialism had been shifted to the colonial areas, and certainly not to the tropical colonies acquired after 1870. The essential revolutionary struggle remained in the West and lay between the advanced proletariat led by the Soviet Union and the bourgeoisie of the advanced capitalist powers; all else was subsidiary.[51] Stalin's theory of the chain of imperialism breaking at its weakest link in no way altered the doctrine. The question was seen simply as to how "the dependent and colonial countries can be transformed from a reserve of the imperialist bourgeoisie into a reserve of the revolutionary proletariat."[52] Not until Maoism did any official Communist voice dare to suggest that the centre of gravity had shifted to the Third World and to advance the claim that "the whole course of the international proletarian revolution hinges on the outcome of the revolutionary struggles of the peoples of these areas, who constitute the overwhelming majority of the world's population."[53]

If Lenin's theory of imperialism remains in the last resort an explanation of the internal configuration of the industrialized world in which colonialism is but one and not the most important deriva-

---

[51] Lenin, "Preliminary Draft of Theses on the National and Colonial Questions," June 1920, Works, xxxi, p. 146: "World political developments are of necessity concentrated on a single focus—the struggle of the world bourgeoisie against the Soviet Russian Republic around which are inevitably grouped, on the one hand, the Soviet movements of the advanced workers in all countries, and, on the other, all the national-liberation movements in the colonies and among the oppressed nationalities . . ." Cf. his outline for draft theses on the international economic and political situation for the 2nd Congress of the Comintern, 19 July 1920, Works, xxxv, 450–1.

[52] J. Stalin, "The Foundations of Leninism" (1924) in Leninism (London, 1940), p. 52.

[53] "A Proposal concerning the General Line of the International Communist Movement," para. 8, 14 June 1963; Reply of Chinese Communist Party to Communist Party of the Soviet Union. Printed D. Floyd, Mao Against Kruschev (paperback edn. 1963), p. 410. Cf. G. Fairbairn, Revolutionary Warfare and Communist Strategy: The Threat to South-East Asia (1968), pp. 130 ff.

tive,[54] then a large part of the critique directed against it falls wide of the mark. The validity or otherwise of the Marxist theory and the canons of historical explanation it employs are a separate question. Yet when the arguments of both Lenin and of Robinson and Gallagher have been freed from the elements of caricature, their general analyses of European colonialism between 1870 and 1914 exhibit a surprising degree of correspondence. Lenin, it would appear, was no Leninist; he too stands the classical model of economic imperialism on its head.

---

[54] Soviet Russia, in terms of the theory, is included in "the industrialized world." For a modern Marxist statement, cf. Harry Magdoff, "The Age of Imperialism," *Monthly Review*, New York, xx (June 1968), esp. pp. 22–3.

VII/THE RUSSIAN REVOLUTION

I T is conceivable that the tsarist regime, if much reformed and adapted to a form of constitutional monarchy, might have survived for a considerable period, had not World War I broken out when it did. Its archaic socioeconomic structures proved unable to withstand the shock of mobilization; famine, disease, and the human suffering caused by war combined with the traditional forms of oppression and exploitation to make the situation untenable. The result was the February Revolution of 1917. The Provisional Government that issued from it under the leadership of Alexander Kerensky was committed to the establishment of a bourgeois-democratic regime, but it was thoroughly compromised by its failure to take Russia out of the war and, further, to take the measures so desperately needed to relieve the misery of the population. Its class interests made it basically unsympathetic to the needs of workers and peasants and thus provoked the continuing confrontation which the Bolsheviks were able to organize into a proletarian socialist revolution in the following October. The rest, as the saying goes, is history.

It is the habit of counterrevolutionaries to claim superior knowledge of the revolutions they condemn. Not merely factual knowledge (of which they may have an uncommon grasp), but intuitive comprehension of what the revolution ought to have been. We have all heard the pious denunciations of Castro's "betrayal" of the "democratic" (read: bourgeois) essence of the Cuban Revolution. It is an old tradition and goes back at least as far as Edmund Burke, who thought that 1789 was fine, but that 1790 was its contradiction and nemesis: The French had gone too far.

It cannot be denied that revolutions possess their own inner dynamic, if not logic. If revolution is, in Trotsky's phrase, "the forcible entrance of the masses into the realm of rulership over their own destiny," there is no telling where the process will stop once unleashed. If this was true of the classic bourgeois revolution of all time, France in 1789–1794, where the masses (but not the proletariat) had already assumed a hegemonic role, how much truer must it be of Russia in 1917 or of Cuba in the 1950s and 1960s. To speak of betrayal is utter nonsense, and even the concept of successive revolutions by diverse classes (used by the historian Georges Lefebvre to explain the French Revolution) seems to me to miss the point. The revolutions (bourgeois-democratic and proletarian-socialist in the latter two instances) were for all intents and purposes simultaneous, two aspects of the *combined development,* an idea which Trotsky explains in the selection from his work printed here.

A variation on the "what the revolution should have been" theme is that of necessity. Was revolution necessary to achieve the goals of the revolutionaries? The answer is usually "No." Aside from the fact that the revolutionary masses do not generally embark on the process with a clear program in mind, much depends on the definition of the goals. Just as a new society is born in the womb of the old, so a revolution builds a new edifice with the stones of the old regime. Industrialization and political liberty might have been possible without, and even were coming into existence before, the Russian Revolution. In a celebrated piece of rhetoric, Lenin once said: "Communism is electrification plus soviets." But the goal was communism, which electrification alone would not have secured.

We conclude that the Revolution was necessary. For a Marxist, history is the record of class struggle, and revolutions take place when the contradictions between the social relations of production and the productive forces become so sharp that something has to give. But classes are made of men, and men make their own history, albeit not under conditions of total freedom. This implies that consciousness, the translation into subjective desire of an objective situation, is a necessary prerequisite of revolution. It may take a longer or shorter time to develop; nothing in the entire process is automatic. Hence the need for political activity, for consciousness-raising.

In this light, inevitability takes on a new meaning. The maturation of social conditions proceeds on one time scale; thought, on another. Either one may chronologically, within certain limits, precede the other. Thus, Lenin and the rest of the revolutionary vanguard were seeking to overthrow the tsarist regime before all the room available within it for the development of the productive forces had been taken—witness the industrialization of Russia in the years just before World War I. On the other hand, Lenin would not have thought in terms of socialist revolution (or, at the very best, would have remained an isolated genius) had the development of the capitalist mode of production not already been well along. Had he never lived, a confrontation between oppressed and oppressor classes would have taken place at another time, in different forms, and perhaps with other results. Revolutions do not inevitably triumph, at least not in the sense of the immediate replacement of one class by another in the seats of power. However, a class that loses a battle often goes on to win the war—see, for example, the history of the German bourgeoisie in the nineteenth century. Whether this will also be possible in the present era of confrontations between capitalists and proletarians is a more vexed question, although it seems to be the assumption implicit in contemporary theories of coexistence and the "peaceful transition to socialism."

There are two other related points on which revolutionaries and nonrevolutionaries will differ. One is the role of error and miscalculation, of what used to be called accident, in history. It is the question of Kaiser Wilhelm's withered hand and Cleopatra's nose. The facts are not in dispute; all is in the weight we choose to give them. Whereas others may wish to make them determinant, a Marxist will maintain that individual peculiarities are only important because of their social context and conditioning. We deal here with a king of Germany and a queen of Egypt in societies which had, respectively, certain child-rearing practices and fixed standards of beauty. There lies the crux of the matter: The Kaiser may have undergone all sorts of psychic (or psychoanalytic) trauma, and Marc Antony may have fallen victim to the Queen's quivering nostrils, and the actions of one and the other in World War I and at the battle of Actium would have to be studied biographically in this light. The *historical* study of the same events must, however, have another dimension, for neither man was a free agent, able independently to make war or carry out a policy as his particular neurosis or infatuation may have suggested. Nor is anyone ever at liberty to do so. The limits of individual action are always set by the structure of social relations.

The second point has to do with the principle of elitism. Great men count in history, but they are not alone. George Kennan, now at the Institute for Advanced Study in Princeton, is the former United States ambassador to the Soviet Union and the author of a two-volume study of Russian-American relations in the early revolutionary period. He was also the principal architect of the United States policy of containment in Eastern Europe after World War II. In the following article, he considers the causes of the Russian Revolution and concludes that what counted was the tsar's ineptitude and the alienation of active minorities from the state and its affairs. He cannot conceive of masses changing history, either as the steam that drives the vanguard piston or even directly, without intermediaries. It is the same attitude of mind that allows him to write that the Russian people were not yet ready for parliamentary institutions in 1905. That is either phrase-mongering, or it means that they would have made a mess of bourgeois institutions by turning them to their own purposes. Order ("When everything is wrong, but in the right places," was Brecht's definition) would no doubt have suffered, but that hypothesis is not sufficient reason to ask us to concentrate on elites and to minimize the role of the masses in historical change.

The other two articles reprinted here are by dissident Marxists who broke with their respective Communist parties. Leon Trotsky (1879–1940) was, with Lenin and Stalin, one of the great triumvirate of Russian revolutionary leaders. He was exiled from the Soviet Union in 1929 and died in Mexico at the hands of an assassin in 1940. The following selection from his *History of the Russian Revolution* deals in particular with his theory of *combined development* (to which we have already alluded) in an effort to explain the basis for revolutionary change in Russia in 1917. Isaac Deutscher (1907–1967) was a leading Marxist historian and political commentator friendly to Trotsky and highly critical of the Stalinist policies of the Soviet Union, which in his eyes were responsible for the maintenance of the Bolshevik revolution in an "unfinished" state, as he explains here. After being expelled from the Polish Community party in 1932, he settled in England where he wrote his important biographies of Stalin and Trotsky. In recent years, Deutscher's work has been most influential in the intellectual formation of the American and European new left.

George F. Kennan

16

The Breakdown of the Tsarist Autocracy

The discussion that follows proceeds from the premise that what occurred in Russia in February–March 1917 was, precisely, a *breakdown* of the autocracy under a fortuitous combination of momentary strains—not the overthrow of the existing order by revolutionary forces. In essence, the regime may be said to have collapsed because it was not able to muster sufficient support to enable it to withstand this sudden combination of strains. In quarters whose support would have been essential to enable it to do this, there was either distrust, indifference, outright hostility, or, in the particular case of the bureaucracy and the army, a mixture of disorientation, demoralization, and ineptness. The central question involved is therefore the question as to which of the regime's policies—that is, what elements of its behavior, what errors of commission or omission, or possibly what circumstances outside its control—were decisive or outstandingly important in bringing it to the helpless and fatal predicament in which it found itself at the beginning of 1917.

Such an inquiry presents special difficulty in view of the bewildering interaction of long-term and short-term causes. One is compelled to ask not just what were the long-term weaknesses that rendered the regime susceptible to the danger of collapse under relatively trivial pressures in the first place, but also what it was that caused the collapse to come at this particular moment.

I should like to begin with an examination of some of the long-term weaknesses and failures of the regime and then conclude with some brief reflections about the developments of the final wartime period just preceding its fall.

LONG-TERM WEAKNESSES AND FAILURES
OF THE REGIME

When one looks for those more basic mistakes and failings that undermined the tsarist autocracy and caused it to lose what the Chinese would call the "mandate of Heaven," one is obliged first to deal with certain broadly held misimpressions on this score—misimpressions that Soviet historians, in particular, have been at no pains to dispel. One of these is that the autocracy lost the confidence and respect of the people because it failed to bring a proper degree of modernization to Russian society in the economic, technological, and educational fields—that it made no adequate effort to overcome Russia's backwardness. Another is that the regime was intolerably cruel and despotic in its treatment of the populace generally; and that a revolution was required to correct this situation. In each of these impressions there are, of course, elements of truth; but both represent dangerous, and in general misleading, oversimplifications. That this is true is so well known to experts in the field that it needs, I think, no great elaboration here. But I shall just mention briefly, to avoid unclarity, my own impressions of the situation.

Let us take first the subject of industrialization. Here, it seems to me, we have one of those fields in which the tsar's regime had least to be apologetic about from the standpoint of responsibility for the modernizing of the country. The rates of industrial growth achieved in Russia in the final decades of tsardom would appear to compare not at all unfavorably with those achieved in Western countries at comparable stages of development. The 8 percent growth rate that I understand to have been achieved in the 1890's, and the comparable 6 percent figure for the period from 1906 to 1914, are respectable figures, to say the least. One must doubt that the pace of industrialization could have been pushed much further without producing adverse social consequences out of all proportion in seriousness to the gains involved. Nor does there seem to be any reason to suppose that if revolution had not intervened, and if the dynamics of growth observable in the final decades of tsardom had been projected into mid-century, the results achieved would have been significantly inferior to those that have actually been achieved under Soviet power. This is, of course, only another way of saying that if industrialization was the main concern then no revolution was needed at all: there were easier and no less promising ways of doing it.

It has often been pointed out by way of reproach to the tsar's regime—both at the time and since—that this growth was achieved only by an excessive acceptance of investment and equity participation by foreigners in Russian industry, as well as by excessive state borrowing from other governments. Certainly, the proportion of foreign equity participation in Russian industrial concerns was very high, particularly in mining and metallurgy; and it is perfectly true that the Russian government was the most heavily indebted, externally, of any government in the world at the time. But I am not sure how well these charges stand up as reproaches to the policies of the tsar's government. Whether the high rate of foreign industrial investment was a bad thing depends on whether one accepts the Marxist thesis that any important degree of such external financing represented a form of enslavement to the foreign investors. The experience of the United States, where foreign capital also played a prominent part in nineteenth century industrial development, would not suggest that this is the case. And as for the government borrowing: much of this, of course, found its way, directly or indirectly, into the process of industrialization, and particularly into the building of railways. But the main stimulus to such borrowing was not the need for industrial capital but rather the effort by the government to maintain a military posture, and to engage in military ventures, that were far beyond its means. These practices, and the heavy indebtedness to which they led, were indeed among the significant weaknesses of the regime; but they do not constitute a proper source of reproach to the regime in connection with its program of industrialization. Had the foreign borrowings of the government been restricted to what it required in order to do its share in the stimulation of the growth of industry, the resulting burden of debt would surely have been well within its means.

Another reproach often leveled at the tsar's government in this connection was that industrialization was given precedence over agriculture and that it was partially financed by the exploitation of the peasantry through such devices as high indirect taxation, rigged prices for agricultural products, forced exportation of grain, and so on. Certainly there is much substance in these charges. The program of rapid industrialization was indeed put in hand long before any attack of comparable vigor was made on the problems of the peasantry, and the peasant was made to contribute heavily to its costs. But these circumstances seem to me to be illustrative less of any error or unfeeling quality on the part of tsarist statesmen than of the cruelty of the dilemmas with which they were faced. Without at least a certain prior development of industry, and particularly without the construction of railway network, no modernization of Russian agriculture would have been conceivable at all. And while somewhat more might perhaps have been extracted from the upper classes through ruthless taxation, there is no reason to suppose that this could have changed basically the logic of the situation, which was that the cost of industrialization, to the extent it was not covered by foreign borrowing, had to be covered by limitations on consumption by the great mass of the Russian people—which meant, in fact, the peasantry. To have tried, through the device of heavy taxation, to switch this entire burden to the relatively well-to-do or property-owning classes would merely have tended to destroy existing possibilities for the accumulation of private industrial capital; but such private accumulation was precisely what the government was concerned, and for very respectable reason, to stimulate and promote.

The truth is that the tsar's government, if it wished to get on in a serious way with the industrial development of the country, had no alternatives other than foreign borrowing and an extensive taxation of the peasantry. The claim that it should have avoided one or the other of these devices is thus equivalent to the allegation that it moved not too slowly but much too fast in the whole field of industrialization. For this there might be much to be said. But this is not the way the reproach is usually heard.

In the case of agriculture, the pattern is obviously more complex. Certainly, the reform of the 1860's left much to be desired; it was not properly followed through; the burdens resting on the peasantry down to 1905 were inordinate; the economic situation of large portions of the peasant population remained miserable. In all this there were just grounds for reproach to the regime; and I have no desire to minimize its significance. It seems reasonable to suppose that the additional burden of bitterness that accumulated in peasant minds in the final decades of the nineteenth century contributed importantly both to the peasant disorders of the first years of the new century, and to that spirit of sullen contempt for the dynasty, and indifference to its fate, that manifested itself at the time of the revolution.

Against these reflections must be set, however, two compensatory considerations. One has, first, the fact that the most important single factor involved in producing the land hunger and economic misery of the central-Russian village in these decades was nothing having to do with governmental policy but simply the enormous increase in the rural population that occurred at that time—a doubling, and more, just in the years between the emancipation and the outbreak of the world war. Second, there is the fact that after 1906 the government did finally address itself vigorously, intelligently, and in general quite effectively to the problems of the Russian countryside. The fact that this effort came late—too late to be successful in the political and psychological sense—should not blind us to its imposing dimensions. What was achieved in those final years from 1907 to 1914 in a whole series of fields affecting the peasant's situation—in the purchase of land by small peasant holders; in the break-up of the peasant commune and the facilitating of the transition from communal to hereditary tenure; in the consolidation of strip holdings, with all the enormous labor of surveying and adjudication this involved; in resettlement and in colonization of outlying regions of the empire; in the development of the cooperative movement in the countryside—strikes me as impressive in the extreme.

One can truthfully say that the tsar's government deserved reproach for its failures in relation to the peasant throughout most of the nineteenth century. And there can be no doubt that the price of these failures figured prominently in the reckoning the autocracy had to face in 1917. No one would deny, in particular, the importance of the impact that the spectacle of all this rural misery and degradation had on the growth of the Russian revolutionary movement in the nineteenth century. And one can well say that such efforts as were made to improve the situation of the peasantry came much too late in the game. What one cannot say is that they did not come at all or that revolution was necessary because the tsar's government, as of 1917, had still done nothing effective about agriculture. The fact is that the revolution came precisely at the moment when the prospects for the development of Russian agriculture, the war aside, had never looked more hopeful.

Similar conclusions could be drawn, I should think, with relation to education. That Russia was slow in coming to popular education no one would deny. But that the progress made in this field in the final years of tsardom was rapid and impressive seems to me equally undeniable. If, as I understand to be the case, enrollments in primary schools throughout the empire more than doubled in the final two decades before 1914; if in this same period enrollments in institutions of higher learning more than tripled and those in secondary schools nearly quadrupled; or if, for example, the incidence of literacy among military recruits increased from 38 percent in 1894 to 73 percent in 1913— then it may be argued, I think, that all this might have been done earlier; but it cannot be said that nothing consequential was being done at all. The official goal, as adopted five or six years before the outbreak of the world war, was the achievement of universal, compulsory primary school education. The tsarist authorities hoped to achieve this goal by 1922. The rate of progress made prior to the war suggests that it would probably have been achieved at the latest by the mid-1920's had not war and revolution intervened. This is certainly no later than the date at which it was finally achieved by the Soviet regime. Again, one simply cannot accept the thesis that the old regime kept the Russian people in darkness to the end and that a revolution was necessary in 1917 to correct this situation.

In all these fields of modernization, the pattern is in fact much the same: initial backwardness, long sluggishness and delay, then a veritable burst of activity in the final years. If it was in these fields that one was to look for the decisive failures of the autocracy and the reasons for revolution, then it would have to be said that there was much less reason for an overthrow of the regime in 1917 than there was in 1905. Had the 1905 Revolution succeeded, one might well have concluded that the tsar's regime had been overthrown because it failed to bring the Russian people into the modern age. To account for an overthrow coming in 1917, one has to look for other and deeper causes.

The first and most decisive of these causes seems to me to have been, unquestionably, the failure of the autocracy to supplement the political system in good time with some sort of a parliamentary institution—the failure, in other words, to meet the needs of the land-owning nobility and then, increasingly, of the new intelligentsia from all classes for some sort of institutional framework that would associate them with the undertakings of the regime, give them a sense of participation in the governmental process, and provide a forum through which they, or their representatives, could air their views and make their suggestions with regard to governmental policy. In the absence of any such institution, literally hundreds of thousands of people—student youth, commoners (raznochintsy), sons of priests, members of the national minorities, members of the gentry, even members of the land-owning nobility itself—people bursting with energies and of the love of life in all its forms; people vibrating with intellectual excitement under the flood of impressions that swept over Russian society as its contacts with the West developed during the nineteenth and early twentieth centuries; people passionately concerned with public affairs, intensely aware of Russia's backwardness, and possessed by no more consuming passion than the desire to contribute to its correction —all these people found themselves, insofar as they did not become associated with the armed forces or the administrative bureaucracy, repelled by the regime, held at a distance from its doings and responsibilities, condemned either to a passive submissiveness in public affairs that did violence to their consciences as well as their energies or to the development of forms of association and political activity that could not, in the circumstances, appear to the regime as other than subversive. What was required, initially, was not a widely popular assembly. There was much to be said for the view that the Russian people at large were not yet ready for this. At any time in the nineteenth century, even a central assembly of the local government boards (zemstva) would have constituted an important safety valve, and in fact a very suitable one, insofar as it would have enlisted as collaborators in the tasks of government at the central level not mere theorists devoid of practical experience but people who had had the best sort of preparation: namely, experience at the local, provincial level in the fields of administration intimately connected with the lives and interests of common people. To attempt, with relation to so great and complex a process as that of the loss of public confidence by the Russian autocracy, to identify any single error as a crucial one is, of course, always to commit an act of oversimplification; but if one were to inquire what, by way of example, might appear as outstanding historical errors of the regime, I should think one would have to name such things as the flat repulsion by Alexander II in 1862 of the initiative taken by the gentry of Tver, under the leadership of Unkovskii, in favor of a central *zemstvo* organ; or the rebuff administered by Nicholas II to the representatives of the *zemstva* and the nobility who called on him in 1895 to urge—if only in the mildest of language—the recognition of the need for a more representative system of government. In the entire record of the last decades of tsarist power, I can think of no mistakes more calamitous than these.

There was, of course, eventually, the Duma; and it was, as an institution, not really so bad as it has often been portrayed. Its initial members could, as Vasilii Maklakov pointed out, have made much better use of it than they actually did. The franchise was indeed a limited one, but it was not so severely limited as to prevent both First and Second Dumas from being violently oppositional, and even extensively revolutionary, in spirit. Nor can I develop any lively sympathy for the great unhappiness manifested by the Kadets over the fact that the Duma was not given the right to appoint and control the government. For an American, in particular, it is hard to regard a fusing of the legislative and executive powers as absolutely essential to a sound political system. But leaving aside the adequacy of the arrangements governing the constitution and functioning of the Duma, it is obvious that the granting of it by Nicholas II came far too late and in precisely the wrong way—under pressure, that is, and with obvious reluctance and suspicion on his part. Given the situation that existed at that particular moment, it was natural enough for him to do so. There could have been no more than a minority of the members of the First Duma whose political aspirations, if satisfied, would not have ended in the violent destruction of the autocracy; and the tsar understood this very well. And yet it was Nicholas himself, his father, and his grandfather who were responsible for the fact that this was the way things were. Had they acted earlier—and the 1860's would not have been too soon—they might have had a different, more respectful, and less menacing sort of a parliamentary body before them. And the difference would, I think, have been decisive. The conservative and liberal intelligentsia, from which the dynasty really had something to hope, might have rallied to its side and the radical revolutionary movement, from which it could expect nothing good, would have been split. The effect of waiting forty years and establishing the Duma in 1906 instead of in the 1860's was just the opposite: it unified the radical-revolutionary movement against the regime and split the conservative and liberal intelligentsia, whose united support was essential if the dynasty was to survive.

It was true, of course, that to grant a parliamentary institution would have involved at any time on the tsar's part a readiness to share the power which the dynasty had previously exercised absolutely. But in the mid-nineteenth century, there were still people on the other side who would have been willing to content themselves with this sharing of supreme power. By 1906 there was practically no one left, not only in the revolutionary movement but among the liberals as well, who did not insist, by implication at least, on destroying the tsar's powers entirely rather than just sharing in them. It was the destruction of the autocracy as such, not really its limitation, that was implicit in the demands of the First Duma for a responsible government, for control in effect of the police, and above all for a general amnesty.

In the 1860's the dynasty might still have had before it, in a parliamentary institution, people who were anxious to see it succeed in its tasks and willing to help it do so. By 1906 it was confronted, in every political party to the left of the Octobrists and even partly in the ranks of that grouping, not by people who constituted a loyal opposition, not by people who really wanted the dynasty to succeed with the tasks of modernization to which I referred earlier on, not by people who wished to have a share in the dynasty's power, but by rivals for the exercise of that power, by people whose chief grievance against the regime was not that it was dilatory or incompetent but that it stood in their own path, whose complaint was not really that the autocracy misruled Russia, but that it prevented *them* from ruling—or misruling, as history would probably have revealed—in its place.

With Unkovskii and his associates in 1862, Alexander II might, it seems to me, have come to some sort of political terms. With Miliukov and his associates, decorous and mild-mannered as they outwardly were, this same possibility no longer existed. It had become by that time a case of *kto kogo* (who whom)—either the tsar or they. Yet without their help, as February 1917 revealed, the dynasty itself could not be defended.

In the mid-nineteenth century, in other words, the autocracy could still have opted for the status of a limited monarchy. In 1906 this option no longer remained open to it. And the failure to accept it when it *had been* open left only one possibility, which was its final and total destruction.

This great deficiency—namely the denial of political expression—
must be clearly distinguished from the question of physical cruelty
and oppression in the treatment of the population. It was suggested,
at the outset of this discussion, that it was a misimpression that the
regime was intolerably cruel and despotic in this respect. This is, of
course, a controversial statement; and I do not wish to make it
unnecessarily so. I am well aware of the fact that the tsarist police and
prison authorities, as well as the military courts, were guilty of many
acts of stupidity, injustice, and cruelty. I am not unmindful of the
observations of my distinguished namesake, the elder George Kennan,
on the exile system in Siberia. But the standards of the present age are
different from those of the latter—unfortunately so. The tsarist autocracy did not engage in the sort of prophylactic terror—the punishment
of great numbers of the innocent as a means of frightening the
potentially guilty—of which we have seen so much in our age. Its
treatment of many individual revolutionaries, including incidentally
Chernyshevskii, seems to have been, if anything, on the lenient side.
The censorship was irritating and often silly, but it was not sufficiently
severe to prevent the appearance in Russia of a great critical literature.
Most important of all, one has to distinguish, when one speaks of
police terrorism, between that element of it that is spontaneous and
the element that is provoked. That the Russian revolutionaries
behaved provocatively, and deliberately so, on countless occasions is
something that few, I think, would deny. Now, it is a habit of political
regimes to resist their own violent overthrow; it is something to be
expected of them. Stolypin used harsh measures—yes—in suppressing
the disorders of the period following the war with Japan, but measures
no more harsh than the situation required from the standpoint of the
regime. Had there been a time in the history of the United States
when political assassinations—assassinations of public officials—were
running at the rate of more than one and a half thousand per annum,
as was the case in Russia in 1906, I rather shudder to think what would
have been the reaction of the official establishment here. In situations
of this nature, where there is a constant interaction between the
strivings of revolutionaries and the defensive efforts of a political
regime, the question of responsibility for violence becomes a matter of
the chicken and the egg. If one abstracts from the behavior of the
regime in the administration of justice and in the imposition of
political discipline that element that was provided by provocation
from the revolutionary side, then the use of police terror cannot be
regarded as more than a minor determinant of the alienation of great
sectors of society that underlay the breakdown of 1917.

So much for the denial of parliamentary government and political
liberty. A second crucial deficiency of the autocracy was one that it

shared with a large part of upper-class Russian society, and with a portion of the lower classes as well, and that was for this reason not only much more difficult to recognize at the time but has been more difficult of recognition even in the light of history. This was extreme nationalism—that romantic, linguistic nationalism that was the disease of the age.

The spirit of modern nationalism was pernicious for the Russian autocracy for two reasons: first, because it reflected itself unfortunately on the treatment by the tsar's government of the national minorities; but second, because it led to an adventurous foreign policy, far beyond what the capacities of the Russian state at that time could support.

In an empire of which nearly half, or something more than one half (depending on where the Ukrainians were ranked) of the population was made up of national minorities, an absolute monarchy was confronted, in the age of nationalism, with a basic choice. It could make political concessions to the Great-Russian plurality and thus at least keep the strongest single national element firmly associated with it in an effort to hold down the minorities; or, if it did not wish to do this, it could employ a light touch with the minorities, do everything possible to reconcile them to the Russian state, and play them off against the potentially rebellious central Great-Russian group. The tsar's government did neither. Operating against the background of a sullen Russian peasantry, a frustrated Russian upper class, and a lower-class Russian intelligentsia veritably seething with sedition, it set about to treat the national minorities in the name of Russian nationalism with an utterly senseless provocation of their national cultures and feelings and a rigid repression of all their efforts to establish a separate national political identity. This was a policy calculated to make sure that if there were anyone among the minority elements who was not already alienated from the autocracy by virtue of its general social and political policies, he would sooner or later be brought into the opposition by the offense to his national feelings. Among the manifestations of this stupidity none was more serious than the anti-Semitism that set in after the murder of Alexander II—an aberration of policy that was at first simply clumsy and reactionary in an old-fashioned religious sense but then assumed, under Nicholas II, forms that were truly disgraceful and bespoke a profound perversion of political and philosophic understanding. This tendency was particularly unfortunate because it came at a period when, for the first time, a great many young Jews would have been prepared, given half a chance, to forget the specific circumstances of their religious and cultural origin and to become essentially russified. And this anti-Semitism was of course only a part of nationalistic policies that affected in some way and at some time practically every one of the minorities that lined the periphery of the empire. The revenge for this extraordinary blindness became apparent, quite naturally, in the form of the high percentage of members of the national minorities to be found in the revolutionary movement. It is impossible to say what 1917 would have been like without the Chkheidzes and Martovs, the Trotskys, Dzerzhinskiis, Radeks, Sverdlovs, Stalins, and Ordzhonikidzes; but certainly the non-Great-Russian component in the revolutionary opposition to tsardom was a great one, particularly after 1881, and it must be assumed to have added greatly to the difficulty of the predicament of the autocracy at that final moment.

The second manner in which the disease of extreme nationalism manifested itself in tsarist policy was, as already noted, in the field of foreign affairs. Particularly was this true under Nicholas II. The origins of the war with Japan were, from the Russian side, disreputable and inexcusable. There was no need for this involvement; it could easily have been avoided; the attendant military effort was clearly beyond the physical resources of the country at that moment of rapid economic and social transition; and the folly of the venture from the domestic-political standpoint was at once apparent in the events of the Revolution of 1905. And as though this war were not folly enough in itself, it had the further effect of making it more difficult than ever for Russia to resist involvement in the much greater and even more dangerous European war that was shortly to come. The financial distress in which the tsar's government finished the war with Japan left it more dependent than ever on the financial bounty of the French government and the French bankers and more helpless than ever before the French demands that Russia become in effect an instrument of French policy against Germany.

Whether this added element of financial dependence was decisive in bringing Russia into World War I may well be doubted. The same result would very possibly have been achieved by the nationalistic tendencies now raging unchecked among the Russian bureaucracy, the military caste, and the upper classes generally, coupled with the tsar's strange weakness for military adventurism. To people still imbued with a strong conviction of the iniquity of the kaiser's Germany or Franz Josef's Austria, it may seem strange to hear it suggested that the Russian monarchy might have done better, in the interests of its own preservation, to remain aloof from involvement in a war against Germany. In the light of the prevailing nationalistic emotionalism of the time, it would no doubt have seemed preposterous to suggest that Serbia should have been left to Austria's mercy and that Russian prestige, just recently so painfully injured in the crisis over the annexation of Bosnia and Herzegovina, should suffer another and perhaps even greater reverse of this nature. The fact remains that in 1914

Russia was in no condition to participate in a major war—the experience of the war with Japan had demonstrated this; and neither the fate of Serbia nor the question of control over the Dardanelles really represented for her a vital interest, comparable to what she stood to suffer by courting another domestic upheaval on the heels of the one she had just experienced in 1904–05.

The Franco-Russian alliance served, in Russia's case, a financial interest but not really a political one. The kaiser's Germany may have been a threat to Britain; it was not in great measure a threat to Russia. Some of the more sober statesmen, Witte and even the otherwise nationalistic Stolypin, saw this, and would have tried betimes to avoid the catastrophe to which this alliance, which took no proper account of Russia's internal condition, was leading. But it was the pervasive nationalism of the age that defeated them; and I am inclined, for this reason, to attribute to that nationalism a major role in the causes of the final collapse of the regime. A tsarist autocracy that saw things clearly and wished to exert itself effectively in the interest of its own preservation would have practiced a rigid abstention from involvement in world political problems generally, and from exhausting foreign wars in particular, at that crucial juncture in its domestic-political development.

The third of the weaknesses of the autocracy that I should like to mention was the personality of the last Russian tsar himself. Poorly educated, narrow in intellectual horizon, a wretchedly bad judge of people, isolated from Russian society at large, in contact only with the most narrow military and bureaucratic circles, intimidated by the ghost of his imposing father and the glowering proximity of his numerous gigantic uncles, helpless under the destructive influence of his endlessly unfortunate wife: Nicholas II was obviously inadequate to the demands of his exalted position; and this was an inadequacy for which no degree of charm, of courtesy, of delicacy of manner, could compensate. It is ironic that this man, who fought so tenaciously against the granting of a constitution, had many of the qualities that would have fitted him excellently for the position of a constitutional monarch and practically none of those that were needed for the exercise of that absolute power to which he stubbornly clung. Time and time again, in the record of his reign, one finds the evidences of his short-sightedness and his lack of grasp of the realities of the life of the country interfering with the political process in ways that were for him veritably suicidal. True, he was the product of the vagaries of genetics; another tsar might not have been so bad. But the experience of his reign only illustrates the fact that these accidents of royal birth, tolerable in earlier centuries where the feudal nobility bore a good portion of the load, and tolerable again in the modern age wherever the main burden is borne or shared by parliamentary institutions, were not tolerable in the age of economic development and mass education and in a political system where the monarch claimed the rights of personal absolutism.

So much for the leading and crucial weaknesses of the autocracy itself in the final decades of its power. Mention must be made, in conclusion, of the Russian revolutionary movement. It was, of course, not the revolutionary parties that overthrew the autocracy in 1917. Nevertheless, there were indirect ways in which their existence and activity affected the situation of the regime; and these must be briefly noted.

First of all, by providing a somewhat romantic alternative to any association with the governing establishment, the revolutionary movement drew many talented youths into an attitude of defiance and revolutionary disobedience to it, thereby impoverishing it in talent, energy, and intelligence. Every time that a young person of ability was drawn into the ranks of its revolutionary opponents, the bureaucracy, deprived of these sources of recruitment, became just that more stupid, unimaginative, and inept.

Second, there was the effect the revolutionary elements had on the development of governmental policy. They obviously had no interest in seeing the modernization of the country proceed successfully under tsarist tutelage, and they did as little as they could to support it. I find it significant that more useful social legislation appears to have been passed by the two final and supposedly reactionary Dumas than by the first two relatively liberal, and partially revolutionary, ones. But more important still was the influence of the revolutionaries in frightening the regime out of possible initiatives in the field of political reform. These revolutionary parties and groupings had, as a rule, no interest in seeing genuine progress made in the creation of liberal institutions. Their aim was generally not to reform the system but to cause it to fall and to replace it. For this reason, the more the regime could be provoked into stupid, self-defeating behavior, the better from their standpoint. They often found themselves, in this respect, sharing the same aspirations and purposes as the extreme right wing of the political spectrum, which also—though for other reasons—did not wish to see any liberalization of the autocracy. And in this respect one has to concede to the revolutionary movement a series of important successes. In one instance after another where there appeared to be a possibility of political liberalization or where the pressures in this direction were intense the timely intervention of revolutionary activity of one sort or another sufficed to assure that no progress should be made. One has only to recall, as examples, the effect of the Polish uprising of 1863 on the policies of Alexander II or the effect of his assassination in 1881 on the projects then being entertained by Loris-Melikov.

THE WAR AND THE FINAL CRISIS

So much, then, for the major weaknesses, failures, and strains that entered into the undermining of the tsarist system of power. It remains only to note the manner in which the effect of all of them was magnified by the world war that began in 1914: magnified to a point where the system could no longer stand the strain. Wartime patriotic fervor, engulfing the liberal-parliamentary circles even more hopelessly than the government itself, brought them in at this point as critics of the government on new grounds: on the grounds that it was not *sufficiently* nationalistic, not *sufficiently* inspired and determined in its conduct of the war effort. And to this there was now added the quite erroneous but heady and dangerous charge that it was pro-German and even treasonable in its relations to the enemy. These charges were utilized by the liberal-parliamentary circles as the excuse for setting up new organizational entities, such as the various war industry councils, which were able to function as rival authorities to the governmental bureaucracy, to provide channels for political activity hostile to the regime, and eventually to contribute significantly to the circumstances surrounding its collapse. Meanwhile, the strictly military aspects of the war effort had a whole series of effects—such as the weakening by losses in battle of the loyal portion of the officers' corps, the stationing of undisciplined garrisons in the vicinity of the capital city, the removal of the tsar himself to field headquarters, and so on—that were to have important connotations, unfavorable to the security of the regime, at the moment of supreme trial. In a number of ways, furthermore, the war effort exacerbated relations between the government and members of the national minorities, who for obvious reasons did not always share the Russian emotional commitment to the war. Finally, not perhaps as a consequence of the war (this is hard to judge), but certainly simultaneously with it, there were the grotesque developments in the tsar's own personal situation, particularly the ripening and the denouement of the Rasputin affair—developments that finally succeeded in alienating from his cause not only large elements of the immediate bureaucratic and military entourage that had constituted his last comfort and protection, but even a portion of the imperial family itself, thus completing his isolation and removing, or disqualifying, his last potential defenders.

CONCLUSIONS

Prior to the undertaking of this review, I was inclined to feel that had the war not intervened, the chances for survival of the autocracy and for its gradual evolution into a constitutional monarchy would not have been bad. On reviewing once more the events of these last decades, I find myself obliged to question that opinion. Neither the tardiness in the granting of political reform, nor the excesses of an extravagant and foolish nationalism, nor the personal limitations of the imperial couple began with the war or were primarily responses to the existence of the war. None of the consequences of these deficiencies were in process of any significant correction as the war approached. The spectacle of the final years of tsardom prior to 1914 is that of an impressive program of social, economic, and cultural modernization of a great country being conducted, somewhat incongruously, under the general authority of a governmental system that was itself in the advanced stages of political disintegration. The successes in the field of modernization might indeed, if allowed to continue, have brought Russia rapidly and safely into the modern age. It is doubtful that they could for long have overbalanced the serious deficiencies of the political system or averted the consequences to which they were—even as war broke out—inexorably leading.

Isaac Deutscher

17

The Unfinished Revolution: Russia, 1917–1967

THE HISTORICAL PERSPECTIVE

Quite a few theorists and historians still view the October revolution as an almost fortuitous event. Some argue that Russia might well have been spared the revolution if only the Tsar had been less obstinate in insisting on his absolute prerogatives and if he had come to terms with the loyal Liberal opposition. Others say that the Bolsheviks would never have had their chance if Russia had not become involved in the First World War or if she had withdrawn from it in time, before defeat reduced her to chaos and ruin. The Bolsheviks, according to this view, triumphed because of the errors and miscalculations committed by the Tsar and his advisers or by the men who took office immediately after the Tsar's downfall; and we are asked to believe that these errors and miscalculations were chance occurrences, accidents of individual judgment or decision. That the Tsar and his advisers committed many foolish mistakes is, of course, true. But they committed them under the pressure of the Tsarist bureaucracy and of those elements in the possessing classes who had a stake in the monarchy. Nor were the governments of the February regime, the governments of Prince Lvov and Kerensky, free agents. They kept Russia in the war because, like the Tsarist governments, they were dependent on those powerful Russian and foreign centres of finance-capital which were determined that Russia should remain to the end a belligerent member of the Entente. The "errors and miscalculations" were socially conditioned. It is also true that the war drastically exposed and aggravated the fatal weakness of the *ancien régime*. But it was hardly the decisive cause of that weakness. Russia had been shaken by the tremors of revolution just before the war; the streets of St. Petersburg were covered with barricades in the summer of 1914. Indeed the outbreak of hostilities and the mobilization swamped the incipient revolution and delayed it by two years and a half, only to charge it eventually with greater explosive force. Even if Prince Lvov's

296

or Kerensky's government had contracted out of the war, it would have done so under conditions of a social crisis so profound and severe that the Bolshevik Party would probably still have won, if not in 1917 then some time later. This is, of course, only a hypothesis; but its plausibility is now reinforced by the fact that in China Mao Tse-tung's party seized power in 1949, four years after the end of the Second World War. This circumstance throws perhaps a retrospective light on the connexion between the First World War and the Russian revolution—it suggests that this connexion might not have been as clear cut as it appeared at the time.

We need not assume that the course of the Russian revolution was predetermined in all its features or in the sequence of all its major phases and incidents. But its general direction had been set not by the events of a few years or months; it had been prepared by the developments of many decades, indeed of several epochs. The historian who labours to reduce the mountain of the revolution to a few contingencies, stands as helpless before it as once stood the political leaders who sought to prevent its rise.

After every revolution its enemies question its historic legitimacy— sometimes they do so even two or three centuries later. Allow me to recall how Trevelyan answered the historians who still wondered whether the Great Rebellion was really necessary: "Was it then impossible for Parliamentary power to take root in England at a less cost than this national schism and appeal to force . . . ? It is a question which no depth of research or speculation can resolve. Men were what they were, uninfluenced by the belated wisdom of posterity, and thus they acted. Whether or not any better way could have led to the same end, it was by the sword that Parliament actually won the right to survive as the dominant force of the English Constitution." Trevelyan, who follows here in Macaulay's footsteps, renders precise justice to the Great Rebellion, even while he underlines that it left the nation "poorer and less noble" for a time, which is, unfortunately, in one sense or another true also of other revolutions, including the Russian. In stressing that England owed its parliamentary constitution primarily to the Great Rebellion, Trevelyan takes the long-term view of the role of the Puritans. It was Cromwell and the Saints, he says, who established the principle of Parliament's supremacy; and even though they themselves were in conflict with the principle and appeared to obliterate it, the principle survived and triumphed. The "good deeds" of the Puritan revolution outlasted its follies.

Mutatis mutandis, the same may be said of the October revolution. "Men acted as they did because they could not act otherwise." They could not copy their ideals from Western European models of parliamentary democracy. It was by the sword that they won for the Councils

of Workers' and Peasants' Deputies—and for socialism—"the right to
survive as the dominant force" in the Soviet constitution. And although
they themselves then reduced the Workers' Councils to a shadowy
existence, those Councils, the Soviets, and their socialist aspirations,
have remained the most significant parts of the message of the Russian
revolution.

As for the French revolution, its necessity was questioned or denied
by a long line of thinkers and historians, from Burke, fearful of the
Jacobin contagion, to Tocqueville, distrustful of any modern democracy, and Taine, horrified by the Commune of Paris, down to Madelin,
Bainville, and their disciples, some of whom laboured after 1940, under
Marshal Pétain's encouraging gaze, to lay the ghost of the revolution.
Curiously, of all those writers Tocqueville has recently enjoyed the
greatest vogue in English-speaking countries. Quite a few of our
learned men have tried to model their conception of contemporary Russia on his *L'Ancien Régime et la Révolution*. They are attracted by his
argument that the revolution had made no radical departure from the
French political tradition, that it merely followed the basic trends that
had been at work under the *ancien régime*, especially the trend towards
the centralization of the State and the unification of national life.
Similarly, the argument runs, the Soviet Union, in so far as it has any
progressive achievement to its credit, has merely continued the work of
industrialization and reform that had been undertaken by the *ancien
régime*. If Tsardom had survived, or if it had been replaced by a bourgeois democratic republic, that work would have gone on; and progress
would have been more orderly and rational. Russia might have become
the world's second industrial power without having to pay the terrible
price the Bolsheviks have exacted, without having to endure the ex-
propriations, the terror, the low standards of living, and the moral
degradation of Stalinism.

It seems to me that Tocqueville's disciples do an injustice to their
master. Although he belittled the creative and original work of the
revolution, he did not deny its necessity or legitimacy. On the contrary,
by placing it within the French tradition, he sought to "adopt" it, on
his own conservative terms, and to "incorporate" it into the national
heritage. His imitators show greater zeal for belittling the original and
creative work of the Russian revolution than for "adopting" it, on
whatever terms. But let us consider the Tocquevillesque argument more
closely. Of course, no revolution creates *ex nihilo* [from nothing]. Every
revolution works in the social environment that has produced it and
on the materials it finds in that environment. "We are building a new
order," Lenin liked to say, "out of the bricks the old order has left us."
Traditional methods of government, vital national aspirations, a style
of life, habits of thought, and various accumulated factors of strength

and weakness—these are the "bricks." The past refracts itself through the innovating work of the revolution, no matter how bold the innovations. The Jacobins and Napoleon continued indeed to build the unitary and centralized State that the *ancien régime* had up to a point promoted. No one emphasized this more forcefully than Karl Marx in his *18th Brumaire*, which appeared some years before Tocqueville's *Ancien Régime*. And it is equally true that Russia had made a real start in industrialization in the reign of the last two Tsars, without which the rapid entry of her industrial working class upon the political stage would not have been possible. Both countries thus achieved under the *ancien régime* some progress in various directions. This does not mean that the progress could go on in an "orderly" manner, without the gigantic "disturbance" of revolution. On the contrary, what was destroying the *ancien régime* was precisely the progress achieved under it. Far from making the revolution superfluous, it made it all the more necessary. The forces of progress were so constricted within the old order that they had to burst it. The French striving for the unitary State had been in chronic conflict with the barriers set to it by particularisms of feudal origin. France's growing bourgeois economy needed a single national market, a free peasantry, free movement of men and commodities; and the *ancien régime* could not satisfy these needs, except within the narrowest of limits. As a Marxist would put it: France's productive forces had outgrown her feudal property relations, and could no longer be contained within the shell of the Bourbon monarchy, which conserved and protected those relations.

In Russia the problem was similar but more complicated. The efforts made in Tsarist times to modernize the fabric of national life were blocked by the heavy residuum of feudalism, the under-development and weakness of the bourgeoisie, the rigidity of the autocracy, the archaic system of government, and, last but not least, by Russia's economic dependence on foreign capital. The great Empire was, in the reign of the last Romanovs, half empire and half colony. Western shareholders owned 90 per cent of Russia's mines, 50 per cent of her chemical industry, over 40 per cent of her engineering plants, and 42 per cent of her banking stock. Domestic capital was scarce. The national income was far too small in relation to modern needs. More than half of it came from farming, which was utterly backward and contributed little to the accumulation of capital. Within limits the State provided, out of taxation, the sinews of industrialization—it built the railways, for instance. But in the main it was on foreign capital that industrial expansion depended. Foreign investors, however, had no continuous interest in ploughing back their high dividends into Russian industry, especially when the vagaries of a self-willed bureaucracy and social unrest deterred them. Russia could achieve the industrial "take off," to use Professor Rostow's term, only by drawing on the resources of her agriculture and through the extraordinary exertions of her own workers. None of these requirements could be fulfilled under the *ancien régime*. The Tsarist governments were too strongly dependent on Western finance-capital to assert Russia's national interests against it; and they were too feudal in their background and social connexions to release farming from the paralyzing grip of the landed aristocracy (from whose *milieu* came even the Prime Minister of the first republican government of 1917!). And none of the pre-Bolshevik governments had the political strength and moral authority to obtain from the working class the exertions and sacrifices that industrialization demanded in any circumstances. None had the outlook, the determination, and the modern mind that the task required. (Count Witte, with his ambitious schemes for reform, was the exception that confirmed the rule; and he, as Prime Minister and Minister of Finance, was almost boycotted by the Tsar and the bureaucracy.) It seems inconceivable that any regime not inherently revolutionary should have been able to raise a semi-illiterate peasant nation to anything approaching the present level of Soviet economic development and education. Here again, the Marxist will say that Russia's productive forces had advanced just far enough under the old regime to burst the old social structure and its political superstructure.

No automatic economic mechanism, however, produces the final disintegration of an old established order or assures the success of a revolution. An obsolete social system may be declining in the course of decades, and the bulk of the nation may be unaware of it. Social consciousness lags behind social being. The objective contradictions of the *ancien régime* have to translate themselves into subjective terms, into the ideas, aspirations, and passions of men in action. The essence of revolution, says Trotsky, is "the direct intervention of the masses in historic events." It is because of that intervention—a phenomenon so real and so rare in history—that the year 1917 was so remarkable and momentous. The great mass of the people were seized by the most intense and urgent awareness of decay and rot in the established order. The seizure was sudden. Consciousness leapt forward to catch up with being, and to change it. But this leap too, this sudden change in the psychology of the masses, did not come *ex nihilo*. It took many, many decades of revolutionary ferment and of a slow growth of ideas— it took the birth and the withering away of many parties and groups— to produce the moral-political climate, the leaders, the parties, and the methods of action of 1917. There was little or nothing fortuitous in all this. Behind this last half-century of revolution there loomed a whole century of revolutionary endeavour.

The social crisis under which Tsarist Russia laboured manifested itself in the stark contrast between her status and importance as a great power and the archaic weakness of her social structure, between the splendours of her empire and the wretchedness of her institutions. This contrast was laid bare for the first time by Russia's triumph in the Napoleonic wars. Her boldest spirits were aroused to action. In 1825 the Decembrists rose in arms against the Tsar. They were an aristocratic, intellectual elite; but they had the bulk of the nobility against them. No social class in Russia was capable of promoting the nation's progress. The towns were few and medieval in character; the urban middle classes, unlettered merchants and artisans, were politically negligible. The peasant-serfs rebelled sporadically; but since Pugachev's defeat there had been no large-scale action aiming at their emancipation. The Decembrists were revolutionaries without any revolutionary class behind them. This was their tragedy; and this was to be the tragedy of all successive generations of Russian radicals and revolutionaries almost till the end of the nineteenth century—in different forms the tragedy was to project itself into the post-revolutionary epoch as well.

Let me recapitulate briefly its main acts and motifs. Before the middle of the nineteenth century, new radicals and revolutionaries, the *Raznotchintsy*, made their appearance. They came from the slowly growing middle classes; many were children of civil servants and priests. The bourgeoisie was still negligible. The civil servants and priests were terrified of their rebellious sons. The peasantry was apathetic and passive. Only a section of the nobility favoured some reform, namely, the landlords who, eager to adopt modern methods of farming or to engage in industry and trade, wished to see serfdom abolished and the administration of the State and education liberalized. When Alexander II, yielding to their persuasion, abolished serfdom, he thereby secured for the dynasty the peasantry's unwavering allegiance for decades ahead. The 1861 Act of Emancipation thus isolated again the radicals and the revolutionaries and, in effect, postponed revolution by over half a century. Yet the land problem remained unresolved. The serfs had been freed, but had received no land; and they had to contract heavy debts and servitudes, and to become sharecroppers, in order to be able to till the land. The nation's way of life remained anachronistic. This state of affairs and the oppressiveness of the autocracy drove ever new men of the intelligentsia to revolt, to produce new ideas, and to experiment with ever new methods of political struggle .

Each successive group of revolutionaries drew its strength only from itself; for each an impasse waited at the end of its road. The *Narodniks* or Populists, inspired by Herzen and Bakunin, Chernyshevsky and Lavrov, were objectively the peasantry's militant vanguard. But when they appealed to the *muzhiks* and tried to open their eyes to the fraud of the emancipation and to the new manner in which the Tsar and the landlords kept them in subjection, the ex-serfs refused to budge or even to listen; not rarely they delivered the *Narodniks* into the hands of the gendarmes. An oppressed social class, with great revolutionary potentialities, thus betrayed its own revolutionary elite. The successors of the *Narodniks*, the *Narodnovoltsy*, abandoned the apparently hopeless search for a revolutionary popular force in society. They decided to act alone as the trustees of an oppressed and mute people. Their politically inspired terrorism took the place of the agrarian Populism of their predecessors. The propagandist or agitator of the previous era, who "went out to the people" or even tried to settle among the peasants, was replaced by the lonely, taciturn, heroic conspirator, with the suggestion of a Superman, who, determined to vanquish or perish, took upon himself the task the nation was unable to accomplish. The circle whose members assassinated Alexander II in 1881 consisted of fewer than two score of men and women. Six years later only a dozen young people, among them Lenin's elder brother, formed the group that planned an attempt on the life of Alexander III. These tiny conspiratorial bodies held the huge empire in suspense, and made history. Yet, if the failure of the Populists of the 1860s and 1870s had demonstrated the unreality of the hope that the peasantry might be moved to rise, the martyrdom of the *Narodnovoltsy* of the 1880s exposed once again the impotence of a vanguard which acted without the support of any of the basic social classes. These negative experiences taught invaluable lessons to the revolutionaries of the next decades—and in this sense they were not fruitless. The moral drawn by Plekhanov, Zasulich, Lenin, Martov, and their comrades was that they must not act as an isolated vanguard, but must look for support to a revolutionary class—and must look beyond the peasantry. By now, however, the beginning of Russia's industrialization was solving the problem for them. The Marxist propagandists and agitators of Lenin's generation found their audience among the new factory workers.

We should note the transparent dialectics of this protracted struggle. There is first of all the contradiction between social need and social consciousness. No social need or interest could have been more elementary than the peasants' hunger for land and freedom; and no social consciousness could have been more false than the one that allowed them to content themselves, for half a century, with an Act which, while freeing them from chattel slavery, denied them land and freedom—a consciousness that induced generations of *muzhiks* to hope that the Tsar-*Batiushka* [Beloved Tsar] would right their wrongs. This discrepancy between need and consciousness lay at the root of the many metamorphoses of the revolutionary movement. The logic of the situation produced these opposite models of organization: the self-sufficient conspiratorial elite on the one hand, and the mass-oriented movement on the other, the dictatorial and the democratic types of the revolutionary. We should note also the special, exclusive, and historically effective role that the intelligentsia played in all this—in no other country do we find anything like it. Generation after generation, they stormed the Tsarist autocracy and smashed their heads against its walls, preparing the way for those who were to come after them. They were inspired by an almost Messianic faith in their, and in Russia's, revolutionary mission. When at last the Marxists came to the fore, they inherited a great tradition and a unique experience; they assessed both critically and used them effectively. But they also inherited certain problems and dilemmas.

The Marxists started out, as they had to, with the negation of the Populist and terrorist traditions. They rejected "agrarian socialism," the sentimental idealization of the peasantry, the radical versions of Slavophilism, and the quasi-Messianic idea of Russia's unique revolutionary mission. They repudiated terrorism, the self-glorification of the radical intellectual, and the self-sufficient conspiratorial elite. They opted for the democratically oriented organization, the party and the trade unions, and for modern forms of proletarian mass action. This attitude, "strictly" or even exclusively proletarian and distrustful of the peasantry, was characteristic of the beginnings of the entire Russian Social Democratic Party; it was to remain typical of the Mensheviks in their best period. But the movement, as it passed to action, could not rest on the abstract negation of the native revolutionary traditions—it had to absorb what was vital in them and transcend them. It was Bolshevism that accomplished this task, and it did so long before 1917. The Bolsheviks inherited from the Populists their sensitivity towards the peasantry, and from the *Narodnovoltsy* their concentrated aggressiveness and their conspiratorial determination. Without these elements Marxism in Russia would have remained an exotic plant, or at best, a theoretical outgrowth of Western European socialism, as it was in Plekhanov's brilliant opus and in some of Lenin's youthful writings. The Russian acclimatization of Marxism was, above all, Lenin's achievement. He produced the synthesis of the doctrine with the native tradition. He insisted on the need for the workers, the leading force in the revolution, to gain allies in the peasants; and he assigned to the intellectuals and the revolutionary elite a weighty, educative and organizing role in the workers' mass movement. This synthesis epitomized the century of Russian revolutionary endeavour.

If I were to stop here, I might give you a one-sided view of the elements that went into the making of the revolution. Though it is customary in the West to treat Bolshevism as a purely Russian phenomenon, it is hardly possible to exaggerate the contribution that Western Europe had made to it, Throughout the nineteenth century

Russia's revolutionary thought and action were, at every stage, decisively influenced by Western ideas and movements. The Decembrists belonged, no less than, say, the *Carbonari*, to the European aftermath of the French revolution. Many of them had been, after Napoleon's downfall, young officers of the Russian occupation troops in Paris; and contact even with the defeated revolution was enough to set their minds ablaze. The *Petrashevtsy*, Belinsky and Herben, Bakunin and Chernyshevsky, and so many others were formed by the events of 1830 and 1848, by French socialism, German philosophy, especially by Hegel and Feuerbach, and by British political economy. Then Marxism, itself embodying all these influences, made its stupendous intellectual conquest of radical and even of liberal Russia. No wonder the apologists of Tsardom denounced socialism and Marxism as products of the "decadent" West. Not only Pobedonostsev, the crude preacher of obscurantism and Pan-Slavism, not only Dostoevsky, but even Tolstoy repudiated the ideas of socialism in such terms. And they were not quite mistaken: whether the West wishes to remember this or not, it has invested a great deal of its own spiritual heritage in the Russian revolution. Trotsky once wrote about the "paradox," that while Western Europe "exported its most advanced technology to the United States . . . it exported its most advanced ideology to Russia. . . ." Lenin makes the same point, plainly and forcefully: ". . . in the course of about half a century, roughly from the 1840s till the 1890s, progressive thought in Russia searched avidly . . . for the correct revolutionary theory, and followed with remarkable zeal and meticulousness every last word that came from Europe and America. Russia has indeed come to Marxism . . . through extreme sufferings, agonies, and sacrifices . . . through learning, testing in practice . . . and engaging in a comparative study of Europe's experience. Because Tsardom forced us to lead an émigré existence, revolutionary Russia . . . had at her command such a wealth of international contacts and so excellent an awareness of all the forms and theories of revolutionary movements all over the world as no one else possessed."

In 1917 and in the following years not only the leaders but also the great mass of Russian workers and peasants saw the revolution not as the business of Russia alone, but as part of a social upheaval embracing the whole of mankind. The Bolsheviks considered themselves the champions of at least a European revolution, whose battles they were waging on Europe's eastern outposts. Even the Mensheviks had held this conviction and had eloquently expressed it. And not only the Russians saw themselves in this light. Early in this century Karl Kautsky, the leading theorist of the Socialist International, drew this perspective: "The epicentre of revolution has been moving from the West to the East. In the first half of the nineteenth century it was situated in

France, at times in England. In 1848 Germany entered the ranks of the revolutionary nations. . . . Now the Slavs . . . join their ranks, and the centre of gravity of revolutionary thought and action is more and more shifting . . . to Russia." "Russia, having taken over so much revolutionary initiative from the West, may now in her turn become a source of revolutionary energy for the West," Kautsky remarked on the contrast with the situation in 1848, when the Peoples' Spring in Western Europe was nipped by the "hard frost from Russia"; now the storm from Russia might help to clear the air in the West.

Kautsky wrote this in 1902 for *Iskra*, of which Lenin was co-editor; and his words made such an impression on Lenin that nearly twenty years later he quoted them with ironic delight against their author, now outraged by the fulfillment of his forecast. The forecast was in fact even more portentous than either Kautsky or Lenin perceived. We have seen how in our time the epicentre of revolution has shifted even farther to the East, from Russia to China. A historian with a flair for the grand generalization might extrapolate the perspective sketched by Kautsky and draw a more sweeping line, illustrating the eastward advance of the revolution in the course of three centuries. The line might start in Puritan England, traverse the whole of Europe, sweep on to China, and finally touch the south-eastern fringes of Asia.

However, such a graph may be misleading; it may suggest too linear and too strongly predetermined a course of history. But in whatever degree the course was determined or not, it has, clearly, had its inner coherence and logic. Goethe once said that the history of knowledge is a great fugue, in which the voices of the various nations appear one after another. One might say the same of the history of revolution. It is not the world symphony some of the great revolutionaries had hoped for. Nor is it the medley of discordant solos, the cacophony the Philistines hear. It is rather the great fugue in which the voices of the various nations, each with its own hopes and despairs, enter one after another.

BREAKS IN REVOLUTIONARY CONTINUITY

In 1917 Russia lived through the last of the great bourgeois revolutions and the first proletarian revolution in European history. The two revolutions merged into one. Their unprecedented coalescence imparted extraordinary vitality and *élan* to the new regime; but it was also the source of severe strains and stresses and cataclysmic convulsions.

I should perhaps give here, at the risk of stating the obvious, a brief definition of bourgeois revolution. The traditional view, widely accepted by Marxists and anti-Marxists alike, is that in such revolutions, in Western Europe, the bourgeoisie played the leading part, stood at the head of the insurgent people, and seized power. This view underlies many controversies among historians; the recent exchanges, for instance, between Professor Hugh Trevor-Roper and Mr. Christopher Hill on whether the Cromwellian revolution was or was not bourgeois in character. It seems to me that this conception, to whatever authorities it may be attributed, is schematic and historically unreal. From it one may well arrive at the conclusion that bourgeois revolution is almost a myth, and that it has hardly ever occurred, even in the West. Capitalist entrepreneurs, merchants, and bankers were not conspicuous among the leaders of the Puritans or the commanders of the Ironsides, in the Jacobin Club or at the head of the crowds that stormed the Bastille or invaded the Tuileries. Nor did they seize the reins of government during the revolution or for a long time afterwards, either in England or in France. The lower middle classes, the urban poor, the plebeians, and *sans culottes* made up the big insurgent battalions. The leaders were mostly "gentlemen farmers" in England and lawyers, doctors, journalists, and other intellectuals in France. Here and there the upheavals ended in military dictatorship. Yet the bourgeois character of these revolutions will not appear at all mythical, if we approach them with a broader criterion and view their general impact on society. Their most substantial and enduring achievement was to sweep away the social and political institutions that had hindered the growth of bourgeois property and of the social relationships that went with it. When the Puritans denied the Crown the power of arbitrary taxation, when Cromwell secured for English shipowners a monopolistic position in England's trading with foreign countries, and when the Jacobins abolished feudal prerogatives and privileges, they created, often unknowingly, the conditions in which manufacturers, merchants, and bankers were bound to gain economic predominance and, in the long run, social and even political supremacy. Bourgeois revolution creates the conditions in which bourgeois property can flourish. In this, rather than in the particular alignments during the struggle, lies its *differentia specifica*.

It is in this sense that we can characterize the October revolution as a combination of bourgeois and proletarian revolutions, though both were accomplished under Bolshevik leadership. Current Soviet historiography describes the February revolution as bourgeois and reserves the label "proletarian" for the October insurrection. This distinction is made by many Western historians too and is justified on the ground that in February, after the Tsar's abdication, the bourgeoisie seized power. In truth, the combination of the two revolutions had already appeared in February, but in a shadowy form. The Tsar and his last government were brought down by a general strike and a mass insurrection of workers and soldiers who at once created their Councils or Soviets, the potential organs of a new State. Prince Lvov, Miliukov, and

Kerensky took power from the hands of a confused and groping Petrograd Soviet, which willingly yielded it to them; and they exercised it only for as long as the Soviets tolerated them. But their governments carried out no major act of bourgeois revolution. Above all, they did not break up the aristocracy's landed estates and give land to the peasants. Even as a bourgeois revolution, the February revolution was *manquée*.

All this underlines the prodigious contradiction with which the Bolsheviks undertook to cope when in October they promoted and directed the double upheaval. The bourgeois revolution over which they presided created conditions which favoured the growth of bourgeois forms of property. The proletarian revolution they accomplished aimed at the abolition of property. The main act of the former was the sharing out of the aristocracy's land. This created a wide potential base for the growth of a new rural bourgeoisie. The peasants who had been freed from rents and debts and had enlarged their farms were interested in a social system that would offer security to their holdings. Nor was this a matter only of capitalist farming. Rural Russia was, as Lenin put it, the breeding ground of capitalism at large—many of Russia's industrial entrepreneurs and merchants had been of peasant stock; and, given time and favorable circumstances, the peasantry might have bred a far more numerous and modern class of entrepreneurs. All the more ironic was it that in 1917 none of the bourgeois parties, not even the moderate Socialists, dared to sanction the agrarian revolution which was developing spontaneously, with elemental force, for the peasants were seizing the aristocracy's land long before the Bolshevik insurrection. Terrified by the dangers that threatened property in town, the bourgeois parties refused to undermine property in the country. The Bolsheviks (and the Left Social Revolutionaries) alone placed themselves at the head of the agrarian revolts. They knew that without the upheaval in the country the proletarian revolution would be isolated in town and defeated. The peasants, afraid of a counter-revolution that might bring back the landlords, thus acquired a stake in the Bolshevik regime. But from the outset the socialist aspects of the revolution aroused their misgivings, fears, or hostility.

The socialist revolution was supported wholeheartedly by the urban working class. But this was a small minority of the nation. Altogether one-sixth of the population, twenty-odd million people, lived in the towns: and of these only half or so could be described as proletarian. The hard core of the working class consisted at the most of about three million men and women employed in modern industry. Marxists had expected the industrial workers to be the most dynamic force in capitalist society, the main agents of socialist revolution. The Russian workers more than justified this expectation. No class in Russian society, and no working class anywhere in the world, has ever acted with the energy, the political intelligence, the ability for organization, and the heroism with which the Russian workers acted in 1917 (and thereafter in the civil war). The circumstance that Russia's modern industry consisted of a small number of huge factories, concentrated mainly in Petrograd and Moscow, gave the massed workers of the two capitals an extraordinary striking power at the very nerve centres of the *ancien régime*. Two decades of intensive Marxist propaganda, fresh memories of the struggles of 1905, 1912, and 1914, the tradition of a century of revolutionary endeavour, and Bolshevik singleness of purpose had prepared the workers for their role. They took the socialist aim of the revolution for granted. They were not content with anything less than the abolition of capitalist exploitation, socialization of industry and banking, workers' control over production, and government by Soviets. They turned their backs on the Mensheviks, whom they had followed at first, because the Mensheviks were telling them that Russia was not "ripe for a socialist revolution." Their action, like that of the peasants, had its own spontaneous force: they established their control over production at the factory level well before the October insurrection. The Bolsheviks supported them and turned the factory rebellions into a socialist revolution.

Yet Petrograd and Moscow, and a few other scattered industrial centres, constituted an extremely narrow base for this undertaking. Not only did people over the whole immensity of rural Russia scramble to acquire property while the workers of the two capitals strove to abolish it; not only was the socialist revolution in implicit conflict with the bourgeois one; in addition, it was fraught with its own inner contradictions. Russia was and was not ripe for socialist revolution. She was better able to cope with its negative than with its positive tasks. Guided by the Bolsheviks, the workers expropriated the capitalists and transferred power to the Soviets; but they could not establish a socialist economy and a socialist way of life; and they were unable to maintain their dominant political position for any length of time.

At first, the dual character of the revolution was, as has been said, the source of its strength. If a bourgeois revolution had taken place earlier (or if, at the time of the Emancipation, in 1861, the freed serfs had been given land on fair terms), the peasantry would have turned into a conservative force; and it would have opposed proletarian revolution, as it did in Western Europe, particularly in France, throughout the nineteenth century. Its conservatism might then have influenced even the urban workers, many of whom had roots in the country. A bourgeois order would have had far greater staying power than that possessed by the semi-feudal and semi-bourgeois regime. The conjunction of the two revolutions made possible the alliance of the workers and peasants for which Lenin strove; and this enabled the Bolsheviks to win the civil war and withstand foreign intervention. Although the aspirations of the workers were in implicit conflict with those of the peasants, neither of the two classes was as yet aware of this. The workers rejoiced in the *muzhiks'* triumph over the landlords; and they saw no contradiction between their own striving for a collectivist economy and the peasantry's economic individualism. The contradiction became apparent and acute only towards the end of the civil war, when the peasantry, no longer inhibited by fear of the landlord's return, forcefully asserted that individualism.[1]

---

[1] This was the prevailing attitude, even though the peasantry itself was divided between rich and poor, and small groups of enlightened peasants formed, of their own accord, co-operatives and communes soon after the revolution and in the early 1920s.

18

The History of
the Russian Revolution

The most indubitable feature of a revolution is the direct interference of the masses in historic events. In ordinary times the state, be it monarchical or democratic, elevates itself above the nation, and history is made by specialists in that line of business—kings, ministers, bureaucrats, parliamentarians, journalists. But at those crucial moments when the old order becomes no longer endurable to the masses, they break over the barriers excluding them from the political arena, sweep aside their traditional representatives, and create by their own interference the initial groundwork for a new régime. Whether this is good or bad we leave to the judgment of moralists. We ourselves will take the facts as they are given by the objective course of development. The history of a revolution is for us first of all a history of the forcible entrance of the masses into the realm of rulership over their own destiny.

In a society that is seized by revolution classes are in conflict. It is perfectly clear, however, that the changes introduced between the beginning and the end of a revolution in the economic bases of the society and its social substratum of classes, are not sufficient to explain the course of the revolution itself, which can overthrow in a short interval age-old institutions, create new ones, and again overthrow them. The dynamic of revolutionary events is *directly* determined by swift, intense and passionate changes in the psychology of classes which have already formed themselves before the revolution.

The point is that society does not change its institutions as need arises, the way a mechanic changes his instruments. On the contrary, society actually takes the institutions which hang upon it as given once for all. For decades the oppositional criticism is nothing more than a safety valve for mass dissatisfaction, a condition of the stability of the social structure. Such in principle, for example, was the significance acquired by the social-democratic criticism. Entirely exceptional conditions, independent of the will of persons or parties, are necessary in order to tear off from discontent the fetters of conservatism, and bring the masses to insurrection.

The swift changes of mass views and moods in an epoch of revolution thus derive, not from the flexibility and mobility of man's mind, but just the opposite, from its deep conservatism. The chronic lag of ideas and relations behind new objective conditions, right up to the moment when the latter crash over people in the form of a catastrophe, is what creates in a period of revolution that leaping movement of ideas and passions which seems to the police mind a mere result of the activities of "demagogues."

The masses go into a revolution not with a prepared plan of social reconstruction, but with a sharp feeling that they cannot endure the old régime. Only the guiding layers of a class have a political program, and even this still requires the test of events, and the approval of the masses. The fundamental political process of the revolution thus consists in the gradual comprehension by a class of the problems arising from the social crisis—the active orientation of the masses by a method of successive approximations. The different stages of a revolutionary process, certified by a change of parties in which the more extreme always supercedes the less, express the growing pressure to the left of the masses—so long as the swing of the movement does not run into objective obstacles. When it does, there begins a reaction: disappointments of the different layers of the revolutionary class, growth of indifferentism, and therewith a strengthening of the position of the counter-revolutionary forces. Such, at least, is the general outline of the old revolutions.

Only on the basis of a study of political processes in the masses themselves, can we understand the rôle of parties and leaders, whom we least of all are inclined to ignore. They constitute not an independent, but nevertheless a very important, element in the process. Without a guiding organization the energy of the masses would dissipate like steam not enclosed in a piston-box. But nevertheless what moves things is not the piston or the box, but the steam.

. . .

However, the processes taking place in the consciousness of the masses are not unrelated and independent. No matter how the idealists and eclectics rage, consciousness is nevertheless determined by conditions. In the historic conditions which formed Russia, her economy, her classes, her economy, her classes, her State, in the action upon her of other states, we ought to be able to find the premises both of the February revolution and of the October revolution which replaced it. Since the greatest enigma is the fact that a backward country was the *first* to place the proletariat in power, it behooves us to seek the solution of that enigma in the *peculiarities* of that backward country—that is, in its differences from other countries.

.   .   .

A backward country assimilates the material and intellectual conquests of the advanced countries. But this does not mean that it follows them slavishly, reproduces all the stages of their past. The theory of the repetition of historic cycles—Vico and his more recent followers—rests upon an observation of the orbits of old pre-capitalistic cultures, and in part upon the first experiments of capitalist development. A certain repetition of cultural stages in ever new settlements was in fact bound up with the provincial and episodic character of that whole process. Capitalism means, however, an overcoming of those conditions. It prepares and in a certain sense realizes the universality and permanence of man's development. By this a repetition of the forms of development by different nations is ruled out. Although compelled to follow after the advanced countries, a backward country does not take things in the same order. The privilege of historic backwardness—and such a privilege exists—permits, or rather compels, the adoption of whatever is ready in advance of any specified date, skipping a whole series of intermediate stages. Savages throw away their bows and arrows for rifles all at once, without traveling the road which lay between those two weapons in the past. The European colonists in America did not begin history all over again from the beginning. The fact that Germany and the United States have now economically outstripped England was made possible by the very backwardness of their capitalist development. On the other hand, the conservative anarchy in the British coal industry—as also in the heads of MacDonald and his friends—is a paying-up for the past when England played too long the rôle of capitalist pathfinder. The development of historically backward nations leads necessarily to a peculiar combination of different stages in the historic process. Their development as a whole acquires a planless, complex, combined character.

The possibility of skipping over intermediate steps is of course by no means absolute. Its degree is determined in the long run by the economic and cultural capacities of the country. The backward nation, moreover, not infrequently debases the achievements borrowed from outside in the process of adapting them to its own more primitive culture. In this the very process of assimilation acquires a self-contradictory character. Thus the introduction of certain elements of Western technique and training, above all military and industrial, under Peter I, led to a strengthening of serfdom as the fundamental form of labor organization. European armament and European loans—both indubitable products of a higher culture—led to a strengthening

of tzarism, which delayed in its turn the development of the country.
The laws of history have nothing in common with a pedantic
schematism. Unevenness, the most general law of the historic process,
reveals itself most sharply and complexly in the destiny of the backward countries. Under the whip of external necessity their backward
culture is compelled to make leaps. From the universal law of unevenness thus derives another law which, for the lack of a better name, we
may call the law of *combined development*—by which we mean a
drawing together of the different stages of the journey, a combining of
separate steps, an amalgam of archaic with more contemporary forms.
Without this law, to be taken of course in its whole material content,
it is impossible to understand the history of Russia, and indeed of any
country of the second, third or tenth cultural class.

Under pressure from richer Europe the Russian State swallowed
up a far greater relative part of the people's wealth than in the West,
and thereby not only condemned the people to a twofold poverty, but
also weakened the foundations of the possessing classes. Being at the
same time in need of support from the latter, it forced and regimented
their growth. As a result the bureaucratized privileged classes never
rose to their full height, and the Russian state thus still more
approached an Asiatic despotism. The Byzantine autocratism, officially
adopted by the Muscovite tzars at the beginning of the sixteenth
century, subdued the feudal Boyars with the help of the nobility, and
then gained the subjection of the nobility by making the peasantry
their slaves, and upon this foundation created the St. Petersburg
imperial absolutism. The backwardness of the whole process is sufficiently indicated in the fact that serfdom, born at the end of the
sixteenth century, took form in the seventeenth, flowered in the
eighteenth, and was juridically annulled only in 1861.

. . .

The meagerness not only of Russian feudalism, but of all the old
Russian history, finds its most depressing expression in the absence of
real medieval cities as centers of commerce and craft. Handicraft did
not succeed in Russia in separating itself from agriculture, but preserved its character of home industry. The old Russian cities were
commercial, administrative, military and manorial—centers of consumption, consequently, not of production. Even Novgorod, similar
to Hansa and not subdued by the Tartars, was only a commercial, and
not an industrial city. True, the distribution of the peasant industries
over various districts created a demand for trade mediation on a large
scale. But nomad traders could not possibly occupy that place in social
life which belonged in the West to the craft-guild and merchant-
industrial petty and middle bourgeoisie, inseparably bound up with
its peasant environment. The chief roads of Russian trade, moreover,

led across the border, thus from time immemorial giving the leadership to foreign commercial capital, and imparting a semi-colonial character to the whole process, in which the Russian trader was a mediator between the Western cities and the Russian villages. This kind of economic relation developed further during the epoch of Russian capitalism and found its extreme expression in the imperialist war.

The insignificance of the Russian cities, which more than anything else promoted the development of an Asiatic state, also made impossible a Reformation—that is, a replacement of the feudal-bureaucratic orthodoxy by some sort of modernized kind of Christianity adapted to the demands of a bourgeois society. The struggle against the state church did not go farther than the creation of peasant sects, the faction of the Old Believers being the most powerful among them.

Fifteen years before the great French revolution there developed in Russia a movement of the Cossacks, peasants and worker-serfs of the Urals, known as the Pugachev Rebellion. What was lacking to this menacing popular uprising in order to convert it into a revolution? A Third Estate. Without the industrial democracy of the cities a peasant war could not develop into a revolution, just as the peasant sects could not rise to the height of a Reformation. The result of the Pugachev Rebellion was just the opposite—a strengthening of bureaucratic absolutism as the guardian of the interests of the nobility, a guardian which had again justified itself in the hour of danger.

The Europeanization of the country, formally begun in the time of Peter, became during the following century more and more a demand of the ruling class itself, the nobility. In 1825 the aristocratic intelligentsia, generalizing this demand politically, went to the point of a military conspiracy to limit the powers of the autocracy. Thus, under pressure from the European bourgeois development, the progressive nobility attempted to take the place of the lacking Third Estate. But nevertheless they wished to combine their liberal régime with the security of their own caste domination, and therefore feared most of all to arouse the peasantry. It is thus not surprising that the conspiracy remained a mere attempt on the part of a brilliant but isolated officer caste which gave up the sponge almost without a struggle. Such was the significance of the [Decembrist] uprising.

The landlords who owned factories were the first among their caste to favor replacing serfdom by wage labor. The growing export of Russian grain gave an impulse in the same direction. In 1861 the noble bureaucracy, relying upon the liberal landlords, carried out its peasant reform. The impotent bourgeois liberalism during this operation played the rôle of humble chorus. It is needless to remark that tzarism solved the fundamental problem of Russia, the agrarian problem, in a more niggardly and thieving fashion than that in which the Prussian

monarchy during the next decade was to solve the fundamental problem of Germany, its national consolidation. The solution of the
problems of one class by another is one of those combined methods
natural to backward countries.

The law of combined development reveals itself most indubitably,
however, in the history and character of Russian industry. Arising
late, Russian industry did not repeat the development of the advanced
countries, but inserted itself into this development, adapting their
latest achievements to its own backwardness. Just as the economic
evolution of Russia as a whole skipped over the epoch of craft-guilds
and manufacture, so also the separate branches of industry made a
series of special leaps over technical productive stages that had been
measured in the West by decades. Thanks to this, Russian industry
developed at certain periods with extraordinary speed. Between the
first revolution and the war, industrial production in Russia approximately doubled. This has seemed to certain Russian historians a
sufficient basis for concluding that "we must abandon the legend of
backwardness and slow growth."[1] In reality the possibility of this swift
growth was determined by that very backwardness which, alas, continued not only up to the moment of liquidation of the old Russia,
but as her legacy up to the present day.

The basic criterion of the economic level of a nation is the productivity of labor, which in its turn depends upon the relative weight of
the industries in the general economy of the country. On the eve of
the war, when tzarist Russia had attained the highest point of its
prosperity, the national income per capita was 8 to 10 times less than
in the United States—a fact which is not surprising when you consider
that $4/5$ of the self-supporting population of Russia was occupied with
agriculture, while in the United States, for every one engaged in agriculture, $2\frac{1}{2}$ were engaged in industry. We must add that for every one
hundred square kilometers of land, Russia had, on the eve of the war,
0.4 kilometers of railroads, Germany 11.7, Austria-Hungary 7. Other
comparative coefficients are of the same type.

But it is just in the sphere of economy, as we have said, that the law
of combined development most forcibly emerges. At the same time that
peasant land-cultivation as a whole remained, right up to the revolution, at the level of the seventeenth century, Russian industry in its
technique and capitalist structure stood at the level of the advanced
countries, and in certain respects even outstripped them. Small enterprises, involving less than 100 workers, employed in the United States,
in 1914, 35 per cent of the total industrial workers, but in Russia
only 17.8 per cent. The two countries had an approximately identical

---

[1] The assertion is made by Professor M. N. Pokrovsky.

relative quantity of enterprises involving 100 to 1000 workers. But the giant enterprises, above 1000 workers each, employed in the United States 17.8 per cent of the workers and in Russia 41.4 per cent! For the most important industrial districts the latter percentage is still higher: for the Petrograd district 44.4 per cent, for the Moscow district even 57.3 per cent. We get a like result if we compare Russian with British or German industry. This fact—first established by the author in 1908 —hardly accords with the banal idea of the economic backwardness of Russia. However, it does not disprove this backwardness, but dialectically completes it.

The confluence of industrial with bank capital was also accomplished in Russia with a completeness you might not find in any other country. But the subjection of the industries to the banks meant, for the same reasons, their subjection to the western European money market. Heavy industry (metal, coal, oil) was almost wholly under the control of foreign finance capital, which had created for itself an auxiliary and intermediate system of banks in Russia. Light industry was following the same road. Foreigners owned in general about 40 per cent of all the stock capital of Russia, but in the leading branches of industry that percentage was still higher. We can say without exaggeration that the controlling shares of stock in the Russian banks, plants and factories were to be found abroad, the amount held in England, France and Belgium being almost double that in Germany.

The social character of the Russian bourgeoisie and its political physiognomy were determined by the condition of origin and the structure of Russian industry. The extreme concentration of this industry alone meant that between the capitalist leaders and the popular masses there was no hierarchy of transitional layers. To this we must add that the proprietors of the principal industrial, banking, and transport enterprises were foreigners, who realized on their investment not only the profits drawn from Russia, but also a political influence in foreign parliaments, and so not only did not forward the struggle for Russian parliamentarism, but often opposed it: it is sufficient to recall the shameful rôle played by official France. Such are the elementary and irremovable causes of the political isolation and anti-popular character of the Russian bourgeoisie. Whereas in the dawn of its history it was too unripe to accomplish a Reformation, when the time came for leading a revolution it was overripe.

In correspondence with this general course of development of the country, the reservoir from which the Russian working class formed itself was not the craft-guild, but agriculture, not the city, but the country. Moreover, in Russia the proletariat did not arise gradually through the ages, carrying with itself the burden of the past as in England, but in leaps involving sharp changes of environment, ties, relations, and a sharp break with the past. It is just this fact—combined with the concentrated oppressions of tzarism—that made the Russian workers hospitable to the boldest conclusions of revolutionary thought—just as the backward industries were hospitable to the last word in capitalist organization.

The Russian proletariat was forever repeating the short history of its origin. While in the metal industry, especially in Petrograd, a layer of hereditary proletarians was crystallized out, having made a complete break with the country, in the Urals the prevailing type was half-proletarian, half-peasant. A yearly inflow of fresh labor forces from the country in all the industrial districts kept renewing the bonds of the proletariat with its fundamental social reservoir.

The incapacity of the bourgeoisie for political action was immediately caused by its relation to the proletariat and the peasantry. It could not lead after it workers who stood hostile in their everyday life, and had so early learned to generalize their problems. But it was likewise incapable of leading after it the peasantry, because it was entangled in a web of interests with the landlords, and dreaded a shake-up of property relations in any form. The belatedness of the Russian revolution was thus not only a matter of chronology, but also of the social structure of the nation.

England achieved her Puritan revolution when her whole population was not more than 5½ millions, of whom half a million were to be found in London. France, in the epoch of her revolution, had in Paris also only half a million out of a population of 25 million. Russia at the beginning of the twentieth century had a population of about 150 million, of whom more than 3 million were in Petrograd and Moscow. Behind these comparative figures lurk enormous social differences. Not only England of the seventeenth century, but also France of the eighteenth, had no proletariat in the modern sense. In Russia, however, the working class in all branches of labor, both city and village, numbered in 1905 no less than 10 million, which with their families amounts to more than 25 million—that is to say, more than the whole population of France in the epoch of the great revolution. Advancing from the sturdy artisans and independent peasants of the army of Cromwell—through the Sansculottes of Paris—to the industrial proletarians of St. Petersburg, the revolution had deeply changed its social mechanism, its methods, and therewith its aims.

The events of 1905 were a prologue to the two revolutions of 1917, that of February and that of October. In the prologue all the elements of the drama were included, but not carried through. The Russo-Japanese war had made tzarism totter. Against the background of a mass movement the liberal bourgeoisie had frightened the monarchy with its opposition. The workers had organized independently of the bourgeoisie, and in opposition to it, in soviets, a form of organization then first called into being. Peasant uprisings to seize the land occurred throughout vast stretches of the country. Not only the peasants, but also the revolutionary parts of the army tended toward the soviets, which at the moment of highest tension openly disputed the power with the monarchy. However, all the revolutionary forces were then going into action for the first time, lacking experience and confidence. The liberals demonstratively backed away from the revolution exactly at the moment when it became clear that to shake tzarism would not be enough, it must be overthrown. This sharp break of the bourgeoisie with the people, in which the bourgeoisie carried with it considerable circles of the democratic intelligentsia, made it easier for the monarchy to differentiate within the army, separating out the loyal units, and to make a bloody settlement with the workers and peasants. Although with a few broken ribs, tzarism came out of the experience of 1905 alive and strong enough.

What changes in the correlation of forces were introduced by the eleven years' historical development dividing the prologue from the drama? Tzarism during this period came into still sharper conflict with the demands of historic development. The bourgeoisie became economically more powerful, but as we have seen its power rested on a higher concentration of industry and an increased predominance of foreign capital. Impressed by the lessons of 1905, the bourgeoisie had become more conservative and suspicious. The relative weight of the petty and middle bourgeoisie, insignificant before, had fallen still lower. The democratic intelligentsia generally speaking had no firm social support whatever. It could have a transitional political influence, but could play no independent rôle: its dependence upon bourgeois liberalism had grown enormously. In these circumstances only the youthful proletariat could give the peasantry a program, a banner and leadership. The gigantic tasks thus presented to the proletariat gave rise to an urgent necessity for a special revolutionary organization capable of quickly getting hold of the popular masses and making them ready for revolutionary action under the leadership of the workers. Thus the soviets of 1905 developed gigantically in 1917. That the soviets, we may remark here, are not a mere child of the historic backwardness of Russia, but a product of her combined development, is indicated by the fact that the proletariat of the most industrial country, Germany, at the time of its revolutionary high point—1918 to 1919—could find no other form of organization.

The revolution of 1917 still had as its immediate task the overthrow of the bureaucratic monarchy, but in distinction from the older bourgeois revolutions, the decisive force now was a new class formed on the basis of a concentrated industry, and armed with new organizations, new methods of struggle. The law of combined development here emerges in its extreme expression: starting with the overthrow of a decayed medieval structure, the revolution in the course of a few months placed the proletariat and the Communist Party in power.

In its initial task the Russian revolution was thus a democratic revolution. But it posed the problem of political democracy in a new way. While the workers were covering the whole country with soviets, including in them the soldiers and part of the peasantry, the bourgeoisie still continued to dicker—shall we summon or not summon a Constituent Assembly? In the course of our exposition this question will rise before us in full completeness. Here we wish only to mark the place of the soviets in the historic succession of revolutionary ideas and forms.

In the middle of the seventeenth century the bourgeois revolution in England developed under the guise of a religious reformation. A struggle for the right to pray according to one's own prayer book was identified with the struggle against the king, the aristocracy, the princes of the church, and Rome. The Presbyterians and Puritans were deeply convinced that they were placing their earthly interests under the unshakable protection of the divine Providence. The goals for which the new classes were struggling commingled inseparably in their consciousness with texts from the Bible and the forms of churchly ritual. Emigrants carried with them across the ocean this tradition sealed with blood. Hence the extraordinary virility of the Anglo-Saxon interpretation of Christianity. We see even today how the minister "socialists" of Great Britain back up their cowardice with these same magic texts with which the people of the seventeenth century sought to justify their courage.

In France, which stepped across the Reformation, the Catholic Church survived as a state institution until the revolution, which found its expression and justification for the tasks of the bourgeois society, not in texts from the Bible, but in the abstractions of democracy. Whatever the hatred of the present rulers of France for Jacobinism, the fact is that only thanks to the austere labor of Robespierre are they still able to cover their conservative rulership with those formulas with the help of which the old society was exploded.

Each of the great revolutions marked off a new stage of the bourgeois society, and new forms of consciousness for its classes. Just as France stepped over the Reformation, so Russia stepped over the formal democracy. The Russian revolutionary party, which was to place its stamp upon a whole epoch, sought an expression for the tasks of the revolution neither in the Bible nor in that secularized Christianity called "pure" democracy, but in the material relations of the social classes. The soviet system gave to these relations their simplest, most undisguised and transparent expression. The rule of the toilers has for the first time been realized in the soviet system, which, whatever its immediate historic vicissitudes, has penetrated as irrevocably into the consciousness of the masses as did in its day the system of the Reformation or of pure democracy.

. . .

THE PROLETARIAT AND THE PEASANTRY

The Russian proletariat learned its first steps in the political circumstances created by a despotic state. Strikes forbidden by law, underground circles, illegal proclamations, street demonstrations, encounters with the police and with troops— such was the school created by the combination of a swiftly developing capitalism with an absolutism slowly surrendering its positions. The concentration of the workers in colossal enterprises, the intense character of governmental persecution, and finally the impulsiveness of a young and fresh proletariat, brought it about that the political strike, so rare in western Europe, became in Russia the fundamental method of struggle. The figures of strikes from the beginning of the present century are a most impressive index of the political history of Russia. With every desire not to burden our text with figures, we cannot refrain from introducing a table of political strikes in Russia for the period 1903 to 1917. The figures, reduced to their simplest expression, relate only to enterprises undergoing factory inspection. The railroads, mining industries, mechanical and small enterprises in general, to say nothing of agriculture, for various reasons do not enter into the count. But the changes in the strike curve in the different periods emerge no less clearly for this.

We have before us a curve—the only one of its kind—of the political temperature of a nation carrying in its womb a great revolution. In a backward country with a small proletariat—for in all the enterprises undergoing factory inspection there were only about 1½ million workers in 1905, about 2 million in 1917—the strike movement attains such dimensions as it never knew before anywhere in the world. With the weakness of the petty bourgeois democracy, the scatteredness and political blindness of the peasant movement, the revolutionary strike of the workers becomes the battering ram which the awakening nation directs against the walls of absolutism. Participants in political strikes in 1905 numbering 1,843,000—workers participating in several strikes are here, of course, counted twice—that number alone would permit us to put our finger on the revolutionary year in our table, if we knew nothing else about the Russian political calendar.

Year	Number in thousands of participants in political strikes
1903	87*
1904	25*
1905	1,843
1906	651
1907	540
1908	93
1909	8
1910	4
1911	8
1912	550
1913	502
1914 (first half)	1,059
1915	156
1916	310
1917 (January–February)	575

* The figures for 1903 and 1904 refer to all strikes, the economic undoubtedly predominating.

For 1904, the first year of the Russo-Japanese war, the factory inspection indicates in all only 25,000 strikers. In 1905, political and economic strikes together involved 2,863,000 men—115 times more than in the previous year. This remarkable fact by itself would suggest the thought that a proletariat, impelled by the course of events to improvise such unheard-of revolutionary activities, must at whatever cost produce from its depths an organization corresponding to the dimensions of the struggle and the colossal tasks. This organization was the soviets—brought into being by the first revolution, and made the instrument of the general strike and the struggle for power.

Beaten in the December uprising of 1905, the proletariat during the next two years makes heroic efforts to defend a part of the conquered positions. These years, as our strike figures show, still belong directly to the revolution, but they are the years of ebb. The four following years (1908–11) emerge in our mirror of strike statistics as the years of victorious counter-revolution. An industrial crisis coincident with this still further exhausts the proletariat, already bled white. The depth of the fall is symmetrical with the height of the rise. National convulsions find their reflection in these simple figures.

The industrial boom beginning in 1910 lifted the workers to their feet, and gave a new impulse to their energy. The figures for 1912–14 almost repeat those for 1905–07, but in the opposite order: not from above downwards, but from below up. On a new and higher historical basis—there are more workers now, and they have more experience—a new revolutionary offensive begins. The first half-year of 1914 clearly approaches in the number of political strikes the culminating point of the year of the first revolution. But war breaks out and sharply interrupts this process. The first war months are marked by political inertness in the working class, but already in the spring of 1915 the numbness begins to pass. A new cycle of political strikes opens, a cycle which in February 1917 will culminate in the insurrection of soldiers and workers.

The sharp ebbs and flows of the mass struggle had left the Russian proletariat after a few years almost unrecognizable. Factories which two or three years ago would strike unanimously over some single arbitrary police action, today have completely lost their revolutionary color, and accept the most monstrous crimes of the authorities without resistance. Great defeats discourage people for a long time. The consciously revolutionary elements lose their power over the masses. Prejudices and superstitions not yet burnt out come back to life. Gray immigrants from the village during these times dilute the workers' ranks. Sceptics ironically shake their heads. So it was in the years 1907–11. But molecular processes in the masses are healing the psychological wounds of defeat. A new turn of events, or an underlying economic impulse, opens a new political cycle. The revolutionary elements again find their audience. The struggle reopens on a higher level.

In order to understand the two chief tendencies in the Russian working class, it is important to have in mind that Menshevism finally took shape in the years of ebb and reaction. It relied chiefly upon a thin layer of workers who had broken with the revolution. Whereas Bolshevism, cruelly shattered in the period of the reaction, began to rise swiftly on the crest of a new revolutionary tide in the years before the war. "The most energetic and audacious element, ready for tireless struggle, for resistance and continual organization, is that element, those organizations, and those people who are concentrated around Lenin." In these words the Police Department estimated the work of the Bolsheviks during the years preceding the war.

In July 1914, while the diplomats were driving the last nail into the cross designed for the crucifixion of Europe, Petrograd was boiling like a revolutionary cauldron. The President of the French Republic, Poincaré, had to lay his wreath on the tomb of Alexander III amid the last echoes of a street fight and the first murmurs of a patriotic demonstration.

Would the mass offensive of 1912–14 have led directly to an overthrow of tzarism if the war had not broken out? It is hardly possible to answer that question with certainty. The process would inexorably have led to a revolution, but through what stages would the revolution in those circumstances have had to go? Would it not have experienced another defeat? How much time would have been needed by the workers in order to arouse the peasantry and win the army? In all these directions only guesses are possible. The war, at any rate, gave the process at first a backward movement, but only to accelerate it more powerfully in the next period and guarantee its overwhelming victory.

. . .

The agrarian movement, having, like the strike movement of the workers, died down toward the end of 1907, partially revives in 1908, and grows stronger during the following years. The struggle, to be sure, is transferred to a considerable degree within the commune: that is just what the reaction had figured on politically. There are not infrequent armed conflicts among peasants during the division of the communal land. But the struggle against the landlord also does not disappear. The peasants are more frequently setting fire to the landlord's manors, harvests, haystacks, seizing on the way also those individual tracts which had been cut off against the will of the communal peasants.

The war found the peasantry in this condition. The government carried away from the country about 10 million workers and about 2 million horses. The weak homesteads grew still weaker. The number of peasants who could not sow their fields increased. But in the second year of the war the middle peasants also began to go under. Peasant hostility toward the war sharpened from month to month. In October 1916, the Petrograd Gendarme Administration reported that in the villages they had already ceased to believe in the success of the war—the report being based on the words of insurance agents, teachers, traders, etc. "All are waiting, and impatiently demanding: When will this cursed war finally end?" And that is not all: "Political questions are being talked about everywhere and resolutions adopted directed against the landlords and merchants. Nuclei of various organizations are being formed. . . . As yet there is no uniting center, but there is reason to suppose that the peasants will unite by way of the coöperatives which are daily growing throughout all Russia." There is some exaggeration here. In some things the gendarme has run ahead a little, but the fundamentals are indubitably correct.

The possessing classes could not but foresee that the village was going to present its bill. But they drove away these black thoughts, hoping to wriggle out of it somehow. On this theme the inquisitive French ambassador Paléologue had a chat during the war days with the former Minister of Agriculture Krivoshein, the former Premiere Kokovtsev, the great landlord Count Bobrinsky, the President of the State Duma

Rodzianko, the great industrialist Putilov, and other distinguished people. Here is what was unveiled before him in this conversation: In order to carry into action a radical land reform it would require the work of a standing army of 300,000 surveyors for no less than fifteen years; but during this time the number of homesteads would increase to 30 million, and consequently all these preliminary calculations by the time they were made would prove invalid. To introduce a land reform thus seemed in the eyes of these landlords, officials and bankers something like squaring the circle. It is hardly necessary to say that a like mathematical scrupulousness was completely alien to the peasant. He thought that first of all the thing to do was to smoke out the landlord, and then see.

If the village nevertheless remained comparatively peaceful during the war, that was because its active forces were at the front. The soldiers did not forget about the land—whenever at least they were not thinking about death—and in the trenches the muzhik's thoughts about the future were saturated with the smell of powder. But all the same the peasantry, even after learning to handle firearms, could never of its own force have achieved the agrarian democratic revolution—that is, its own revolution. It had to have leadership. For the first time in world history the peasant was destined to find a leader in the person of the worker. In that lies the fundamental, and you may say the whole, difference between the Russian revolution and all those preceding it.

In England serfdom had disappeared in actual fact by the end of the fourteenth century—that is, two centuries before it arose in Russia, and four and a half centuries before it was abolished. The expropriation of the landed property of the peasants dragged along in England through one Reformation and two revolutions to the nineteenth century. The capitalist development, not forced from the outside, thus had sufficient time to liquidate the independent peasant long before the proletariat awoke to political life.

In France the struggle with royal absolutism, the aristocracy, and the princes of the church, compelled the bourgeoisie in various of its layers, and in several installments, to achieve a radical agrarian revolution at the beginning of the eighteenth century. For long after that an independent peasantry constituted the support of the bourgeois order, and in 1871 it helped the bourgeoisie put down the Paris Commune.

In Germany the bourgeoisie proved incapable of a revolutionary solution of the agrarian problem, and in 1848 betrayed the peasants to the landlords, just as Luther some three centuries before in the peasant wars had betrayed them to the princes. On the other hand, the German proletariat was still too weak in the middle of the nineteenth century to take the leadership of the peasantry. As a result the capitalist development of Germany got sufficient time, although not so long a period as in England, to subordinate agriculture, as it emerged from the uncompleted bourgeois revolution, to its own interests.

The peasant reform of 1861 was carried out in Russia by an aristocratic and bureaucratic monarchy under pressure of the demands of a bourgeois society, but with the bourgeoisie completely powerless politically. The character of this peasant emancipation was such that the forced capitalistic transformation of the country inevitably converted the agrarian problem into a problem of revolution. The Russian bourgeois dreamed of an agrarian evolution on the French plan, or the Danish, or the American—anything you want, only not the Russian. He neglected, however, to supply himself in good season with a French history or an American social structure. The democratic intelligentsia, notwithstanding its revolutionary past, took its stand in the decisive hour with the liberal bourgeoisie and the landlord, and not with the revolutionary village. In these circumstances only the working class could stand at the head of the peasant revolution.

The law of combined development of backward countries—in the sense of a peculiar mixture of backward elements with the most modern factors—here rises before us in its most finished form, and offers a key to the fundamental riddle of the Russian revolution. If the agrarian problem, as a heritage from the barbarism of the old Russian history, had been solved by the bourgeoisie, if it could have been solved by them, the Russian proletariat could not possibly have come to power in 1917. In order to realize the Soviet state, there was required a drawing together and mutual penetration of two factors belonging to completely different historic species: a peasant war—that is, a movement characteristic of the dawn of bourgeois development—and a proletarian insurrection, the movement signalizing its decline. That is the essence of 1917.

THE TZAR AND THE TZARINA

This book will concern itself least of all with those unrelated psychological researches which are now so often substituted for social and historical analysis. Foremost in our field of vision will stand the great, moving forces of history, which are super-personal in character. Monarchy is one of them. But all these forces operate through people. And monarchy is by its very principle bound up with the personal. This in itself justifies an interest in the personality of that monarch whom the process of social development brought face to face with a revolution. Moreover, we hope to show in what follows, partially at least, just where in a personality the strictly

personal ends—often much sooner than we think—and how frequently
the "distinguishing traits" of a person are merely individual scratches
made by a higher law of development.

Nicholas II inherited from his ancestors not only a giant empire, but
also a revolution. And they did not bequeath him one quality which
would have made him capable of governing an empire or even a
province or a county. To that historic flood which was rolling its bil-
lows each one closer to the gates of his palace, the last Romanov opposed only a dumb indifference. It seemed as though between his consciousness and his epoch there stood some transparent but absolutely
impenetrable medium.

.   .   .

Historians and biographers of the psychological tendency not infrequently seek and find something purely personal and accidental
where great historical forces are refracted through a personality. This
is the same fault of vision as that of the courtiers who considered the
last Russian tzar born "unlucky." He himself believed that he was
born under an unlucky star. In reality his ill-luck flowed from the
contradictions between those old aims which he inherited from his
ancestors and the new historic conditions in which he was placed.
When the ancients said that Jupiter first makes mad those whom he
wishes to destroy, they summed up in superstitious form a profound
historic observation. In the saying of Goethe about reason becoming
nonsense—"*Vernunft wird Unsinn*"—this same thought is expressed
about the impersonal Jupiter of the historical dialectic, which with-
draws "reason" from historic institutions that have outlived themselves
and condemns their defenders to failure. The scripts for the rôles of
Romanov and Capet were prescribed by the general development of
the historic drama; only the nuances of interpretation fell to the lot
of the actors. The ill-luck of Nicholas, as of Louis, had its roots not in
his personal horoscope, but in the historical horoscope of the bureau-
cratic-caste monarchy. They were both, chiefly and above all, the last-
born offspring of absolutism. Their moral insignificance, deriving from
their dynastic epigonism, gave the latter an especially malignant
character.

You might object: if Alexander III had drunk less he might have
lived a good deal longer, the revolution would have run into a very
different make of tzar, and no parallel with Louis XVI would have
been possible. Such an objection, however, does not refute in the least
what has been said above. We do not at all pretend to deny the significance of the personal in the mechanics of the historic process, nor the
significance in the personal of the accidental. We only demand that a
historic personality, with all its peculiarities, should not be taken as
a bare list of psychological traits, but as a living reality grown out of

definite social conditions and reacting upon them. As a rose does not lose its fragrance because the natural scientist points out upon what ingredients of soil and atmosphere it is nourished, so an exposure of the social roots of a personality does not remove from it either its aroma or its foul smell.

The consideration advanced above about a possible longer life of Alexander III is capable of illuming this very problem from another side. Let us assume that this Alexander III had not become mixed up in 1904 in a war with Japan. This would have delayed the first revolution. For how long? It is possible that the "revolution of 1905"—that is, the first test of strength, the first breach in the system of absolutism —would have been a mere introduction to the second, republican, and the third, proletarian revolution. Upon this question more or less interesting guesses are possible, but it is indubitable in any case that the revolution did not result from the character of Nicholas II, and that Alexander III would not have solved its problem. It is enough to remember that nowhere and never was the transition from the feudal to the bourgeois régime made without violent disturbances. We saw this only yesterday in China; today we observe it again in India. The most we can say is that this or that policy of the monarchy, this or that personality of the monarch, might have hastened or postponed the revolution, and placed a certain imprint on its external course.

With what angry and important stubbornness tzarism tried to defend itself in those last months, weeks and days, when its game was hopelessly lost! If Nicholas himself lacked the will, the lack was made up by the tzarina. Rasputin was an instrument of the action of a clique which rabidly fought for self-preservation. Even on this narrow scale the personality of the tzar merges in a group which represents the coagulum of the past and its last convulsion. The "policy" of the upper circles at Tzarskoe Selo, face-to-face with the revolution, were but the reflexes of a poisoned and weak beast of prey. If you chase a wolf over the steppe in an automobile, the beast gives out at last and lies down impotent. But attempt to put a collar on him, and he will try to tear you to pieces, or at least wound you. And indeed what else can he do in the circumstances?

The liberals imagined there was something else he might do. Instead of coming to an agreement with the enfranchised bourgeoisie in good season, and thus preventing the revolution—such is liberalism's act of accusation against the last tzar—Nicholas stubbornly shrank from concessions, and even in the last days when already under the knife of destiny, when every minute was to be counted, still kept on procrastinating, bargaining with fate, and letting slip the last possibilities. This all sounds convincing. But how unfortunate that liberalism, knowing so accurately how to save the monarchy, did not know how to save itself!

It would be absurd to maintain that tzarism never and in no circumstances made concessions. It made them when they were demanded
by the necessity of self-preservation. After the Crimean defeat, Alexander II carried out the semi-liberation of the peasants and a series
of liberal reforms in the sphere of land administration, courts, press,
educational institutions, etc. The tzar himself expressed the guiding
thought of this reformation: to free the peasants from *above* lest they
free themselves from *below*. Under the drive of the first revolution
Nicholas II granted a semi-constitution. Stolypin scrapped the peasant
communes in order to broaden the arena of the capitalist forces. For
tzarism, however, all these reforms had a meaning only in so far as the
partial concession preserved the whole—that is, the foundations of a
caste society and the monarchy itself. When the consequences of the
reform began to splash over those boundaries the monarchy inevitably
beat a retreat. Alexander II in the second half of his reign stole back
the reforms of the first half. Alexander III went still farther on the
road of counter-reform. Nicholas II in October 1905 retreated before
the revolution, and then afterward dissolved the Dumas created by it,
and as soon as the revolution grew weak, made his coup d'état.
Throughout three-quarters of a century—if we begin with the reform
of Alexander II—there developed a struggle of historic forces, now
underground, now in the open, far transcending the personal qualities
of the separate tzars, and accomplishing the overthrow of the monarchy.
Only within the historic framework of this process can you find a place
for individual tzars, their characters, their "biographies."

Even the most despotic of autocrats is but little similar to a "free"
individuality laying its arbitrary imprint upon events. He is always the
crowned agent of the privileged classes which are forming society in
their own image. When these classes have not yet fulfilled their mission,
then the monarchy is strong and self-confident. Then it has in its hands
a reliable apparatus of power and an unlimited choice of executives—
because the more gifted people have not yet gone over into the hostile
camp. Then the monarch, either personally, or through the mediation
of a powerful favorite, may become the agent of a great and progressive
historic task. It is quite otherwise when the sun of the old society is
finally declining to the west. The privileged classes are now changed
from organizers of the national life into a parasitic growth; having lost
their guiding function, they lose the consciousness of their mission and
all confidence in their powers. Their dissatisfaction with themselves
becomes a dissatisfaction with the monarchy; the dynasty becomes
isolated; the circle of people loyal to the death narrows down; their
level sinks lower; meanwhile the dangers grow; new forces are pushing
up; the monarchy loses its capacity for any kind of creative initiative;
it defends itself, it strikes back, it retreats; its activities acquire the

automatism of mere reflexes. The semi-Asiatic despotism of the Romanovs did not escape this fate.

If you take the tzarism in its agony, in a vertical section, so to speak, Nicholas is the axis of a clique which has its roots in the hopelessly condemned past. In a horizontal section of the historic monarchy, Nicholas is the last link in a dynastic chain. His nearest ancestors, who also in their day were merged in a family, caste and bureaucratic collectivity—only a broader one—tried out various measures and methods of government in order to protect the old social régime against the fate advancing upon it. But nevertheless they passed on to Nicholas a chaotic empire already carrying the matured revolution in its womb. If he had any choice left, it was only between different roads to ruin.

Liberalism was dreaming of a monarchy on the British plan. But was parliamentarism born on the Thames by a peaceful evolution? Was it the fruit of the "free" foresight of a single monarch? No, it was deposited as the result of a struggle that lasted for ages, and in which one of the kings left his head at the crossroads.

The historic-psychological contrast mentioned above between the Romanovs and the Capets can, by the way, be aptly extended to the British royal pair of the epoch of the first revolution. Charles I revealed fundamentally the same combination of traits with which memoirists and historians have endowed Louis XVI and Nicholas II. "Charles, therefore, remained passive," writes Montague, "yielded where he could not resist, betrayed how unwillingly he did so, and reaped no popularity, no confidence." "He was not a stupid man," says another historian of Charles Stuart, "but he lacked firmness of character. . . . His evil fate was his wife, Henrietta, a Frenchwoman, sister of Louis XIII, saturated even more than Charles with the idea of absolutism." We will not detail the characteristics of this third—chronologically first— royal pair to be crushed by a national revolution. We will merely observe that in England the hatred was concentrated above all on the queen, as a Frenchwoman and a papist, whom they accused of plotting with Rome, secret connections with the Irish rebels, and intrigues at the French court.

But England had, at any rate, ages at her disposal. She was the pioneer of bourgeois civilization; she was not under the yoke of other nations, but on the contrary held them more and more under her yoke. She exploited the whole world. This softened the inner contradictions, accumulated conservatism, promoted an abundance and stability of fatty deposits in the form of a parasitic caste, in the form of a squirarchy, a monarchy, House of Lords, and the state church. Thanks to this exclusive historic privilege of development possessed by bourgeois England, conservatism combined with elasticity passed over from her institutions into her moral fiber. Various continental Philistines, like the Russian professor Miliukov, or the Austro-Marxist Otto Bauer, have not to this day ceased going into ecstasies over this fact. But exactly at the present moment, when England, hard pressed throughout the world, is squandering the last resources of her former privileged position, her conservatism is losing its elasticity, and even in the person of the Laborites is turning into stark reactionism. In the face of the Indian revolution the "socialist" MacDonald will find no other methods but those with which Nicholas II opposed the Russian revolution. Only a blind man could fail to see that Great Britain is headed for gigantic revolutionary earthquake shocks, in which the last fragments of her conservatism, her world domination, her present state machine, will go down without a trace. MacDonald is preparing these shocks no less successfully than did Nicholas II in his time, and no less blindly. So here too, as we see, is no poor illustration of the problem of the rôle of the "free" personality in history.

But how could Russia with her belated development, coming along at the tail end of the European nations, with her meager economic foundation underfoot, how could she develop an "elastic conservatism" of social forms—and develop it for the special benefit of professional liberalism and its leftward shadow, reformist socialism? Russia was too far behind. And when world imperialism once took her in its grip, she had to pass through her political history in too brief a course. If Nicholas had gone to meet liberalism and replaced Stürmer with Miliukov, the development of events would have differed a little in form, but not in substance. Indeed it was just in this way that Louis behaved in the second stage of the revolution, summoning the Gironde to power: this did not save Louis himself from the guillotine, nor after him the Gironde. The accumulating social contradictions were bound to break through to the surface, and breaking through to carry out their work of purgation. Before the pressure of the popular masses, who had at last brought out into the open arena their misfortunes, their pains, indignations, passions, hopes, illusions and aims, the high-up combinations of the monarchy with liberalism had only an episodic significance. They could exert, to be sure, an influence on the order of events, maybe upon the number of actions, but not at all upon the development of the drama nor its momentous climax.

VIII/FASCISM AND COUNTERREVOLUTION

S we approach the end of this book, the real differences between mainstream and radical historians become increasingly clear. They are many but may be easily grouped around a few basic issues. A mainstream historian will tend to proceed by multifactor analysis, while a radical will insist on class as the integrating framework within which to bring together the many facets of any given set of historical relationships. A mainstream historian will put a good deal of emphasis on the play of ideas as a causal factor, while a radical will prefer to speak in terms of ideology. And finally, a radical will be much interested in the action of the masses on the stage of history, not because he entertains romantic views of the purity and goodness of the working classes, but because he believes their participation, especially in revolutionary situations and increasingly in the modern and contemporary eras, to be of primary importance in social development. In all honesty, it must be said that nonradical historians are now more frequently displaying similar interests, although there is always the danger of turning the "people" into a formalistic abstraction, either by refusing to analyze its component parts or, on the contrary, by separating them out into so many elements that there is nothing left but a flux of atomized individuals.

Nowhere are the differences of conception clearer than in the studies of Nazism published in recent years. The immeasurable horror of the Nazi experience has even led some otherwise astute observers to adopt the thesis of the fatal flaw in the German people, which would explain brutality, racism, and aggressive war by reference to the development of national character.

Like so many emotionally tempting theses, this one is intellectually dishonest, irrational, and, moreover, smells of the very racism its partisans reject—even when the usual disclaimers (that, of course, it has nothing to do with blood) are made.

Much more representative is the excellent work of K. D. Bracher, whom it would not, I think, be unjust to classify as a liberal in the modern American sense of the word. Bracher holds that no monocausal explanation of the rise of Nazism is possible, and then goes on to catalogue all the factors that contributed to the emergence of the movement. This is a useful exercise, insofar as it makes us conscious of the overriding complexity of modern politics and demands that we examine the relevance of each proffered explanation. The procedure can, however, be misleading. When Bracher writes that Hitler came to power as a result of a series of avoidable errors, he has gone to the logical conclusion of a multifactor analysis, taken as a bunch of independent variables. He has also subtly displaced the question. Instead of asking: What explains the phenomenon of fascism, or the rise of a fascist political movement?, he asks: What accounts for its success? These are not, by any means, the same question. In a sense, the success (Hitler's conquest of power) was accidental, due, among other reasons, to the failure of the German left to unite against him. The rise of fascism, on the other hand, while not inevitable, must be linked to the long-term development of class relations in Germany, which alone rendered it possible. Nicos Poulantzas, in the article that follows, starts from this premise and attempts to create some order out of the chaos of class-oriented, but conflicting, interpretations. He does this by employing the Gramscian concept of hegemony (see section IV, The Risorgimento) to develop an analysis of the relationships existing within the group of classes and fractions of classes who make up the ruling bloc. The language he employs is unfamiliar but not notably abstruse. Once his definitions are known, his reasoning may be easily followed. A *dominant class* is one that exercises ultimate power in society. A *reigning class* is one whose parties occupy the principal places on the political scene, while a *class-in-charge* is one from whose ranks are recruited the political, bureaucratic, and military personnel who fill the high offices of state. The three roles may be played by one or several classes at any given moment in time.

The articles printed here take up two other related questions: the role of the petite bourgeoisie in the Nazi movement and state, and Nazi economic policy. It is now a commonplace that the oppressed and disgruntled petit bourgeois is open

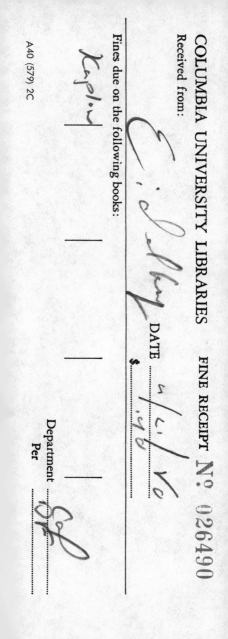

to the blandishments of right-wing demagogues, be they Hitler, Mussolini, or George Wallace. Petit bourgeois can be pretty nasty sorts, and it is not our business to play down their negative contributions. The fear of becoming a proletarian and the trembling after the security of one's property are ingredients well calculated to make a bitter witch's brew. Nevertheless, it would be wrong to concentrate on them exclusively, without bringing into focus the role of monopoly capital. It is not blood nor even culture alone that makes the petit bourgeois vicious, but the fact that he *is* caught, as his rhetoric so often declares, between the upper and nether millstones of capital and labor. He must go in one direction or the other, but he cannot remain a stable anachronism in a society whose economic base has increasingly less room for him. Insofar as his self-image is that of a property owner, he may fail to see that the ultimate responsibility for his difficulties lies with the bourgeoisie rather than with the workers. And, because he is less skilled than the ruling class in making ideological somersaults, he will tend to remain a convinced reactionary even in periods of liberalization of big capital. That is why in the United States today, the Ku Klux Klan and the White Citizens' Councils are recruited from members of the petite bourgeoisie, while the steel magnates of Birmingham are able to make the necessary minimal adjustment to the Black revolt.

Does the lower middle class get what it has been looking for once the right takes power? The experience of Nazism forces a negative answer. The article by the German refugee scholar Franz Neumann demonstrates that the Nazis accepted the basic characteristics of German class society and, indeed, attempted to consolidate them. To be sure, the Nazis were not simple-minded slaves of the bourgeoisie. In one sense, they did subordinate purely economic goals to a political program which called for the speeding up of rearmament and the maintenance of the food supply. But we want to be careful about making the rather fanciful assumption that the bourgeois were so many *hominis economici* interested exclusively in the accumulation of profit, which the Nazis disdained. There were, in Bracher's words, "organizational and psychological changes" in the structure of German society, of which the greatest were the growth of bureaucracy and the creation of a purely formal sense of comradeship, so that all might feel, but not be, equal in the eyes of the gargantuan state apparatus. As the Big Bad Wolf might have said, it was "all the better to eat you with." In any case, Nazism hardly adds up to an anticapitalist revolution.

K. D. Bracher

19

The German
Dictatorship

A LOOK AHEAD TOWARD 1933

The question [is] what special circumstances made possible the rise of National Socialism. The answer must be sought in the combination of the shortcomings of German policy from the early nineteenth century on and the fatal roots and crisis-ridden history of the Weimar Republic. The democracy of 1918 was held responsible for the aftereffects of defeat suffered in the war. The new government became the scapegoat and hate-object of the forces of restoration and reaction in state and society, as well as of the revolutionary dictatorial movements gathered in the militant Free Corps,[1] in *völkisch*–anti-Semitic sects, and in paramilitary outfits. The "Red specter" of Communist revolution did the rest to make Army and bureaucracy, middle class and business, susceptible to these sentiments. The democratic forces extended to their enemies the tolerance of a liberal legal system. They were also confronted with the desire for authority nurtured by an authoritarian bureaucratic state, and this created serious organizational problems in the Republic.

The conflict between authoritarian tradition and the new democracy had a number of consequences: a nonfunctioning of parliamentary government; agitation for a Presidential system as a sort of ersatz empire and quasi dictatorship; the splintering and lack of cooperation of ideologically and politically rigid parties; the rise of antidemocratic movements which, being in opposition to the government, limited the maneuverability of the political coalitions; the militarization of the nongovernmental sector by militant groups; the spread of a terrorist power philosophy which propounded a barbaric friend-foe principle as opposed to the democratic idea of compromise; the radicalization

---

[1] Volunteer defense units organized by former imperial officers, and owing allegiance to these officers.—*Translator's note.*

335

of the economically and socially threatened urban and rural middle classes; the susceptibility of the bureaucracy and judiciary to hierarchical-authoritarian ideas of order; and, finally, the Army's suspicious attitude toward the democratic Republic.

It was against this background that National Socialism took shape as a new type of integrating force. Being a specifically German manifestation of European antidemocratism, it was completely attuned to the German situation and even less of an export article than Italian Fascism. This is yet another example of the limits of the conception of a universal fascism. The nationalist foundation makes for profound differences from country to country. Nor is there any monocausal explanation, whether it be based on economic, political, or ideological premises. National Socialism, like Hitler, was the product of World War I, but it was given its shape and force by those basic problems of modern German history which marked the painful road of the democratic movement. Among these were the fragility of the democratic tradition and the powerful remnants of authoritarian governmental and social institutions before and after 1848; the susceptibility to nationalistic, imperialistic ideas, a product of the belated and never fully realized creation of a German national state; the problems arising out of the unexpected defeat and the resultant stab-in-the-back legend, and the widespread disgruntlement over the Versailles peace; the permanent crisis of a republic which never won the full support of the majority of the people; the explosive consequences of the Depression on this highly industrialized, socially and religiously divided state with its feudalistic, traditionalistic remnants; and, finally, the middle class's fear of proletarization and Communism, and the added resentment and panic of a rural population threatened by the spread of modern technology. It should, therefore, not come as a surprise that National Socialism scored its greatest electoral successes first in rural Bavaria and then in the rural provinces of Schleswig-Holstein and Lower Saxony.

Among the special factors of the early days of National Socialism was the tremendously important part played by the spectacular rise and near-religious veneration of a Führer. The organizational structure and activities of this new type of movement were based completely on the leader principle. In the center stood the figure of Adolf Hitler. In terms of social psychology, he represented the disenfranchised little man eager to compensate for his feelings of inferiority through militancy and political radicalism. His Austrian birth, educational and professional failure, and the redeeming experience of the male camaraderie of the war shaped his own life as well as the ideology of National Socialism.

National Socialism was based on a nationalistic, racist, oversimplified Social Darwinism popularized in the writings of radical sectarians. Yet at the same time, through an eclectic mixture of doctrinaire and political programs, it sought to appeal to all parts of the population. The early slogans of National Socialism, by their championship of expansionist social imperialism and by their submission to nationalist dictatorial rule, were intended to divert the middle class and the working class from domestic troubles. The "national community" was proclaimed as the panacea for the cure of economic and political ills, in place of the pluralism of democracy and the class society. Militaristic and racist doctrines were the instruments used to woo and win over the population. An aggressive nationalism appealing to the traditional German sense of uniqueness and the vision of a unified Greater Germany was used in the campaign against the Versailles treaty. The next step was a demand for the expansion of the national and ethnic boundaries, for *Lebensraum* [living space] in the East for the allegedly superior German and Germanic peoples.

In addition to the Führer cult, which appealed to the authoritarian desire for order, the social and biological version of anti-Semitism became one of the early fanatical fixtures of Hitler's program. This issue lent itself to the concept of the absolute enemy which every totalitarian movement has to have in order to direct and deflect the aggressiveness it has mobilized. Above all, National Socialist ideology and political strategy were based on the right of the stronger, as propounded by Social Darwinism. The exaltation of "action" as the highest ideal, above reason and intellect, defined the basically irrational nature of National Socialism. Its ultimate purpose was the acquisition of unlimited power through oppression inside the country and expansion outside. The history of the Third Reich reveals that National Socialism followed Hitler's early plans, despite its offhand dismissal by the social critics of the time. The history of National Socialism, in effect, is the history of its fatal underestimation.

This is true also of Hitler's victory of 1933. The Third Reich came into being as a result of a series of effective deceptive maneuvers. Without them, Hitler probably could not have come to power. His, he said, was a "legal revolution." By combining these two contradictory concepts, the National Socialists paid homage to the popular desire for legality as well as the wish for complete change in a period of grave economic ills. After the failure of his putsch of 1923, as well as the reactionary Kapp Putsch of 1920,[2] which manifested the distaste of the bourgeoisie and civil service for overt coups and revolutions, Hitler

---

[2] This attempt by an antirepublican military coalition under Wolfgang Kapp and General von Lüttwitz to overthrow the Government failed after only four days. —*Translator's note*

confined himself to pseudo-legal tactics. Instead of attempting a putsch against the Republic, he made use of the possibilities offered by the emergency provisions of the Weimar Constitution to abrogate it. The road of a Presidential dictatorship had always been a favored recommendation of conservative opponents of parliamentary democracy, and, after 1930, it was actively supported by the authoritarian, monarchic President of Germany, Field Marshal Hindenburg. It was he who helped the National Socialist Party shed the shackles of a minority party that never had won much more than a third of the popular vote in any election. The special powers granting the President the right to dissolve the Reichstag and appoint a Chancellor made possible the legal dictatorhip of the President. It was exercise of these prerogatives, not the voice of a majority government, which brought Hitler to power.

The successful imposition of autocratic rule was augmented by the appeal for a "national revolution." As far as Hitler was concerned, the alliance with rightist parties, industrial circles, agrarian interests, and the military was merely one of expediency. When a serious party crisis threatened at the end of 1932, he did make major concessions to the champions of a "national concentration" of the Right assembled by von Papen, Hindenburg's confidant. But even if as Chancellor he accepted a majority of Conservative ministers, he nonetheless insisted on the right to exercise the dictatorial Presidential powers. Disguising the power claims of the National Socialists as the call for a Christian-national resurgence had the desired effect in the Government as well as among the public, and did not interfere with the ruthless oppressive measures Hitler pushed through with the help of those "legal" dictatorial powers in February, 1933. Hitler's allies had initially overestimated their own power, and later they tried to steer the revolution into orderly channels. But by their cooperation they first made possible the pseudo-legality of that revolution. For similar reasons, the opposition of the middle class capitulated before the Enabling Act, and the civil service cooperated in the legalization of the Nazi revolution. The Left also let itself be duped. For too long it remained almost paralyzed in the face of the novel situation of a "legal" and "national" revolution.

In the final analysis, Hitler came to power as a result of a series of avoidable errors. He was neither elected freely by a majority of the German people nor were there compelling reasons for the capitulation of the Republic. However, in the end, the democratic forces were in the minority vis-à-vis the totalitarian, dictatorial parties of the National Socialists and the Communists. And in this situation a large portion of Germany's top echelons went over to Hitler after 1933. The susceptibility of the middle class had historical as well as immediate reasons. As confusing as the history of Hitler's takeover may be, the preconditions of National Socialism also do not lend themselves to simple explanations. A number of not too clearly defined factors and elements played a part, forces of a dark underground of German and European social and national conditions. The fatal emergence of Hitler is closely linked to a main current of German events in the nineteenth and twentieth centuries, even if National Socialism cannot be equated with German history. Looking back after 1945, Friedrich Meinecke put the problem of the antecedents of National Socialism and its links to German thought and attitudes thus:

One can always object that the power-state and Machiavellism were not confined to Germany, that they were more often preached but not more strongly practiced by us Germans. This view is quite true. Specifically German, however, was the frankness and nakedness of the German power-state and Machiavellism, its hard and deliberate formulation as a principle of conduct, and the pleasure taken in its reckless consequences. Specifically German also was the tendency to elevate something primarily practical into a universal world-view theory. It was a serious thing for the future that these ideas about power-state and Machiavellism, at first expressed merely as theories, might become practical weapons in the hands of ruling authorities. The German power-state idea, whose history began with Hegel, was to find in Hitler its worst and most fatal application and extension.[3]

It was the rural and urban "middle class," in the broad sense of the term, which started and carried out the breakthrough of the NSDAP [the Nazi party]. The "panic of the middle class," which set in with the outbreak of the economic crisis, was sharpened by the fact that the middle class felt threatened not only economically but, more important, socially as well. The violent reaction which drove many of its members toward the radical Right arose out of a subjective feeling of crisis in a time of social upheaval in an industrial, democratic age. The power of the old middle class continued to decline within an expanding population; its nervous irritability and susceptibility to radical slogans was the result of this prestige loss as well as of economic plight. Out of a general desire for security after the catastrophe of the inflation, this group, after having for so long maintained an apolitical isolation from democracy, reacted in a markedly political fashion to the new crisis. And that was why it turned to the "new" party.

The successful onslaught of National Socialism on the middle classes begun in 1929 was closely connected with the frequently invoked "anticapitalist sentiments" of these groups. What they wanted was not

---

[3] *The German Catastrophe: Reflections and Recollections* (Cambridge, Mass., 1950), pp. 14–15.

socialism but protection of the small property owners against the growing incursion of big capital; the middle classes, contrary to Marxist expectations, did not come over into the ideological realm of socialism. Generally, in times of crisis the hopeless elements in the middle class tend to listen to fascist slogans, while the working class, on the other hand, tends toward Communism. The conflict between ideas of property and socialization, fought out with particular sharpness in the mixed industrial-agrarian regions, brought a parting of the ways. National Socialist propaganda knew how to operate flexibly and attractively without ignoring the pro-union, anticapitalist sentiments of those middle-class workers toward whom the appeal of the "workers' party" was initially directed. The slogan of the dual fight of the "idealistic, national" people against the decadent "foreign powers" of both proletarian as well as capitalist materialism proclaimed the primacy of national "idealism" over economic materialism.

Growing pressure from both camps, from egalitarian socialism as well as powerful capitalist organizations, put great stress on the middle classes and threatened to split them into hopelessly disenfranchised heaps (*Interessenhaufen*). But here was a program which, in combination with the social-imperialist solution of the *Lebensraum* philosophy, promised to resolve the conflict between economic situation and social prestige in favor of the latter. In the final phase of the Republic, when it had become obvious that no inroads were being made into the working-class parties and their unions—aside from the unemployed— even when scoring major electoral victories, National Socialist mass propaganda was directed almost exclusively toward the middle classes. This concentration on a social group which unquestionably occupied a key position brought the loosely knit middle-of-the-road parties, with the exception of the Center, to the brink of disintegration. Moreover, the NSDAP mobilized many new voters and nonvoters, until it ran up against those sociologically conditioned limits which in 1932 put an end to its further expansion.

Thus, though the NSDAP failed to become the all-inclusive popular movement demanded by its ideology, it did nonetheless become the powerful party of the middle classes, and not only because of its broad economic promises. The heterogeneous, tense nature of middle-class economic thinking set natural limits to the unifying efforts on the economic-ideological plane. Therefore, contemporary socialist interpretations which saw the NSDAP in purely socio-economic terms as a reactionary middle-class and peasant movement considered only one side of the phenomenon and ultimately failed in the task of unmasking it ideologically and effectively halting its progress. What is important is that National Socialist propaganda, with its appeal to the "national idealism" of the middle classes, brought into play attractions and ties which promised an integration beyond the manifold immediate interests.

National Socialism's dynamics and appeal—like Fascism's—did not lie in a socially closed interest movement of the middle classes—that is, a class movement—but, on the contrary, in its emphasis on being a unifying movement of the most varied and antagonistic groups. The fact that it was able to develop this cohesive force across heterogeneous interests, considerations, and feelings is connected with the lack of fervor that accompanied the founding of the Republic in a time of military collapse and fear of a Left revolution.

The predominantly Social Democratic working class was unable, even in the democratic Republic, to rid itself of the charge of being anational, and since the Wilhelminian authoritarian state had not imbued them with a more profound patriotic tradition, the workers confined themselves to sober skepticism. Large segments of the middle classes, on the other hand, once more manifested an urge for the glorifying myth of the fatherland which the Republic, with its manifold international obligations, could not satisfy with sufficient splendor and pomp. National Socialism built on this dissatisfaction. With an eye toward the failure of its labor policy, it did away with earlier concessions to socialist economic ideas and concentrated on the anticapitalism of the lower and middle bourgeoisie. This turn did cause some internal conflicts, such as the splitting off of (Otto) Strasser's "socialist" wing in the summer of 1930. But at the same time, the National Socialist ideologues with their concept of nationalism went far beyond the traditionalist conservative patriotism of the bourgeois middle classes. They elevated a blood-based, profoundly unhistorical idea of nation to an all-encompassing absolute. The activist, revolutionary postwar youth were the pillar of this "nationalism." To them, the "national revolution" did not conjure up glorious memories of the empire or a renewal of "bourgeois" prestige in a leveled society but rather the triumph of the pursuit of unconditional power. For them the war, and not prewar Germany, was the conscious, determining experience and point of orientation. They held the key positions within the NSDAP; the victory of their blood romanticism over the historical patriotism of the bourgeoisie was an expression both of profound misunderstanding and social insecurity as well as of political-ideological confusion and weakness. The vote of the white-collar workers, the middle class, and the peasants for the NSDAP, the most radical opposition party and noisiest anti-Communist movement, primarily was a vote against the existing state, not a vote for the barely defined National Socialist state. The NSDAP supported these voters in their desperate two-front battle against capital and proletariat, so vital a part of fascist movements.

To be sure, every formulation of National Socialist aims, every concrete treatment of the special interests behind the ideological ideal, reawakened the many differences and tensions within the middle class; proposals acceptable to business were looked upon with mistrust by the higher wage earners favoring trade-union ideas. The antisocialist turn of the NSDAP brought with it the danger that the multiplicity of interest groups in its fold might seriously press for clear-cut positions. The question arose how long and in what form the multifarious middle classes could be kept together with nothing more than a propaganda program. In 1932, the limits of the movement and the first signs of its deterioration became apparent, and there were many who believed that with the expected economic upturn or with responsible participation in government, it would face dissolution. But then at the last moment came the leap to power which relieved the party of all democratic responsibility for its political course. In view of the new upturn in the international economic situation, it was seemingly able to fulfill a number of the promises so magnanimously scattered by its propaganda.

The fact that the crisis of the middle classes was not really being solved in the Third Reich through any "corporate new order" no longer mattered. As far as the middle class was concerned, the slogans had done their job in 1933. Using the political tools which it had won in a ruthless power grab, the NSDAP was able to replace the laborious tactics of mass appeal with the tight power-monopoly of the totalitarian governing party.

· · ·

ECONOMY AND SOCIETY IN TRANSITION

At no time did National Socialism develop a consistent economic or social theory. The catchwords of the party program (Articles 13–17) were a disjointed conglomeration of middle-class and semisocialist slogans; Hitler himself referred only to the *Volksgemeinschaft* (people's community) and the end of the class struggle, to war on both Marxism and liberalism; Gottfried Feder, his early mentor, and Feder's "war on finance capital" receded into the background after 1933, together with the "socialist" Strasser wing; and Alfred Rosenberg, the party's chief ideologue, thought it below the dignity of a philosopher to occupy himself with economic and social theories. By the summer of 1933, it had become obvious that not only were the anticapitalist appeals being sacrificed, but also the promises of a corporate order alleged to protect the middle class against socialism as well as against heavy industry and big business. The men who engineered the takeover were not swayed by the dismay of old Nazi ideologues or new Nazis dreaming of a corporate state modeled on Fascist Italy or on a preindustrial society.

Just as the "legal" revolution succeeded in overthrowing a political order with the instruments of that very order, the economic and social realm also was the scene of a unique, paradoxical revolution. It has been called a "dual revolution," that is to say, in the final analysis ideological concepts determined the aim—the fight against bourgeois and industrial society—but at the same time, this fight was conducted with the tools of industry and technology and with the help of the bourgeoisie .This ambivalence had already surfaced in the romantic pessimism of the precursors of National Socialism. As a political organization, and certainly as totalitarian rule, National Socialism made singularly effective use of modern industrial and technological methods. This was a presupposition both for the propagandistic and organizational *Gleichschaltung* [control of the administrative apparatus of the state] and for the plans of expansion. The other basic precept, racism, that product of a pseudo-scientific naturalism resting on irrational foundations, culminated in the technical application of "eugenics" and mass murder. In its methods National Socialism was as up-to-date as any regime: Hitler's reverence of technology, the highly touted Autobahn, the Four-Year Plans and new industrial plants, and the rise of the technician Speer furnish ample proof. Only the bases of the objectives were reactionary and anachronistic: expansion leading to autarchy; race policies to solve the problems of a mixed mobile population; the substitution of the utopia of a people's community for the social stratification of an expanding industrial society.

But these were theoretical problems. The practical problem lay in the contradiction between economic and social theses of revolution and the revisionist and later expansionist revolutionizing of a foreign policy dependent on the mobilization of a political apparatus. As a consequence, the economic and social structures were subject to profound political and administrative encroachment, but they were neither destroyed nor basically reorganized. They were a mixture of private and state capitalism, which under conditions of rearmament and a war economy were increasingly directed from above and outside, but which never became anticapitalistic or antimonopolistic, let alone socialist. For contrary to the promises of the propaganda machine, the middle class and the workers never reaped the promised profits from this development. On the contrary. During 1933 and 1934, the destruction of the trade unions and the reserve army of 5–6 million unemployed were used to make working and wage conditions even more stringent. The programs for increased employment in connection with rearmament benefited big business rather than the small businessman, while the interests of the workers were diverted ideologically to the

political successes of the regime and to the organization of leisure—
a strategy involving strict controls and threats that protests or strikes
would be seen as evidence of Marxist activities. One of the first laws of
the Hitler regime (April 4, 1933) sanctioned the on-the-spot dismissal
of Communist workers and all SPD [Social Democratic Party] and
union shop stewards; this threat effectively hovered over all undesirable workers, who possessed neither representatives nor the right to
strike nor funds.

But at the same time, efforts were made to win labor support and
cooperation by sham reforms. At any rate, in 1933, almost one-third
of the NSDAP membership—750,000—were workers. The NSDAP
was not just another capitalist party, as some oversimplified analysis
maintains. The founding and activity of the German Labor Front
(DAF) must be seen in this light. It had been formed to counteract
the special interests of Nationalist Socialist employees' organizations
(like the NSBO). For this reason, the DAF was put under the jurisdiction of the Chief of Party Organization, Robert Ley, and in November,
1933, the employers' organization was incorporated into it. All industrial enterprises were designated communities of a leader and his
followers; trusteeship councils were set up to advise works managers
and intensify the new harmony; trustees of labor and honor courts
were to supervise these utopian class and unionless work communities
and were empowered to remove not only workers but also entrepreneurs from their own plants. To be sure, the employer once more was
master in his own house, more so than in the days of the unions. But
because of its size and monopoly position, the DAF soon began to
develop its own power claims. Tensions developed between the DAF
and the interests and authority of the employers, as well as with the
planners and directors of the arms programs, the economic and labor
ministries, and the offices of the Four-Year Plan. Here, too, guided
jurisdictional chaos—David Schoenbaum has called it the institutional
Darwinism of National Socialism—ruled. It turned out that the
destruction of the unions and the voluntary dissolution of the employers' organizations could not in themselves make the class and wage
conflicts of an industrial society disappear. That which the DAF
offered as a substitute for freedom—appeals to national pride and the
work ethos of the "soldiers of labor" (thus Ley), the beautification of
work sites as well as cultural and sports installations under the aegis
of the DAF, a "Beauty of Labor" division, vacation trips and various
cultural activities after 1934 through the "Strength through Joy"
("Kraft durch Freude") program, and, finally, the promise of the
Volkswagen (people's car)—could not alter the fact that employer and
employee continued to stand in opposite corners, that with full employment after 1936, workers wanted higher wages, that work performance

in the boom of the arms and construction industries tended to decline, and that all branches of industry and trade suffered under the pressure of price competition and labor shortage. The highly touted "battle of labor" of 1933–35 was won largely by virtue of rearmament and universal military service; however, the regime profited psychologically from this sham success. The fact that this upswing meant "guns instead of butter" (in the words of Göring) was lost in the short-range self-interests of the social partners. But along with full employment and unprofitable weapons, Autobahn, and military construction, there arose classic problems of wage and price policies, balance of payments, raw materials, and the budget. Wages leveled off, conflicts between employers and employees increased, and economic measures alone could not hold the "socialism" of the people's community together.

Beginning in 1936, Göring's Four-Year Plan office drew up far-reaching plans for wage and production controls, regulations barring the hiring of workers employed in other jobs, and the stabilization of working conditions. But the Government was hesitant about restricting the workers' job mobility. Plans to draft workers for war enterprises (Hermann Göring Works, Siegfried Line) were not implemented until June, 1938, and were expanded only after the beginning of the war. Before that time, it would have taken coercion to break worker resistance and this, given the labor shortage, would have had disastrous effects on the economy and rearmament. True, the Gestapo (Geheime Staatspolizei, the secret police) could ship intractable workers to concentration camps, but it could not replace them. The war seemingly solved the problem; in fact, however, it only covered it over. On September 4, 1939, comprehensive wage and price controls were instituted and the existing labor legislation largely modified. But the future saw protests and substantial modifications, proof that the Government was as dependent on a contented labor force as on the cooperation of big business. Of course, in addition to political and social controls, the Government also commanded harsher weapons to control labor and production: the labor and military draft, as well as a classic method of colonial rule—the employment of disenfranchised foreign and slave labor.

The basic principle of National Socialist economic policy was to use the traditional capitalist structure with its competent economic bureaucracy to coordinate and move toward its prime objective: acceleration of rearmament and safeguarding of the food supply. (This policy was modified, however, with the founding in 1937 of far-flung Government enterprises designed to expand and direct the arms potential like the Hermann Göring Works [steel industry] and the Volkswagen Works.) But even during the war, despite a trend toward vast monopolistic organizations, the private capitalist enterprises continued to exist, except that more determined official efforts were made to impose controls. The same spirit that bred profitable mutual-interest alliances with big business and the incidental enrichment of numerous Nazi chieftains also brought the dissolution of medium-sized and small enterprises. Their existence was made dependent on their contribution to the war effort; moreover, they were not able to keep up with the mammoth orders and the rationalization of modern giant plants and trusts. They were also at a disadvantage in the network of connections and influence-peddling; contacts with rival economic bigwigs were a vital part of the game. The Nazi leadership had respect for the top managers who faithfully paid their Adolf Hitler Fund contributions and gained entree into the circle of industrialists around Himmler. Capital concentration continued to increase. The confiscation of Jewish and captured economic holdings, which for reasons of the war economy went mostly to large firms like Krupp, Mannesmann, IG Farben, and Siemens, contributed considerably to this growing concentration.

The involved system of controls and interference and the creation of superagencies (Reich Economic Chamber) and planning councils could not, however, prevent either waste, jurisdictional conflict, corruption, or faulty planning. Detailed studies have shown the gap that existed between objectives and reality in the economic preparations for the war despite the daring financial manipulations of Hjalmar Schacht. The development of synthetics could not alleviate the raw-material shortage, which played a vital part in the decision of industrial circles —whether or not they favored the autarchic ideology of National Socialism—to support and exploit Hitler's thesis of the necessity of expansion. More and more, the view that war was a near certainty for economic reasons as well gained ground. Long before the Hossbach meeting, in which Hitler cited Germany's food and raw-material situation as the compelling reasons for expansion, he had made this point in a secret memorandum on the Four-Year Plan (August, 1936). It was a vicious circle in which the German economy, blindly fixing its sight on greater production and efficiency, followed the regime: rearmament exacerbated the raw-material situation, which made aggression necessary, and which in turn resulted in the need for more arms. Thus from the very beginning, a permanent war economy in the guise of capitalism formed the backdrop of National Socialist economic policy.

In contrast, the solutions promised before 1933 played no role in either economic or social policy: nationalization of trusts, profit-sharing in big business, improvement of the old-age pension system, creation of a viable middle class, and the communalization of large retail enterprises and leasing them to small businessmen, expropriation of large landholdings and their distribution for common use, abolition of land mortgages and loan speculation. None of these partly radical, partly romantic-reactionary reform plans was ever seriously tackled, unless one considers the persecution of Jews, the "Aryanization" of their assets, and the resettlement of German farmers and businesses in occupied territories as fulfillment of these promises. In the course of mobilization for war other roads were taken to realize the social and political ideas of National Socialism. Power politics was the sole determinant in the course being followed: economic recovery as a prerequisite for the consolidation of power; this in turn called for huge sums and material as well as economic expansion, which could be gained most expeditiously through war—which, of course, in the end devoured everything.

Only the objectives, not their realization, were total. It would be misleading to speak of the economic policies of the Third Reich as a smoothly functioning system of planning and controls. But, conversely, to conclude from the obvious discrepancy between objectives and reality that the war mobilization was merely a gigantic hoax designed to deceive the rest of the world would be as misleading as to say that the Nazi foreign policy was simply a conventional method of blackmailing the appeasers. The very fact that a capitalist economy could be led into war in so noneconomic a fashion and mobilized fully only during the war itself (after 1941–42) proves the absolute primacy of the political goals. Here, too, Hitler was anything but an instrument of the capitalist. Their cooperation followed the same pattern found in the governmental and cultural policies: the cooperating experts and economists were instruments and objects, not originators, of this policy. Economic efficiency and primacy of politics, not capitalist, middle-class, or socialist doctrines, determined the course. As never under Socialist governments, the economy was controlled by the Government and subject to the subsidies, retrenchments, plans, and controls of the Nazi regime. The voice of special interests disappeared; assent and cooperation offered the only chance for success—a clearly lopsided alliance of economy and dictatorship, and Hitler, contrary to the predictions of both Right and Left, did not become either capitalism's captive or its servant.

Next to the middle class, agriculture had had the greatest expectations of the new government. And in fact, National Socialism held fast to the romantic-racist peasant ideology even after 1933, despite the enormous contradiction between an agrarian ideal of state and society and accelerated industrialization. Hitler's, and particularly Himmler's, visions of the future (one of Himmler's offices was the chairmanship of the League of German Agriculturists [Reichsbund Deutscher Diplomlandwirte]), saw the issue of *Lebensraum* essentially as a battle for the establishment of Germanic farm settlements in the East and de-urbanization in line with the "blood and soil" ideology. One of the many paradoxical consequences of Nazi rule is the fact that its policies and ultimate defeat brought the exact opposite: less space and more industrialization, yet greater economic progress than ever before. A cynic willing to ignore the victims might speak of the cunning of reason, by which a rule of horror with anachronistic goals accelerated the modernization of Germany.

Ideological and political-economic motives intertwined. Rural life as the *völkisch*-racist "source" was held up as a model against urban civilization; expansion via settlement simultaneously was to serve as strategic protection against the "East." It was a rather revolutionary though romantic conception, extending from the pre-Nazi ideologists to the aims of the SS state and its repopulating policies. Germanic race policies, a European political economy, a "new aristocracy of blood and soil" (Darré)—these central ideas of a future German empire were part of the Nazi agrarian ideology. And yet, National Socialism was by no means a rural movement, even though it had profited from the large influx of rural voters in the years 1930–33. Farmers were not too strongly represented in the party, and they were greatly underrepresented in the SS, so committed to future resettlement. In this area, just as in the program for the middle class, the difference between ideology and practical politics soon became apparent. But unlike the short-lived middle-class ideology, the party's agrarian ideology remained a political objective which, in close alliance with the politics of war and expansion, was destined to lend support to the Nazi reorganization of Europe.

Like the rest of the economy and industry, agriculture after the *Gleichschaltung* of its organizations was made subservient to the political objectives through market and price controls. The more far-reaching plans for reform, on the other hand, remained incipient. Neither the entailed farm laws, introduced with great fanfare, nor the fragmentary measures for lifting indebtedness, for redistribution, and for resettlement brought alleviation, let alone the reagrarianization of Germany. Contrary to the anti-urban propaganda, which at any rate conflicted with industrial mobilization, the population of the big cities and industrial centers continued to grow, particularly in those cities with strategic chemical industries; between 1933 and 1938, the populations of Magdeburg, Halle, Halberstadt, Dessau, Bitterfeld, and Bernburg more than doubled. And the population of the future "world capital city" Berlin, in megalomaniacal contradiction to the de-urbanization ideology, was even expected to reach 10 million.

In fact, many fewer new farms came into being in the Third Reich than in the Weimar Republic; the opening up of land for military and industrial purposes (not to mention highways) clearly had priority. In line with the autarchic goals, imports of agricultural products were reduced, and thanks to substantial subsidies, the farmers could count on firmer prices and better incomes. But in contrast to the wages and profits of industry, farm income did not keep step with the growth of national income after 1935. After a brief recovery spurt, the indebtedness of the small and medium-sized farms in particular continued to increase; technological improvements and mechanization made as little headway as their precondition—a far-reaching consolidation of landholdings—and the shortage of farm labor increasingly made itself felt. In profound contradiction to the romantic agrarian ideology, agriculture lagged far behind the general standard of living, bringing with it a movement to the cities, the sale of farms, and declining agricultural production. The much-bemoaned "flight from the land" set new records between 1933 and 1938; the exodus has been estimated at almost 1 million. A magnanimous decree "for the support of the rural population" (July, 1938), granting greater agricultural subsidies and credits, also did not bring an increase in farm production; the decline of farming, a consequence of National Socialist economic and rearmament policies, continued. Not the highly touted settlement movement but the ideologically undesirable landholdings of the Junkers shaped agricultural life east of the Elbe, though there, too, the continuing pressure of political planning and decisions made itself felt. Instead of reversing the trend of the industrial era, the Nazi power and war policies accelerated it, and the failure of the expansion finally sealed it. In the agricultural sector, the Nazi regime was unable to solve the built-in problems which it had inherited from the German economic crises of 1918 and 1929. To be sure, the dynamization and mobilization of German society, its political regimentation and psychological orientation toward war, substantially furthered Nazi economic policies. The help proffered by "unpolitical" experts and interested parties in business and bureaucracy dazzled by feelings of superiority and short-range prospects of success proved invaluable.

The social aspects of the political revolution of 1933 initially were determined by a negative aim shared by Nazi leaders as well as followers: the rejection of the status quo and the chance to overhaul everything. The conservative-national partners believed that these changes were directed only against the democratic-republican establishment of Weimar. But the National Socialist thrust went much further. It was revolutionary not only in the utopia of the "people's community" but also in the reality of a changed elite structure and a pseudo-egalitarian leveling of all strata under the leader principle. The emergence of youth, social awareness, productive society—those were the battle cries of the "newcomers" against the old, outmoded "system." The Third Reich saw itself as a unique system, and its new order clamorously called on two groups—peasants and workers—above all others. This invocation was given immediate expression in the institutionalization of appropriate holidays and mass demonstrations at harvest festivals (the slogan: "Blood and Soil") and on the "Day of National Labor" (the slogan: "Workers of Brawn and Brain"). Here both the romantic, anti-urban and the pseudo-proletarian, technological elements of Nazi ideology asserted themselves; the two met in the military ideal, which through such slogans as "soldiers of labor" and "battle of labor" was integrated into civilian life and made part of the combative and leader principle. A verbal "social revolution" took place, and under its sign both the old anticapitalism and the diverse new body of supporters could be manipulated. "Bourgeois," "capitalist," "intellectual" continued to be terms of derision, synonyms for reactionary; the reviled past became the "bourgeois epoch."

But the profound changes in the relationship of state and economy and of labor and capital took place on another plane. The aim of the much-invoked socialism was not genuine socialization or expropriation but a change in the social consciousness, unconditional cooperation with the political regime, and the leadership's irrevocable right to encroach and control. The right to property, like all other civil rights, became a function of dedication to the new state, and in this sense "national socialism" and "good" capitalism were held to be not only compatible but practically identical. In contrast, Western capitalism was derided as plutocracy in the manner of the old anticapitalist slogans, just as "German socialism" was contrasted to Marxism and Soviet socialism. The basic concept underlying all Gleichschaltung and mobilization plans was that of the equality of all "national comrades" regardless of class, limited only by the politically determined function of the leader principle. In this respect, the Nazi system, particularly during the war, did in fact help to remove social barriers and in a way played a modernizing role. The persistent myth about the "good" aspects of National Socialism is based on this no less than on the technical achievements. At the time, this point proved a persuasive propaganda issue.

The Nationalist Socialist system like no other demonstrated the superior ability of an ideology, however vague, to shape minds, whatever the social reality. Now every German had to be socialistic in the sense of "social." The Winterhilfe (Winter Help) and countless other fund-raising drives, national labor competitions and model plants, "Strength through Joy" and nationwide one-pot meals, a people's car for everyone, and finally the classless society of the Hitler Youth and party organizations, of the DAF and Labor Service—all these active manifestations of the "people's community" were undeniably effective, even though they were purposeful tools of control, coordination, and war mobilization and relied on more or less gentle coercion. Designations like "worker" or "entrepreneur" were no longer supposed to indicate class differences, only functions. Not status but principles allegedly mattered; the model was Adolf Hitler, the man of the people, who lived simply and turned down honorary doctorates.

The position of women in this "new" social system also remained paradoxical. As a decidedly male movement, National Socialism sought to contain the emancipation of woman and reduce her role to biological and familial functions. In line with the anti-urban, antimodernist ideology of National Socialism, this generally was understood to mean motherhood, housework, and at best "feminine" professions. Politics, at any rate, was not a suitable field for women. The task of the Nazi women's organization was to lead women back into the traditional realms of the specifically feminine, to their "natural" duties and rights. Thus, the first step in the effort to create jobs in 1933 was to ease out women from the labor market and the universities. The introduction of the so-called household year, marriage credits, and child bonuses was part of the anti-emancipation campaign. But with the growing labor shortage after 1935, the anachronism of these efforts became patently obvious, above all in regard to unmarried women. They were reabsorbed into the labor process and continued their impotent role in the labor market as during the Weimar Republic. In addition, labor service for women was expanded. At first (from 1936) voluntary, and later (from January, 1939) compulsory, women under twenty-five, except those in essential jobs, served one-year labor terms, allegedly to alleviate the labor shortage on the land and in the factories, but in reality in order to involve them fully in the mobilized economy. The number of working women in 1938 rose to 5.2 million, from 4.24 million in 1933 and 4.52 million in 1936. An increasing number of women were employed in industry. Among women there also was a growing trend to leave farms and migrate to the cities. With the beginning of the war, the number of women in the universities also increased.

In one respect, however, Nazi ideology remained consistent: Women's opportunities for advancement were much smaller, and they were paid incomparably less than men for performing the same work. They were also poorly represented in the civil service, although the war brought some loosening there. But the original intention—the ousting of women from the modern labor process—was defeated by the consequences of progressive industrialization and social and economic mobilization. Woman's economic emancipation continued and even gained momentum in the course of the war. True, the political rights of women in the Third Reich were limited to plebiscitary assent, but that essentially was true of everyone. The undesired social by-products of modernization implicit in the Nazi war policies affected women as well as men. Thus, in its fashion, the totalitarian state contributed substantially to the social mobility and equality which wrought changes in the social structure.

The paradox which enabled Nazi legal and social theorists to hail the equality of all "national comrades" and simultaneously champion a sharply defined, military-aristocratic command structure was made possible above all by two major organizational tenets: the leader principle in place of electoral and majority decisions, and the battle or war community as the prototype of the new social order. Labor and military service as the training ground of a classless nation not only were to be the visible supports of militarization but also models of the inner uniformity and mobilization of the "people's community." The single act of rearmament hit two targets, and the war community was already being offered and prepared as an answer to the social problem. These factors contributed substantially to changing German society both organizationally and psychologically, even though in fact the basic structures of income distribution, capitalism, and bureaucratic autocracy remained. To the many thousands who before 1933 either had become unemployed or had never been employed at all, the loss of trade-union organizations and social freedom was, in the final analysis, less important than the fact that with Hitler came full employment, mobility, and opportunities for advancement—regardless of the methods or consequences. This argument proved effective then, as it still does today; it served to sustain a regime which the great majority of workers had opposed in 1933.

From 1935 on, all employed persons had to register in labor offices, were increasingly regimented, and, as "soldiers of labor," were subjugated to the needs of rearmament, yet the pseudo-military order ideology of the regime profited psychologically from this. Neither labor nor social policy improved measurably—Autobahns and rearmament gobbled up too much—but both were effectively manipulated and used. Political spectacles and Strength through Joy "care" provided for leisure-time activities; thus, in 1938, Ley was able to announce triumphantly that the private citizen had ceased to exist; only sleep was still a private affair, and no longer could anyone do or not do whatever he wanted. It was a renunciation of freedom in favor of the semblance of social order, security, and unity. At what cost and with what results was another matter.

Franz Neumann

20

Behemoth:
The Structure and Practice of
National Socialism, 1933–1944

THE MONOPOLISTIC ECONOMY
Property and Contract
                               To understand the nature of the
National Socialist economic system, a few considerations on the relation between property and contract will prove helpful. What is capitalism? How do we define it? Many identify capitalism with freedom
of trade and contract, that is, with free competition. Capitalism is
defined as an economy that is continuously maintained by the free
initiative of a large number of entrepreneurs competing in a free market. It is thereby identified with one phase of its development, competitive capitalism. In that phase, free competition is held to be the
distinguishing mark. This theory of capitalism is to a certain extent
the classical one, though it has highly significant differences.

We propose to illustrate the nature of the economic system by an
examination of the institution of property. By an institution, we mean
an authoritarian or co-operative enduring association of men or of
men and property, for the continuation of social life. This definition
is purely descriptive. It has nothing to do with institutionalist philosophies, with pluralism, neo-Thomism, or syndicalism. Our definition
covers all kinds of institutions: family, property, foundations, et cetera.
Above all, it defines the major institution of modern society, private
property in the means of production. Property, for a lawyer, is merely
a subjective right that one man has against all others. It endows the
proprietor with absolute defensive rights. The scope of man's power
over the things he owns is, in principle, unlimited. The owner is a
sovereign.

But the sociologist has to distinguish between various types of
property. The man who owns a house in which he lives, furniture
which he uses, clothes which he wears, food which he eats, an auto-

mobile which he drives, has no other power than the direct possession of the things he owns. He does not by virtue of his ownership control other men's lives. Houses, food, clothes, and automobiles are not institutions, are not intended to endure. They disappear or become valueless as they are consumed or used.

There is, however, a second type of property which is an institution, because it is an enduring and authoritarian organization for the perpetuation and reproduction of society: property of the means of production. In our language, domination over means of consumption and means of production is called by the same name: "property"; the term has thus become the legal mask behind which the owner of the means of production exercises power over other men. The term property (and ownership) never indicates what kind of object and what kind of power lies behind it, whether it is restricted to control over things or whether it also gives control over the fate of men. Property in the means of production gives power: power over workers, power over the consumers, power over the state. Property in the means of production is enduring, it aids in the continuous reproduction of society, it is the primary institution of modern society.

According to liberal ideas, if society is continuously to reproduce itself, there must be a free market. The prime requisites of the free market are free entrepreneurs, freedom of contract, and freedom of trade. The owner must be able to sell and to purchase, to lend and to borrow, to hire and to dismiss. Freedom of contract is, therefore, a supplementary or auxiliary guarantee of private property. It makes it possible for the owner of the means of production to produce and distribute. A competitive society must also be based on freedom of trade, the right to carry on one's business without interference and to establish a competing business. Freedom of trade is therefore another supplementary or auxiliary guarantee of property during the era of free competition. It, too, aids in the reproduction of society. In the process of competition, unfit competitors are thrown out, new establishments arise. Disturbances in equilibrium eliminate entrepreneurs who are not sufficiently rational in the conduct of their business; higher profits in one branch attract capital from other branches, thereby preserving the dynamic quality of a competitive society. Freedom of trade and freedom of contract are thus integral elements in a competitive society.

Hence property is surrounded by supplementary and auxiliary guarantees and by supplementary and auxiliary institutions, which make the operation of this major institution possible. They are at the service of the major institution, property, and are, in consequence, changed when the institution changes its function. Thus they are not merely juristic categories, as they are conceived to be today. The natural lawyers of the seventeenth century and the classical economists of the eighteenth century clearly realized that freedom of contract and freedom of trade are not simply legal categories but exercise specific social functions. Present-day apologists of economic liberalism maintain that freedom of contract implies the right to establish industrial combinations, to erect cartels, concerns, and trusts. They believe that freedom of trade exists even when a branch of industry is so completely monopolized that freedom of trade becomes a mere formal right. They maintain that competition implies the right to eliminate competing businesses and to establish the prerogative of a monopolistic group.

This was not the view held by the classical economists. "One individual must never prefer himself so much even to any other individual as to hurt or injure that other in order to benefit himself, though the benefit of the one should be much greater than the hurt or injury of the other." "In the race for wealth and honor and preferment, each may run as hard as he can and strain every nerve and every muscle in order to outstrip all his competitors, but if he should justle or throw down any of them, the indulgence of the spectators is entirely at an end." In these statements, Adam Smith introduces a distinction between two kinds of competition, one based on efficiency and the other based on the destruction of the competitor. He does not tolerate unfettered competition, since, in the theory of Adam Smith, competition is more than a right of the entrepreneur: it is the basic device for the continuous reproduction of society on an ever higher level. But this necessarily presupposes the absence of monopolies. Freedom of contract does not imply the right to establish industrial combinations; freedom of contract is the form of "free commodities." Where the commodities are not free, where they are monopolized, governmental interference must take place. "For a free commodity . . . there is no occasion for this [governmental interference], but it is necessary for bakers who may agree among themselves to make the quantity and prices what they please."

Yet the assumptions under which the classical economists are willing to guarantee freedom are still wider in character. They refer to the basic institution of society, to private property. Monopolies are repudiated as incompatible with the economic and social system, exceptions being allowed only for colonies, and even here only for a transitional period. As for the laws passed during the mercantilist period for protecting monopolies—"Like the laws of Draco, these laws may be said to be written in blood." Even the joint stock corporation is rejected in principle and allowed only for four economic activities: banking, insurance, the building and navigation of canals, and the water supply of great cities. It is characteristic of the profound sociological insight of Adam Smith that he considers joint stock corporations legitimate only because in these activities the initiative of the entre-preneur has become unnecessary since the economic activity has been reduced to a mere routine.

The mechanism of the classical system is based, therefore, on the assumption of a large number of entrepreneurs of about equal strength, freely competing with each other on the basis of freedom of contract and freedom of trade, with the entrepreneur investing his capital and his labor for the purpose of his economic ends, and bearing the economic risks involved.

In this stage of society, freedom of contract was indeed the means by which society was held together. The contract was then the form through which the owner exercised his liberty and it was at the same time the means of ending the isolation in which each owner finds him-self. "To bring about that I may own property, not only by means of a thing and my own subjective will but by means of another will and thereby a common will—this constitutes the sphere of contract." In Hegel's words, therefore, contract is the form in which society recog-nizes property and by which the property owners constitute society.

It is characteristic of the later development of capitalism that it com-pletely divorced the juristic categories of freedom of contract and free-dom of trade from the socio-economic background and thereby made the juristic categories absolute. Freedom of contract, the means by which free competition was secured, became the device by which it has been destroyed. Legal theory and practice, even more so in Europe than in the United States, separated the legal notion "freedom of trade" from the socio-economic requirements. Freedom of contract became the means of and the justification for the formation of indus-trial combinations, announcing the end of free competition. In the same way, freedom of trade degenerated into a mechanism for main-taining economic privileges and prerogatives. Its existence was asserted even in those branches of industry in which, because of the immense capital investment in one plant, no outsider could hope to establish a competing business, since he could not put up the necessary capital. Freedom of trade was perverted into a slogan for the defense of eco-nomic prerogatives and against state intervention.

This is one side of the development, but there is a second which is perhaps still more characteristic. Freedom of contract, although long disputed, implies the right to form trade unions and to oppose the power of the monopolist by the collective power of labor. Freedom of trade also implies the right of any entrepreneur to leave a combina-tion and to re-establish his economic freedom, thereby endangering monopolistic possessions. Although it has lost much of its actual con-tent, it still allows the establishment of competing business, once again endangering monopolistic privileges. These rights assume an especially dangerous form of monopolistic privileges in periods of recession and depression. The more perfect and rigid the structure of the economy becomes, the more sensitive it is to cyclical changes. A severe depression will inevitably shatter monopolistic positions. Cartels will be dissolved, outsiders will remain aloof, labor unions will fight off cuts in wages, protected by the sanctity of contracts. In such periods, the free contract, the freedom to keep aloof from the monopolists, turns into a major weapon against them.

Moreover, the new technology requires enormous investments, which involve risks and may give but uncertain returns. Only rich and powerful corporations will be able to make such investments, and their willingness to do so will depend upon what protection they receive—against cut-throat competition and the chiseler, even against competition as such. They may—and do—even demand specific guarantees from the state, in the form of guarantees of profit or turnover, of permission to write off investments in a short time, even in the form of outright subsidies. Outsiders, new competitors, labor unions—all these manifestations of freedom of trade and contract are then a nuisance. They must be destroyed.

For both sides, therefore—for the large masses and the small businessman on the one hand and the monopolistic powers on the other—state intervention in economic life becomes the major problem. The large masses and the small businessman will call in the state machinery for their protection. They will demand interference in the freedom of contract and freedom of trade in order to halt monopolization or even to dissolve existing industrial combines. By that demand they are merely drawing the consequences of the views of the classical economists. But in this situation monopolists will demand abrogation of freedom of contract and freedom of trade. They will insist that the right of industrial enterprises to leave cartels or to stay aloof from them means ruin for the economic system. They will point out that the freedom of labor to organize increases the costs of production and thereby the price of commodities. They will therefore demand complete abrogation of economic liberty.

In the period of monopolization, the new auxiliary guarantee of property is no longer the contract but the administrative act, the form in which the state interferes. But because that is so, it is the form and the content of the interventionist measure that now assumes supreme importance. Who is to interfere and on whose behalf becomes the most important question for modern society. The possession of the state machinery is thus the pivotal position around which everything else revolves. This is the only possible meaning of primacy of politics over economics. Shall the state crush monopolistic possessions, shall it restrict them for the sake of the masses, or shall interference be used to strengthen the monopolistic position, to aid in the complete incorporation of all business activities into the network of industrial organizations? Shall the state become the weapon by which the masses will be made completely subservient to the policies of the industrial empires within it?

The aims of the monopolistic powers could not be carried out in a system of political democracy, at least not in Germany. The Social Democratic party and the trade unions, though they had lost their aggressive militancy, were still powerful enough to defend their gains. Their defensive strength made it impossible to place the whole machinery of the state at the service of one particular group in society. Similarly, the National Socialist party could not possibly carry out its economic policy on a democratic basis. Its propaganda and program were ostensibly aimed at protecting the small and medium-scale entrepreneur, handicraftsman, and trader—that is, those very groups that have suffered most under the National Socialist regime. The complete subjugation of the state by the industrial rulers could only be carried out in a political organization in which there was no control from below, which lacked autonomous mass organizations and freedom of criticism. It was one of the functions of National Socialism to suppress and eliminate political and economic liberty by means of the new auxiliary guarantees of property, by the command, by the administrative act, thus forcing the whole economic activity of Germany into the network of industrial combinations run by the industrial magnates.

The German economy of today has two broad and striking characteristics. It is a monopolistic economy—*and* a command economy. It is a private capitalistic economy, regimented by the totalitarian state. We suggest as a name best to describe it, "Totalitarian Monopoly Capitalism."

. . .

THE RULING CLASS

If one believes that Germany's economy is no longer capitalistic under National Socialism, it is easy to believe further that her society has become classless. This is the thesis of the late Emil Lederer. A brief analysis of his book will serve to introduce our discussion of the new German society.[1]

Lederer rejects attempts to define National Socialism as the last line of defense of capitalism, as the rule of the strong man, as the revolt of the middle classes, as domination by the army, or as the ascendency

---

[1] The book referred to by Emil Lederer is *State of the Masses: The Threat of the Classless Society* (New York, 1940).—*Ed.*

of the untalented. For him, it is a "modern political system which rests on amorphous masses." It is the masses "which sweep the dictator into power and keep him there" (page 18). The masses are therefore the actors, not the tools of a ruling class.

But who are the masses? They are the opposite of classes. They can be united solely by emotions (page 31); they tend to "burst into sudden action" (page 38), and being amorphous, they must be integrated by a leader who can articulate their emotions (page 39). As the very opposite of classes, the masses make up a classless society. The policy of National Socialism is to transfer a class-stratified society into masses by keeping the latter in a state of perpetual tension (page 105). Since the regime must also satisfy the material demands of the masses, it goes in for large-scale public spending and thus achieves full employment. National Socialism realizes that "people are filled with envy, with hatred for the rich and successful" (pages 110–11). The emotions can best be kept alive in the field of foreign affairs; for an aggressive foreign policy and preparation for foreign war prevent "the reawakening of thinking and of articulation into social groups" (page 123).

National Socialist society is thus composed of the ruling party and the amorphous masses (page 127). All other distinctions are removed. "It is on this psychological basis that the Fascist party has been built up. With their success they attract active mass-men who then are kept in a state of emotion and cannot return to their former ways of life. Even family cohesion is broken, the pulverization of society is complete. Masses make dictators, and dictators make masses the continuing basis of the state" (page 131). That is why the social stratification of society is of the utmost importance and why the Marxist theory of a classless society becomes so dangerous (page 138). National Socialism has completely destroyed the power of social groups and has established a classless society.

Were Lederer's analysis correct, our earlier discussion would be completely wrong. Social imperialism would then be not a device to ensnare the masses but an articulation of the spontaneous longing of the masses. Racism would not be the concern of small groups alone but would be deeply imbedded in the masses. Leadership adoration would be a genuine semi-religious phenomenon and not merely a device to prevent insight into the operation of the social-economic mechanism. Capitalism, finally, would be dead, since all particular groups have been destroyed and only leaders and masses remain.

Lederer is wrong, however, though a little of the truth sifts into some of his formulations. Occasionally one feels that even he realizes that the so-called spontaneity of the masses and their active participation in National Socialism are a sham and that the role of the people is merely to serve as an instrument of the ruling group. The problem is perhaps the most difficult of all in an analysis of National Socialism. The difficulties lie not only in the paucity of information and the inadequacy of the sociological categories but also in the extraordinarily complicated character of the social relations themselves. Class structure and social differentiation are not identical—failure to recognize this point is the basic error underlying Lederer's analysis. A society may be divided into classes and yet not be socially differentiated in any other way. On the other hand, a classless society may have sharp differentiations.

The essence of National Socialist social policy consists in the acceptance and strengthening of the prevailing class character of German society, in the attempted consolidation of its ruling class, in the atomization of the subordinate strata through the destruction of every autonomous group mediating between them and the state, in the creation of a system of autocratic bureaucracies interfering in all human relations. The process of atomization extends even to the ruling class in part. It goes hand in hand with a process of differentiation within the mass party and within society that creates reliable élites in every sector. Through these élites, the regime plays off one group against the other and enables a minority to terrorize the majority.

National Socialism did not create the mass-men; it has completed the process, however, and destroyed every institution that might interfere. Basically, the transformation of men into mass-men is the outcome of modern industrial capitalism and of mass democracy. More than a century ago the French counter-revolutionaries, de Maistre and Bonald, and the Spaniard Donoso Cortes, asserted that liberalism, Protestantism, and democracy, which they hated, bore the seeds of the emotionally motivated mass-man and would eventually give birth to the dictatorship of the sword. Mass democracy and monopoly capitalism have brought the seeds to fruition. They have imprisoned man in a network of semi-authoritarian organizations controlling his life from birth to death, and they have begun to transform culture into propaganda and salable commodities.

National Socialism claims to have stopped this trend and to have created a society differentiated not by classes but according to occupation and training. That is absolutely untrue. In fact, National Socialism has carried to its highest perfection the very development it pretends to attack. It has annihilated every institution that under democratic conditions still preserves remnants of human spontaneity: the privacy of the individual and of the family, the trade union, the political party, the church, the free leisure organization. By atomizing the subject population (and to some extent the rulers as well), National Socialism has not eliminated class relations; on the contrary, it has deepened and solidified the antagonisms.

National Socialism must necessarily carry to an extreme the one process that characterizes the structure of modern society, bureaucratization. In modern anti-bureaucratic literature, this term means little more than the numerical growth of public servants, and especially of civil servants. Society is pictured as composed of free men and autonomous organizations on the one hand and of a bureaucratic caste, on the other hand, which takes over more and more political power. The picture is inaccurate, for society is not wholly free and unbureaucratic nor is the public bureaucracy the sole bearer of political and social power.

Bureaucratization, correctly understood, is a process operating in both public and private spheres, in the state as well as in society. It means that human relations lose their directness and become mediated relations in which third parties, public or private functionaries seated more or less securely in power, authoritatively prescribe the behavior of man. It is a highly ambivalent process, progressive as well as reactionary. The growth of bureaucracy in public life is not necessarily incompatible with democracy if the aims of the democracy are not limited to the preservation of individual rights, but also include the furtherance of certain social goals. Even in the social sphere the growth of private organizations is not entirely retrogressive. It brings some kind of order into an anarchic society and thereby rationalizes human relations that would otherwise be irrational and accidental.

If members of a trade union decide to change their labor conditions, they do so by accepting the recommendation of their officials, in whose hands the decision is left. When a political party formulates some policy, it is the party hierarchy that does so. In athletic organizations, the machinery of presidents, vice-presidents, secretaries, and treasurers goes into operation in arranging matches and carrying on the other activities of the group. This process of mediation and depersonalization extends to culture as well. Music becomes organized in the hands of professional secretaries who need not be musicians. The radio prescribes the exact amount of culture to be digested by the public, how much classical and how much light music, how much talk and how much news. The powers extend to the most intimate relations of man, to the family. There are organizations for large families and for bachelors, birth-control associations, advisory councils for the promotion of family happiness, consumers' co-operatives, giant food chain stores making a farce of the consumers' supposedly free choice.

There is, in short, a huge network of organizations covering almost every aspect of human life, each run by presidents and vice-presidents and secretaries and treasurers, each employing advertising agencies and publicity men, each out to interfere with, and to act as the mediator in, the relations between man and man. Civil liberties lose many of the functions they had in a liberal society. Even the exercise of civil rights tends more and more to be mediated by private organizations. Whether it is a problem of defense in a political trial or protection of the rights of labor or the fight against unjust taxation, the average man, lacking sufficient means, has no other choice but to entrust his rights to some organization. Under democratic conditions, such mediation does not destroy his rights, as a rule, since the individual still has a choice between competing organizations. In a totalitarian society, however, even if his rights are still recognized on paper, they are completely at the mercy of private bureaucrats.

What National Socialism has done is to transform into authoritarian bodies the private organizations that in a democracy still give the individual an opportunity for spontaneous activity. Bureaucratization is the complete depersonalization of human relations. They become abstract and anonymous. On this structure of society, National Socialism imposes two ideologies that are completely antagonistic to it: the ideology of the community and the leadership principle.

Nicos Poulantzas

21

Fascism
and Social Class

CONTRADICTIONS AMONG RULING CLASSES
AND SECTIONS
The process of development and
the advent of fascism correspond to a state of intensification and utter
exacerbation of the internal contradictions within the ruling classes
and sections of these classes: this constitutes an important element of
the political crisis under consideration.

It can be explained only in terms of a clear understanding of alliances among classes and sections of classes at the level of political rule.
In a social structure consisting of many social classes and epecially in
a capitalist social structure where the bourgeoisie is subdivided into
sections of classes, political rule is not the exclusive domain of any
single class or section. There is a special alliance of several classes or
sections of classes, which I have defined elsewhere as the "ruling
bloc." Thus, the contradictions within the ruling classes and sections
of classes have a significant and often determining influence on the
form of the state and the regime.

Concerning the contradictions among ruling classes and sections
of classes in the case of fascism, it should also be pointed out that
these contradictions are not merely confined, as it often happens, to
the economic level. In the fascistization process, the exacerbation of
the internal contradictions within the ruling bloc is revealed by a
characteristic extension of these contradictions to the political and
ideological levels: The effect of this upon the bloc is a deep crisis of
ideology and party representativeness.

While the fascistization process is characterized by the fact that the
political struggle of the ruling bloc against the masses plays a more
dominant role than the economic struggle—what we might term a
process of overt politicalization of the class struggle by the ruling bloc
—its truly specific feature is the spread of the impact of this politicalization to the contradictions within the bloc itself. This is a remarkable

feature, because any politicalization of this kind does not necessarily have this effect: indeed, the process most often results in the rewelding of the ruling bloc in the face of a common enemy.

THE CRISIS OF SUPREMACY

In the case of the fascistization process and of fascism itself, no ruling class or section of a class appears able to impose its leadership upon the other classes and sections within the ruling bloc, either by means of its own political organization or through the parliamentary democratic state.

For in fact, and this is true of any alliance, the ruling bloc is not usually made up of classes or sections of equal importance sharing scraps of power. It can function normally only to the extent that a dominant class or section imposes its special rule on the other members of the alliance in power—in other words, to the extent that this class succeeds in asserting its supremacy over the others and in consolidating them under its wing.

The inability of a class or section to assert its supremacy—that is, in the final analysis, the inability of the ruling alliance to surmount by itself its own intensified contradiction—is the characteristic circumstance of fascism. This inability to exercise supremacy within the ruling bloc is also linked to the supremacy crisis experienced by the ruling bloc and its members with regard to their political rule over the social structure as a whole.

Changes in Supremacy

Apart from this situation within the ruling bloc, fascism also corresponds to a complete reorganization, and a very specific one, of this bloc. It involves: (1) a change in the relationship of forces within the alliance, a redistribution of the respective weights of the forces that constitute it; and (2) the establishment, through fascism, of the supremacy of a new section of a class within the ruling bloc, the section of finance capital, or even of big monopoly capital.

While the outset of the fascistization process is marked by unstable supremacy, a stage in which various classes or sections take turns exercising supremacy, followed by a stage of literally impossible supremacy, the coming to power of fascism is characterized by the establishment of the political supremacy of a section that had never before played this role.

This function of fascism, which is related to a shift in political supremacy (as distinguished from the already strong domination of big capital in the economic field), was more or less ignored by the Comintern, which merely lumped together economic domination and political supremacy: "Fascist dictatorship does not show any difference ... from bourgeois democracy, where the dictatorship of finance capital is also achieved."

The Political Parties and the Breaking of the Links
Between the Representatives and the Represented

The circumstances of fascism and the beginning of the fascistization process correspond, as far as the ruling bloc is concerned, to what we would define as a crisis of party representation—which is a remarkable feature of this type of political crisis. In other words, there is a breaking of relationships both in terms of representation (in the state system) and of organization between the ruling classes and sections of classes and their political parties. The significance of this feature has been pointed out both by Marx, in his analysis of the situation in France before the coming to power of Louis Bonaparte, and by Gramsci: "How do these conflict situations arise between 'representatives and represented' which, from the party level . . . are reflected in the whole body of the state, and reinforce the corresponding situation of bureaucratic power?"

It is a significant fact that the traditional political parties of the bourgeoisie and its allies have at no time totally accepted fascism, and have even at times (but always too late) tried openly to oppose its advent. Whenever these parties have agreed to form governments with the participation of the fascists, they have done so only with the stated and pursued aim of controlling the rise of the fascist parties— that is, of getting rid of them after having used them against the masses.

But the bourgeois political parties have not enjoyed the support of the classes and sections they have been supposed to represent. This does not mean, as is often claimed, that the bourgeoisie and its allies as a whole unanimously and openly supported the accession of fascism to power throughout the fascistization process; it was rather the deep political confusion of the ruling bloc that enabled the fascist party, openly supported by the section of big monopoly capital, to fill, step by step and turning point after turning point, the void created by the breaking of the representative-represented link with the traditional political parties. As a result, the bourgeoisie and its allies as a whole passively witnessed the elimination of these parties by the fascist party. Nor does all this mean that nothing was happening within the traditional political parties—that is, that they remained faithful to their role in the parliamentary democratic form of the state; far from it.

In fact, the beginning of the fascistization process corresponds to a turn of the bourgeois parties toward the extremism of the "emergency state." The solution aimed at by these parties, however, was a toughening of the state different from that which would have enabled them to maintain or restore their leadership on the political scene, or even ultimately to achieve the military dictatorship solution.

Let us come back to the question of the breaking of the representative-represented link. This gradual breaking first affected the "representation" relationship. With the onset of the fascistization process, while the parliamentary democracy form of the state seemingly remains intact, the relationship between ruling classes and sections, on the one hand, and the state on the other is no longer established mainly by means of the political parties, but becomes an increasingly direct one. This has the following results: (1) The institution alongside these parties of a series of secret networks that act as the true transmission belt of power and decisions: this process extends from the emergence of private pressure groups and militias as the nuclei of political reorganization to the setting up of genuine para-state networks, (2) An increased role for the state apparatus itself—army, police, courts, government bureaucracy—that short-circuits, in a way, the role of the formal administration, characteristically circumvents the established legal system, and shifts real power from the place where these parties, now mere political cliques, still express themselves (that is, Parliament) to the state apparatus, in the strict sense of the word. In short, we witness what can be termed, by analogy with the "dual power" that characterizes a revolutionary situation, a characteristic discrepancy between formal power and real power that is specific to a political crisis.

Therefore, this process should not be reduced to a mere modification of the legislative-executive relationship—that is, to a mere transition from a parliamentary state to a strong state dominated by the executive. This change which characterizes, with some variations, the transition from the liberal state form of competitive capitalism to the interventionist state form of monopoly capitalism is not in itself identical with a typical fascistization process, even though there are traits common to both because fascism itself belongs to the imperialist stage. The important factor here seems to be that the characteristic discrepancy between real and formal power is a direct result of the breaking of the representative-represented link. It is these two phenomena that do not always occur in every change from a liberal state to an interventionist one.

Finally, the break between representatives and represented also affects the organizational relationship. The very bitter struggle among the various political parties of the ruling classes and sections of classes seems to deviate in its objectives from the real political contradictions. The parties seem to confine themselves to objectives arising from economic contradictions alone, these contradictions assuming at the same time the form of personal "quarrels" between politicians. In so doing, they lose sight of the concrete means of working for their general political class interest. Marx and Lenin have aptly described the pitiful situation of the bourgeois political leaders, unable to organize politically the alliance of the classes and sections of classes they represent or their supremacy, cut off from their constituents, expiring puppets of parliamentary cretinism, whose delirium is spurred by their fear of the working class. It is a situation which, before the advent of fascism, often gave rise to particularly nonsensical episodes.

Last but not least, throughout the fascistization process, the stages of unstable and impossible supremacy are marked by a proliferation of organizations—including parties—of the ruling classes and sections, whereas a nonfascist solution of the crisis would require, as Gramsci pointed out, the merger of these organizations into a single party of the bourgeoisie.

THE IDEOLOGICAL CRISIS
                                    The circumstances of fascism correspond to a crisis of the dominant ideology. This aspect of the problem cannot be overstressed: Indeed, fascism cannot be explained or understood without having a correct view of the determining role played by ideology in definite historical circumstances, and without a careful examination of the ideological crisis experienced by the social structures in systems where fascism triumphed.

By ideological crisis we mean particularly a crisis of the dominant ideology in a given social structure, that is, a crisis of the ruling class ideology in this structure. The ideology of the ruling class, the true "cement" of the social structure, is first challenged by the masses, that is, by the oppressed classes which this ideology is mainly intended to maintain in their state of subordination and political subjection. But this is just one aspect of the question: Beyond this crisis of the dominant ideology, it is possible to speak, in certain circumstances, of a general ideological crisis distinct from that of the dominant ideology alone.

Within any social structure, there are, in fact, not just one dominant ideology—that is, an ideological discourse given a relatively systematic character by the very dominance of this ideology—but real ideological subsystems constituted by ideologies pertaining to classes other than the ruling one: working-class ideology, lower-middle-class ideology. Of course, the dominant ideology (that is, the ideology of the ruling class) is really dominant throughout the social structure to the extent that it succeeds in permeating, through various devices, the ideological subsystems. The ideology of the ruling class becomes dominant, for example, within the working-class ideology subsystem. Thus, the trade-unionist ideology, which is not, as such, the ideology of the middle class, is nothing but an aspect of this ideology within the working class—that is, the means through which bourgeois ideology permeates and dominates the working-class ideology subsystem.

It is obvious, therefore, that a crisis of the dominant ideology will affect the total ideological universe of a social structure, though it will not always affect it in the same way. For example, an acute crisis of the ruling social force's ideology might make possible a greater development of the ideology of the antagonistic social forces. There might even be a relative replacement of the former by the latter, even before the occurrence of a real revolution. A typical case is that of France where bourgeois ideology surreptitiously replaced feudal ideology before the French Revolution.

But a situation of general ideological crisis might also exist. In other words, there might be a situation in which, simultaneously and for different reasons, there is a crisis both of the dominant ideology and of the ideology of the main dominated social force. This was exactly the case for fascism: The deep crisis of the dominant bourgeois ideology was accompanied by a simultaneous deep crisis in the masses—not a crisis of the working-class ideology dominated by bourgeois ideology (that is, of the reformist-revisionist ideology, which would have facilitated the development of Marxist-Leninist ideology), but a crisis of Marxist-Leninist ideology itself.

We should concentrate first, however, on the crisis of the dominant ideology, and on this particular aspect: In the case of fascism, this crisis affects not only the impact of the dominant ideology on the dominated classes, but also the relationship between the bourgeoisie (and its allies) and its own ideology, for the ideological crisis spreads within the ruling alliance. The ruling classes and sections seem to have become unable to "experience," in the way they had before, their relationship to their way of life. In other words, the function of the dominant ideology with respect to the ruling classes themselves is also affected.

One of the main results of this situation was, as a matter of fact, the breaking of the representative-represented link between these classes and sections and their political parties and the organizational failure of these parties; another result was the characteristic and dramatic conversion to fascist ideology of the ruling bloc's "watchdogs," its caste of recognized official ideologists, and their systematic attacks against traditional bourgeois ideology. This about-face of the official ideologists of the bourgeoisie, combined with the ideological crisis within the ruling classes themselves, was one of the important factors in the bourgeoisie's ultimate overt shift to fascism.

It is even possible to maintain that this ideological crisis, in the form it assumes within the ruling class itself, is the source of an additional element of the political crisis: the break between the political representatives of the bourgeoisie (the parties and the political personnel) and its ideological representatives (its watch-dog official ideologists). The latter seem to embrace and advocate fascism more fully, directly, and overtly than the former, and often come into acute conflict with the parties and politicians by attacking them. And it is not mere chance that the bond between the bourgeoisie and its official ideologists proved to be the strongest.

. . .

THE FASCIST PARTIES, FASCISM, AND THE RULING
CLASSES AND SECTIONS: DOMINATION, SUPREMACY,
AND THE PREVAILING CLASS; THE RELATIVE
AUTONOMY OF FASCISM

Another important question concerns the relationship of the ruling classes and sections of classes with fascism—first with the fascist party, then with the fascist state. The three main views on this question seem equally mistaken to me:

1. The gradually prevailing view within the Comintern alleges the following: Contrary to the parliamentary democratic state, in which other ruling classes and sections play a determining political role, the fascist state corresponds to the total control over the state of the big monopoly capital section alone. The capitalist state reaches here a stage of total subordination to the strict interest of this section, the fascist state being the mere agent (in the strongest sense of the term) of this section, a "tool" that can be manipulated at will by this section alone, to the exclusion of the other ruling classes and sections. It is clear, therefore, that the fascist state cannot be said to enjoy a relative autonomy from the ruling bloc and its sovereign section.

This view of the Third International is a stubborn delusion harking back to an "instrumentalist" conception of the state, closely linked with economism, which still governs, *as is,* the current analyses of the Communist parties concerning the state at the "state monopoly capitalism" stage. In this respect, Comintern analyses of the fascist state and the current state are absolutely identical. This conception has definitely prevailed in the Comintern since Dimitrov and the Seventh Congress. It should be pointed out here that this conception is often combined with the seemingly inconsistent notion of the "internal contradictions" of fascism. Though these analyses often stress the fact that fascism represents conflicting interests of various classes, these contradictions are supposed to disappear miraculously at the institutional level of the fascist party and state.

This conception of the relationship between the fascist state and big capital *after* the advent of fascism controls their particularly mistaken view concerning the relationship between big capital and the fascist party throughout the fascistization process. The fascist party is mainly considered to be a "paid agent" in the service of big capital. The fascist party, the "military fighting instrument of big capital," is often reduced to a "horde of white guards," a mere "armed militia" in the pay of big capital, which can manipulate it at will.

Thus, on the one hand, the main question on which attention is focused is that of the financiers of the fascist organizations, whereas the organizational relationship between the fascist party and the bourgeoisie is considerably more complex. On the other hand, not only is the military aspect considered to be the main aspect of the fascistization process throughout its development, but it is also regarded as independent of the political aspect. The fact is, however, that the military aspect is constantly determined by the political aspect of the process, one of the characteristics of this process being the predominant role played by the political aspect, except in the very last stage. In this connection, Clara Zetkin was right in her warning to the executive committee of the Comintern on June 23, 1923:

The mistake of the Italian Communist Party consisted mainly in their considering fascism merely as a military-terrorist movement and not as a mass movement with deep social roots. The fact should be stressed explicitly that, before fascism wins a military victory, it has already gained an ideological and political one over the working class. . . .

2. Equally mistaken is the series of conceptions that describe fascism in terms of the Bonapartist model; that is, in terms of an "equal balance" of the two main contending forces. This conception has been formulated mainly by Thalheimer, but it is also held by many Marxist theoreticians of fascism. This means endowing the fascist state with a *kind* and *extent* of relative autonomy it does not really possess, and such a view might even make it impossible to establish the true relationship between fascism and big capital. These analysts have gone so far, for example, as to speak of a discrepancy between the economic domination exercised by big capital and the political domination monopolized by the totally "independent" fascist state, and have thus misinterpreted Marx's famous statement in *18 Brumaire* on the "opposition between state and society," and "the independence of the state

from civil society." The relative autonomy of the state might even go so far as meaning a breaking of the link between the state and the sovereign section. This results in absolutely false descriptions of fascism as acting explicitly in the long run through a war economy, against the interests of big capital and in open conflict with it.

3. I also consider mistaken the conception, fairly common in social-democratic circles and rightly opposed by the International, of fascism as the "political dictatorship of the lower middle class." A close and complex link, underestimated by the International, does exist between fascism and the lower middle class. But in trying to establish the relative autonomy of the fascist state, this conception, like the preceding one, attempts to do so on the basis of a discrepancy between economic and political domination, with the difference that here it is no longer a more or less independent state facing two balancing forces, but a state representing the political domination of the lower middle class (the "third force") as opposed to the economic domination of big capital.

Let us now state what seems to be the correct view. Throughout the fascistization process and after the seizing of power, fascism (the fascist party and the fascist state) possesses a characteristic relative autonomy from both the ruling bloc and the section of big monopoly capital whose supremacy it establishes. This relative autonomy results from two series of factors: (1) The internal contradictions of the classes and sections of the ruling alliance, that is, its internal political crisis. The relative autonomy is necessary in order to reorganize this bloc and establish the supremacy, within it, of the big monopoly capital section, (2) The contradictions between the ruling classes and sections and the dominated classes, that is, the political crisis of the total social structure, and the complex relationship between fascism and the dominated classes. It is this relationship that makes of fascism the indispensable intermediary for reestablishing a stable political domination and supremacy.

This relative autonomy, however, is not of the same type nor of the same breadth as that of a state in a situation in which there is a balance of power of the two main social forces. This does not mean that in the latter case the state becomes a neutral intermediary in the class struggle; it never ceases to be the organizer of political domination. But the circumstances afford it a working margin that has never been available to the fascist state because of the different context of the political crisis. In short, though it is true that the fascist state possesses a characteristic relative autonomy that does indeed distinguish it from the "normal" types of capitalist state, it cannot be considered as a particular case of the relative autonomy peculiar to the Bonapartist type of state.

We will consider here only the first series of factors of this relative autonomy. The following is a listing of its stages, which correspond to those of the fascistization process:

1. *From the beginning of the process to the point of no return.* The fascist party, which had existed previously only in the embryonic form of armed gangs supported by sections of the ruling class during the aggressive stage of the proletariat, but deserted by them during the stabilization stage, progressively becomes a mass party. It is openly supported by big capital circles, but it is far from being the party "representing" this section and even less, therefore, the party of the whole ruling alliance.

At the point of no return, the fascist party gains the support of the big capital section, to which it gives strong guarantees. It tries to strengthen its relationship with some of the ruling classes and sections and to neutralize the reticent ones. In other words, it establishes organized party links with a ruling alliance which has taken the offensive and is deprived of its own representative political organizations (this distinguishes fascism from Bonapartism, which does not usually become a party, in the true sense of the word). The party's political link to the masses, however, remains quite strong.

2. *From the point of no return to the accession to power of fascism.* This is the completion of the previous stage by the successful resolution of contradictions between the big monopoly capital section and the other ruling classes and sections, through compromises of fascism with the latter. At the same time, however, there is a veering, so to speak, toward the masses alarmed by the increasingly open relationship between the fascist party and the ruling bloc. This is a stage marked by the actual establishment through the fascist party of an alliance, heretofore tenuous, between the monopoly section and the lower middle class: it is a rather ambiguous alliance, however, with explosive potentialities.

3. *Early stage of fascist power.* This is the moment of truth, but it is as yet a rather relative truth. The policy of fascism aimed at establishing, though in a veiled way, the supremacy of big monopoly capital over the other ruling classes and sections is reinforced. At the same time, fascism is forced, against the will of the ruling bloc, to make some concessions to the masses—although this in no way prevents the suppression of their vanguard and their organizations.

Moreover, things are changing on the political scene. Through the fascist party, still strongly marked by its class background, and through the reorganization of the state system and its apparatus, the lower middle class becomes during that stage, and without ever really exercising political rule, the prevailing class, and starts to become the class in charge of the state. This is an explosive situation, which ends in a mass purge of the "leftist wing" of the fascist party itself, and brings to a close the era of compromises (this compromise policy is, on the contrary, a constant characteristic of Bonapartism).

4. *The stabilization of fascism.* The big monopoly capital section establishes its supremacy and also acquires the status of prevailing class (the identity of the prevailing section with the one holding supremacy also distinguishes fascism from Bonapartism), of which it deprives the lower middle class. The latter, however, continues to be in charge of the state: This process is even reinforced by a reorganization of the political personnel in the broad sense.

The era of compromises, as a characteristic stage, has drawn to an end. But fascism, once "stabilized," is often forced to impose on the ruling bloc some concessions to the masses (underestimated by the Comintern) in order never to break all ties with them. At the same time, the establishment of the supremacy of big capital sharpens the contradictions within the ruling alliance. Fascism is forced to deal with the sovereign section by devious means and sometimes to keep its distance from it. Though in the last analysis the policy of fascism corresponds, on the whole, to the long-term interests of this section, fascism is not its obedient agent.

Eventually, the situation on the political scene (lower middle class as the class in charge) and on the ideological one (fascist ideology) adds its effects to the preceding factors, with the result that the policy carried out by fascism ends up by working against big capital.

. . .

THE NAZI PARTY, NAZISM, AND THE RULING CLASSES AND SECTIONS: SUPREMACY AND PREVAILING CLASS

The last question we will deal with here is that of the relationship of the National Socialist party and of National Socialism with the ruling bloc and especially with big capital. Before the beginning of the fascistization process, the armed gangs and free corps were under the direct command of big landlords and capital, who ceased to finance them as soon as their direct military role became useless. With the beginning of the process, the situation becomes very different. Coincident with the offensive stage of the ruling bloc, the National Socialist party becomes a real mass movement, and an actual organizational relationship is gradually established between this party and the bloc.

The term "coincident" is deliberately used to make it clear that we are referring neither to a chronological sequence nor to a direct cause-effect relationship. In other words, it is not the "previous" establishment of a relationship with the ruling bloc, and more especially with big capital, that immediately turns the National Socialist party into a mass movement. These two elements seem rather to be linked by the circumstances. It is just as easy to reverse the order and say that it is because the National Socialist party becomes a mass movement, and to the extent that it becomes one, that the ruling bloc gradually turns toward it. For, contrary to the assertions of most of the ideologists of "totalitarianism," it is not true either to say that the National Socialist party first becomes a mass movement and only afterward wins the support of big capital.

The National Socialist party, which seems crushed after the abortive coup in Bavaria in 1923, swiftly builds itself up again: it goes from 27,000 members in 1925 to 72,000 members, including 30,000 S.A., at the Nuremberg Congress in 1927. Its members keep climbing rapidly, and reach 108,000 in 1928, 178,000 in 1929. In 1926, Baldur von Schirach creates the notorious Union of National-Socialist Students, whose influence in university circles keeps spreading and whose success in student elections is constantly greater. It is true that the National Socialist party is not very successful in elections before 1930, a fact which long leads the Comintern to underestimate its importance, but it nevertheless becomes a mass party in the early stage of the fascistization process. Things are even clearer if we consider the growing influence of fascist ideology in the various nationalist movements—see, for example, the wide circulation rapidly reached by the newspaper *Der Angriff*, which was begun in 1927.

During this stage, political links are established between the National Socialist party and big capital circles, links which lead, once the point of no return is reached, to the support of the party by this section as a whole. Significantly, in 1927 Strasser, whose "leftist" ideas irritated these circles, is replaced as the head of the Berlin-Brandenburg region (*Gau*) by Goebbels. It is in 1927 too that the National Socialist program is drastically revised for the first time, a revision marked by the toning down of the overly anticapitalist demands it previously included.

It is exactly around this time that agrarian and big capital circles bring increasing support to the party. The landlords, including some members of the imperial family, join it almost en masse. Gradually, all the landlords and, in particular, big capital as a whole bring their support to the National Socialist party; the links between them clearly assume an organizational political aspect. It is also around 1927 that the process of the subordination of the German National party and other right-wing organizations to the National Socialist party begins. Hugenberg, elected to the presidency of the German National party in 1928, openly allies with Hitler in 1929 during a broad national campaign against the Young plan. The United National Front is created, bringing together the German Nationals, the Steel Helmets *Stahl-helm*), the National Socialist party, and the Pan-German League. In 1930, the "national opposition" under Brüning is increasingly dominated by the National Socialist party. Support and funds pour in. Also in 1930, Hitler advocates respecting constitutional legality for the accession of his party to power, which is but a sign of the political links established with big capital.

During the second stage of the fascistization process, the National Socialist party succeeds to a large extent in defusing the political contradictions between the other sections of the ruling bloc and the landlords and big capital, as well as in appeasing their resistance to its accession to power. While the economic contradictions within the ruling bloc intensify, the National Socialist party actually emerges as the common political denominator of the ruling bloc in its offensive stage. This is mainly manifested by the state apparatus's open support of the National Socialist party, by the more than ambiguous attitude of middle capital's political representatives toward National Socialism (for example, the episode of the temporary banning of the S.A. by Brüning), and, finally, by the utter passivity of middle capital when the last obstacles to the accession to power of National Socialism are ousted: this passivity is quite clear when Hindenburg ousts Brüning.

During this stage, however, the political link between the National Socialist party and the masses remains quite strong—so much so that big capital is often irritated by the National Socialist party's policy. Big capital plays at the same time the Hindenburg-military dictatorship card, but only as a possible position of retreat: take, for example, its parallel support for Hindenburg's candidacy against Hitler in 1932.

With the accession to power of National Socialism, we observe the establishment of the political supremacy of big capital, the bridging of the gap between political supremacy and economic domination, and the intensification of the process of economic domination. Proceeding by stages and with some ups and downs, big capital succeeds in imposing through the fascist party, state, and ideology a general policy that overcomes the internal economic contradictions of the ruling bloc, which is thus unified under its banner.

During the first stage of their accession to power, the National Socialists banned all the political organizations of the ruling bloc; that is, they expelled from the political scene its traditional representatives. One year after taking power, the National Socialist party became Germany's only party. The last members of the former political personnel —von Papen, Hugenberg, von Neurath—were expelled from the government, and harsh measures (including death in some cases) were taken against them. A purge of the "leftist" wing within the National Socialist party itself was taking place at the same time; there was the "night of the long knives," the dissolution of the 2-million-strong S.A. who demanded a "second revolution" (an "anticapitalist" one), and the killing of their chiefs, Röhm and Strasser. Later came the elimination of whatever political resistance still existed within the state apparatus.

This process, however, followed a very specific path. The increasing political importance of the state apparatus, the shifting of the main weight within this apparatus from the army to the police and the government bureaucracy, the investing of the top levels of the state apparatus by National Socialist party members all resulted, during the first stage of National Socialism's power, in making of the lower middle class, bound by special links to the National Socialist party, the prevailing class. It is from within this class that the political personnel of the top levels of the state apparatus are recruited. This was a group of personnel whose links with the lower middle class it still represents have not yet been broken. The lower middle class thus derives definite benefits from the situation existing during the first stage of National Socialist power.

Two parallel processes can be observed: On the one hand, the state apparatus as a whole, which grows in "monstrous" fashion, is invested by members whose background and ideology are specifically lower middle class; on the other, the organs of the state apparatus originally linked to other classes (especially the army) become subordinated to the strictly lower-middle-class ones. The lower middle class thus becomes the "class in charge" of the state; this is the *Gleichschaltung* process and the problem of "fascist bureaucracy."

During the stabilization stage, this results in the subordination of the National Socialist party to the Nazi state proper. For, when this stage is reached, the lower-middle-class upper levels of the state apparatus and the top ranks of the party have broken their ties of representation with that class. The lower middle class thus loses its status as the prevailing class, but remains the supporting class of the National Socialist state, for despite the fact that its interests are definitely injured by the National Socialist policy, it remains the class in charge of the state. The subordination of the party to the state—which, however, stops short of their merging—implies the loss by the lower middle class of the political means (the party) that enabled it for a short time to act as the prevailing class. It continues, however, to act as a social force through its relationship to the state apparatus as a whole. In addition, successive purges occur at the same time within the National Socialist party, and these are not limited to the leftists in its top ranks: 20 percent of those who were the political leaders of the party before 1933 had been expelled by the end of 1934. From that time on, 80 percent of its political leaders were recruited among members who had joined after 1933.

This situation is itself the result of the whole relationship of forces leading to the establishment and the maintenance of the power of National Socialism, a situation characterized by both big capital and the lower middle class definitely growing close to it by offering either their alliance or their support, depending on the various stages. This situation characterizing the political scene and the totality of political apparatuses is at the same time a determining factor of the relative autonomy of the Nazi state with respect to big capital.

Let us take a closer look. It is true that the industrialists and the financiers are not, strictly speaking, kept out of the state apparatus; they are, on the contrary, present directly and in force, mainly through corporate organizations, as well as through their participation in the National Socialist party and the gradual merger of parts of the upper levels of the National Socialist party (Göring, and so on) with big capital by means of the constitution of a state bourgeoisie nucleus. This is one of the reasons for the lack of validity of Thalheimer's thesis, which explains fascism in terms of the Bonapartist model, and according to which the "relative autonomy" of fascism is based on a definite inconsistency between big capital's economic domination and its political supremacy, the safeguarding of the former necessitating its relinquishing the latter in favor of a "leader" (Louis Bonaparte, Hitler). But the main reason for Thalheimer's error is that he overlooks the essential difference between fascism and Bonapartism— namely, the existence of the fascist party and its objective role with regard to big capital. In fact, the fascist party gradually comes to act as the political representative of big capital, and ensures its political supremacy and its direct participation in the top leadership of the state apparatus.

At the same time, however, the very existence of the National Socialist party constitutes a factor of the relative autonomy of the state with respect to big capital. The party as a whole, especially the minor ranks and the base, continue to be closely linked to the lower middle class, which has in the meantime invested every level of the state apparatus. Even the corporate organizations, in which the members of big capital participate directly, are dominated by the party.

It is not necessary to analyze in detail the constant contradictions between big capital and the National Socialist party-state. They are due to the fact that National Socialism plays off against each other big capital and the other classes and sections of the ruling bloc, as well as the latter and the masses. These contradictions come into the open with the Four Year Plan of 1936 (conflict between Göring and

Schacht) and the organization of the war economy (the disgrace of Marshals Blomberg and Fritsch in 1938). This does not mean, of course, that the war did not correspond to the interests of Big German capital. The conflict was mainly due, in this case, to the attempt by the National Socialist state to control the process of the establishment of the domination of big capital over the other elements of the ruling bloc.

IX/WORLD WAR II AND THE COLD WAR

A RECENT book on history as a social science has defined the function of history as threefold: (1) It is the custodian of the collective memory and nourishes the collective ego of a society. (2) It serves to socialize the young. (3) It is that branch of inquiry that seeks to arrive at an accurate account and valid understanding of the past. All well and good, but there is one omission from the list. As Marx said, philosophers have always been content to study the world, but the time has come now to change it. And history, together with all the other sciences, is a tool in the process. Clearly, in the world-wide struggle between revolution and counterrevolution, there is no longer room for neutrals. Nor has there ever really been any; the difference today is that with the sharpening of class antagonisms on an international scale, we are (and have to be) more conscious of the available alternatives. If none suits us, we must create our own.

I have no desire to indulge in a pernicious, if reverse, form of American imperialism, but I think it may be said that Americans have a special need to know where they stand and how they got there. For, whether we like it or not, it is the United States today that is the counterrevolutionary power par excellence. That fact alone creates special obligations for us if we do not wish merely to be its accomplices. We are in the belly of the whale, and while that may not for the moment be an uncomfortable place, who can tell when the digestive processes will begin? The end of our own alienation presupposes a change in the global role of our state, government, and society that we alone can bring about.

The role of history—or rather of the historian—in this confrontation with ourselves and others is to help us to know why we are in our present situation. It is a study of the past that ought ideally to be carried on simultaneously with action to change the present and the future. I might even go so far as to maintain that only active involvement in the world as it is can make it possible for us to know the world as it was.

Both David Horowitz and Gabriel Kolko are members of that younger generation of American historians who have undertaken, in their life and art, to act in accordance with these principles. Seeking the roots of the contemporary world conflict, they focus naturally on the period surrounding World War II, which they treat as the transposition of class conflict onto the global stage. By so doing, they give a new dimension to the study of international relations and diplomatic history and demonstrate how historical analysis not only may but must be made relevant to the world beyond the classroom and the library. Some of their statements may shock the sensibilities of those of us brought up to believe that World War II was a great crusade for freedom and democracy. But they are not muckrakers, nor are they out to score facile points at the expense of the heroes of the age. World War II did take on the aspect of a holy war against the barbarous hordes as a result of the alliance, however tenuous, between bourgeois-democracy and the left. What started out to be a classic imperialist war of redivision became an imperfect exercise in popular justice, not only because of the tremendous force of the mass movements on the left, but also because of the contradictions that existed between systems of imperial domination. These in turn were linked to a complex network of historical causes in the period of more or less successful bourgeois revolutions. To know this is in no way to dim the luster of the antifascist cause and the story of those who died in its name. On the contrary, it makes their actions comprehensible and allows us to share in the lucidity that was so often theirs.

Gabriel Kolko

22

Politics of War:
The World and United States
Foreign Policy, 1943–1945

INTRODUCTION

The historian may attempt to abstract the essentials of a reality, but the realities of World War II defy description. Yet without an appreciation of the quality of existence for the people of Europe and Asia from 1939 through 1945 one cannot understand the ultimate significance of the battles which were fought, the dispatches issued, or the more obvious externals of human behavior which are the stuff from which histories are composed. The primary condition of World War II, the crucial background for understanding *all* else, was the unprecedented human pain and misery, the millions upon millions of deaths, the widespread tragedy and suffering transforming the existence of the peoples of Europe and Asia, tragedy and torment the depths of which no one, however sensitive, can plumb. The war swept away all the institutions and relationships that anchor man to his society: the home was shattered, the family destroyed, work was gone, hunger and danger were ever more pressing as ever-growing millions wandered over lands in search of safety and security, or as enemies or governments forcibly wrenched them from their environment. Man became degraded and uprooted, and having lost his commitment to and interest in conventional ways and wisdom, he sought to redeem himself and his society in order to save himself. For no civilization can indulge in two terrible and prolonged wars in twenty-five years and emerge untorn.

The impact of World War II on the individuals who experienced and fortunately survived it was the motor of political and social change, the creator of mass movements and parties, the catalyst that made men act, that destroyed constituted orders everywhere. All who wished to survive accepted in principle the currency of violence and repression, for it was the reality that had transformed their existence and one which they could not deny. Both reactionaries and revolutionaries quickly accepted this premise, in theory if not in practice, and this too became an essential quality of the politics of a war-torn world. War therefore carried with it the ever-present possibility of shaping the actions of men of power, or of generating social revolution —and eventually World War II devastated the established societies far more thoroughly than any of the upheavals following World War I.

Most historians still tend to think in noncataclysmic categories appropriate to the pre-1939 period, if not the nineteenth century, but World War II and its aftermath witnessed the definitive smashing of a world political and economic order that began tottering after 1917. Germany ceased to be a Great Power, Eastern Europe was no longer a hotbed of potential conflict and entered into a period of internal pre-occupations, the balance of power in the Far East shifted away from Japan in a manner that permitted revolutionary changes, colonialism began to die, and England assumed a lesser role in regulating the world scene. In brief, everywhere the war and the suffering of men transformed the political and social landscape drastically, even decisively, to define the preconditions of world politics over the subsequent decades.

The human condition the war created also produced the larger backdrop for diplomacy, battles, and the multifarious immediate events that were expressions of conflict between enemies and allies alike— and the reader would do well to fix this essential ingredient firmly in his mind. When turning to the overwhelming and bewildering succession of events, historians have treated them simplistically, as evidence of the naïveté, good faith, or malice of one nation or another, or as singular occurrences unconnected with the entire fabric of the war, much less with the events of the post-1945 period.

To understand the role of the United States in World War II one must also understand that the American government had a series of immediate objectives, centered first of all around the desire to win battles and defeat the Axis, and an elaborate and highly sophisticated set of economic and political goals it defined as urgently desirable war aims. The interaction between the larger objectives of the United States and the world as the military and political leaders of the United States perceived it formed the vital context of the politics of World War II.

In considering World War II, and especially the years 1943–1945, there are three major issues, or themes, which subsume many, if not most, of the concerns of those in Washington who thought about the problem of American war and peace aims. First was the question of the Left, which is to say, the disintegration of the prewar social systems and the growth of revolutionary movements and potential upheaval everywhere in the world. Next was the problem of the Soviet Union, which at times appeared very much connected with the issue of the Left. Finally, there was the issue of Great Britain, invariably set in the context of the future of the world economy, and its present and future relationship to the United States. No facile dissection of these three elements is possible, and no priority or weighting is useful as a general rule. All three themes interacted so that a change in one area often affected policy and conditions in another, lowering the significance of one factor at one moment, posing new dimensions at another. Yet the reader must recall these intertwined components again and again, or else the events of the war will appear discrete and disconnected, and the politics of the war bewildering and confused. Moreover, the contemplated problems of the peace and the military realities of the war meshed with each other with increasing frequency as the war wore on.

War in the twentieth century has become a necessary precondition for the emergence of a powerful Left, and for the first time since 1919 the Left, both in Europe and Asia, issued forth from the shadow of political defeat and impotence to the very center of world politics. War has come to mean not just the defeat of armies or the change of borders, but frequently the destruction or disintegration of social systems. Internal class conflict ripened to complicate the more traditional issues of international political, economic, and military conflict. In China, Italy, Greece, France, and Eastern Europe there were in varying degree real or disguised civil wars taking place at the very time of the war against Germany and Japan. Germany for its part saw the significance to the Allied camp of the movement toward the left and ultimately, in the last moments before defeat, attempted to play on the fears of the West in a manner that profoundly shaped relations among the Allies and the contours of postwar politics.

In Europe the form of the armed Resistance, the phenomenal growth of the Communist parties in Western Europe, and the rise of Soviet power as the tide of the Red Army moved relentlessly toward the West all typified the problem of the Left for the United States. The Resistance and the growth of the Italian and French Communist parties, however, were not the result of the presence of Soviet troops, as was the case in much of Eastern Europe, but of the collapse of the Old Order during the war and its alliance in many nations with fascism. To this extent, therefore, the potency of the threat of the Left did not reflect support from a broken Russia, but from the momentary collapse of European capitalism and, in the Far East, colonialism or oligarchy.

The United States and Britain could see powerful Communist movements emerging throughout Western and Southern Europe and the central role of the Communists in the leadership of the armed Resistance. The Resistance attracted men and women who exhibited the courage and abandon of nationalist revolutionaries. They developed appropriate leftist ideologies, and might in time become social-revolutionary actors as well, to purge not only the foreign invaders but also those domestic forces of conservatism that had collaborated with fascism and made its victory so easy. Would the Resistance act, would the Communists take power? If historians have hardly examined the internal world of these movements in relation to global politics, it is also a fact that the American and British leaders at the time similarly failed to perceive them clearly and correctly, for there was seemingly no alternative but to prepare for the worst or face a possible effort to wrest from the West the political victory that was the objective of their military sacrifices and triumph.

Given the collapse of the prewar power of the social forces that had contained the Left after 1920, the question confronting the United States and Britain was how to fill the vacuum and what to do with the traditional parties of conservative order. Between 1943 and 1947 the Western Allies developed, at first haphazardly and then with deliberate consciousness, a coherent policy toward this dilemma save, as in China, where they frankly acknowledged the magnitude of the undertaking to be beyond their capacity.

The vast upheavals in Europe and Asia invariably impinged on relations with the Soviet Union, for suspicion of Communism in Europe inevitably confirmed the conventional belief that international Communism, presumably Moscow-directed, could turn the revolutionary forces of Europe and Asia on and off at will. Western-Soviet diplomacy therefore was contingent on developments beyond the control of the Soviet Union insofar as no nation could undo the nearly universal social and political consequences of the war, even when the U.S.S.R. was quite willing, indeed anxious, to attempt to do so. Yet in Eastern Europe, where Soviet presence gave it the power to define events, the United States could perceive policies which only confirmed its worst fears and violated the American definition of an ideal world order. Relations with the U.S.S.R. therefore subsume the problem of revolutionary upheaval in Europe and Asia, especially in Eastern Europe, and the bearing of military strategy on the more obvious political issues dividing the Allies. At the same time the United States defined for its own purposes the preconditions for Russia's return to the family of nations after twenty-five years of isolation, preconditions that vividly illustrate the nature of the world which the United States hoped might emerge from the war.

The nascent rivalry between the United States and Russia was not the only critical broad area of concern in Washington. To the extent that the United States articulated clear political and economic objectives for the postwar world—and much effort went into such a definition—it came into direct conflict with Great Britain. The Americans saw the problem of the prewar and postwar world economy primarily as a problem of British policy in conflict with American goals, and the entire issue of postwar political alliances raised the issue of the British desire to ally itself with France to create a Western European bloc quite independent of both the United States and the U.S.S.R., much less a United Nations system as the Americans envisaged it. The problem of France is not only a question of the threat of the Left, even less of the personality of De Gaulle, but also of France's postwar political and economic commitments. Much the same was true for Italy, Yugoslavia, and Greece, where the United States had to think not merely of the potential domination of the Left, but also of the domination by Britain. Indeed even the question of British diplomacy toward Russia was a source of dispute, and in the Middle East prewar antagonisms were rekindled as the two Western Allies found themselves working against each other in Saudi Arabia and elsewhere. And as military allies, fighting side by side at all times, the differences in military strategy were exacerbating and often serious. Without the even greater common problem of the Left and the U.S.S.R. many of these disagreements between the United States and Britain would most certainly have led to sharper, more serious clashes. As it was, the problem of Anglo-American relations during the period 1943–1945 and thereafter is the key to comprehending a whole spectrum of issues and America's definition of its unique postwar political and, above all, economic aims.

Taking into account the conditions which the war, the Left, the Soviet Union, and Britain created, the United States had to balance its desire for an ideal world system against its perception of a more complicated economic, military, and political reality, and to merge the two insofar as it was possible. In considering the postwar world political order, and especially the United Nations as a forum for the resolution of future problems, the United States had to shape its position to adjust for its Western Hemispheric policies and needs, its desire for military security via bases, and its rapidly growing spheres of interest elsewhere. It expressed the synthesis in a distinctive form of internationalism quite compatible with American interests, but obviously elusive insofar as the existing international political system was merely a tentative world coalition unified only in that it shared a common enemy. On an economic plane the United States had to weigh its objectives against the fact that the war, and the depression preceding it, had dangerously undermined world capitalism and would compel the United States to seek its goals in a seriously altered strategic and economic context. The attention and energy which the Americans devoted to meeting these objectives during the war, in the framework of the problems of the Left, the U.S.S.R., and England, is the key to the problem of the politics and diplomacy of World War II.

One must study the development of United States political policy in the context of the kind of world that emerged from the chaos of World War II. . . . For I have written this book as much to describe the actual condition of the world during World War II as [to study] the way the United States defined and quite as often misconceived the course of global realities. Yet what can be said about the seeming variability of a national policy that to the professional, much less the casual observer, has often seemed chaotic? To the extent that any system is haphazard or improvised, of course, no single theory or explanation will cover the phenomenon, and the fashionable tendency to believe that men of power are the victims of errors rather than the creators of them—and that perhaps reason or pressure by reasonable men will bring them back to the truth—has reinforced this homily. This assumption, so crucial to the premises of liberal political theory, implies that "democratic" power structures are not merely poorly informed but innocent, and that a true dialogue between virtue and power is possible. Such an image, postulating behavior as a series of bumbles, ignores the possibility that policies which are dangerous, destructive, or even do not work are very often quite consistent and necessary in forwarding interests or holding the line in defensive situations.

In attempting to appraise the conduct of policy one does not have to assume that history is determined or made up of repeated accidents. It is sufficient to study its pattern of functional behavior, to comprehend the assumptions formulated in response to challenging situations, and to perceive a policy and pattern that in some sense makes future responses predictable and in this sense inevitable. And quite beyond rhetoric are the institutional forces that do or can influence policy and power. If rhetoric is confused with reality, the banalities of speech writers, platitudes, and the convenient transformation of words into useful symbols rather than truth all become the basis of analysis and a substitute for comprehending action, clear definitions, and institutional imperatives. A description of functionally defined goals and consistent actions, whether or not someone has consciously defined and explicitly acknowledged them, reveals the motives and consequences of any nation, the United States included, in specific and general cases. The reader will soon discover that policy-makers usually explicitly acknowledged these de facto principles as immediate objectives relevant as a basis for action in specific situations when they had to consider concrete national interests, and usually the leaders of American foreign policy articulated them into a coherent, long-term world view. Illusion and mere rhetoric are plausible only when an environment for action never breaks down; in times of crisis, which is to say for the major part of the period after 1939, policy requires a meaningful basis of action for sheer survival, and American leaders often articulated it in private and in public as well. It is not difficult to focus on underlying patterns and specific events that illustrate them. In doing so one must evaluate two levels of political crisis: specific causes, such as who did what first, and who was responsible for escalating specific, relatively minor crises into major ones, and why. Throughout this study I will refer to broad patterns as well as to specific events that especially illustrate them.

We live in the shadow and with the consequences of World War II, and a reassessment of the meaning of that war is crucial to an understanding of our own decade and the sustained foreign policy crisis that has engaged the United States for over twenty-five years. The events at the beginning of that critical period are all largely contemporaneous with present confrontations—indeed, their very genesis. To separate these events from a continuum, in the hope that decision-makers will apply reason in one case and not in others, is to do violence to the history of the great shifting and reintegration of the world political system that occurred between 1943 and 1949, and to the magnitude of the issues involved. By understanding the meaning of that period we comprehend our own decade in microcosm and the challenges we face in breaking the paralyzing grip of a thirty-year-old crisis in international relations over the future of all mankind. In viewing the genesis of the challenge of our time we hold a mirror to ourselves, the problems we confront, and the source of our malaise.

.   .   .

CONCLUSION

The coalition against the Axis was born of necessity rather than deliberation or choice, and only the common need to defeat a common enemy bound it together. Great Britain, the Soviet Union, and the United States shared no single set of objectives other than this preeminent reality, no unifying political and economic peace aims—save, in the case of Britain and America, the negative one of containing Russia and the Left—and when Germany and Japan lay in smoking ruins the wartime Allies turned from a tenuous coalition to open conflict. That incipient struggle grew in importance throughout the war, until no later than the end of 1944 it necessarily became the defining obsession of the Western members of the coalition. That conflict has shaped the contours of modern world history, and we have yet to feel or know its full meaning and ultimate consequences.

No major power sacrificed less of its blood and material wealth during World War II than the United States. If one considers military potential in terms of overall industrial and technological capacity to sustain modern warfare over a period of time, in August 1945 only the United States had that power and only the United States emerged from the bloodiest conflagration in human history stronger than ever before. The war ultimately drained Britain more than even Russia, relative to its limited manpower and resources, transforming that small island into a power of the second tier. The United States was incomparably the greatest single nation in the world, with sharply articulated global political and, primarily, economic aspirations equal, even much more than equal, to the role.

The leaders in Washington were above all else fully aware of their own physical strength as well as their political and economic objectives, and they always viewed the problem of future relations with the U.S.S.R. or Great Britain, or the nature of the world, with these critical goals in clear perspective. For how to advance its peace aims and apply its directing power to the inordinately complex and unpredictable realities of the broken, war-torn world colored every specific American response and assumption, and it was these expansive premises that were to define the postwar structure of relations—and conflict —between great states.

The problem of Soviet power gradually subsumed the other great wartime challenge to American diplomacy: the emergence of the Left and its threat to securing American economic and political war aims. In Eastern Europe, perhaps more than any other single region, American leaders found evidence of what they interpreted to be the dangers of Soviet expansionism that might undercut the attainment of their nation's largest postwar goals. The war utterly and finally destroyed the traditional Eastern European political and economic structure and nothing the Russians might do could alter that fact, for not the Soviet Union but the leaders of the Old Order in Eastern Europe themselves made that collapse inevitable. The Russians could work within that new structural limitation in a variety of ways, and in practice they did explore many political options, but they could not transcend the new socioeconomic reality. More aware than anyone else of their own weaknesses in the event of a conflict with the United States, the Russians pursued a conservative and cautious line wherever they could find local non-Communist groups willing to abjure the traditional diplomacy of the cordon sanitaire and anti-Bolshevism.

They were entirely willing to restrain equally the militant Left and militant Right, and given the complex political admixtures of the region they showed neither more nor less respect for an unborn functional democracy in Eastern Europe than the Americans and British evidenced in Italy, Greece, or Belgium. For neither the Americans, British, nor Russians were willing to permit democracy to run its course anywhere in Europe at the cost of damaging their vital strategic and economic interests, perhaps also bringing about the triumph of the Left or the restoration of prewar clerical fascism. In fact we now know that the Russians lost control of the revolutionary forces in Yugoslavia and Greece, and that they had no intention of Bolshevizing Eastern Europe in 1945 if—but only if—they could find alternatives.

For the United States, Eastern Europe was a question of economic war aims to which political realities had also to conform to satisfy American aspirations, and quite apart from the local leaderships' policies toward Russia, that was hardly possible in nearly all the Eastern European nations. Even where the United States had yet to develop all of its objectives in specific detail, it was imperative that it prevent any Great Power from totally dominating Eastern Europe or any other region of the world for that matter, because the United States considered all political and economic blocs or spheres of influence that it did not control as directly undermining its larger political, and especially economic, objectives for an integrated world capitalism and a political structure which was the prerequisite to its goals. For this reason America opposed Britain's control over French affairs and set itself against an Eastern European reality which neither it, nor in the last analysis, the Russians, could fully shape according to a plan or desire.

Given the pervasive, chronic Russian conservatism on political questions during the war, one best reflected in the United Front tactics of accommodation which caused the Russian-disciplined Left to submerge its distinctive socialist character at all costs, the failure to reach agreement over Poland or Czechoslovakia—and Eastern Europe in general —reflected the effort of the United States to disengage Soviet influence in Eastern Europe and to create states ready to cooperate with a postwar economic program compatible with American objectives and interests. To the Russians during the war, Eastern Europe was a question of preventing the resurrection of traditionally hostile conservative leaders, and in this they had the total collapse of much of Eastern European society working on their behalf. To the Americans it was a matter of putting together a perhaps somewhat reformed version of the social and political sources of Eastern Europe's alliance with atavistic forces of imperialism and nationalism during two wars and reintegrating the region into a traditional prewar European economy in a condition of semicolonialism. That task was beyond the power of the United States or Russia, but it was a failure of American policy for which Washington was ultimately to hold Russia responsible. This exacerbation of world politics over Eastern Europe was a result of American expansion into the historically hopeless imbroglio and mire of Eastern European affairs.

In the last analysis both the Soviet Union and the United States could only partially control the uncontrollable—the Left—and could seemingly inhibit it only in Western Europe. For World War II brought to fruition a whole spectrum of internal crises inherent in the civil war in society, which was a by-product of different admixtures within each nation of industrial capitalism, World War I, and the continued weakening of world capitalism and colonialism after 1939. America, with some significant aid from Russia, might retard that collapse, yet it could not stay its irresistible momentum, and all the issues were joined during the period 1942–1945 that were again to break out with renewed force after the war to define the direction of modern world diplomacy and conflict. The Old Order of prewar capitalism and oligarchy with which the United States identified, with reservations, and which it hoped to reform and integrate into a transformed world capitalist economy, was dying in the colonial world and a dependent China; it committed suicide in Eastern Europe, and the United States could refurbish it in temporarily acceptable ways only in Western Europe. The impact of these changes on the conditions and structure of world power ultimately were to be more far-reaching than the Bolshevik Revolution itself, in part because—after 1947—the protective existence and support of Soviet power was a cushion between success and failure in many, but by no means all, socialist or revolutionary nations.

By 1945 the war itself delivered the *coup de grâce* to the prewar structure of European politics and economics, for which there was now but slight social backing, and therefore slight resistance to change. Only external intervention saved what remained of European capitalism, and it is this attempted unilateral Great Power definition of the internal affairs of other nations that became the defining fact of wartime and postwar politics. The Americans and British set the precedent in Italy, and formalized it in Europe when the United States also extended the principle elsewhere by preventing the emergence of a truly collaborative forum in the European Advisory Commission in the hope that occupation forces might contain potentially revolutionary changes via a controlled "democracy" whose limits and outcome the West might determine.

This larger instability in European economics and politics required the United States to aid the resuscitation of cooperative conservative elements of Europe and to attempt to prevent a total collapse of the Old Order in Europe and Asia that might open the door to Soviet predominance in a region or even the complete transformation of whole nations. For this reason the United States did not advance a truly permanent stern peace for Germany or Japan, since toward the end of the war many important American leaders accepted the need to reintegrate and reform German and Japanese power to create a balance to Soviet predominance and to advance American objectives. And this deliberate ambiguity, which permeated all their wartime considerations of the future role of the defeated Axis, implied that it was not the total destruction of Axis power, but the advancement of American global interests that soon became the preeminent concern in American planning. In this sense World War II was a tragic error to the American government in that even before the war was over it understood that perhaps a less imperialist Germany and Japan would be preferable to the U.S.S.R. as allies in the future.

Indeed, this perceptible shift in priorities ultimately became the basis of American postwar policy, reflecting a shift in tactical goals all along the line, one that also significantly downgraded initial American hostility to British political aims in Europe, and more particularly in France, on behalf of a far deeper commitment to the objectives of containment and stability—containment of the dual menace of the Left and the Soviet Union, and stability for the essential social and economic system of prewar European capitalism and colonialism.

Although the United States undertook a task that was insuperable in many places, it was still possible in much of Europe, and in any event the American government had no option but to resist as best it could those destabilizing political and economic conditions which brought revolutionary movements of every shape and variety into existence, and attempt to compensate for their subversive effect on American interests and postwar objectives by containing, redirecting, or destroying them. There was no other recourse for the United States but to undertake the difficult, and in many places, the impossible, for the consequence of inaction might have been the unchallenged triumph of the Left in numerous countries. Only the United States had the power to engage fully in international counterrevolution and sustain the forces of conservatism for prolonged periods of time, and it was this militant intervention into the affairs of literally every area of the world that set the pattern for postwar world politics. By 1945 Washington's decision to undertake that role was an unquestioned postulate in America's plans for the future of its power in the world.

The Russians understood the American intention and the risks of any covert aid to the Left, and they gave precious little of it during and immediately after the war, when they discovered that even an obviously conservative policy failed to blunt the American belief that behind all the world's social and economic ills, somehow, and in some critical fashion, a Russian plot and device existed. From this viewpoint United States policy-makers saw Russia and the Left as the cause rather than the reflection of the collapse of capitalism, and responsible for the failings of a system that began to commit suicide in vast areas of the globe no later than 1914. Still, it was Soviet conservatism on revolutionary movements everywhere that gave Western European capitalism the critical breathing spell during which it might recover, though the caution of the Western European Communist parties became a permanent and willingly self-imposed fact of political life. This desire to opt into the existing order where possible, and the correct realization that the American and British armies would certainly not permit a triumph of the Left either by the ballot or a takeover in the streets, shaped the political conduct of the Communist parties wherever there were Western troops. And the U.S.S.R. demanded and assiduously enforced this strategy where it controlled local Communist parties and, through them, the Resistance. It brought an end to the illusions of possibilities and national renovation that inspired the European Resistance. Yet where the Soviets could not control the armed opposition, or the Right was too rigid to absorb the armed Left—as in China, Greece, and Yugoslavia—the end result was revolution and international crisis.

These crises were not a by-product of Soviet policy, but reflected a lack of Russian control over the Left and the response of the British and, preeminently, the United States, to the irresistible tides of change. Outside Western Europe the Americans could recognize, in moments of clarity, the total breakdown of existing societies, but they bent every energy—via dollars and ultimately force of arms—to avoid the political and economic consequences of a perceptible reality for which they could have no sympathy. In Western Europe both dollars and guns succeeded, but where the Americans could not undo disintegration resulting from the war and economic collapse, they often limited and shaped the character of change. American resistance to social and revolutionary upheavals from diverse sources and causes, whether Communist or revolutionary nationalist, polarized change in the world, denying pluralism and options which were natural to radical and humanist movements unable and unwilling to risk survival along with diversity and social exploration. Successful movements of social transformation, due in some degree to ideology but necessarily because of the external pressures, became monolithic and anti-American as

a precondition to success. Counterrevolution in this manner defined
the course of revolution and history for decades, and imposed on the
remnants of the tortured men and women seeking to create a new life
for themselves in Asia and elsewhere the American problem as the
constant threat to social renovation and survival.

With each new success in confining British power in the Middle East
or British financial freedom to pursue an independent course, or in
its ability to define the future contours of the postwar world economy,
the United States downgraded the relative importance it attached to
bringing Great Britain into complete conformity with postwar American economic and political objectives. As time revealed the full extent
of British weakness, and as the common denominator of anti-Communism made what the two states shared more important than ever
before, the problems of the Soviet Union in the postwar world and the
international movement of social change altered, but by no means
eclipsed, the previous weight Washington assigned to its relations with
the British Empire.

The initial Anglo-American rivalry was based on the interwar
world economic experience, and on the basis of that period the United
States defined its postwar economic objectives with an unusual precision unequaled in other fields. Nearly all important leaders in Washington assumed and hoped that the United States would revive and
reform capitalism everywhere in the world, but preeminently in the
British Empire, and that there would not be a collapse of world
capitalism so deep or profound as to raise the fundamental question
of the inherent viability of the system on an international level in any
form. Only toward the very end of the war did the enormity and
social impact of the event begin impressing many in Washington so
that they understood that the needs of reconstruction in Europe might
necessarily precede the creation of a liberal international economy
modeled after late-nineteenth-century British free trade. In the meantime the Hullian theory of American economic objectives was less
significant than its specific goals, and these showed more practically
what it was the United States sought to attain for itself in its ideal
world economy. At least in the short run the accumulated privileges of
the British in the Middle East, and their unique challenge to United
States hegemony over the foreign trade sectors of other Western
Hemispheric nations, presented the major obstacles to attaining these
goals. In the theory of a world economy which Cordell Hull propounded on behalf of the government, the United States would have
enjoyed a competitive advantage over all the other industrialized
nations; in the practice of applying American power to specific interests, in particular oil, the British were certain their wartime ally was

bent on a course of economic imperialism which might also result in the eclipse, even demise, of British power. Rhetoric aside, expedient references to the Open Door in the international economy functionally meant American economic predominance, often monopoly control, over many of the critical raw materials on which modern industrial power is based. Oil revealed the theory and reality of American economic war aims.

The rivalry between the United States and Britain over oil and the postwar world economic structure added to the inevitable weakening of Britain during the war to create a vacuum in world power which the Americans quickly and gladly filled in the Middle East and Latin America. This new role was not unplanned or accidental, but was sought with a compulsion and desire the British perceived as the creation of an American equivalent of the form of spheres and blocs Washington attributed to the British. The elimination of Britain's power in large areas of the world, and the American entry into the wake, carried with it the enormous political and strategic responsibilities which unavoidably befell those who wished global profit, and that new burden was as much a by-product of an American desire for world economic expansion as it was a response to the emergence of the Left everywhere, much less the growth of Russian power. It was inherent in the clear vision of the type of world order the Americans wished to create, and inevitably the American defeat of Britain for predominance in the Middle East also predicated the task of policing ever-growing regions of the world. America's foreign policy at the end of World War II necessitated the ability and desire to employ loans, credits, and investments everywhere, to create a world economic order according to its own desires. In this the United States did only what was functional to its own needs and objectives, as the British had done before it in an earlier era.

It is this deliberate quality, this articulate set of economic and political goals which ultimately set the United States at the end of World War II against the Soviet Union, against the tide of the Left, and against Britain as a coequal guardian of world capitalism—in fact, against history as it had been and had yet to become. That there was something accidental or unintended about the American response to the world is a comforting reassurance to those who wish to confuse the American rhetoric and descriptions of intentions with the realities and purposes of operational power, but given the society and its needs American foreign policy could hardly have been different. For the United States emerged from the war with a sense of vast power, and indeed, as the most powerful single state in the world, anxious to attain a highly organized world economic and political community as a precondition to the realization of its vital peace aims. But as strong as it was, the United States, even when the Soviet Union worked with it for its own reasons and toward its own ends, was too weak to mold the destiny of mankind everywhere on earth. It might limit and shape that fate, but it could not control the world by creating its desired political and economic order modeled after American aspirations.

At times the key decision-makers in Washington fully appreciated America's possible inadequacy and need for allies, as in their enigmatic attitudes toward the future of Germany in Europe and Japan in the Far East. Everywhere in the world America could deploy material power in various forms, and at the conference table it spoke with a weight beyond that of any other state. Estimating this strength in relation to that of other states, Washington fully intended that at the end of the war America could, and would, determine the basic character of the postwar world. For this reason Roosevelt and his aides throughout 1943 and 1944 opposed the desire of the British Foreign Office to meet Soviet aims in Eastern Europe at the bargaining table, for the leaders of the United States fully expected—and this was as true of Roosevelt as of Truman—to employ American power to define the political and economic outcome of the war when their allies were relatively weak. The problem, which it was impossible for anyone in Washington to sufficiently perceive and appreciate, was that the kind of world emerging from the war required power beyond the factory and army, the kind of resources and inspiration that only revolutionary movements in villages and mountains can possess and generate.

For insofar as world conflict was transformed from wars between states into ideological and civil wars for social transformation and liberation, the political arithmetic of sheer insufficiency of numbers made it impossible for the Americans to be everywhere at once, and to employ vast technological power—in bases and ships the Americans planned to have throughout the world—against sheer mass. To succeed in that situation one had to be neither American, English, nor Russian, but to be present in every village in the hungry world, or, as in the case of the Russians, to endorse an inevitability that they could neither initiate nor prevent.

It was in this context of vast material might and yet greater ambition that World War II ended for the United States and defined the manner in which the postwar period began. There was nothing qualitatively unique about this goal or the tools that the United States employed, for the reliance on the state to attain the domestic and international objectives of private American business interests, or to advance a broader "national interest" on behalf of an allegedly new internationalism which scarcely concealed the imperial intent behind it, much less the consequences, was a characteristic of American life and had been for many decades. What was new was the vastly more destructive technology which now accompanied the expansion of states—of which the United States was both the most powerful and first after 1943—and the human consequences of international conflicts.

The United States has yet to construct the international political and economic system modeled after the images and goals which it carefully formulated during World War II, and to make its creation the test of a stable and ideal postwar order or, to compensate for the political and economic frustrations of only one nation of the world, set the stage for an endless series of international crises. In this sense the quality and purpose of modern American diplomacy—in principle and form—we may see in microcosm during the years 1943 to 1945. No nation could build such a world and the efforts of the United States to do so almost consistently revealed its weaknesses. It attempted to apply its strength while refusing to see the limits of American capabilities and ideology in a world that, given its inherently decentralized nature and problems, was moving beyond the mastery of any one nation or alliance of states. For nowhere were the long-term political and economic objectives that the United States formulated during World War II fully realized, save in the replacement of Britain in certain areas by a lesser American influence.

World War II was a prelude to the profound and irreversible crisis in world affairs and the structure of societies everywhere which is the hallmark of our times.

For the war had come to an end, but the world was still aflame.

David Horowitz

23

World War
and Cold War

*The socialist revolution begins on the national arena,
it unfolds on the international arena, and is completed on
the world arena. Thus the socialist revolution becomes a
permanent revolution in a newer and broader sense of the
word; it attains completion only in the final victory of the
new society on our entire planet.*

—TROTSKY

This second international struggle
of the great powers had obvious diplomatic and political roots in
the first, but at the same time a more complex class character. Although
generally neglected or misunderstood, this class dimension of the conflict provides the vital key to the events that followed. For while the
First World War was climaxed by a concert of the victorious powers,
who organized and presided over a postwar settlement, the close of
the Second witnessed an abrupt dissolution of the wartime coalition,
a dramatic and unprecedented reversal of alliances in the West—with
the former enemies becoming intimate allies—and a new, even more
bitterly engaged international conflict. (The fact that this conflict was
contained within cold war limits by the deterrent factor of nuclear
weapons does not alter the reality of the confrontation.) To omit or
overlook the social character of the wartime alliances and struggles
and to dwell exclusively on their national or political content is simply to render this whole succeeding development opaque and unin-
telligible.

If the conflicts of the war and its aftermath are subjected to a
class-oriented analysis, however, they can readily be seen to reflect the
combined and uneven development of world social forces and the
antagonistic property bases which formed the premise of that development in the East and in the West.

In the evolution of the conflict, the principal combatant states fell clearly into three distinct groups, corresponding to the three main historical routes to industrialization. On the one hand, there were the globally preeminent Western allies, whose modern developments were more or less dominated by commercial capitalist classes and based on largely complete bourgeois-democratic revolutions.[1] Ranged against them were the three global latecomers Italy, Germany and Japan—the "renaissance powers," as Nazi writers described them—all either victims of the Versailles settlement or excluded from its benefits. Dominated by conservative bourgeois-aristocratic alliances, these countries' modern developments were at best based on belated and *incomplete* bourgeois revolutions (in the case of Japan there was no bourgeois revolution at all).

Allied with the Western powers up to the end of the war was Soviet Russia, a noncapitalist power, whose recent industrial ascent had been dominated by a bureaucratic-revolutionary elite, and whose course of development was based on a previous thoroughgoing proletarian-peasant revolution, which had swept away both the old landed and industrial ruling classes. The most important feature of this premature, autocratic socialist state, in terms of subsequent developments, was its connection through the International with the forces of revolution in both the industrial and colonial regions of the world, from Europe to China. For as we have seen, this served to sharpen the international class significance and impact of the Soviet state system, and therefore to intensify its inter-state tensions with the dominant capitalist powers in the West—tensions which the Soviet regime throughout the thirties, and afterward, sought futilely to repress and contain.[2]

It is in the two-front orientation of the fascist "anti-Comintern" axis, however, that the complex engagement of social forces in the conflicts of the Second World War finds its real focus and its underlying patterns become intelligible. For fascism as a form of capitalist development can be seen to represent an acute and qualitatively new stage of the permanent crisis of belated bourgeois revolution—a post-

---

[1] Put baldly in this manner, the characterization may appear at first not to apply to England, where the relationship between bourgeoisie and aristocracy was extremely complex. To make possible an explanation of the difference between liberal and non-liberal or bourgeois and non-bourgeois capitalist developments, it is necessary further to distinguish between aristocracies, i.e., between those of the Junker type, based on labor-intensive agriculture and repressive forms of landlord-peasant relationship, and those of the gentry type, as in England, where the peasants were driven from the land and agricultural relations acquired a liberal commercial structure very early.

[2] In 1943, for example, as a gesture to his capitalist allies, Stalin even took the formal step of dissolving the Communist International.

1914 and especially post-"October" deepening of this particular form of capitalist impasse. Thus, the factors associated with belated bourgeois revolution—the inveterate weakness of the liberal-democratic forces, the strength of the conservative feudal-military tradition, the internal social tensions generated by distorted development and capitalist crisis and the determining threat of the incipient socialist revolution (now significantly heightened by the Bolshevik triumph and the post-1917 rise of Communism)—all played critical roles in the fascist emergence both in advanced industrial areas like Germany and in more backward countries like Italy and Spain.

In the advanced and intensely monopolistic contexts of Germany and Japan the fascist development was more deeply based both in the structural evolution of the social economy itself[3] and in the pressure for military-imperialist expansion (the military emphasis being itself a consequence of late internal and external development). Thus, the necessity for total mobilization for imperialist war had a profound impact on the emergence of fascism in both countries[4] as well as on its totalitarian character, which was correspondingly less evident in less expansionist states.

Nazism in Germany, as a result of the peculiar features of Germany's development—its amalgamation of Eastern barbarism and Western industry, its late unification (by military conquest), its recent defeat and the economic, psychological and political consequences of that defeat—represented the most extreme form of the fascist phenomenon, and in this respect was atypical. Nonetheless, its principal features conformed to the general pattern.

Thus, antagonism to Western (especially English) liberalism and imperialism, which formed one characteristic pole of the Nazi program, was as rooted in the whole course of Germany's belated emergence as was Germany's expansion toward the Slavic, Communist and non-Communist East. Neither the Versailles system, organized by Germany's capitalist rivals at the end of the First World War, nor the dissolution of the monarchy and establishment of the Weimar Republic (in which the armed presence of the Western powers also played a

---

[3] For example, ". . . business enterprise in Japan has, from the earliest days, unfolded its activities in an atmosphere largely, and at times, wholly dominated by principles, controls, and social philosophies which are internally coherent with what we in the Western World have come more recently to identify as Fascism."— Robert A. Brady, *Business As a System of Power* (New York: Columbia University Press, 1943), pp. 84–85.

[4] In Japan its influence was decisive, even the limited constitutional framework proving a serious obstacle to a program of military imperialism. On the role of the military in the emergence of Japanese fascism, see Tanin and Yohan, *Militarism and Fascism in Japan*.

decisive role) represented any real steps toward destroying the structural bases of Germany's military-imperial expansionism. Because of the feebleness of German liberalism, including its social democratic form, and the reluctance of the capitalist victors to weaken the structure of Germany's social and economic status quo (in the face of what they regarded as an immediate Bolshevik threat), the revolution of 1918–19, even in its democratic aspect, was extremely partial; the forces of the old order—the imperial army, the absolutist bureaucracy and the Prussianized capitalist ruling class—were left intact and in possession of their bases of social and economic power. An immediate effect of this was to prevent the necessary widening of the internal market through income redistribution and control of the monopolies. The more general and related consequence was to ensure that the Weimar Republic would be little more than an interregnum before the triumph of the counterrevolution and the restoration of the interrupted course of Germany's prewar military-imperial expansion.[5]

The origins of this interregnum in defeat and its history in crisis had a profoundly negative effect on the political character of the restoration. Another factor, ironically, was the institution of parliamentary rule. This forced reaction to seek plebeian roots and compelled the holders of social and economic power in Germany to form alliances with popular, demagogic and "extremist" political forces, like Hitler's National Socialists. But this should not obscure the class character of the restoration itself. Thus the Nazis' anti-Communism (which meant ruthless hostility to the working-class organizations and socialist parties) as well as their authoritarianism, militarism and racial nationalism, were all basic components of the traditional program of Germany's traditional imperialist ruling class. This was evident in the dual ideological function of Nazi racism. For the doctrine of racial superiority provided, internally, an obvious surrogate for the class struggle, directing anticapitalist resentments against a dispensable ("non-Aryan") minority group; externally, it provided a necessary justification for the program of military expansion against powerful European states.[6]

---

[5] Cf. Taylor, *The Course of German History,* which makes eminently clear the character of fascism as a restoration rather than a revolution.

[6] As Neumann points out, political nationalism (as opposed to racial nationalism), which emphasizes the sovereignty of the nation, tends to "equalize" all nations and thus to raise a barrier against the assertion of national superiority. "Indeed, whenever democratic states resort to [imperialist] expansion, they almost invariably abandon the national concept and glorify racial and biological traits that allegedly make them superior to the conquered." In England and America, as Neumann notes, such theories served as an aid to expansion, but never attained the proportions or significance they did in Germany. The reason he adduces is that England and

Moreover, the *anti*capitalist planks of the Nazi program, which had been an important basis of the Nazi appeal to petty-bourgeois, peasant, and declassed social elements, were all dropped under the pressure of big capital, as the Nazis acceded to power.[7] (No similarly effective pressure was forthcoming to curb Nazi barbarism, however, for while Nazi methods were undoubtedly distasteful to some segments of the ruling elite in German society, opposition to them lacked the substance of a class interest, and carried no comparable weight.) The only "socialist" doctrine to be implemented by the Nazis was, significantly, that of "social imperialism," i.e., what the Nazis called "proletarian war" against the dominant capitalist states—which was merely the Nazi version of a "have-not" imperialism in a world of established imperial systems. Such an "anticapitalism," of course, was not at all objectionable to Germany's expansion-minded, militaristic ruling class, even as such a war was for them the only course open within the given economic and international framework.

In the Far East the conflict with Japanese fascism showed striking similarities in origin and development to the conflict with Germany in Europe. For it was Japan's effort to establish a "Greater East Asia Co-Prosperity Sphere" to provide foreign markets and outlets for her intensely monopolistic economy[8] as well as the raw materials, which she lacked, for self-sufficient production that had brought her into collision with the dominant Western powers in Asia (the Netherlands, the United States and Britain)[9] just as surely as had Germany's expansion in Europe. The way in which both Japanese and German statesmen pointed to the Monroe Doctrine area of the United States as providing a prototype for their own imperial concepts underlined the extent to which the Second World War was, like the First, an imperialist war of redivision in the strict Leninist sense.

America conquered very weak states, so that the services of such theories "were never required to organize the total power of the nation for war." In the case of Germany, however, "expansion was and is directed against powerful states. When Germany came forward as an active imperialist force, it found the earth divided among the various military machines. Redistribution, where it could not be achieved peaceably, required the force of arms and an enormous outlay in blood and money. It required an ideology that could justify the huge effort in the eyes of the people. The alleged superiority of the German Nordic race performed this function."—*Behemoth*, p. 89.

[7] This "betrayal" provoked a significant reaction and resulted in the famous "night of the long knives," in which the "radical" Nazis were purged.

[8] Japanese proponents of empire also spoke of the pressure of surplus population. However, "surplus population" was directly related to the narrowness of the internal market, which resulted in turn from the monopolistic structure of the economy.

[9] Vichy France collaborated with the Japanese in Asia, as with the Germans in Europe.

Yet, important as this similarity of structure was, it should not be allowed to obscure the differences between the two world conflicts, which were rooted in the social developments of the intervening period. Among these, the most significant was the emergence of the Soviet Union and the world Communist parties and their role as major participants in the second conflict. This difference manifested itself most centrally in the revolutionary developments in Eastern Europe and China at the war's end, and played no small part in the subsequent reversal of alliances which initiated the postwar struggle. The principal problem for analysis raised by this development is to explain how the Western capitalist states came to find themselves in an unexpected and relatively firm alliance not only with the Soviet state but with revolutionary Communist parties (e.g., in Yugoslavia) in a struggle against other capitalist states.

Not the least part of the answer to this question lies in the very weakness of the Soviet Union at the beginning of the war (Western experts expected a rapid capitulation of Russia before the German onslaught), so that until the very end the Soviet forces never represented such a threat to the conservative camp as to cause its unification. The other part of the explanation, as the preceding analysis of fascism suggests, lies in the recognition that the inter-capitalist conflict of the Second World War represented not merely a struggle between national imperialist powers for hegemony within a single global system,[10] but to a significant extent a conflict between imperialist social systems as such. For, despite their common capitalist frameworks, there was a profound historical gulf between the social and political orders of the fascist powers and the bourgeois democracies in the West. This gulf extended in varying degrees to the wider systems of the capitalist states, and found its clearest and most significant expression in the difference between the corporate imperialism under which the United

---

[10] This element of the struggle should not be underestimated, however. For while many people at the time might have expected the British to make terms with Hitler, as a class ally, and while Britain's response to the Finnish war seemed to indicate the formation of a general capitalist alliance against Russia, the national outlook of leaders like Churchill, supported by the swell of popular feeling against the Germans after the occupation of the low countries, prevented such a course. A German conquest of Europe (against which British diplomacy and arms had been marshalled for a century) would have been fatal to British national interests, and therefore to the interests of the British ruling class as well; on the other hand, Russia was considered to be so weak that few expected her to survive the German attack, and no one expected the Red Army to emerge as the liberating force in Eastern Europe. When this did begin to seem a prospect, the military strategy of the British was oriented to prevent it, and to keep the main thrust of the German forces toward the Soviet Union.

States dominated and exploited the Monroe Doctrine area of Latin America (a system which was destined to become *the* postwar mode of imperialist relationship) and the "New Order" which Nazi Germany sought to impose on the states of central and eastern Europe. A similar though subtler difference was reflected in developments in Asia, where the Japanese "New Order" began its expansion with the incalculable advantage of an "anti-(white)imperialist" program, but was incapable of establishing a neo-colonial system in collaboration with nationalist, anti-Western forces, because of its own intensely chauvinistic, repressive and basically feudal concept of empire.

This conflict between imperialist systems had its basis in the divergent historical developments of capitalism in its bourgeois-democratic and belated feudal-military forms, and in this lay the source of the different character of the two world wars. For in the general crisis after 1917 this gulf was greatly deepened, and because of the prodigious military-industrial strength of the belated systems which made it possible for them to raise a serious challenge for global hegemony, the conflict of the war attained, in a real sense, the character of a struggle *for* the bourgeois-democratic revolution, and created the ground for a temporary alliance between bourgeois and socialist forces against the threat of antidemocratic, anti-Communist reaction.[11]

This alliance, however, did not (and in the nature of things could not) outlast the military defeat of the major fascist powers and the establishment of the absolute and unchallenged supremacy of the bourgeois system in the non-Soviet world. For, as was clear on analytic and historical grounds and confirmed in the prewar vacillation of these powers—their unwillingness to bloc with Soviet Russia and their readiness to accommodate, appease and make a substantial space for the fascist orders in Europe and Asia—the alliance between capitalist and anticapitalist "democratic" forces was necessarily conjunctural, and once the fascist threat to bourgeois hegemony was removed, and the U.S.S.R. had emerged as a potential world power, it was destined to be overridden by more basic class antagonisms.

Thus with the defeat of Germany and Japan the ground was laid for the inevitable realignment of national and social forces based on the realities of the international class struggle: the basic community of interest between propertied social classes, and their common fear of the resurgent threat of Communist revolution. For various reasons, not least of which were the strength of antifascist sentiment in the

---

[11] In Yugoslavia, for example, it was the Communist partisans who attained leadership of the *national* resistance to German oppression and of the struggle for self-determination, and it was precisely because the Communists were the leaders of the nationalist cause that the British were compelled to cooperate with them.

West and the solidarity forged by the preceding struggle, this realignment did not take place everywhere at once. In general, the illusion of a continuing Grand Alliance between Washington, London and Moscow survived many frictions and conflicts of the immediately ensuing period. There were areas, however, where the exigencies of the class struggle, as it emerged out of the wartime resistance, forced a sudden and dramatic reversal which threw a clear light on the nature of the cold war to come.

In Greece, for example, the suddenness of this reversal within the antifascist camp[12] was a major factor in deciding the outcome of the developing internal civil war. The Left, which had emerged through the resistance as the predominant power in Greece, with a program of democratic revolution, did not foresee the antidemocratic, counter-revolutionary role which their previous ally Great Britain would play in the decisive next phase of the struggle. Consequently they were unprepared for the intervention when it came. In effect, neither the Communists (whose outlook, for reasons already analyzed, was one of coexistence with "progressive" capitalisms) nor the non-Communist Left understood the dynamics of the international class struggle as it was emerging with the defeat of German and Japanese imperialism and the tremendous wartime upsurge of the global revolutionary forces. Hence, they did not understand the threat which their own armed revolutionary presence posed, despite their limited demands, to "democratic" British and American imperialism. So sharp and unexpected was the transition in Greece from one phase of the international struggle to the next that demonstrating crowds of the left-wing, antifascist resistance were heard chanting "Long live Roosevelt! Long live Churchill! No King!"[13] even as they were shot down by British troops who had been sent (in American planes) to crush them, and to reimpose the hated rightist monarchy in collaboration with conservative, quisling and fascist elements.

The illusion that despite the tremendous power shifts of the war the capitalist states would remain allies of the Left, so long as the

---

[12] Of course, this reversal did not yet represent a split between the great state powers of the alliance, since the Soviet Union acquiesced in the British intervention.

[13] A fourth slogan was "Down with Papandreou," the provisional Prime Minister. Two decades later, even Papandreou's conservative brand of liberalism and bourgeois nationalism was considered to be too dangerous by the United States and its monarchist and military allies in Greece. To close the liberal doorway to communism, a fascist coup was carried out in April 1967, just prior to general elections which Papandreou's party was expected to win.

Left confined itself to the democratic struggle,[14] was dramatically shattered not only in Greece at this time, but on the other side of the globe as well. In French Indochina, where the forces of the Vietnamese resistance proclaimed a democratic republic in a document modeled on the American Declaration of Independence and closely according with the spirit of the Atlantic Charter, a similar realignment took place.

"We are convinced," said the Vietnamese in their declaration, "that the Allied nations which at Teheran and San Francisco [the U.N. Conference] have acknowledged the principles of self-determination and equality of nations will not refuse to acknowledge the independence of Vietnam. A people who have courageously opposed French domination for more than eighty years, a people who have fought side by side with the Allies against the Fascists during these last years, such a people must be free and independent." As in Greece, incoming British troops were initially welcomed to Hanoi by the resistance leaders, who regarded them as allies and liberators. But instead of disarming the Japanese occupation forces the British used them to maintain "order" while the French troops prepared themselves to reestablish their colonial control of Vietnam. In the ensuing struggle the United States, which had offered a modicum of aid to the Vietminh during the struggle against the Japanese and their French collaborators, now threw their full support behind France's effort to retain this resource-rich outpost of its dwindling colonial empire.[15]

In the East as in the West, at the end of the war, the natural alliance of conservative class forces was reestablishing itself in the face of the rising threat of socialist revolution. By the early fifties, when the United States was openly providing massive economic and military

---

[14] In one area, namely Italy, this alliance not only worked (until 1947), but actually produced a bourgeois-democratic "revolution." This was mainly because of Italy's defeat in the war and the fact that the American occupation forces had played a major role in the actual liberation and were physically in control of many areas as the crucial negotiations were being conducted, and to some extent that the Americans did not have the kind of direct ties to the Italian monarchy as the British did to the Greek.

[15] Indeed, the parallel between Vietnam and Greece, with respect to the commitments of the Western powers and the tactics of revolutionary struggle goes much further. Just as the Vietminh in 1954 laid down their arms (under Sino-Soviet pressure) for a worthless Western guarantee that political rights would be safeguarded and free elections held, so the Greeks nine years before were induced to accept a similar arrangement under the Varkiza agreements. Like the South Vietnamese, once they had laid down their arms they were hunted by rightist forces and compelled to resume their resistance under far less favorable circumstances.

support to sustain the fascist regime in Spain, the cold war "free world" alliance of propertied social forces, ranging from the parliamentary states of the developed capitalist world through the military dictatorships and feudal kingdoms of their dependent allies, was firmly sealed.[16]

The main stages of the transition to this realignment and its effect on the bourgeois-democratic revolution throughout the ensuing period were most clearly registered in the transformation of Allied occupation policies in the defeated fascist states. This was particularly true in the Far East, where the United States, the most bourgeois of the capitalist powers, exercised unilateral jurisdiction over the most "feudal," Japan, and where the complicating European factor of military confrontation between the great powers was not directly present.

Initially, the U.S. Occupation Command acted with apparent determination to bring Japan's archaic social and political structure fully into the bourgeois framework. A bourgeois-democratic constitution was introduced, the emperor being reduced to the status of a constitutional monarch; a trade union law was promulgated, guaranteeing the right to organize, bargain and strike, and a democratizing educational reform was undertaken. In addition, a move to deconcentrate Japan's intensely monopolized economy was initiated, as well as a bourgeois land reform aimed at the repressive, quasi-feudal relations in agriculture. Finally, war crimes trials were held, and there was an administrative purge of the military and civil bureaucracies, as well as a general demilitarization and dismantling of the Japanese war machine.

Even from the beginning, however, these reforms were of a partial rather than a sweeping nature. For the U.S. authorities were restrained in their program by the desire not to weaken the conservative structure of Japanese society in the process of bringing it within the framework of the bourgeois system. Thus, the purges, while extensive, were nonetheless superficial, and the bureaucracy was left essentially intact.[17] Even the land reform, which fared far better, stopped short of fulfillment as a result of the reluctance of the authorities to stir up the

---

[16] By March 1955, of 71 countries in the "free world," according to one Congressional reporter, 49 were "outwardly or actually dictatorships or close oligarchies . . . of the remaining 22 nations, most of them truly have some claim to the adjective 'free' as far as their political governments are concerned, but certainly as far as the economic control of several of them is concerned, it is oligarchic and a small percentage of the nation is living off the backs of the other 99%."—Representative Thomas B. Curtis (cited from the Congressional Record in Mills, *The Marxists*, p. 24).

[17] The purge was carried out by category, so that the top officials were removed as a group, leaving their juniors in charge. This made the bureaucracy more tractable to the Occupation Command, but hardly represented a change in its outlook.

class struggle in the countryside. Another factor inducing restraint, and drastically reducing the practical impact of the reforms, was the post-liberal character of U.S. capitalism itself. Thus the crucial but half-hearted attempt to deconcentrate Japanese industry[18] and break up the *zaibatsu* proved almost wholly abortive, meeting even in its diluted form with stiff opposition from U.S. financial and corporate interests.

Additional forces behind the arrest of the Occupation Command's reformist impulse were the growing international and internal class tensions: the triumphant revolution in China, the Communist-initiated civil war and Western intervention in Korea and the rise of a Japanese Marxist Left. As early as February 1947 the Occupation banned a general strike on "economic grounds," while the following year civil servants and local government employees were prohibited from resorting to the strike weapon at all. In 1949 the Occupation's progressive labor laws were revised (at U.S. insistence) to restrict the power of the trade union movement, and in 1949 and 1950 there was a general purge of Communists in the unions, government, education and industry. At the same time, the Occupation authorized the Japanese government to review the applications of those removed in the original purge of fascists, and by 1951 almost all those originally affected had regained their political rights. Coincident with the anti-Communist repressions, which were accompanied by the reinvigoration of the Japanese police apparatus, a remilitarization campaign was begun (also under U.S. pressure, in alliance with the Japanese right-wing), so that, as in Germany, the last phase of the occupation witnessed a restoration of the forces of the old order, albeit within a partially reformed institutional context.

While the U.S. occupation of Japan is instructive because of the clear insight it provides into the characteristic relation between bourgeois and fascist forces[19] in the postwar epoch, and the fateful consequences of that relation for the bourgeois-democratic revolution, it does not give a full picture of the dynamics of the emergent cold war struggle. For this conflict was dominated in its initial stages by the confrontation between the great powers in Europe. It cannot be understood therefore without insight into the duality of Soviet state policy as well, and hence the temporary but far-reaching reorientation in the

---

[18] A list of 1,200 firms to be broken up was compiled and then progressively reduced until there were only 19 left. When nine of these had been dealt with, the board set up by the U.S. authorities, and composed of five prominent U.S. corporate leaders, decided that enough had been done.

[19] And hence "feudal" forces as well.

East, which reflected and interacted with the early postwar realignments in the West.

Initially, Stalin had attempted to approach the postwar period in the same nationalist manner in which he had approached the period leading up to the disasters of 1939. Indeed, this was the very basis of his agreements at Yalta with the Western allies. Just as he strove to keep the Spanish revolution within bourgeois limits in the interests of "coexistence" and defensive entente with the capitalist powers, so at the end of the war he sought to contain and even abort the Communist revolutions in Yugoslavia, China and Greece, which were outside the sphere assigned to Russia under the Yalta agreements. In a similar spirit, he recognized the Badoglio regime in Italy, and urged the French and Italian Communists to enter the conservative cabinets of De Gaulle and De Gasperi, and the latter even to vote for the reenactment of Mussolini's Lateran pacts with the Vatican.

His approach to the security zone in Eastern Europe, including the former Nazi satellites (over whom it was agreed Russia would have an influence comparable with that of the British in Greece), was initially in keeping with this conservative coexistence policy. While taking steps to ensure the pro-Soviet political orientation of the regimes, he left their social structures basically intact and proceeded to satisfy the demands of Russia's own devastated and perilously weakened economy by exacting reparations and tribute from the conquered regions (and even from the former devastated allies of Russia—Poland, Czechoslovakia and Yugoslavia). By these methods he began the slow replenishment of Russia's depleted economic base, while at the same time severely damaging any prospect of popular socialist revolution in the tributary areas for years to come.

However, even in this early period, when Stalin was pursuing a basically nationalist policy at the expense of revolutionary interests in Eastern Europe, deep cold war tensions with the West were already making themselves felt. These tensions, though expressed in political and national power terms, were, in fact, rooted in the ineradicable antagonism between the economic systems of the contending states and their mutually exclusive institutional (class) bases. The class orientation of Western policy was amply evident in its whole effort to restrict Soviet influence in the guaranteed Eastern sphere and in Washington's parallel attempt to extend the Open Door system to the Soviet border. Nor was the Soviet Union any more capable in this particular context, of separating its national aspirations from the underlying class bias of its economic structure. For just as the West, to further *its* influence, reached out to anti-Communist conservatives, as well as to anti-Russian nationalists in the region of the former cordon sanitaire, so the Soviet Union inevitably found its "national" allies in the East European Communist parties and among those class forces which were pressing for a revolutionary transformation of the repressive and inequitable East European social order. Thus, even if Soviet policy in Eastern Europe had started from purely nationalist premises—in particular the Kremlin's intense regard for the area as a primary security zone—inevitably, in order to defend the zone the Kremlin would have found it necessary to block the open door penetration of U.S. private capital, and to attack the economic and social bases of anti-Soviet power, i.e., to restrict and curtail the influence of the old ruling groups and conservative class forces in the area.

To this general situation was added another element in the outlook of the officer corps of the occupying Red Army. For, as Deutscher has observed, while these men were instructed by the Kremlin to carry out a policy of "non-interference" in the domestic affairs of the occupied countries, they were no more able to do so than their Western counterparts. As Communists they could hardly administer the countries they controlled "in such a way as to allow capitalist business to function as usual and non-Communist parties, whose leaders did not even conceal their hatred and contempt of the Communist conquerors, to carry on their activities without hindrance." These anticapitalist tendencies of course provoked their own reaction among the Western powers, who saw in them an attempt by Stalin to go beyond the Yalta agreements and to Communize the entire region.

The inseparability of national from class elements in Soviet policy in Eastern Europe was perhaps most clearly evident in a process which provided the key to the subsequent and relatively peaceful social transformation of the area (for in no East European country before 1956 was there anything remotely approaching the violent resistance encountered by the British-sponsored restoration in Greece). Under the terms of the Allied agreements, the governments of Eastern Europe were obligated to purge their bureaucracies of Nazis, fascists, militarists and all those who had worked against Russia in the conflict. These purges were directed by Communists who, with Soviet assistance, had attained control of the Departments of Interior and Defense in each of the East European regimes. Since the old ruling classes had consisted mainly of antidemocratic elements which had manifested a pro-German or at least an anti-Russian attitude in the war, it was possible without grossly violating the terms of the agreements to deprive them of their organizational base and to render them "politically impotent." As the intermediate groupings lacked cohesion and were extremely weak, these purges prepared the ground for the ascendance of the Communist parties and the eventual transformation of East European society.

For such a development to occur, that is, for the Communist parties actually to be given the signal to take power, it was necessary first that the Kremlin be induced to abandon its policy of coexistence and "self-containment," and thus be prepared to invite open confrontation with the West. What impelled the Kremlin to seek security in "revolution" in Eastern Europe after the war, rather than in alliance and coopera-tion with the Western powers, was the Western reversal over the Yalta spheres-of-influence understanding, the effective collapse of the war-time coalition, the toleration and support by the Western powers for fascist forces and regimes, the rightward shift in U.S. policy and the early launching of the global anti-Communist crusade.

Never really reconciled to a Russian sphere in Eastern Europe, enjoying a position of unprecedented military and economic superi-ority, confident, further, that war-devastated "Russia is really afraid of our power," Washington embarked, as early as 1945, on a program to expel Russian influence from its East European sphere, to revive German, and later Japanese, military power, and in fact to mount the third major capitalist offensive against the Soviet regime in a genera-tion. Whether the offensive, which began politically and economically, would develop into a military thrust as some top officials were urging, was hardly a question to which the Soviet General Staff was likely to be indifferent. At the time, Washington was feverishly developing the atomic weapon, securing air and naval bases around the perimeter of the Soviet Union and alerting the populations of the West to an alleged military menace emanating from Moscow, which it must have known simply on logistical grounds to have been nonexistent.

It was in this threatening situation, which reached a decisive turning point with Truman's "Doctrine" speech in March 1947, that the Krem-lin's attitude toward Eastern Europe underwent a profound change.[20] Keenly aware of the military importance of Eastern Europe for the defense of the Soviet Union, impressed by the perhaps insurmountable difficulties of taking Russia, alone, through a second forced ascent, Moscow rapidly extended its control in the buffer area and took steps to integrate the East European social, political and economic struc-tures into the Soviet system (recognizing thereby the failure of its autarchical economic policy and the cherished doctrine of Russian self-sufficiency).

---

[20] There was also a partial left shift in its general international policy. A Com-munist information agency (Cominform) was established to replace the dissolved Comintern. The new body, however included only the East European parties and the large French and Italian CPs, and this (and its official status as an "information" agency) reflected the defensive nature of the new militant line adopted by the CPs in the ensuing period and the total subordination of that line to short-term Soviet interests.

This early postwar reversal of Soviet policy was not unprecedented. In 1939 Stalin had entered the Baltic states (whose governments had been inclined toward Berlin rather than Moscow) in order to establish military bases and secure his threatened defenses. A year later, in a situation of heightened danger following the fall of France and the British retreat at Dunkirk, he staged "revolutions" in each of these countries (overthrowing their governments and socializing their economies) and incorporated them into the Soviet Union.[21]

Thirty-five years before, in his original tract on permanent revolution, Trotsky had written: "If the Russian proletariat, having temporarily obtained power, does not on its own initiative carry the revolution onto European soil, it will be *compelled* to do so by the forces of European feudal-bourgeois reaction." (Emphasis in original.) Of course, Trotsky did not expect the revolution to be carried abroad on the points of the Red Army's bayonets, and indeed emphatically opposed "revolution by conquest" when the issue arose with respect to Tukhachevsky's march on Warsaw in 1920. Nor did Stalin, for that matter, occupy the Soviet borderlands in 1940 or 1945 for revolutionary purposes. But the logic of permanent revolution, the permanence of capitalist aggression against the social revolution and its bases, and the permanence of the revolutionary reaction (even in this distorted form) as its only viable defense asserted itself dramatically in the events of 1940 as in the early cold war period. By 1949, with NATO in formation and Eastern Europe fully Sovietized, the revolution once again, in spite of Stalin's best efforts and most devious methods, had been compelled to carry itself abroad.

---

[21] The act of incorporation or more accurately reincorporation, since the Baltic states had been severed from the Russian empire through the punitive peace at Brest-Litovsk, distinguished this expansion from the postwar course of events in Eastern Europe, and, of course, in its motivation contained a strong element of Great Russian chauvinism.

Accumulation. The acquisition of capital necessary for the development of production. Before the capitalist mode of production can become dominant, capital has to be available and concentrated in the hands of the potential employers of labor, and a work force dependent on wages has to be created. *Primitive accumulation* refers to the process by which the capital necessary for capitalist development is acquired. The process varied from country to country, the wealth coming sometimes from agriculture, sometimes from mercantile activity. But on the whole it was marked by a high degree of violence, directed against both the feudal system and the resisting peasants and urban wage-earners. *Capitalist accumulation* refers to the process within the capitalist mode of production whereby wealth is acquired through the creation of profits.

Appropriation. The term refers to the proceeds (or surplus value) from the product of the workers' labor taken over by the capitalist after wages have been paid.

The *bourgeoisie* is a social class, that is, a group of men defined by the role they play in the relations of production. By definition, a class cannot exist by itself but only in relation to another class. Nor is a class strictly and solely an economic category, for men, as they engage in the productive process, develop all sorts of characteristics affecting all areas of social life: the way they think, express themselves, make war, build political institutions, etc., *ad infinitum.* It is the sum of the interactions of all these areas, as well as the dialectic of the struggle between the classes, that defines each of them.

As is true of all other classes, the bourgeoisie has had a long history. In classic feudal societies, the bourgeoisie was those persons who were engaged in trade and who were outside the dominant lord-peasant relationship. We therefore speak of the *commercial bourgeoisie,* at a point in time before capitalism had penetrated all aspects of production. In France before 1789 there were other types of bourgeoisie, such as the financiers who collected the taxes and dealt in state finance, and the office holders who occupied the higher echelons of state administration. Under fully developed capitalism, the bourgeoisie is defined as the capitalist owners of the means of production.

All revolutions bring about a change in power relations in a society. In a *bourgeois revolution* the dominant class is replaced by the bourgeoisie. But a revolution of this sort may take years before it is completed, and it may be more or less successful, that is, the class seeking power may be forced into a whole series of compromises with both the older and newer opposition, and the particular shape taken by the new regime will be much affected by the balance of forces so realized. A *pre-bourgeois revolution* is one that takes place when the bourgeoisie is still relatively undeveloped and in conditions of economic backwardness. The term has been applied to the history of sixteenth-century Germany in particular. It is to be noted that a revolution identified with a given social class is not necessarily the conscious work of all, or even some, of its members. Rather, it is the result of the revolution and the place it occupies within a precise analytical framework that determine its class character.

Capitalism is that mode of production characterized by the pursuit of profit (rather than the satisfaction of social needs), where capital is concentrated in the hands of the owners of the means of production and where profit is realized at the expense of the workers (proletarians) who are dependent on the sale of their labor power for a living. Emphasis must be placed on the notion of production and its subordination to capital. Insofar as this does not exist, neither does the capitalist mode of production. Care must be taken not to confuse *capital investment*, which has always existed, with capitalist production. Hence, the expressions *commercial, financial,* or *speculative* capitalism which, applied to medieval or early modern Europe, refer to marginal capitalist practices subordinated to the needs of feudal society and its dominant class. They had little or nothing to do with the productive sphere, although their existence was not without importance in the process of primitive capitalist accumulation.

The phrase *rationally acquisitive capitalism* is associated with the names of the German sociologists/historians Max Weber and Werner Sombart. Writing in the first decades of the twentieth century, both thought that what distinguished the medieval from the early modern economy was a new spirit of desire for gain and rational organization, quite independent of the ownership of the means of production as Marx would have it.

Determinism. The term refers to any system of historical or philosophical analysis which subordinates human action to external forces, whether material or spiritual. Marx has often been accused of being an economic determinist, but in reality he was not. Marx wrote that "the mode of production of material life conditions the process of social, political, and spiritual existence as a whole," and he sought to discover the laws according to which the *capitalist* mode of production functions. This said, he never established an automatic correspondence between the economic sphere and any other sphere of human action. Nor did he deprive men of the possibility of making their own history. On the contrary. In short, if the general shape of historical development is determined (for instance, the destruction of capitalism and its replacement by socialism), the way in which this may take place is totally undetermined. The timing of events, the ups and downs of the process are so many unknowns, and men are free, within the bounds of certain material constraints, to act as they will. Similarly, one sphere of human action—economic, social, political, intellectual, military—may at any given moment assume greater importance than, or be in advance of the development of, the rest, precisely because of the existence of significant human freedom.

Hegemony. According to Antonio Gramsci, a class is said to exercise hegemony when it has seized the initiative in the process of social change.

Neo-Marxist describes any thinker or theory that accepts Marxist principles as a point of departure but rejects certain of their component theses.

Production. For Marx, it is productive activity that distinguishes men from other animals. It is in the course of producing that men create the basic relationships that bind them one to another, the characteristics that give their societies shape and consistency.

The *means of production* refer to the items that make possible the creation of material objects: land, capital, tools, raw materials. The *productive forces* or *forces of production* include the means of production together with the labor of the workers and the techniques applied. The *relations of production* or *social relations* are the ensemble of relations into which men enter in the process of "producing and reproducing real life." Specifically, these include the system of property holding (of the means of production), the distribution of material goods, and the class structures that are their expression.

A *mode of production* is the total of the forces of production and of the relations of production. But it is an abstract category not meant to describe reality. A *social formation* is the expression used to describe a concrete historical moment in which elements of one or more modes of production may be present and interacting with one another, thus creating a unique situation. Each social formation encompasses activi-

THIS BOOK was set on the Linotype in Baskerville. The punches for this face were cut under the supervision of George W. Jones, the eminent English printer and the designer of Granjon and Estienne. Linotype Baskerville is a facsimile cutting from type cast from the original matrices of a face designed by John Baskerville, a writing master of Birmingham, for his own private press. The original face was the forerunner of the "modern" group of type faces, known today as Scotch, Bodoni, etc. After his death in 1775, Baskerville's punches and matrices were sold in France and were used to produce the sumptuous Kehl edition of Voltaire's works.

ties directly economic in nature, as well as ideologies, beliefs, and institutions.

Revisionism. A school of thought which rejects most of the fundamental notions of Marxism, particularly the dialectic and the analysis of capitalist development, making of the little that is left a series of ethical recommendations. The revisionists favor using parliamentary reform to pass from capitalism to socialism, and reject both revolutionary violence and the dictatorship of the proletariat.

Surplus value. In the capitalist mode of production, the relationship between the owner of the means of production and the worker (proletarian) is an exploitative one. The capitalist buys the worker's labor power. The labor power is used to create products sold on the market as commodities. Surplus value is that part of the proceeds which remains in the hands of the capitalist after deducting payment to the worker, a payment which permits the latter to survive and renew his labor power. But the amount of the wages paid the worker does not affect the fact of his exploitation.